Mt.
Ararat

Nineveh

Euphrates River

Babylon

Ur

PRESENTED TO:

_____

BY:

_____

DATE:

_____

◆ ◆ ◆

_____

_____

The Wonder Bible

With selected
Scripture text from the acclaimed
International Children's Bible

Edited by
MACK THOMAS

Illustrations by
GREG TESS

Gold 'n'
Honey
BOOKS

THE WONDER BIBLE

published by Gold'n'Honey Books
a part of the Questar publishing family

© 1993 by Questar Publishers, Inc.

International Standard Book Number: 0-945564-59-7

Cover illustration by Greg Tess

Printed in the United States of America

For information:
Questar Publishers, Inc.
Post Office Box 1720
Sisters, Oregon 97759

93 94 95 96 97 98 99 00 01 — 10 9 8 7 6 5 4 3 2

A Special Word
for Parents & Teachers

CHILDREN FIRST LEARN to "taste and see that the Lord is good" in bright, engaging children's story Bibles (such as the *The Beginner's Bible*). But what happens when they outgrow their simple picture Bibles? What happens when they hunger to know more about God's promises, people, and plans?

Most often, we expect them to jump immediately to a full-text Bible. That's quite a stretch. That's like moving overnight from strained peaches to porter-house steak! Rather than encouraging these young ones to develop a lifetime of Bible reading, we may discourage them. They may conclude that the Bible is something for very small children or very large grownups...but not for them. Some may come back to the Bible when they are adults. Tragically, some never do.

THE WONDER BIBLE is designed to help bridge that wide gap. A child can realistically expect to read this entire volume without getting lost, confused, or bogged down.

Three goals guided both the selection of Scripture text and the addition of extra features on these pages:

1. *To give children a successful and enjoyable reading experience through each book of the Bible.* The heart of every book of the Bible is included here.

2. *To help children personalize what they read in Scripture.* This is encouraged especially in the extra features throughout THE WONDER BIBLE.

3. *To get children excited about reading a full-text Bible.* You'll see in this book a recurring section called "And There's More..." This helps reinforce the idea that there are wider vistas to see, deeper marvels to explore, and more and more life-changing truths to learn in this wondrous book we call the Bible. It's the feel of gold and the taste of honey that will keep their appetite for God's Word strong and growing. *THE WONDER BIBLE isn't meant to be a replacement for full-text Bible-reading, but a stimulating preparation for it.*

The heart of THE WONDER BIBLE is a careful selection of Bible passages. They were chosen to offer children the most readable and meaningful encounter with Bible truth, while also giving them a thorough understanding of what the entire Bible is all about. The passages chosen are especially *action-centered* and *people-centered* (offering the most interest to children), and *principle-centered* (clearly presenting foundational Christian doctrines).

Another guide in selecting text for THE WONDER BIBLE was our attempt to avoid repetition. In the four Gospels, for example, Mark, Luke, and John in THE WONDER BIBLE do not generally repeat what is also found in Matthew.

As a result of this attempt to present the entire Scriptures in a more manageable size for children, the nearly 800,000-word text of a standard Bible for adults has been abridged to one-sixth that amount, or about 130,000 words, in THE WONDER BIBLE.

The Scripture version chosen for THE WONDER BIBLE is the acclaimed *International Children's Bible*, the first complete Bible translated especially for children. Unlike many other children's Bibles, the ICB is not a paraphrase, storybook, or repackaged adult version. Rather, it's an accurate translation you can trust for your children.

In addition, portions of the extra-feature text in THE WONDER BIBLE have been adapted from Mack Thomas's bestseller *The Bible Tells Me So.*

Our heartfelt desire is to offer a warm, welcoming hand to children with a newly awakened thirst for the Book of Books. We believe children will quickly discover that THE WONDER BIBLE is the right Bible for them — with the right language and vocabulary, the right amount and selection of text, and the right extra features. When it comes to Scripture, no child should feel left out or left behind.

CONTENTS

A Special Word for
Parents and Teachers 5

OLD TESTAMENT:

Genesis 13
Exodus 39
Leviticus 61
Numbers 69
Deuteronomy 81
Joshua 94
Judges 105
Ruth 115
1 Samuel 123
2 Samuel 135
1 Kings 149
2 Kings 165
1 Chronicles 179
2 Chronicles 185
Ezra 193
Nehemiah 197
Esther 203
Job 214
Psalms 225
Proverbs 237
Ecclesiastes 251
Song of Solomon 255
Isaiah 260
Jeremiah 277
Lamentations 291
Ezekiel 295
Daniel 305
Hosea 318
Joel 323
Amos 327
Obadiah 331
Jonah 335

Micah 341
Nahum 345
Habakkuk 349
Zephaniah 353
Haggai 357
Zechariah 361
Malachi 365

NEW TESTAMENT:

Matthew 372
Mark 399
Luke 409
John 429
Acts 450
Romans 472
1 Corinthians 483
2 Corinthians 489
Galatians 495
Ephesians 501
Philippians 507
Colossians 513
1 Thessalonians 519
2 Thessalonians 523
1 Timothy 527
2 Timothy 531
Titus 537
Philemon 541
Hebrews 548
James 555
1 Peter 561
2 Peter 565
1 John 569
2 John 573
3 John 577
Jude 581
Revelation 588

CREATION (The exact date isn't known.) | **4000 B.C.**

OLD TESTAMENT TIME LINE

GENESIS -About 6000 B.C.

Noah Born -3500 B.C.

| **900 B.C.** | **800 B.C.** | **700 B.C.** | **600 B.C.** |

OBADIAH -855 B.C.
2 KINGS -848 B.C.
JOEL -835 B.C.

JONAH -785 B.C.
AMOS -760 B.C.
HOSEA -750 B.C.
ISAIAH -740 B.C.
MICAH -740 B.C.

ZEPHANIAH -635 B.C.
JEREMIAH -626 B.C.
NAHUM -620 B.C.
DANIEL -605 B.C.
HABAKKUK -605 B.C.

EZEKIEL -1446 B.C.
Jerusalem destroyed
-586 B.C.
LAMENTATIONS
-586 B.C.
EZRA -538 B.C.
HAGGAI -520 B.C.
ZECHARIAH -520 B.C.

| **JESUS' BIRTH** | **20 A.D.** | **30 A.D.** | **40 A.D.** |

NEW TESTAMENT TIME LINE

LUKE -6 B.C.
MATTHEW -6 B.C.

MARK -26 A.D.
JOHN -26 A.D.

ACTS-30 A.D.
Jesus rises from the
dead -30 A.D.

GALATIANS -49 A.D.
JAMES -49 A.D.

The date by the name of each book is the
starting time for what happens in that book.

3000 B.C. | **2000 B.C.** | **1000 B.C.**

Abraham Born -2166 B.C.
Isaac Born -2066 B.C.
Jacob Born -2006 B.C.

JOB -2000 B.C.
EXODUS -1446 B.C.
LEVITICUS -1445 B.C.
NUMBERS -1444 B.C.
DEUTERONOMY -1406 B.C.
JOSHUA -1406 B.C.
JUDGES -1380 B.C.
RUTH -1200 B.C.
1 SAMUEL -1105 B.C.
2 SAMUEL -1010 B.C.

1 CHRONICLES-1000 B.C.
PSALMS-1000 B.C.
1 KINGS-970 B.C.
2 CHRONICLES-970 B.C.
PROVERBS-970 B.C.
SONG OF SOLOMON
    -970 B.C.
ECCLESIASTES-940 B.C.

500 B.C.

ESTHER -479 B.C.
NEHEMIAH -445 B.C.
MALACHI -440 B.C.

50 A.D. | **60 A.D.** | **90 A.D.**

1 THESSALONIANS
    -51 A.D.
2 THESSALONIANS
    -52 A.D.
1 CORINTHIANS
    -55 A.D.
2 CORINTHIANS
    -56 A.D.
ROMANS -57 A.D.

EPHESIANS -60 A.D.
COLOSSIANS -60 A.D.
PHILEMON -60 A.D.
PHILIPPIANS -61 A.D.
1 PETER -62 A.D.
1 TIMOTHY -64 A.D.
TITUS -64 A.D.
JUDE -65 A.D.
2 TIMOTHY -66 A.D.

HEBREWS -66 A.D.
2 PETER -67 A.D.

1 JOHN -90 A.D.
2 JOHN -90 A.D.
3 JOHN -90 A.D.
REVELATION
    -95 A.D.

INTRODUCING...

GENESIS • EXODUS • LEVITICUS
NUMBERS • DEUTERONOMY

On the very first page of the Bible, a simple truth rises up pure and clear, like a fresh mountain spring. That great and simple truth is this: *God made everything.*

That's what the Bible is about — *God,* and *everything!*

Without God, there would be no Bible. We have a Bible because God loves us, and He decided to tell us in His own words about His love and all that He's done for us. So the Bible is *God's Book* through and through. What water is to a river or a lake or the ocean, that's what God is to the Bible.

As you may know, the Bible is not just one book. It's 66 different books put together into one, and arranged in a certain order. The first 39 books are what we call the Old Testament. All these books were written before Jesus came to earth to live and die and then to rise up from the dead.

The last 27 books are the New Testament. All these were written after Jesus rose from the dead and went back to heaven.

To better understand how all these books fit together, we can put them into even smaller groups. For example, these first five books of the Bible — Genesis through Deuteronomy — were all written by Moses. Sometimes we call these books "the Law," because they tell the laws God gave His people to live by. You might also say that what these first five books are about most is *God's promises.* As you read, look and see how many promises you can find from God.

The Book of
GENESIS

The Beginning
of All Things

Looking forward to Genesis...

"The Beginning of All Things"

God makes promises — and He keeps promises! That message comes through loud and clear in the book of Genesis. For example, we read in Genesis about special promises God made to a man named Abraham. That was more than 4,000 years ago. And those promises are still being fulfilled today!

Adam: He was the first person God created. God created him as a perfect man. But when he and his wife sinned, the entire human race was hurt by sin from then on.

Eve: Adam's wife, and the first woman.

Noah: A good man who obeyed God. Because he obeyed God, he saved both his family and the entire human race.

Abraham: The man God chose to build a nation from. His family became the nation of Israel.

Isaac: Abraham's son, born in Abraham's old age.

Jacob: Isaac's son. God changed his name to Israel. Jacob had 12 sons, and the families of those sons became the 12 tribes of Israel.

Canaan: This was the land God promised Abraham. Later this land was called Israel.

Egypt: The people of ancient Egypt were the world's most powerful nation in the time of Abraham, Isaac, Jacob, and Joseph.

I wonder how everything got started...
And I wonder what God really had in mind
when He started it...

I N THE BEGINNING God created the sky and the earth. The earth was empty and had no form. Darkness covered the ocean, and God's Spirit was moving over the water.

Creation

Then God said, "Let there be light!" And there was light. God saw that the light was good. So he divided the light from the darkness. God named the light "day" and the darkness "night." Evening passed, and morning came. This was the first day.

Then God said, "Let there be something to divide the water in two!" So God made the air to divide the water in two. Some of the water was above the air, and some of the water was below it.

God named the air "sky." Evening passed, and morning came. This was the second day.

Then God said, "Let the water under the sky be gathered together so the dry land will appear." And it happened. God named the dry land "earth." He named the water that was gathered together "seas." God saw that this was good.

Then God said, "Let the earth produce plants. Some plants will make grain for seeds. Others will make fruit with seeds in it. Every seed will produce more of its own kind of plant." And it happened. The earth produced plants. Some plants had grain for seeds. The trees made fruit with seeds in it. Each seed grew its own kind of plant. God saw that all this was good. Evening passed, and morning came. This was the third day.

Then God said, "Let there be lights in the sky to separate day from night. These lights will be used for signs, seasons, days and years. They will be in the sky to give light to the earth." And it happened.

So God made the two large lights. He made the brighter light to rule the day. He made the smaller light to rule the night. He also made the stars. God put all these in the sky to shine on the earth. They are to rule over the day and over the night. He put them there to separate the light from the darkness. God saw that all these things were good. Evening passed, and morning came. This was the fourth day.

Then God said, "Let the water be filled with living things. And let birds fly in the air above the earth."

So God created the large sea animals. He created every living thing that moves in the sea. The sea is filled with these living things. Each one produces more of its own kind. God also made every bird that flies. And each bird produces more of its own kind. God saw that this was good. God blessed them and said, "Have many young ones

and grow in number. Fill the water of the seas, and let the birds grow in number on the earth." Evening passed, and morning came. This was the fifth day.

Then God said, "Let the earth be filled with animals. And let each produce more of its own kind. Let there be tame animals and small crawling animals and wild animals. And let each produce more of its kind." And it happened.

So God made the wild animals, the tame animals and all the small crawling animals to produce more of their own kind. God saw that this was good.

Human Beings

Then God said, "Let us make human beings in our image and likeness. And let them rule over the fish in the sea and the birds in the sky. Let them rule over the tame animals, over all the earth and over all the small crawling animals on the earth."

So God created human beings in his image. He created them male and female. God blessed them and said, "Have many children and grow in number. Fill the earth and be its master."

God said, "Look, I have given you all the plants that have grain for seeds. And I have given you all the trees whose fruits have seeds in them. They will be food for you. I have given all the green plants to all the animals to eat. They will be food for every wild animal, every bird of the air and every small crawling animal." And it happened. God looked at everything he had made, and it was very good. Evening passed, and morning came. This was the sixth day.

So the sky, the earth and all that filled them were finished. By the seventh day God finished the work he had been doing. So on the seventh day he rested from all his work. God blessed the seventh day and made it a holy day. He made it holy because on that day he rested.

The First People

The Lord God had not yet made it rain on the land. But a mist often rose from the earth and watered all the ground.

Then the Lord God took dust from the ground and formed man from it. The Lord breathed the breath of life into the man's nose. And the man became a living person. Then the Lord God planted a garden in the East, in a place called Eden. He put the man he had formed in that garden. The Lord God caused every beautiful tree and every tree that was good for food to grow out of the ground. In the middle of the garden, God put the tree that gives life. And he put there the tree that gives the knowledge of good and evil.

The Lord God put the man in the garden of Eden to care for it and work it. The Lord God commanded him, "You may eat the fruit from any tree in the garden. But you must not eat the fruit from the tree which gives the knowledge of good and evil. If you ever eat fruit from that tree, you will die!"

The First Woman

Then the Lord God said, "It is not good for the man to be alone. I will make a helper who is right for him."

From the ground God formed every wild animal and every bird in the sky. He brought them to the man so the man could name them. Whatever the man called each living thing, that became its name. But Adam did not find a helper that was right for him. So the Lord God caused the man to sleep very deeply. While the man was asleep, God took one of the ribs from the man's body. Then God closed the man's skin at the place where he took the rib. The Lord God used the rib from the man to make a woman. Then the Lord brought the woman to the man.

And the man said, "Now, this is someone whose bones came from my bones. Her body came from my body. I will call her 'woman,' because she was taken out of man."

So a man will leave his father and mother and be united with his wife. And the two people will become one body.

The man and his wife were naked, but they were not ashamed.

The Beginning of Sin

Now the snake was the most clever of all the wild animals the Lord God had made. One day the snake spoke to the woman. He said, "Did God really say that you must not eat fruit from any tree in the garden?"

The woman answered the snake, "We may eat fruit from the trees in the garden. But God told us, 'You must not eat fruit from the tree that is in the middle of the garden. You must not even touch it, or you will die.' "

But the snake said to the woman, "You will not die. God knows that if you eat the fruit from that tree, you will learn about good and evil. Then you will be like God!"

The woman saw that the tree was beautiful. She saw that its fruit was good to eat and that it would make her wise. So she took some of its fruit and ate it. She also gave some of the fruit to her husband, and he ate it.

Then, it was as if the man's and the woman's eyes were opened. They realized they were naked. So they sewed fig leaves together and made something to cover themselves.

Then they heard the Lord God walking in the garden. This was during the cool part of the day. And the man and his wife hid from the Lord God among the trees in the garden. But the Lord God called to the man. The Lord said, "Where are you?"

The man answered, "I heard you walking in the garden. I was afraid because I was naked. So I hid."

God said to the man, "Who told you that you were naked? Did you eat fruit from that tree? I commanded you not to eat from that tree."

The man said, "You gave this woman to me. She gave me fruit from the tree. So I ate it."

Then the Lord God said to the woman, "What have you done?"

She answered, "The snake tricked me. So I ate the fruit."

The Lord God said to the snake, "Because you did this, a curse will be put on you. You will crawl on your stomach, and you will eat dust all the days of your life. I will make you and the woman enemies to each other. Your descendants and her descendants will be enemies. Her child will crush your head. And you will bite his heel."

Then God said to the woman, "I will cause you to have much trouble when you are pregnant. And when you give birth to children, you will have great pain. You will greatly desire your husband, but he will rule over you."

Then God said to the man, "You listened to what your wife said. And you ate fruit from the tree that I commanded you not to eat from. So I will put a curse on the ground. You will have to work very hard for food. The ground will produce thorns and weeds for you. You will sweat and work hard for your food. Later you will return to the ground. This is because you

were taken from the ground. You are dust. And when you die, you will return to the dust."

The man named his wife Eve. This is because she is the mother of everyone who ever lived.

The Lord God made clothes from animal skins for the man and his wife. And so the Lord dressed them. Then the Lord God forced the man out of the garden of Eden. Then God put angels on the east side of the garden. He also put a sword of fire there. It flashed around in every direction. This kept people from getting to the tree of life.

The First Family

Eve became pregnant and gave birth to Cain. After that, Eve gave birth to Cain's brother Abel. Abel took care of sheep. Cain became a farmer.

Later, Cain brought a gift to God. He brought some food

PAUSE & WONDER

When Adam and Eve sinned and disobeyed God, it made them embarrassed and afraid. Suddenly there was shame, fear, and death in the perfect world God created. Something beautiful and free was lost — but not forever! We do not have the perfect world Adam and Eve first enjoyed. But because Jesus now has died for our sins, someday we will!

from the ground. Abel brought the best parts of his best sheep. The Lord accepted Abel and his gift. But God did not accept Cain and his gift. Cain became very angry and looked unhappy.

The Lord asked Cain, "Why are you angry? Why do you look so unhappy? If you do good, I will accept you. But if you do not do good, sin is ready to attack you. Sin wants you. But you must rule over it."

Cain said to his brother Abel, "Let's go out into the field." So Cain and Abel went into the field. Then Cain attacked his brother Abel and killed him.

Later, the Lord said to Cain, "Where is your brother Abel?"

Cain answered, "I don't know. Is it my job to take care of my brother?"

Then the Lord said, "What have you done? Your brother's blood is on the ground. That blood is like a voice that tells me what happened. And now you will be cursed in your work with the ground. It is the same ground where your brother's blood fell. Your hands killed him. You will work the ground. But it will not grow good crops for you anymore. You will wander around on the earth."

More People

Eve gave birth to a son. She named him Seth. After Seth was born, Adam lived 800 years. During that time he had other sons and daughters. Then he died.

The number of people on earth began to grow. The Lord saw that the human beings on the earth were very wicked. He saw that their thoughts were only about evil all the time. The Lord was sorry he had made human beings on the earth. His heart was filled with pain. So the Lord said, "I will destroy all human beings that I made on the earth. And I will destroy every animal and everything that crawls on the earth. I will also destroy the birds of the air. This is because I am sorry that I have made them." But Noah pleased the Lord.

Noah and the Flood

Noah was the most innocent man of his time. He walked with God.

God said to Noah, "People have made the earth full of violence. So I will destroy all people from the earth. Build a boat of cypress wood for yourself. Make rooms in it and cover it inside and outside with tar. This is how big I want you to build the boat: 450 feet long, 75 feet wide and 45 feet high. I will bring a flood of water on the earth. I will destroy all living things that live under the sky.

This includes everything that has the breath of life. Everything on the earth will die. But I will make an agreement with you. You, your sons, your wife and your sons' wives will all go into the boat. Also, you must bring into the boat two of every living thing, male and female. Keep them alive with you. There will be two of every kind of bird, animal and crawling thing. Also gather some of every kind of food. Store it on the boat as food for you and the animals."

Noah did everything that God commanded him.

The Flood Begins

Then the Lord said to Noah, "I have seen that you are the best man among the people of this time. So you and your family go into the boat. Take with you seven pairs, each male with its female, of every kind of clean animal. And take one pair, each male with its female, of every kind of unclean animal. Take seven pairs of all the birds of the sky, each male with its female. This will allow all these animals to continue living on the earth after the flood. Seven days from now I will send rain on the earth. It will rain 40 days and 40 nights. I will destroy from the earth every living thing that I made."

Noah did everything that the Lord commanded him.

Noah and his wife and his sons and their wives went into the boat. They went in to escape the waters of the flood. The clean animals, the unclean animals, the birds and everything that crawls on the ground came to Noah. They went into the boat in groups of two, male and female. This was just as God had commanded Noah. Seven days later the flood started.

The underground springs split open. And the clouds in the sky poured out rain. The rain fell on the earth for 40 days and 40 nights.

As the water rose, it lifted the boat off the ground. The water continued to rise, and the boat floated on the water above the earth. The water rose so much that even the highest mountains under the sky were covered by it. The water continued to rise until it was more than 20 feet above the mountains.

So God destroyed from the earth every living thing that was on the land. All that was left was Noah and what was with him in the boat. And the waters continued to cover the earth for 150 days.

The Flood Ends

But God remembered Noah

and all the animals with him in the boat. God made a wind blow over the earth. And the water went down. The underground springs stopped flowing. And the clouds in the sky stopped pouring down rain.

The water that covered the earth began to go down. After 150 days the boat came to rest on one of the mountains of Ararat. The water continued to go down.

Noah opened the window he had made in the boat. He sent out a dove. This was to find out if the water had dried up from the ground. The dove could not find a place to land because water still covered the earth. So it came back to the boat. Noah reached out his hand and took the bird back into the boat.

After seven days Noah again sent out the dove from the boat. And that evening it came back to him with a fresh olive leaf in its mouth. Then Noah knew that the ground was almost dry. Seven days later he sent the dove out again. But this time it did not come back.

Noah removed the covering of the boat and saw that the land was dry.

Then God said to Noah, "You and your wife, your sons and their wives should go out of the boat. Bring every animal out of the boat with you—the birds, animals and everything that crawls on the earth. Let them have many young ones and let them grow in number."

So Noah went out with his sons, his wife and his sons' wives. Every animal, everything that crawls on the earth and every bird went out of the boat. They left by families.

Then Noah built an altar to the Lord. Noah took some of all the clean birds and animals. And he burned them on the altar as offerings to God. The Lord was pleased with these sacrifices. He said to himself, "I will never again curse the ground because of human beings. Their thoughts are evil even when they are young. But I will never again destroy every living thing on the earth as I did this time.

"As long as the earth continues, there will be planting and harvest. Cold and hot, summer and winter, day and night will not stop."

The New Beginning

Then God blessed Noah and his sons. He said to them, "Have many children. Grow in number and fill the earth. Every animal on earth and every bird in the sky will respect and fear you. So will every animal that crawls on the ground and every fish in the sea. I have given them to you."

Then God said to Noah and his sons, "Now I am making my agreement with you and your people who will live after you. I make my agreement with every living thing on earth. I make this agreement with you: I will never again destroy all living things by floodwaters. A flood will never again destroy the earth."

And God said, "I am putting my rainbow in the clouds. It is the sign of the agreement between me and the earth."

The sons of Noah came out of the boat with him. They were Shem, Ham and Japheth. And all the people on earth came from these three sons. From these families came all the nations who spread across the earth after the flood.

God Calls Abram

The Lord said to Abram, "Leave your country, your relatives and your father's family. Go to the land I will show you. I will make you a great nation, and I will bless you. I will make you famous. I will bless those who bless you. I will place a curse on those who harm you. And all the people on earth will be blessed through you."

So Abram left Haran as the Lord had told him. Abram was 75 years old. Abram took his wife Sarai, his nephew Lot and everything they owned. They took all the servants they had gotten in Haran. They set out to go to the land of Canaan. In time they arrived there.

The Canaanites were living in the land at that time. The Lord appeared to Abram. The Lord said, "I will give this land to your descendants." So Abram built an altar there to the Lord, who had appeared to him.

God's Agreement with Abram

The Lord spoke his word to Abram in a vision. God said, "Abram, don't be afraid. I will defend you. And I will give you a great reward."

But Abram said, "Lord God, what can you give me? I have no son. So my slave Eliezer from Damascus will get everything I own after I die."

Then the Lord said, "You will have a son of your own. And your son will inherit what you have."

Then God led Abram outside. God said, "Look at the sky. There are so many stars you cannot count them. And your descendants will be too many to count."

Abram believed the Lord. And the Lord accepted Abram's

faith, and that faith made him right with God.

God said to Abram, "I am the Lord who led you out of Ur of Babylonia. I did that so I could give you this land to own."

As the sun was going down, Abram fell into a deep sleep. While he was asleep, a very terrible darkness came. Then the Lord said to Abram, "You can be sure that your descendants will be strangers and travel in a land they don't own. The people there will make them slaves. And they will do cruel things to them for 400 years. But I will punish the nation where they are slaves. Then your descendants will leave that land, taking great wealth with them. Abram, you will live to be very old. You will die in peace and will be buried. After your great-great-grandchildren are born, your people will come to this land again."

So on that day the Lord made an agreement with Abram. The Lord said, "I will give this land to your descendants."

The Promised Son

God said to Abraham, "I will change the name of Sarai, your wife. Her new name will be Sarah. I will bless her. I will give her a son, and you will be the father. She will be the mother of many nations. Kings of nations will come from her."

Abraham said to himself, "Can a man have a child when he is 100 years old? Can Sarah give birth to a child when she is 90?"

God said, "Sarah your wife will have a son, and you will name him Isaac. He is the son whom Sarah will have at this same time next year." After God finished talking with Abraham, God rose and left him.

A Baby for Sarah

The Lord cared for Sarah as he had said. He did for her what he had promised. Sarah became pregnant. And she gave birth to a son for Abraham in his old age. Everything happened at the time God had said it would. Abraham named his son Isaac.

Abraham was 100 years old when his son Isaac was born. And Isaac grew.

God Tests Abraham

After these things God tested Abraham's faith. God said to him, "Take your only son, Isaac, the son you love. Go to the land of Moriah. There kill him and offer him as a whole burnt offering. Do this on one of the mountains there. I will tell you which one."

Early in the morning

Abraham got up and saddled his donkey. He took Isaac and two servants with him. He cut the wood for the sacrifice. Then they went to the place God had told them to go. On the third day Abraham looked up and saw the place in the distance. He said to his servants, "Stay here with the donkey. My son and I will go over there and worship. Then we will come back to you."

Abraham took the wood for the sacrifice and gave it to his son to carry. Abraham took the knife and the fire. So Abraham and his son went on together.

Isaac said to his father Abraham, "Father!"

Abraham answered, "Yes, my son."

Isaac said, "We have the fire and the wood. But where is the lamb we will burn as a sacrifice?"

Abraham answered, "God will give us the lamb for the sacrifice, my son."

So Abraham and his son went on together. They came to the place God had told him about. There, Abraham built an altar. He laid the wood on it. Then he tied up his son Isaac. And he laid Isaac on the wood on the altar. Then Abraham took his knife and was about to kill his son.

But the angel of the Lord called to him from heaven. The angel said, "Abraham! Abraham! Don't kill your son or hurt him in any way. Now I can see that you respect God. I see that you have not kept your son, your only son, from me."

Then Abraham looked up and saw a male sheep. Its horns were caught in a bush. So Abraham went and took the sheep and killed it. He offered it as a whole burnt offering to God. Abraham's son was saved.

The angel of the Lord called to Abraham from heaven a second time. The angel said, "The Lord says, 'You did not keep back your son, your only son, from me. Because you did this, I make you this promise by my own name: I will surely bless you and give you many descendants. They will be as many as the stars in the sky and the sand on the seashore. And they will capture the cities of their enemies. Through your descendants all the nations on the earth will be blessed. This is because you obeyed me.' "

Then Abraham returned to his servants. They all traveled back to Beersheba, and Abraham stayed there.

Sarah lived to be 127 years old. She died in the land of Canaan. Abraham was very sad and cried because of her.

Then Isaac brought Rebekah into the tent of Sarah, his mother. And she became his wife. Isaac loved her very much. So he was comforted after his mother's death.

Abraham lived to be 175 years old. He had lived a long and satisfying life. In the cave of Machpelah, Abraham was buried with his wife Sarah. After Abraham died, God blessed his son Isaac.

Isaac's Family

Isaac's wife could not have children. So Isaac prayed to the Lord for her. The Lord heard Isaac's prayer, and Rebekah became pregnant.

While she was pregnant, the babies struggled inside her. She asked, "Why is this happening to me?" Then she went to get an answer from the Lord.

The Lord said to her, "Two nations are in your body. Two groups of people will be taken from you. One group will be stronger than the other. The older will serve the younger."

And when the time came, Rebekah gave birth to twins. The first baby was born red. His skin was like a hairy robe. He was named Esau. When the second baby was born, he was holding on to Esau's heel. That baby was named Jacob. Isaac was 60 years old when they were born.

When the boys grew up, Esau became a skilled hunter. He loved to be out in the fields. But Jacob was a quiet man. He stayed among the tents. Isaac loved Esau. Esau hunted the wild animals that Isaac enjoyed eating. But Rebekah loved Jacob.

One day Jacob was boiling a pot of vegetable soup. Esau came in from hunting in the fields. He was weak from hunger. So Esau said to Jacob, "Let me eat some of that red soup. I am weak with hunger."

But Jacob said, "You must sell me your rights as the first-born son."

Esau said, "I am almost dead from hunger. If I die, all of my father's wealth will not help me."

But Jacob said, "First, promise me that you will give it to me." So Esau made a promise to Jacob. In this way he sold his part of their father's wealth to Jacob. Then Jacob gave Esau bread and vegetable soup. Esau ate and drank and then left. So Esau showed how little he cared about his rights as the firstborn son.

Isaac Becomes Rich

Isaac planted seed in that land. And that year he gathered

a great harvest. The Lord blessed him very much. Isaac became a very rich man. He had many slaves and many flocks and herds.

The Lord appeared to Isaac. The Lord said, "I am the God of your father Abraham. Don't be afraid because I am with you. I will bless you and give you many descendants. I will do this because of my servant Abraham." So Isaac built an altar and worshiped the Lord there.

Jacob Leaves

When Isaac was old, he called Jacob and blessed him. Then Isaac commanded him, "You must not marry a Canaanite woman. Go to the house of your mother's father in Northwest Mesopotamia. Laban, your mother's brother, lives there. Marry one of his daughters. May God All-Powerful bless you and give you many children. May you become the father of many peoples. May the Lord give you and your descendants the blessing of Abraham. Then you may own the land where you are now living as a stranger. This is the land God gave to Abraham." So Isaac sent Jacob to Northwest Mesopotamia. Jacob went to Laban, the brother of Rebekah.

Jacob's Dream

Jacob left Beersheba and set out for Haran. He came to a place and spent the night there because the sun had set. He found a stone there and laid his head on it to go to sleep. Jacob dreamed that there was a ladder resting on the earth and reaching up into heaven. And he saw angels of God going up and coming down the ladder. And then Jacob saw the Lord standing above the ladder. The Lord said, "I am the Lord, the God of Abraham, your grandfather. And I am the God of Isaac. I will give you and your descendants the land on which you are now sleeping. Your descendants will be as many as the dust of the earth. They will spread west and east, north and south. All the families of the earth will be blessed through you and your descendants. I am with you, and I will protect you everywhere you go. And I will bring you back to this land. I will not leave you until I have done what I have promised you."

Then Jacob woke from his sleep. He said, "Surely the Lord is in this place. But I did not know it." Jacob was afraid. He said, "This place is surely the house of God and the gate of heaven."

Jacob rose early in the

morning. He took the stone he had slept on and set it up on its end. Then he poured olive oil on the top of it. At first, the name of that city was Luz. But Jacob named it Bethel.

Then Jacob made a promise. He said, "I want God to be with me and protect me on this journey. I want God to give me food to eat and clothes to wear. Then I will be able to return in peace to my father's house. If the Lord does these things, he will be my God. This stone which I have set up on its end will be the house of God. And I will give God one-tenth of all he gives me."

Then Jacob continued his journey. He came to the land of the people of the East. He looked and saw a well in the field. Three flocks of sheep were lying nearby, because they drank water from this well. A large stone covered the mouth of the well. All the flocks would gather there. The shepherds would roll the stone away from the well and water the sheep. Then they would put the stone back in its place.

Jacob said to the shepherds there, "My brothers, where are you from?"

They answered, "We are from Haran."

Then Jacob asked, "Do you know Laban?"

They answered, "We know him."

Then Jacob asked, "How is he?"

They answered, "He is well. Look, his daughter Rachel is coming now with his sheep." Then Jacob saw Laban's daughter Rachel and Laban's sheep. So he went to the well and rolled the stone from its mouth. Then he watered Laban's sheep. Then Jacob kissed Rachel and cried. He told her that he was from her father's family. He said that he was the son of Rebekah. So Rachel ran home and told her father.

When Laban heard the news about his sister's son Jacob, Laban ran to meet him. Laban hugged him and kissed him and brought him to his house. Jacob told Laban everything that had happened.

Now Laban had two daughters. The older was Leah, and the younger was Rachel. Jacob worked for Laban seven years so he could marry Rachel. But they seemed to him like just a few days. This was because he loved Rachel very much.

After seven years Laban brought his daughter Leah to Jacob. Jacob said to Laban, "I worked hard for you so that I could marry Rachel!"

Laban said, "In our country we do not allow the younger daughter to marry before the older daughter. But complete the marriage ceremony with Leah. I will give you Rachel to marry also. But you must serve me another seven years."

Then Laban gave him his daughter Rachel as a wife. Jacob worked for Laban for another seven years.

Jacob became very rich. He had large flocks, and many servants, camels and donkeys.

Jacob Goes Back

One day the Lord said to Jacob, "Go back to the land where your ancestors lived. I will be with you."

So Jacob put his children and his wives on camels. Then they began their journey back to Isaac, his father, in the land of Canaan. All the flocks of animals that Jacob owned walked ahead of them. He carried everything with him that he had gotten while he lived in Northwest Mesopotamia.

Jacob made his camp in the mountains. The angels of God met him. When Jacob saw them, he said, "This is the camp of God!"

During the night Jacob rose and sent his family and every-thing he had across the river. But Jacob stayed behind alone. And a man came and wrestled with him until the sun came up. The man saw that he could not defeat Jacob. So he struck Jacob's hip and put it out of joint. Then the man said to Jacob, "Your name will no longer be Jacob. Your name will now be Israel. You have wrestled with God and with men. And you have won." Then he blessed Jacob there.

So Jacob said, "I have seen God face to face. But my life was saved." Then the sun rose as he was leaving that place. Jacob was limping because of his leg.

God said to Jacob, "Go to the city of Bethel and live there. Make an altar to the God who appeared to you there."

So Jacob said to his family and to all who were with him, "We will leave here and go to Bethel. There I will build an altar to God. He has helped me during my time of trouble. He has been with me everywhere I have gone." So Jacob and all the people who were with him went to Bethel in the land of Canaan. There Jacob built an altar.

Rachel Dies

Rachel began giving birth. But she was having much trouble with this birth. When Rachel's nurse saw this, she said, "Don't be afraid, Rachel. You are giving birth to another son." Rachel gave birth to the son, but she died. As she lay dying, she named the boy Son of My Suffering. But Jacob called him Benjamin.

Rachel was buried on the road to Bethlehem. And Jacob set up a rock on her grave to honor her. Then Jacob camped just south of Migdal Eder.

The Family of Israel

Jacob had 12 sons. He had 6 sons by his wife Leah. Reuben was his first son. Then Leah had Simeon, Levi, Judah, Issachar and Zebulun.

He had 2 sons by his wife Rachel: Joseph and Benjamin.

He had 2 sons by Rachel's slave girl Bilhah: Dan and Naphtali.

And he had 2 sons by Leah's slave girl Zilpah: Gad and Asher.

These are Jacob's sons who were born in Northwest Mesopotamia.

Jacob went to his father Isaac at Mamre near Hebron. This is where Abraham and Isaac had lived. Isaac lived 180 years. So Isaac breathed his last breath and died when he was very old. And his sons Esau and Jacob buried him.

Joseph the Dreamer

Jacob loved Joseph more than his other sons. He made Joseph a special robe. Joseph's brothers saw that their father loved Joseph more than he loved them. So they hated their brother and could not speak to him politely.

Joseph told his brothers, "Listen to the dream I had. We were in the field tying bundles of wheat together. My bundle stood up, and your bundles of wheat gathered around mine. Your bundles bowed down to mine."

His brothers said, "Do you really think you will rule over us?" His brothers hated him even more.

Then Joseph told his brothers, "Listen, I had another dream. I saw the sun, moon and 11 stars bowing down to me."

Joseph also told his father about this dream. But his father scolded him, saying, "What kind of dream is this? Do you really believe that your mother, your brothers and I will bow down to you?" Joseph's brothers were jealous of him. But his father thought about what all these things could mean.

One day Joseph's brothers went to Shechem to herd their father's sheep. Jacob said to Joseph, "Go and see if your brothers and the sheep are all right. Then come back and tell me." So Joseph went to look for his brothers.

Sold into Slavery

Joseph's brothers saw him coming from far away. They said to each other, "Here comes that dreamer. Let's kill him and throw his body into one of the wells. We can tell our father that a wild animal killed him. Then we will see what will become of his dreams."

But Reuben said, "Let's not kill him. Throw him into this well here in the desert. But don't hurt him!" Reuben planned to save Joseph later and send him back to his father. So when Joseph came to his brothers, they pulled off his robe. Then they threw him into the well. There was no water in it.

While Joseph was in the well, the brothers sat down to eat. When they looked up, they saw a group of Ishmaelites. They were traveling to Egypt. Their camels were carrying spices, balm and myrrh.

Then Judah said to his brothers, "What will we gain if we kill our brother and hide his death? Let's sell him to these Ishmaelites. Then we will not be guilty of killing our own brother. After all, he is our own flesh and blood." The other brothers agreed. So the brothers took Joseph out of the well. They sold him to the Ishmaelites for eight ounces of silver. And the Ishmaelites took him to Egypt.

The brothers killed a goat and dipped Joseph's robe in its blood. Then they brought the robe to their father. They said, "We found this robe. Look it over carefully. See if it is your son's robe."

Jacob looked it over and said, "It is my son's robe! Some savage animal has eaten him. My son Joseph has been torn to pieces!" All of Jacob's sons tried to comfort him. But Jacob said, "I will be sad about my son until the day I die." Jacob cried.

Meanwhile those who had bought Joseph had taken him to Egypt. There they sold him to Potiphar. Potiphar was an officer to the king of Egypt and captain of the palace guard.

Potiphar saw that the Lord was with Joseph. He saw that the Lord made Joseph successful in everything he did. So Potiphar was very happy with Joseph. He allowed Joseph to be his personal servant. Because of Joseph the Lord blessed everything that belonged to Potiphar, both in the house and in the field. So Potiphar put Joseph in charge of everything he owned.

Joseph in Prison

Now Joseph was well built and handsome. After some time

the wife of Joseph's master began to desire Joseph. But he refused to spend time with her.

One day Joseph went into the house to do his work as usual. He was the only man in the house at that time. His master's wife grabbed his coat. She said to him, "Come with me." But Joseph left his coat in her hand and ran out of the house.

She kept his coat until her husband came home. And she said, "This Hebrew slave you brought here came in to shame me! When he came near me, I screamed. He ran away, but he left his coat."

So Potiphar arrested Joseph and put him into prison.

But the Lord was with Joseph and showed him kindness. The Lord caused the prison warden to like Joseph. The prison warden chose Joseph to take care of all the prisoners. He was responsible for whatever was done in the prison. The warden paid no attention to anything that was in Joseph's care. This was because the Lord was with Joseph. The Lord made Joseph successful in everything he did.

Two Dreams

After these things happened, two of the king's officers displeased the king. These officers were the man who served wine to the king and the king's baker. The king put them in the same prison where Joseph was kept. The captain of the guard put the two prisoners in Joseph's care.

One night both the king's officer who served him wine and the baker had a dream. When Joseph came to them the next morning, he saw they were worried. Joseph asked, "Why do you look so unhappy today?"

The men answered, "We both had dreams last night. But no one can explain the meaning of them to us."

Joseph said to them, "God is the only One who can explain the meaning of dreams. So tell me your dreams."

So the man who served wine to the king told Joseph his dream. He said, "I dreamed I saw a vine. On the vine there were three branches. I watched the branches bud and blossom, and then the grapes ripened. I was holding the king's cup. So I took the grapes and squeezed the juice into the cup. Then I gave it to the king."

Then Joseph said, "I will explain the dream to you. The three branches stand for three days. Before the end of three days the king will free you. He will allow you to return to your work. You will serve the king his wine just as you did before. But when you are free, remember me. Be kind to me. Tell the king about me so that I can get out of this prison. I was taken by force from the land of the Hebrews. And I have done nothing here to deserve being put in prison."

The baker saw that Joseph's explanation of the dream was good. So he said to Joseph, "I also had a dream. I dreamed there were three bread baskets on my head. In the top basket there were all kinds of baked food for the king. But the birds were eating this food out of the basket on my head."

Joseph answered, "The three baskets stand for three days. Before the end of three days, the king will cut off your head! He will hang your body on a pole. And the birds will eat your flesh."

Everything happened just as Joseph had said it would. But the officer who served wine did not remember Joseph. He forgot all about him.

The King's Dreams

Two years later the king had a dream. Then the king woke up. The king slept again and dreamed a second time. Then the king woke up again. The next morning the king was troubled about these dreams. So he sent for all the magicians and wise men of Egypt. The king told

them his dreams. But no one could explain their meaning to him.

Then the chief officer who served wine to the king said to him, "I remember something I promised to do. But I had forgotten about it. There was a time when you were angry with me and the baker. You put us in prison in the house of the captain of the guard. In prison we each had a dream on the same night. A young Hebrew man was in the prison with us. We told him our dreams, and he explained their meanings to us. Things happened exactly as he said they would: I was given back my old position, and the baker was hanged."

So the king called for Joseph. The guards quickly brought him out of the prison. He shaved, put on clean clothes and went before the king.

The king said to Joseph, "I have had a dream. But no one can explain its meaning to me. I have heard that you can explain a dream when someone tells it to you."

Joseph answered the king, "I am not able to explain the meaning of dreams. God will do this for the king."

Then the king said to Joseph, "In my dream I was standing on the bank of the Nile River. I saw seven fat and beautiful cows. They came up out of the river and ate the grass. Then I saw seven more cows come out of the river. They were thin and lean and ugly. They were the worst looking cows I have seen in all the land of Egypt. And these thin and ugly cows ate the first seven fat cows. But after they had eaten the seven cows, they just looked as thin and ugly as they did in the beginning. Then I woke up.

"I had another dream. I saw seven full and good heads of grain growing on one stalk. Then seven more heads of grain sprang up after them. But these heads were thin and ugly. They were burned by the hot east wind. Then the thin heads ate the seven good heads. I told this dream to the magicians. But no one could explain its meaning to me."

Joseph Tells the Dreams' Meaning

Then Joseph said to the king, "Both of these dreams mean the same thing. God is showing the king what he is about to do. You will have seven years of good crops and plenty to eat in all the land of Egypt. But after those seven years, there will come seven years of hunger. People will forget what it was like to

have plenty of food. This is because the hunger that follows will be so great. You had two dreams which mean the same thing. This shows that God has firmly decided that this will happen. And he will make it happen soon.

"So let the king choose a man who is very wise and understanding. Let the king set him over the land of Egypt. And let the king also appoint officers over the land. They should gather the food that is produced during the good years that are coming. They should store grain in the cities and guard it. That food should be saved for later. Then the people in Egypt will not die during the seven years of hunger."

Ruler over Egypt

This seemed like a very good idea to the king. All his officers agreed. And the king asked them, "Can we find a better man than Joseph to take this job? God's spirit is truly in him!"

So the king put Joseph in charge of all of Egypt. The king also gave Joseph a wife named Asenath.

Joseph traveled through all the land of Egypt. And Joseph gathered all the food which was produced in Egypt during those seven years of good crops. Joseph stored much grain, as much as the sand of the seashore. He stored so much grain that he could not measure it.

Before the years of hunger came, Joseph and Asenath had two sons. Joseph named the first son Manasseh. Joseph named the second son Ephraim.

Then the seven years of hunger began, just as Joseph had said. Joseph opened the storehouses and sold grain to the people of Egypt. And all the people in that part of the world came to Joseph in Egypt to buy grain. The hunger was terrible everywhere in that part of the world.

The Dreams Come True

Jacob said to his sons, "I have heard that there is grain in Egypt. Go down there and buy grain for us to eat. Then we will live and not die."

So Joseph's brothers went down to buy grain from Egypt.

Now Joseph was the one who sold the grain to people who came to buy it. So Joseph's brothers came to him. They bowed facedown on the ground before him. When Joseph saw his brothers, he knew who they were. Then Joseph left them and cried. After a short time he went back. When only the brothers were left with Joseph, he told them who he was. Joseph cried so loudly that the Egyptians heard him. But the brothers were very afraid of him.

So Joseph said to them, "Come close to me." So the brothers came close to him. And he said to them, "I am your brother Joseph. You sold me as a slave to go to Egypt. Now don't be worried. Don't be angry with yourselves because you sold me here. God sent me here ahead of you to save people's lives. No food has grown on the land for two years now. And there will be five more years without planting or harvest. So God sent me here ahead of you. This was to make sure you have some descendants left on earth. And it was to keep you alive in an amazing way. So it was not you who sent me here, but God. God has made me the highest officer of the king of Egypt. I am in charge of his palace. I am the master of all the land of Egypt.

"So leave quickly and go to my father. Tell him, 'Your son Joseph says: God has made me master over all Egypt. Come down to me quickly. You will be near me. Also your children, your grandchildren, your flocks and herds and all that you have will be near me. I will care for you during the next five years of hunger. In this way, you and your family and all that you have will not starve.' " Then Joseph kissed all his brothers. He cried as he hugged them.

So the sons of Israel did this. Joseph gave them food for their trip. Joseph also sent his father ten donkeys loaded with the best things from Egypt. They were loaded with grain, bread and other food for his father on his trip back. Then Joseph told his brothers to go. As they were leaving, he said to them, "Don't quarrel on the way home."

So the brothers left Egypt and went to their father Jacob in the land of Canaan. They told him, "Joseph is still alive. He is the ruler over all the land of Egypt." Their father was shocked and did not believe them. But the brothers told him everything Joseph had said. Now Jacob felt better. Jacob, also called Israel, said, "Now I believe you. My son Joseph is still alive. I will go and see him before I die."

Jacob Goes to Egypt

During the night God spoke to Israel in a vision. He said, "I am the God of your father. Don't be afraid to go to Egypt. I will make your descendants a great nation there. I will go to Egypt with you. And I will bring you out of Egypt again. Joseph's own hands will close your eyes when you die."

Then the sons of Israel loaded their father, their children and their wives. They also took their farm animals and everything they had gotten in Canaan. So Jacob went to Egypt with all his descendants. He took his sons and grandsons, his daughters and granddaughters. The total number in the family of Jacob was 70.

Joseph prepared his chariot and went to meet his father Israel. As soon as Joseph saw his father, he hugged his neck. And he cried there for a long time. Then Israel said to Joseph, "Now I am ready to die. I have seen your face. And I know that you are still alive."

Then the king said to Joseph, "Your father and your brothers have come to you. You may choose any place in Egypt for them to live. Give your father and your brothers the best land. Let them live in the land of Goshen."

Then Joseph brought in his father Jacob and introduced him to the king. And Jacob blessed the king.

Joseph gave his father, his brothers and everyone who lived with them the food they needed.

The Israelites continued to live in the land of Goshen in

Egypt. There they got possessions. They had many children and grew in number.

Jacob Blesses His Sons

Then Jacob called his sons to him. He said, "Come here to me. I will tell you what will happen to you in the future."

He gave each son the blessing that was right for him. Then Israel gave them a command. He said, "I am about to die. Bury me in the cave in the field of Machpelah east of Mamre. It is in the land of Canaan. Abraham and Sarah his wife are buried there. Isaac and Rebekah his wife are buried there. I buried my wife Leah there." After Jacob finished talking to his sons, he lay down. He put his feet back on the bed, took his last breath and died.

Jacob's sons carried his body to the land of Canaan. They buried it in the cave in the field of Machpelah near Mamre. After Joseph buried his father, he returned to Egypt. His brothers and everyone who had gone with him to bury his father also returned.

The Brothers Fear Joseph

After Jacob died, Joseph's brothers said, "What if Joseph is still angry with us? We did many wrong things to him. What if he plans to pay us back?" So they sent a message to Joseph. It said, "Your father gave this command before he died. He said to us, 'You have done wrong. You have sinned and done evil to Joseph. Tell Joseph to forgive you, his brothers.' So now, Joseph, we beg you to forgive our wrong. We are the servants of the God of your father." When Joseph received the message, he cried.

Then Joseph said to them, "Don't be afraid. Can I do what only God can do? You meant to hurt me. But God turned your evil into good. It was to save the lives of many people. And it is being done. So don't be afraid. I will take care of you and your children." So Joseph comforted his brothers and spoke kind words to them.

Joseph continued to live in Egypt with all his father's family. He died when he was 110 years old.

The Death of Joseph

Joseph said to his brothers, "I am about to die. But God will take care of you. He will lead you out of this land. He will lead you to the land he promised to Abraham, Isaac and Jacob." Then Joseph had the sons of Israel make a promise. He said, "Promise me that you will carry my bones with you out of Egypt."

WORTH WONDERING...

■ The word Genesis means "beginnings." In the following list, which of these things does NOT begin in Genesis? •men and women; •families; •plants and animals; •human sin; •the nation of Israel •God Himself.

■ When God first made people, what were they like?

■ What are some of the big promises that you see God making in this book?

■ Who is your favorite person in this book of Genesis? What do you like about this person?

■ Think about what you've seen in this book, then answer this question: Which is more important to God: people, or science and nature?

■ What good example can you give of someone in Genesis who did what was right?

■ What example can you give of someone in Genesis who did what was wrong?

■ In this book of the Bible, how do you see that God is great? And how do you see that He is good?

Look back in Genesis to see if you can find these verses:

■ *Look at the sky. There are so many stars you cannot count them. And your descendants will be too many to count.*

■ *You meant to hurt me. But God turned your evil into good.*

■ *God said, "Let there be light!" And there was light.*

■ *God looked at everything he had made, and it was very good.*

■ *Abram, don't be afraid. I will defend you. And I will give you a great reward.*

AND THERE'S MORE...

When you read Genesis in a full Bible, look especially for...

■ The man Enoch. God took him to heaven without his ever having to die.

■ The story of the tower of Babel, where God confused the languages of the world.

■ The story of Lot and the evil cities of Sodom and Gomorroh, which were destroyed by fire from heaven.

■ The story of Ishmael, another son of Abraham.

The Book of
EXODUS

Escape from Egypt

Looking forward to Exodus...

WHAT'S IT ABOUT?

"Escape from Egypt "

SIGNS AND WONDERS

The word Exodus means "exit." In Exodus you'll see God rescue the Hebrew people out of cruel slavery in Egypt. You'll also see how He starts them on their way toward a new land. Exodus is filled with the mightiest collection of God's miracles in the entire Old Testament. It also includes the famous Ten Commandments.

FACES AND PLACES

Moses: The man God chose to lead the people of Israel out of slavery in Egypt. God also gave His laws to Moses to pass on to all the people. Moses was the most humble man on earth.

Aaron: The brother of Moses, and his helper. He was also the person God chose to be the first high priest of Israel.

King of Egypt: He's also known as Pharaoh.

Canaan: The land God had promised to Abraham, Isaac, and Jacob, and to their descendants.

Holy Tent or **Meeting Tent:** God asked the Hebrews to build this tent as a place where He would meet with them. This tent served as a temple for the people. It is also known as the Tabernacle.

I wonder how God could prove His power to rescue His people...

THEN A NEW KING began to rule Egypt. He did not know who Joseph was. This king said to his people, "Look! The people of Israel are too many! And they are too strong for us to handle! We must make plans against them. If we don't, the number of their people will grow even more. Then if there is a war, they might join our enemies!"

So the Egyptians made life hard for the people of Israel. They put slave masters over the Israelites. The Egyptians forced the Israelites to work even harder. But this made the Israelites grow in number and spread more. So the Egyptians became more afraid of them. They forced the Israelites to work even harder making bricks and mortar. They also forced them to do all kinds of hard work in the fields.

The king commanded all his people: "Every time a boy is born to the Hebrews, you must throw him into the Nile River. But let all the girl babies live."

Baby Moses

There was a man from the family of Levi. He married a woman who was also from the family of Levi. She became pregnant and gave birth to a son. She saw how wonderful the baby was, and she hid him for three months. But after three months, she was not able to hide the baby any longer. So she got a basket made of reeds and covered it with tar so that it would float. She put the baby in the basket. Then she put the basket among the tall grass at the edge of the Nile River. The baby's sister stood a short distance away. She wanted to see what would happen to him.

Then the daughter of the king of Egypt came to the river. She was going to take a bath. She saw the basket in the tall grass. So she sent her slave girl to get it. The king's daughter opened the basket and saw the baby boy. He was crying, and she felt sorry for him. She said, "This is one of the Hebrew babies." She adopted the baby as her own son. The king's daughter named him Moses.

Moses Helps His People

Moses grew and became a man. One day he visited his people, the Hebrews. He saw that they were forced to work very hard. He saw an Egyptian beating a Hebrew man, one of Moses' own people. Moses looked all around and saw that no one was watching. So he killed the Egyptian and hid his body in the sand.

The next day Moses returned and saw two Hebrew men fighting each other. He saw that one man was in the wrong.

Moses said to that man, "Why are you hitting one of your own people?"

The man answered, "Who made you our ruler and judge? Are you going to kill me as you killed the Egyptian?"

Then Moses was afraid. He thought, "Now everyone knows what I did."

When the king heard about what Moses had done, he tried to kill Moses. But Moses ran away from the king and went to live in the land of Midian.

The Burning Bush

One day Moses was taking care of sheep. Moses led the sheep to the west side of the desert. He came to Sinai, the mountain of God. There the angel of the Lord appeared to Moses in flames of fire coming out of a bush. Moses saw that the bush was on fire, but it was not burning up. So Moses said, "I will go closer to this strange thing. How can a bush continue burning without burning up?"

The Lord saw Moses was coming to look at the bush. So God called to him from the bush, "Moses, Moses!"

And Moses said, "Here I am."

Then God said, "Do not come any closer. Take off your sandals. You are standing on holy ground. I am the God of Abraham, the God of Isaac and the God of Jacob." Moses covered his face because he was afraid to look at God.

The Lord said, "I have seen the troubles my people have suffered in Egypt. And I have heard their cries when the Egyptian slave masters hurt them. I am concerned about their pain. I will bring them out of that land. I will lead them to a good land with lots of room."

Moses said to God, "When I go to the Israelites, I will say to them, 'The God of your fathers sent me to you.' What if the people say, 'What is his name?' What should I tell them?"

Then God said to Moses, "I AM WHO I AM. When you go to the people of Israel, tell them, 'I AM sent me to you.'"

God also said to Moses, "This is what you should tell the people: 'The Lord is the God of Abraham, the God of Isaac and the God of Jacob. And he sent me to you.' That is how people from now on will know me.

"Go and gather the older leaders and tell them this: 'The Lord, the God of Abraham, Isaac and Jacob spoke to me. He says: I care about you, and I have seen what has happened to you in Egypt. I have decided that I will take you away from the troubles you are suffering in Egypt. I will lead you to the land of the Canaanites. This land grows much food.'

"Then you and the older leaders of Israel will go to the king of Egypt. You will tell him, 'The Lord, the God of the Hebrews, appeared to us. Let us travel three days into the desert. There we must offer sacrifices to the Lord our God.'

"But I know that the king of Egypt will not let you go. Only a great power will force him to let you go. So I will use my great power against Egypt. I will make miracles happen in that land. After I do this, he will let you go. And I will cause the Egyptian people to think well of the people of Israel. So when you leave, they will give gifts to your people. Each Hebrew woman will ask her Egyptian neighbor for gifts. Ask for silver, gold and clothing. You will put those gifts on your children when you leave Egypt. In this way you will take with you the riches of the Egyptians."

Proof for Moses

Then Moses answered, "What if the people of Israel do not believe me or listen to me? What if they say, 'The Lord did not appear to you'?"

The Lord said to him, "What is that in your hand?"

Moses answered, "It is my walking stick."

The Lord said, "Throw it on the ground."

So Moses threw it on the ground. And it became a snake. Moses ran from the snake. But the Lord said to him, "Reach out and grab the snake by its tail." So Moses reached out and took hold of the snake. When he did this, it again became a stick in his hand. The Lord said, "When this happens, the Israelites will believe that the Lord appeared to you. I am the God of their ancestors. I am the God of Abraham, the God of Isaac and the God of Jacob."

Then the Lord said to Moses, "Put your hand inside your coat." So Moses put his hand inside his coat. When he took his hand out, it was white with a harmful skin disease.

Then the Lord said, "Now put your hand inside your coat again." So Moses put his hand inside his coat again. When he took it out, his hand was healthy again. It was like the rest of his skin.

Then the Lord said, "The people may not believe you or be convinced by the first miracle. They may believe you when you show them this second miracle. After these two miracles they still may not believe or listen to you. Then take some water from the Nile River. Pour it on the dry ground. The water will become blood when it touches the ground."

But Moses said to the Lord, "But Lord, I am not a good speaker. I speak slowly and can't find the best words."

Then the Lord said to him, "Who made man's mouth? It is I, the Lord. Now go! I will help you speak. I will tell you what to say."

But Moses said, "Please, Lord, send someone else."

The Lord became angry with Moses. He said, "Your brother Aaron is a skilled speaker. And Aaron will speak to the people for you. You will tell him what God says. And he will speak for you. Take your walking stick with you. Use it to do the miracles."

Return to Egypt

So Moses started back to Egypt. He took with him the walking stick of God.

Meanwhile the Lord said to Aaron, "Go out into the desert to meet Moses." When Aaron went, he met Moses at Sinai, the mountain of God, and kissed him. Moses told Aaron everything the Lord had said to him when he sent him to Egypt. And Moses told him about the miracles which the Lord had commanded him to do.

So Moses and Aaron gathered all the older leaders of the Israelites. Aaron told them everything that the Lord had told Moses. Then Moses did the miracles for all the people to see. So the Israelites believed. They heard that the Lord was concerned about them and had seen their troubles. Then they bowed down and worshiped him.

Moses and Aaron Before the King

After Moses and Aaron talked to the people, they went to the king of Egypt. They said, "This is what the Lord, the God of Israel says: 'Let my people go so they may hold a feast for me in the desert.'"

But the king of Egypt said, "Who is the Lord? Why should I obey him and let Israel go? I do not know the Lord. And I will not let Israel go.

"Moses and Aaron, why are you taking the people away from their work? Go back to your hard work!"

That same day the king gave a command to the slave masters and foremen. He said, "Make these people work harder. Keep them busy. Then they will not have time to listen to the lies of Moses."

So the slave masters kept forcing the people to work harder.

Moses Prays to God

Then Moses returned to the Lord and said, "Lord, why have you brought this trouble on your people?"

Then the Lord said to Moses, "Now you will see what I will do to the king of Egypt. I will use my great power against him, and he will let my people go."

So Moses told this to the people of Israel. But they would not listen to him. They were discouraged, and their slavery was hard.

Then the Lord said to Moses, "Go tell the king of Egypt that he must let the Israelites leave his land."

Aaron's Walking Stick Becomes a Snake

Moses and Aaron went to the king as the Lord had commanded. Aaron threw his walking stick down in front of the king and his officers. And it became a snake.

So the king called in his wise men and his magicians. With their tricks the Egyptian magicians were able to do the same thing. They threw their walking sticks on the ground, and their sticks became snakes. But then Aaron's stick swallowed theirs. But the king was stubborn. He refused to listen to Moses and Aaron, just as the Lord had said.

Water Becomes Blood

Then the Lord said to Moses, "Tell Aaron to stretch the walking stick in his hand over the rivers, canals, ponds and pools in Egypt. The water will become blood everywhere in Egypt. There even will be blood in the wooden buckets and stone jars."

So Moses and Aaron did just as the Lord had commanded. Aaron raised his walking stick and struck the water in the Nile River. He did this in front of the king and his officers. So all the water in the Nile changed into blood. The fish in the Nile died, and the river began to stink. So the Egyptians could not drink water from it. Blood was everywhere in the land of Egypt.

Using their tricks, the magicians of Egypt did the same thing. So the king was stubborn and refused to listen to Moses and Aaron.

The Frogs

Then the Lord told Moses, "Go to the king of Egypt and tell him, 'This is what the Lord says: Let my people go to worship me. If you refuse, then I will punish Egypt with frogs. The Nile River will be filled with frogs. They will come from the river and enter your palace. They will be in your bedroom and your bed. They will enter your ovens and your baking pans. The frogs will jump up all over you.'"

Then the Lord said to Moses, "Tell Aaron to hold his walking stick in his hand over the rivers, canals and ponds. Make frogs come up out of the water onto the land of Egypt."

So Aaron held his hand over all the waters of Egypt. The frogs came up out of the water and covered the land of Egypt. The magicians used their tricks to do the same thing. So even more frogs came up onto the land of Egypt.

So the king called for Moses and Aaron. He said, "Pray to the Lord to take the frogs away from me and my people. I will let your people go to offer sacrifices to the Lord."

Moses and Aaron left the king. Moses asked the Lord about the frogs he had sent to the king. And the Lord did as Moses asked. The frogs died in the houses, in the yards and in the fields. The Egyptians put them in piles. The whole country began to stink. When the king saw that they were free of the frogs, he became stubborn again. He did not listen to Moses and Aaron, just as the Lord had said.

The Gnats

Then the Lord said to Moses, "Tell Aaron to raise his walking stick and strike the dust on the ground. Then everywhere in Egypt the dust will change into gnats." They did this. Then everywhere in Egypt the dust changed into gnats. The gnats got on the people and animals. Using their tricks, the magicians tried to do the same thing. But they could not make the dust change into gnats. So the magicians told the king that the power of God had done this. But the king was stubborn and refused to listen to them. This happened just as the Lord had said.

The Flies

The Lord told Moses, "Get up early in the morning. Meet the king of Egypt as he goes out to the river. Tell him, 'This is what the Lord says: Let my people go so they can worship me. If you don't let them go, I will send swarms of flies. The houses of Egypt will be full of flies. But I will not treat the people of Israel the same as the Egyptian people. There will not be any flies in the land of Goshen, where my people live. By this you will know that I, the Lord, am in this land.'"

So the Lord did as he had said. Great swarms of flies came into the king's palace and his officers' houses. All over Egypt flies were ruining the land.

The Disease on the Farm Animals

Then the Lord told Moses, "Go to the king of Egypt. Tell him, 'This is what the Lord, the God of the Hebrews, says: Let my people go to worship me. You might refuse to let them go and continue to hold them. Then the Lord will punish you. He will send a terrible disease on all your farm animals. He will cause all of your horses, donkeys, camels, cattle and sheep to become sick. But the Lord will treat Israel's animals differently from the animals of Egypt. None of the animals that belong to the Israelites will die.'"

The next day the Lord did as he promised. All the farm animals in Egypt died. But none of the animals belonging to Israelites died. But the king was still stubborn. He did not let the people go.

The Boils

The Lord said to Moses and Aaron, "Fill your hands with the ashes from a furnace. Moses, throw the ashes into the air in front of the king of Egypt. The ashes will spread like dust through all the land of Egypt.

The dust will cause boils to break out and become sores on the skin. These sores will be on people and animals everywhere in the land."

So Moses and Aaron took ashes from a furnace. Then they went and stood before the king. Moses threw ashes into the air. It caused boils to break out and become sores on people and animals. The magicians could not stand before Moses. This was because all the Egyptians had boils, even the magicians. But the Lord made the king stubborn. So he refused to listen to Moses and Aaron. This happened just as the Lord had said.

The Hail

Then the Lord told Moses, "Raise your hand toward the sky. Then the hail will start falling over all the land of Egypt. It will fall on people, animals and on everything that grows in the fields of Egypt." So Moses raised his walking stick toward the sky. And the Lord sent thunder and hail. And lightning flashed down to the earth. So he caused hail to fall upon the land of Egypt. There was hail, and there was lightning flashing as it hailed. This was the worst hailstorm in Egypt since it had become a nation. The hail destroyed everything that was in the fields in all the land of Egypt. The hail destroyed both people and animals. It also destroyed everything that grew in the fields. It broke all the trees in the fields. The only place it did not hail was in the land of Goshen. The people of Israel lived there.

The Locusts

Then the Lord told Moses, "Raise your hand over the land of Egypt, and the locusts will come. They will spread all over the land of Egypt. They will eat all the plants that the hail did not destroy."

So Moses raised his walking stick over the land of Egypt. And the Lord caused a strong wind to blow from the east. It blew across the land all that day and night. When morning came, the east wind had brought the locusts. Swarms of locusts covered all the land of Egypt and settled everywhere. There were more locusts than ever before or after. The locusts covered the whole land so that it was black. They ate everything that was left after the hail. They ate every plant in the field and all the fruit on the trees. Nothing green was left on any tree or plant anywhere in Egypt.

But the king did not let the people of Israel go.

The Darkness

Then the Lord told Moses, "Raise your hand toward the sky, and darkness will cover the land of Egypt. It will be so dark you will be able to feel it." So Moses raised his hand toward the sky. Then total darkness was everywhere in Egypt for three days. No one could see anyone else. And no one could go anywhere for three days. But the Israelites had light where they lived.

The Death of the Firstborn

Now the Lord had told Moses, "I have one more way to punish the king and the people of Egypt. After this, the king will send all of you away from Egypt."

So Moses said to the king, "This is what the Lord says: 'About midnight tonight I will go through all Egypt. Every firstborn son in the land of Egypt will die. The firstborn son of the king, who sits on his throne, will die. Even the firstborn of the slave girl grinding grain will die. Also the firstborn farm animals will die. There will be loud crying everywhere in Egypt. It will be worse than any time before or after this. But not even a dog will bark at the Israelites or their animals.' "

Passover

The Lord spoke to Moses and Aaron in the land of Egypt: "This month will be the first month of the year for you. On the tenth day of this month each man must get one lamb. It is for the people in his house. There must be enough lamb for everyone to eat. The lamb must be a one-year-old male. It must have nothing wrong with it. This animal can be either a young sheep or a young goat. Keep the animal with you to take care of it until the fourteenth day of the month. On that day all the people of the community of Israel will kill these animals. They will do this as soon as the sun goes down. The people must take some of the blood. They must put it on the sides and tops of the doorframes. These are the doorframes of the houses where they eat the lambs. On this night they must roast the lamb over a fire. Then they must eat it with bitter herbs and bread made without yeast.

"This is the way you must eat it: You must be fully dressed as if you were going on a trip. You must have your sandals on, and you must have your walking stick in your hand. You must eat it in a hurry. This is the Lord's Passover.

"That night I will go through the land of Egypt. I will kill all the firstborn of animals and people in the land of Egypt. I will punish all the gods of Egypt. I am the Lord. But the blood will be a sign on the houses where you are. When I see the blood, I will pass over you. Nothing terrible will hurt you when I punish the land of Egypt.

"You are always to remember this day. Celebrate it with a feast to the Lord. Your descendants are to honor the Lord with this feast from now on."

Then Moses called all the older leaders of Israel together. He told them, "Get the animals for your families. Kill the animals for the Passover. Take a branch of the hyssop plant and dip it into the bowl filled with blood. Wipe the blood on the sides and tops of the door-frames. No one may leave his house until morning. The Lord will go through Egypt to kill the Egyptians. He will see the blood on the sides and tops of the doorframes. Then the Lord will pass over that house. He will not let the one who brings death come into your houses and kill you.

"You must keep this command. This law is for you and your descendants from now on. Do this when you go to the land the Lord has promised to give to you. When your children ask you, 'Why are we doing these things?' you will say, 'This is the Passover sacrifice to honor the Lord. When we were in Egypt, the Lord passed over the houses of Israel. The Lord killed the Egyptians, but he saved our homes.'" So now the people bowed down and worshiped the Lord. They did just as the Lord commanded Moses and Aaron.

At midnight the Lord killed all the firstborn sons in the land of Egypt. The firstborn of the king, who sat on the throne, died. Even the firstborn of the prisoner in jail died. Also all the firstborn farm animals died. The king, his officers and all the Egyptians got up during the night. Someone had died in every house. So there was loud crying everywhere in Egypt.

Israel Leaves Egypt

During the night the king called for Moses and Aaron. He said to them, "Get up and leave my people. You and your people may do as you have asked. Go and worship the Lord. Take all of your sheep and cattle as you have asked. Go." The Egyptians also asked the Israelites to hurry and leave. They said, "If you don't leave, we will all die!"

The people of Israel did what

Moses told them to do. They asked their Egyptian neighbors for things made of silver and gold and for clothing. The Lord caused the Egyptians to think well of the Israelites. So the Israelites took rich gifts from the Egyptians.

The Way Out of Egypt

God did not lead them on the road through the Philistine country. That road is the shortest way. But God said, "They might think they will have to fight. Then they might change their minds and go back to Egypt." So God led them through the desert toward the Red Sea. The Israelites were dressed for fighting when they left the land of Egypt.

Moses carried the bones of Joseph with him. Before Joseph died, he had made the sons of Israel promise to do this. He had said, "When God saves you, remember to carry my bones with you out of Egypt."

The people of Israel camped on the edge of the desert. The Lord showed them the way. During the day he went ahead of them in a pillar of cloud. And during the night the Lord was in a pillar of fire to give them light. They could travel during the day or night. The pillar of cloud was always with them during the day. And the pillar of fire was always with them at night.

Then the Lord said to Moses, "Tell the Israelites to camp for the night between Migdol and the Red Sea. The king will think, 'The Israelites are lost, trapped by the desert.' I will make the king stubborn again so he will chase after them. But I will defeat the king and his army. This will bring honor to me. Then the people of Egypt will know that I am the Lord." The people of Israel did just as they were told.

The King Chases the Israelites

The king of Egypt was told that the people of Israel had left. Then he and his officers changed their minds about them. They said, "What have we done? We have let the people of Israel leave. We have lost our slaves!" So the king prepared his war chariot and took his army with him. He took 600 of his best chariots. He also took all the other chariots of Egypt. Each chariot had an officer in it. The Lord made the king of Egypt stubborn. So he chased the Israelites, who were leaving victoriously. The king of Egypt came with his horses, chariot drivers and army. And they chased the Israelites. They caught up with the Israelites while they were camped by the Red Sea.

The Israelites saw the king and his army coming after them. They were very frightened and cried to the Lord for help. They said to Moses, "What have you done to us? Why did you bring us out of Egypt to die in the desert? There were plenty of graves for us in Egypt. We told you in Egypt, 'Let us alone! Let us stay and serve the Egyptians.' Now we will die in the desert."

But Moses answered, "Don't be afraid! Stand still and see the Lord save you today. You will never see these Egyptians again after today. You will only need to remain calm. The Lord will fight for you."

Then the Lord said to Moses, "Command the people of Israel to start moving. Raise your walking stick and hold it over the sea. The sea will split. Then the people can cross the sea on dry land. I have made the Egyptians stubborn so they will chase the Israelites. But I will be honored when I defeat the king and all of his chariot drivers and chariots. I will defeat the king, his chariot drivers and chariots. Then Egypt will know that I am the Lord."

The angel of God usually traveled in front of Israel's army. Now the angel of God moved behind them. Also, the pillar of cloud moved from in front of the people and stood behind them. So the cloud came between the Egyptians and the people of Israel. The cloud made it dark for the Egyptians. But it gave light to the Israelites. So the cloud kept the two armies apart all night.

Moses held his hand over the sea. All that night the Lord drove back the sea with a strong east wind. And so he made the sea become dry ground. The water was split. And the Israelites went through the sea on dry land. A wall of water was on both sides.

Then all the king's horses, chariots and chariot drivers followed them into the sea. Between two and six o'clock in the morning, the Lord looked down from the pillar of cloud and fire at the Egyptian army. He made them panic. He kept the wheels of the chariots from turning. This made it hard to drive the chariots. The Egyptians shouted, "Let's get away from the Israelites! The Lord is fighting for them and against us Egyptians."

Then the Lord told Moses, "Hold your hand over the sea. Then the water will come back over the Egyptians, their chariots and chariot drivers." So Moses raised his hand over the sea. And at dawn the water became deep again. The Egyptians were trying to run from it. But the Lord swept them away into the sea. The water became deep again. It covered the chariots and chariot drivers. So all the king's army that had followed the Israelites into the sea was covered. Not one of them survived.

So that day the Lord saved the Israelites from the Egyptians. And the Israelites saw the Egyptians lying dead on the seashore. When the people of Israel saw the great power that the Lord had used against the Egyptians, they feared the Lord. And they trusted the Lord and his servant Moses.

The People Demand Food

Moses led the people of Israel away from the Red Sea. They came to the Desert of Sin. Then the whole Israelite community grumbled to Moses and Aaron in the desert. The Israelites said to them, "It would have been better if the Lord had killed us in the land of Egypt. There we had meat to eat. We had all the food we wanted. But you have brought us into this desert. You will starve us to death here."

Then the Lord said to Moses, "I will cause food to fall like rain from the sky. This food will be for all of you. Every day the people must go out and gather what they need for that day. I will do this to see if the people will do what I teach them. On the sixth day of each week, they are to gather twice as much as they gather on other days. Then they are to prepare it."

So Moses and Aaron said to all the Israelites: "This evening you will know that the Lord is the one who brought you out of Egypt. Tomorrow morning you will see the greatness of the Lord." And Moses said, "Each evening the Lord will give you meat to eat. And every morning he will give you all the bread you want. He will do this because he has heard you grumble against him. You are not grumbling against Aaron and me. You are grumbling against the Lord."

That evening, quail came and covered the camp. And in the morning dew lay around the camp. When the dew was gone, thin flakes like frost were on the desert ground. When the Israelites saw it, they asked each other, "What is that?"

So Moses told them, "This is the bread the Lord has given you to eat. The Lord has commanded, 'Each one of you must gather what he needs. Gather about two quarts for every person in your family.'"

So the people of Israel did this. Some people gathered much, and some gathered little. Then they measured it. The person who gathered more did not have too much. The person who gathered less did not have too little. Each person gathered just as much as he needed.

Moses said to them, "Don't keep any of it to eat the next day." But some of the people did not listen to Moses. They kept part of it to eat the next morning. But it became full of worms and began to stink. So Moses was angry with these people.

Every morning each person gathered as much food as he needed. But when the sun became hot, it melted away.

The people of Israel called the food manna. The manna was like small white seeds. It tasted like wafers made with honey.

The Israelites ate manna for 40 years. They ate it until they came to the land where they settled. They ate manna until they came to the edge of the land of Canaan.

Water from a Rock

The whole Israelite commu-nity left the Desert of Sin. They traveled from place to place as the Lord commanded. They camped at Rephidim. But there was no water there for the people to drink. So they quarreled with Moses. They said, "Give us water to drink."

So Moses cried to the Lord, "What can I do with these people? They are almost ready to kill me with stones."

The Lord said to Moses, "I will stand in front of you on a rock at Mount Sinai. Hit that rock with the stick, and water will come out of it. Then the people can drink." Moses did these things as the older leaders of Israel watched.

The Amalekites Fight Israel

At Rephidim the Amalekites came and fought the Israelites. So Moses said to Joshua, "Choose some men and go and fight the Amalekites. Tomorrow I will stand on the top of the hill. I will hold the stick God gave me to carry."

Joshua obeyed Moses and went to fight the Amalekites. At the same time Moses, Aaron and Hur went to the top of the hill. As long as Moses held his hands up, the Israelites would win the fight. But when Moses put his hands down, the

Amalekites would win. Later, Moses' arms became tired. So the men put a large rock under Moses, and he sat on it. Then Aaron and Hur held up Moses' hands. Aaron was on one side of Moses, and Hur was on the other side. They held his hands up like this until the sun went down. So Joshua defeated the Amalekites in this battle.

Then the Lord said to Moses, "Write about this battle in a book so people will remember. And be sure to tell Joshua. Tell him because I will completely destroy the Amalekites from the earth."

Israel at Sinai

Exactly three months after the Israelites had left Egypt, the Israelites camped in the desert in front of Mount Sinai. Then Moses went up on the mountain to God. The Lord called to him from the mountain. The Lord said, "Say this to the people of Israel: 'Every one of you has seen what I did to the people of Egypt. You saw how I carried you out of Egypt. I did it as an eagle carries her young on her wings. And I brought you here to me. So now obey me and keep my agreement. Do this, and you will be my own possession, chosen from all nations. Even though the whole earth is mine, you will be a nation that belongs to me alone.' You must tell the Israelites these words."

So Moses went down and called the older leaders of the people together. He told them all the words the Lord had commanded him to say. And all the people answered together, "We will do everything he has said."

Then there was thunder and lightning with a thick cloud on the mountain. And there was a very loud blast from a trumpet. All the people in the camp were frightened. Then Moses led the people out of the camp to meet God. They stood at the foot of the mountain. Mount Sinai was covered with smoke. This happened because the Lord came down on it in fire. The smoke rose from the mountain like smoke from a furnace. And the whole mountain shook wildly. The sound from the trumpet became louder.

So the Lord came down on the top of Mount Sinai. Then he called Moses to come up to the top of the mountain.

The Ten Commandments

Then God spoke all these words:

"I am the Lord your God. I brought you out of the land of Egypt where you were slaves.

"You must not have any other gods except me.

"You must not make for yourselves any idols. Don't make something that looks like anything in the sky above or on the earth below or in the water below the land. You must not worship or serve any idol. This is because I, the Lord your God, am a jealous God. A person may sin against me and hate me. I will punish his children, even his grandchildren and great-grandchildren. But I will be very kind to thousands who love me and obey my commands.

"You must not use the name of the Lord your God thoughtlessly. The Lord will punish anyone who is guilty and misuses his name.

"Remember to keep the Sabbath as a holy day. You may work and get everything done during six days each week. But the seventh day is a day of rest to honor the Lord your God. On that day no one may do any work: not you, your son or daughter, or your men or women slaves. Neither your animals nor the foreigners living in your cities may work. The reason is that in six days the Lord made everything. He made the sky, earth, sea and everything in them. And on the seventh day, he rested. So the Lord blessed the Sabbath day and made it holy.

"Honor your father and your mother. Then you will live a long time in the land. The Lord your God is going to give you this land.

"You must not murder anyone.

"You must not be guilty of adultery.

"You must not steal.

"You must not tell lies about your neighbor in court.

"You must not want to take your neighbor's house. You must not want his wife or his men or women slaves. You must not want his ox or his donkey. You must not want to take anything that belongs to your neighbor."

The people heard the thunder and the trumpet. They saw the lightning on the mountain and smoke rising from the mountain. They shook with fear and stood far away from the mountain. Then they said to Moses, "Speak to us yourself. Then we will listen. But don't let God speak to us, or we will die."

Then Moses said to the people, "Don't be afraid. God has come to test you. He wants you to respect him so you will not sin."

The people stood far away from the mountain while Moses

went near the dark cloud where God was. Then the Lord told Moses to say these things to the Israelites: "You yourselves have seen that I talked with you from heaven. You must not use gold or silver to make idols for yourselves. You must not worship these false gods in addition to me.

"Make an altar of dirt for me. Offer your whole burnt offerings and fellowship offerings on this altar as a sacrifice to me. Use your sheep and your cattle to do this. Worship me in every place that I choose. Then I will come and bless you."

Stone Tablets

So Moses told the people all the Lord's words and laws for living. Then the Lord said to Moses, "Come up the mountain to me. Wait there, and I will give you two stone tablets. On these are the teachings and the commandments. I have written these to teach the people."

So Moses and his helper Joshua set out. Moses went up Sinai, the mountain of God. Moses said to the older leaders, "Wait here for us until we come back to you. Aaron and Hur are with you. Anyone who has a disagreement with others can take it to them."

Moses Meets with God

When Moses went up on the mountain, the cloud covered it. The greatness of the Lord came down on Mount Sinai. The cloud covered the mountain for six days. On the seventh day the Lord called to Moses from inside the cloud. The Israelites could see the greatness of the Lord. It looked like a fire burning on top of the mountain. Then Moses went into the cloud and went higher up the mountain. Moses was on the mountain for 40 days and 40 nights.

The Lord said to Moses, "Tell the Israelites to build a holy place for me. Then I can live among them. Build this Holy Tent and everything in it by the plan I will show you."

So the Lord finished speaking to Moses on Mount Sinai. Then the Lord gave him the two stone tablets with the agreement written on them. The finger of God wrote the commands on the stones.

The People Make a Gold Calf

The people saw that a long time had passed. And Moses had not come down from the mountain. So they gathered around Aaron. They said to him, "Moses led us out of Egypt.

But we don't know what has happened to him. So make us gods who will lead us."

Aaron said to the people, "Take off the gold earrings that your wives, sons and daughters are wearing. Bring them to me." So Aaron took the gold from the people. Then he melted it and made a statue of a calf. He finished it with a tool. Then the people said, "Israel! These are your gods who brought you out of the land of Egypt!"

Aaron built an altar before the calf. Then he made an announcement. He said, "Tomorrow there will be a special feast." The people got up early the next morning. They offered whole burnt offerings and fellowship offerings. First the people sat down to eat and drink. Then they got up and sinned.

And the Lord said to Moses, "Go down from this mountain. Your people, the people you brought out of the land of Egypt, have done a terrible sin. They have quickly turned away from the things I commanded them to do. They have made for themselves a calf of melted gold. They have worshiped that calf and offered sacrifices to it. The people have said, 'Israel, these are your gods who brought you out of Egypt.'"

Then Moses went down the mountain. In his hands he had the two stone tablets with the agreement on them. The commands were written on both sides of each stone, front and back. God himself had made the stones. And God himself had written the commands on the stones.

When Moses came close to the camp, he saw the gold calf and the dancing. He became very angry. He threw down the stone tablets which he was carrying. He broke them at the bottom of the mountain. Then he took the calf that the people had made. He melted it in the fire. And he ground the gold until it became powder. He threw the powder into the water. And he forced the Israelites to drink that water.

The Lord caused terrible things to happen to the people. He did this because of what they did with the calf Aaron had made.

New Stones

The Lord said to Moses, "Cut two more stone tablets like the first two. I will write the same words on them that were on the first two stones which you broke. Be ready tomorrow morning. Then come up on Mount Sinai. Stand before me there on the top of the mountain. No one may come with you. No one should even be seen any place on the mountain. Not even the sheep or cattle may eat grass near that mountain."

So Moses cut two stone tablets like the first ones. Then early the next morning he went up Mount Sinai. He did this just as the Lord had commanded him. Moses carried the two stone tablets with him. Then the Lord came down in the cloud and stood there with Moses.

The Lord passed in front of Moses and said, "I am the Lord. The Lord is a God who shows mercy and is kind. The Lord doesn't become angry quickly. The Lord has great love and faithfulness. The Lord is kind to thousands of people. The Lord forgives people for wrong and sin and turning against him. But the Lord does not forget to punish guilty people."

Then Moses quickly bowed to the ground and worshiped. Moses said, "Lord, forgive our evil and our sin. Take us as your own people."

Then the Lord said, "I am making this agreement with you. I will do miracles in front of all your people. These things have never before been done for any other nation on earth. The people with you will see my work. I, the Lord, will do wonderful things for you. Obey the things I command you today, and I will force your enemies to leave your land. Be careful. Don't make any agreement with the people who live in the land where you are going. It will bring you trouble. But destroy their altars. Break their stone pillars. Don't worship any other god. This is because I, the Lord, the Jealous One, am a jealous God."

Then the Lord said to Moses, "Write down these words. This is because with these words I have made an agreement with you and Israel."

Moses stayed there with the Lord 40 days and 40 nights. During that time he did not eat food or drink water. And Moses wrote the words of the agreement — the Ten Commandments — on the stone tablets.

Then all the skilled workers made the Holy Tent. The total amount of gold used to build the Holy Tent was presented to the Lord. It weighed over 2,000 pounds. The silver given by the members of the community weighed 7,550 pounds. The bronze which was presented to the Lord weighed about 5,000 pounds.

They also made the holy clothes for Aaron as the Lord

had commanded Moses. So all the work on the Meeting Tent was finished. Moses looked closely at all the work. He saw they had done it just as the Lord had commanded. So Moses blessed them.

Then the Lord said this to Moses: "On the first day of the first month, set up the Holy Tent, which is the Meeting Tent." So the Holy Tent was set up. Moses he put put the altar for burning sacrifices at the entrance to the Holy Tent, the Meeting Tent. Then Moses offered a whole burnt offering and grain offerings on that altar. He did these things just as the Lord commanded him.

Then the cloud covered the Meeting Tent. The greatness of the Lord filled the Holy Tent.

WORTH WONDERING...

- Why did God bring the people of Israel out of Egypt?
- How did Moses find out what God wanted him to do?
- Why didn't the king of Egypt want the people of Israel to leave?
- What is God doing now to keep the promises He made in Genesis to Abraham, Isaac, and Jacob?
- Is Moses the kind of leader you would like to follow? Why or why not?
- In Exodus, what are some ways that God showed His people what to do?

GREAT VERSES TO THINK ABOUT AGAIN...

Look back in Exodus to see if you can find these verses:

- *I AM WHO I AM. When you go to the people of Israel, tell them, 'I AM sent me to you.'*
- *You saw how I carried you out of Egypt. I did it as an eagle carries her young on her wings.*
- *Take off your sandals. You are standing on holy ground.*
- *When we were in Egypt, the Lord passed over the houses of Israel. The Lord killed the Egyptians, but he saved our homes.*

AND THERE'S MORE...

When you read Exodus in a full Bible, look especially for...
- The words to the song Moses sang after the people escaped from Egypt.
- All the details about how God wanted the people of Israel to make the Holy Tent and everything that was to go inside and around it.

The Book of
LEVITICUS

*Rules for Worship
and Living*

Looking forward to Leviticus...

WHAT'S IT ABOUT?

"Rules for Worship and Living "

SIGNS AND WONDERS

The most important thing in anyone's life is worshiping God. In the book of Exodus, God teaches His people how to worship Him. The sacrifices and the worship in the Holy Tent are good reminders for Israel that God is holy and perfect — and that our sins must be paid for by blood.

FACES AND PLACES

Moses has written down in this book the rules for worship and living that God gave to him.

Aaron: The brother of Moses, and the man God chose to be the first high priest of Israel.

Nadab and **Abihu:** Sons of Aaron. They were killed by God when they did not follow His rules for offering incense to Him.

Holy Tent or **Meeting Tent:** The place where God said He would meet with the people of Israel. This tent served as a temple for the people. It is also known as the Tabernacle.

God is holy and perfect... I wonder how He could help His people remember that...

THE LORD CALLED Moses and spoke to him from the Meeting Tent. The Lord said, "Tell the people of Israel: 'When you bring an offering to the Lord, bring as your offering one of the cattle, or one of the sheep or goats.

"'If anyone offers a whole burnt offering from the cattle, it must have nothing wrong with it. It is a whole burnt offering, an offering made by fire. And its smell is pleasing to the Lord.

"'When anyone offers a grain offering to the Lord, it must be made from fine flour. The person must pour oil on it and put incense on it. It is an offering made by fire. Its smell is pleasing to the Lord. The rest of the grain offering will belong to

Aaron and the priests. This offering is a most holy part of the offerings made by fire to the Lord.' "

The Sin Offering

The Lord said to Moses, "Tell the people of Israel this: 'A person might sin by accident. He might do some things the Lord has commanded not to be done. If so, that person must offer a young bull to the Lord. It must have nothing wrong with it. This will be a sin offering for the sin he has done.' "

The Lord said to Moses, "Give this command to Aaron and the priests: 'The burnt offering must stay on the altar all night until morning. The altar's fire must be kept burning. It must not be allowed to go out. The priest must put more firewood on the altar every morning.' "

The Lord gave these teachings to Moses on Mount Sinai.

Aaron and His Sons

The Lord said to Moses, "Bring Aaron and his sons. Then gather the people together at the entrance to the Meeting Tent." Moses did as the Lord commanded him. The people met together at the entrance to the Meeting Tent.

Then Moses brought Aaron and his sons forward. He washed them with water. He put the inner robe on Aaron. And he tied the cloth belt around Aaron. Then he put the outer robe on him. Next he put the holy vest on Aaron. Then he tied the skillfully woven belt around him. So the holy vest was tied to Aaron. Then Moses put the chest covering on him. He also put the turban on Aaron's head. Moses did this as the Lord commanded him to do.

Then Moses put the special oil on the Holy Tent and everything in it. In this way Moses made them holy for the Lord. He sprinkled some oil on the altar seven times. Then he poured some of the special oil on Aaron's head. In this way he made Aaron holy for the Lord. Then Moses brought Aaron's sons forward. And he put the inner robes on them. He tied cloth belts around them. Then he put headbands on them. He did these things as the Lord had commanded him.

Then Moses brought the bull for the sin offering. And Aaron and his sons put their hands on its head. Moses killed the bull and took some of the blood. With his finger he put some of the blood on all the corners of the altar. In this way he made the altar pure. Then he poured out the rest of the blood at the bottom of the altar. So he made it holy and ready for service to God. Moses did all these things as the Lord had commanded him.

Then Moses told Aaron, "Go to the altar. There offer sin offerings and whole burnt offerings. Do this to remove your sins and the people's sins so you will belong to God."

So Aaron burned these things on the altar. He did this the way the Lord had commanded Moses.

He killed and offered the sin offering. Then Aaron brought the whole burnt offering and offered it. He also brought the grain offering to the altar.

Moses and Aaron went into the Meeting Tent. Then they came out and blessed the people. Then the Lord's glory came to all the people. Fire came out from the Lord. It burned up the offering on the altar. When the people saw this, they shouted with joy. They bowed facedown on the ground.

God Destroys Nadab and Abihu

Aaron's sons Nadab and Abihu took their pans for burning incense. They put fire in them and added incense. But they did not use the special fire Moses had commanded them to use. So fire came down from the Lord and destroyed Nadab and Abihu. They died in front of the Lord. Then Moses said to Aaron, "This is what the Lord was speaking about when he said, 'I must be respected as holy by those who come near me. Before all the people I must be given honor.'"

Life Is in the Blood

The Lord said to Moses, "Speak to Aaron, his sons and all the people of Israel. Tell them: 'This is what the Lord has commanded: The life of the body is in the blood. And I have given you rules for pouring that blood on the altar. You must do this to remove your sins so you will belong to the Lord. It is the blood that removes the sins from your life so you will belong to the Lord.' "

Other Laws

The Lord said to Moses, "Tell all the people of Israel: 'I am the Lord your God. You must be holy because I am holy.

"'Each person among you

P A U S E & W O N D E R

God says to me in Leviticus, "Be holy, for I am holy." Holy is a little word with a big meaning. One thing it means is that God can't even be touched by evil. That's why no one who hasn't been made clean by the blood of Jesus Christ can enter God's heaven, where everything must be holy forever. God can't allow any evil in His presence. That's why He asks me to get away from what is unclean and sinful.

must respect his mother and father.

"'Do not worship idols. Do not make statues or gods for yourselves. I am the Lord your God.

"'Do not harvest all the way to the corners of your fields. If grain falls onto the ground, don't gather it up. And don't pick up the grapes that fall to the ground. You must leave those things for poor people.

"'You must not steal. You must not cheat people. You must not lie to each other. You must be fair.

"'You must not do anything that would put your neighbor's life in danger.

"'You must not hate your brother in your heart. If your neighbor does something wrong, tell him about it. If you do not, you will be partly to blame. Forget about the wrong things people do to you. You must not try to get even. Love your neighbor as you love yourself. I am the Lord.

"'Show respect to old people. Stand up when they come into the room. Show respect also to your God. I am the Lord.

"'Be my holy people. Be holy because I am holy. I am the Lord your God. Remember and obey my laws. I am the Lord, and I have made you holy.

"'There are six days for you to work. But the seventh day will be a special day of rest. It is a day for a holy meeting. You must not do any work. It is a Sabbath to the Lord in all your homes.

Rewards for Obeying God

"'Remember my laws and commands, and obey them. If you do these things, the land will produce crops. Then you will have plenty to eat. You will live safely in your land. I will

PAUSE & WONDER

There must have been a lot of blood everywhere when the Old Testament people offered all their sacrifices to God. And that reminds me of how Christ had to bleed as the sacrifice to save us from our sin.

give peace to your country. No one will make you afraid.

"'I will walk with you and be your God. And you will be my people. You were slaves in Egypt. You were bent low from the heavy weights you carried as slaves. But I broke the heavy weights that were on your shoulders. I let you walk proudly again.

Punishment for Not Obeying God

"'But if you refuse to obey all my laws and commands, you have broken our agreement. If you do that, I will cause terrible things to happen to you. I will cause you to have disease and fever. You will not have success when you plant your seed. And your enemies will defeat you. These enemies hate you. And they will rule over you.

"'If you still do not obey me, I will punish you seven times more for your sins. If you still turn against me and refuse to obey me, I will beat you seven times harder. The more you sin, the more you will be punished. I will bring armies against you. I will destroy your cities. I will make the land empty.

There Is Always Hope

"'But maybe the people will confess their sins. Maybe they will admit they turned against

me and sinned against me. If they do, I will remember my agreement with Jacob. I will remember my agreement with Isaac and Abraham. I will listen to them even in the land of their enemies. I will not completely destroy them. This is because I am the Lord their God.'"

These are the laws, rules and teachings the Lord gave the people of Israel through Moses. This was at Mount Sinai.

WORTH WONDERING...

■ How is worshiping God different today for God's people than it was in the time of Moses?

■ What did Nadab and Abihu do wrong?

■ From what you see in this book, what do you think it means that God is holy?

■ Which parts of this book would you most like to know more about?

■ Why does God want His people not to work on the seventh day?

GREAT VERSES TO THINK ABOUT AGAIN...

Look back in Leviticus to see if you can find these verses:

■ *I am the Lord your God. You must be holy because I am holy.*

- *Love your neighbor as you love yourself.*
- *The life of the body is in the blood.*
- *I must be respected as holy by those who come near me. Before all the people I must be given honor.*
- *It is the blood that removes the sins from your life so you will belong to the Lord.*
- *I will walk with you and be your God. And you will be my people.*
- *Forget about the wrong things people do to you. You must not try to get even.*
- *There are six days for you to work. But the seventh day will be a special day of rest.*

AND THERE'S MORE...

When you read Leviticus in a full Bible, look especially for...

- More details about the sacrifices and offerings that were to be made to the Lord.

- More rules which the people of Israel were to keep. These rules helped them to be clean and good.

The Book of
NUMBERS

Wandering
in the Desert

Looking forward to Numbers...

"Wandering in the Desert "

SIGNS AND WONDERS

This book is called "Numbers" because the Hebrew people are counted in this book. God protects the people and leads them in the desert for forty years filled with plenty of excitement.

Notice the words of prophecy Balaam spoke: "A star will come from Jacob. A ruler will rise from Israel." These words came true in a special way many centuries later— in Jesus Christ.

FACES AND PLACES

Moses has written down in this book the rules for worship and living that God gave to him.

Aaron: The brother of Moses, and the man God chose to be the first high priest of Israel.

Holy Tent or **Meeting Tent:** The place where God said He would meet with the people of Israel.

Canaan: This was the land God had promised to Abraham and to the people of Israel.

Joshua: Moses' helper. He was one of the twelve spies Moses sent into Canaan.

Caleb: Another one of the twelve spies.

Korah: A man who led a group of the Hebrew people in speaking against Moses. God killed them for this.

Barak: The king of Moab, and an enemy of Israel.

Balaam: A prophet hired by Barak to speak curses against Israel.

I wonder how strict God would be if He needed to punish His people...

MOSES AND AARON called all the people of Israel together. Moses did exactly what the Lord had commanded. Moses listed the people while they were in the Desert of Sinai. All the men 20 years old or older who were able to serve in the army were listed. The total number of men was 603,550.

The families from the tribe of Levi were not listed with the others. The Lord had told Moses: "Do not include them with the other Israelites. But make the Levites responsible for the Holy Tent of the Agreement. They must take care of it and everything that is with it. If anyone else goes near the Holy Tent, he will be put to death. The Israelites will make their camps in separate divisions, each man near his family flag. But the Levites must make their camp around the Holy Tent of the Agreement."

So the Israelites obeyed everything the Lord commanded Moses. They camped under their flags. Each person traveled with his family and family group.

Aaron's Family, the Priests

Aaron had four sons. Nadab was the oldest, then Abihu, Eleazar and Ithamar. They were appointed to serve as priests. But Nadab and Abihu died when they sinned in the presence of the Lord.

The Lord said to Moses, "Tell Aaron and his sons, 'This is how you should bless the Israelites. Say to them: "May the Lord bless you and keep you. May the Lord show you his kindness. May he have mercy on you. May the Lord watch over you and give you peace."'

"So Aaron and his sons will bless the Israelites with my name. And I will bless them."

The Cloud Above the Tent

On the day the Holy Tent was set up, a cloud covered it. (The Holy Tent was also called the Tent of the Agreement.) From dusk until dawn the cloud above the Tent looked like fire. The cloud stayed above the Tent. At night it looked like fire. When the cloud moved from its place over the Tent, the Israelites moved. Wherever the cloud stopped, the Israelites camped. So the Israelites moved at the Lord's command.

The People Complain

The people complained to the Lord about their troubles. When he heard them, he became angry. Fire from the Lord burned among the people. So the people cried out to Moses. He prayed to the Lord, and the fire stopped burning.

Some troublemakers among them wanted better food. Soon all the Israelites began complaining. They said, "We want meat! We remember the fish we ate for free in Egypt. We also had cucumbers, melons, leeks, onions and garlic. But now we have lost our appetite. We never see anything but this manna!"

The manna was like small white seeds. The people would go to gather it. Then they ground it in handmills. Or they crushed it between stones. They cooked it in a pot or made cakes with it. It tasted like bread baked with olive oil. When the dew fell on the camp each night, so did the manna.

Moses heard every family crying. They stood in the entrances of their tents. The Lord became very angry. And Moses got upset. He asked the Lord, "Why have you brought me this trouble? Why did you make me responsible for all these people? Must I carry them in my arms as a nurse carries a baby? Where can I get meat for all these people? If you are going to continue doing this to me, then kill me now. If you like me, put me to death. Then I won't have any more troubles."

The Lord said to Moses, "Tell the people this: 'Make your-selves holy. Tomorrow you will eat meat. The Lord heard you cry, "We want meat! We were better off in Egypt!" So now the Lord will give you meat to eat. You will not eat it for just 1, 2, 5, 10 or even 20 days. You will eat that meat for a whole month. You will eat it until it comes out your nose. You will hate it. This is because you have rejected the Lord.'"

So Moses told them what the Lord had said.

The Quails Come

The Lord sent a strong wind from the sea. It blew quail into the area all around the camp. There were quail a day's walk in any direction. The people went out and gathered quail. They gathered all that day, that night and the next day. Everyone gathered at least 60 bushels. Then they spread them around the camp. But the Lord became very angry. He gave the people a terrible sickness. This came while the meat was still in their mouths.

The Spies Explore Canaan

The Lord said to Moses, "Send men to explore the land of Canaan. I will give that land to the Israelites. Send one leader from each tribe."

So Moses sent them to explore Canaan. He said, "Go through southern Canaan and then into the mountains. See what the land looks like. Are the people who live there strong or weak?"

So they went up and explored the land. In the Valley of Eshcol, they cut off a branch of a grapevine. It had one bunch of grapes on it. They carried that branch on a pole between two of them. They also got some pomegranates and figs. After 40 days of exploring the land, the men returned to the camp.

They came back to Moses and Aaron and all the Israelites and showed everybody the fruit from the land. They told Moses, "We went to the land where you sent us. It is a land where much food grows! Here is some of its fruit. But the people who live there are strong. Their cities are walled and large."

Then Caleb told the people near Moses to be quiet. Caleb said, "We should go up and take the land for ourselves. We can do it."

But the men who had gone with him said, "We can't attack those people. They are stronger than we are." And those men gave the Israelites a bad report about the land they explored. They said, "The land would eat us up. All the people we saw are very tall. We felt like grasshoppers. And we looked like grasshoppers to them."

The People Complain Again

That night all the people in the camp began crying loudly. All the Israelites complained against Moses and Aaron. All the people said to them, "We should have died in Egypt. Or we should have died in the desert. Why is the Lord bringing us to this land? We will be killed with swords. Our wives and children will be taken away. We would be better off going back to Egypt." They said to each other, "Let's get a leader and go back to Egypt."

Then Moses and Aaron bowed facedown in front of all the Israelites gathered there. Joshua and Caleb were among those who had explored the land. They tore their clothes. They said to all of the Israelites, "The land we went to explore is very good. If the Lord is pleased with us, he will lead us into that land. He will give us that land where much food grows. Don't turn against the Lord! Don't be afraid of the people in that land! We will chew them up. They have no protection, but we have the Lord. So don't be afraid of them."

The Lord Punishes the People

Then the glory of the Lord appeared at the Meeting Tent. The Lord said to Moses, "All these men saw the miracles I did in Egypt and in the desert. But they disobeyed me and tested me. So not one will see the land I promised to their ancestors. No one who angered me will see that land."

"I have heard these Israelites' grumbling and complaining. So tell them, 'This is what the Lord says. You will die in this desert. Every one of you who is 20 years old or older will die. You complained against me, the Lord. Not one of you will enter and live in the land I promised to you. Only Caleb and Joshua will go in. As for you, you will die in this desert.' I, the Lord, have spoken. I will certainly do these things to all these evil people."

The men Moses had sent to explore the land were responsible for the bad report. So the Lord killed them with a terrible sickness. Only two of the men did not die. They were Joshua and Caleb.

Korah, Dathan, Abiram and On

Korah, Dathan, Abiram and On turned against Moses. These

4 men were well-known leaders chosen by the community. They came as a group to speak to Moses and Aaron. The men said, "You have gone too far. Why do you put yourselves above all the people?" Then they said, "You brought us to the desert to kill us. And now you want to order us around."

Korah gathered all his followers who were against Moses and Aaron. And they stood at the entrance to the Meeting Tent. Then the glory of the Lord appeared to everyone.

The Lord said to Moses and Aaron, "Move away from these men. In a minute I will destroy them."

Moses warned the people, "Move away from the tents of these evil men! Don't touch anything of theirs. If you do, you will be destroyed because of their sins." So they moved away.

When Moses finished saying these things, the ground under the men opened up. The earth seemed to open its mouth and swallow them. All their families and everything they owned went down. They were buried alive, going to where the dead are. Then the earth closed over them. The people of Israel around them heard their screams.

The Work of the Priests and Levites

The Lord said to Aaron, "Bring with you your fellow Levites from your tribe. They will help you and your sons serve in the Tent of the Agreement. They are under your control. They will do all the work that needs to be done in the Tent. But they must not go near the things in the Holy Place or near the altar. If they do, both you and they will die. Their work is at the Meeting Tent. But only you and your sons may serve as priests. Only you may serve at the altar or go behind the curtain. I am giving you this gift of serving as a priest. Anyone else who comes near the Holy Place will be put to death."

The Lord also said to Aaron, "The people of Israel will give a tenth of what they make. I give that tenth to the Levites. This is their payment for the work they do serving at the Meeting Tent. The Levites will not get any land among the other Israelites."

The Lord said to Moses, "Speak to the Levites. Tell them: 'You will receive a tenth of everything the Israelites make. I give that to you. But you must give a tenth of that back to the Lord. I will accept your offering just as much as I accept the offerings from others. In this way you will present an offering to the Lord as the other Israelites do. Choose the best and holiest part from what you are given. This is the portion you must give to the Lord.' "

Water from the Rock

The people of Israel arrived at the Desert of Zin. They stayed at Kadesh. There was no water for the people. So they came together against Moses and Aaron. They argued with Moses. They said, "Why did you bring us to this terrible place? There's no water to drink!"

So Moses and Aaron went to the entrance of the Meeting Tent. They bowed facedown. And the glory of the Lord appeared to them. The Lord said to Moses, "You and your brother Aaron should gather the people. Also take your walking stick. Speak to that rock in front of them. Then water will flow from it. Give that water to the people and their animals."

So Moses took the stick from in front of the Lord. He did as the Lord had said. He and Aaron gathered the people in front of the rock. Then Moses said, "Now listen to me, you complainers! Do you want us to bring water out of this rock?" Then Moses lifted his hand and hit the rock twice with his stick. Water began pouring out. And the people and their animals drank it.

But the Lord said to Moses and Aaron, "You did not believe me. You did not honor me as holy before the people. So you will not lead them into the land I will give them."

Israel's Enemies

Moses sent messengers to the king of Edom. He said, "We are here at Kadesh, a town on the edge of your land. Please let us pass through your country. We will not touch any fields of grain or vineyards. We will not drink water from the wells. We will travel only along the king's road. We will not turn right or left until we have passed through your country."

But the king of Edom answered: "You may not pass through here. If you try, I will come and meet you with swords."

Then the Edomites went out to meet the Israelites with a large and powerful army. So the Israelites turned back.

The Canaanite king of Arad heard that the Israelites were coming. So he attacked them and captured some of them. Then the Israelites made this promise to the Lord: "If you will help us defeat these people, we will completely destroy their cities." The Lord listened to the

Israelites. And he let them defeat the Canaanites. The Israelites completely destroyed the Canaanites and their cities.

The Bronze Snake

The Israelites left Mount Hor and went around the country of Edom. But the people became impatient on the way. They grumbled at God and Moses. They said, "Why did you bring us out of Egypt? We will die in this desert! There is no bread! There is no water! And we hate this terrible food!"

So the Lord sent them poisonous snakes. They bit the people, and many of the Israelites died. The people came to Moses and said, "We sinned when we grumbled at you and the Lord. Pray that the Lord will take away these snakes." So Moses prayed for the people.

The Lord said to Moses, "Make a bronze snake. And put it on a pole. If anyone is bitten, he should look at it. Then he will live." So Moses made a bronze snake. And he put it on a pole. Then when a snake bit anyone, he looked at the bronze snake and lived.

Sihon and Og

The people of Israel sent messengers to Sihon, king of the Amorites. They said to him, "Let us pass through your country."

But King Sihon gathered his army together. They marched out to meet Israel in the desert. At Jahaz they fought the Israelites. Israel killed the king. Then they captured his land.

Then the Israelites went up the road toward Bashan. Og, the king of Bashan, and his army marched out to meet the Israelites. The Lord said to Moses, "Don't be afraid of him. I will hand him, his whole army and his land over to you. Do to him what you did to Sihon, the Amorite king." So the Israelites killed Og and his sons and all his army.

Balaam and Balak

Then the people camped near the Jordan River across from Jericho.

Balak son of Zippor saw everything the Israelites had done to the Amorites. And Moab was scared of so many Israelites. The Moabites said, "This mob will take everything around us. It will be like an ox eating grass."

Balak sent messengers to Balaam. Balak said, "A nation has come out of Egypt. They cover the land. They have camped next to me. They are too powerful for me. So come and put a curse on them. Maybe then I can defeat them and make them leave the area. I know that if you bless someone, the blessings happen. And if you put a curse on someone, it happens."

The leaders of Moab and Midian went with payment in their hands. They found Balaam. Then they told him what Balak had said.

But God said to Balaam, "Do not go with them. Don't put a curse on those people. I have blessed them."

Balaam said to Balak's leaders, "Go back to your own country. The Lord will not let me go with you."

So Balak sent other leaders. He sent more leaders this time. And they were more important. They went to Balaam and said, "Balak son of Zippor says this: Please don't let anything stop you from coming to me. I will pay you well. I will do what you say. Come and put a curse on these people for me."

But Balaam answered Balak's servants, "King Balak could give me his palace full of silver and gold. But I cannot disobey the Lord my God in anything, great or small. I will find out what more the Lord tells me."

That night God came to Balaam. He said, "These men have come to ask you to go with them. Go. But only do what I tell you."

Balaam and His Donkey

Balaam got up the next morning. He put a saddle on his donkey. Then he went with the Moabite leaders. But the angel of the Lord stood in the road to stop Balaam. Balaam was riding his donkey. And he had two servants with him. The donkey saw the angel of the Lord standing in the road. The angel had a sword in his hand. So the donkey left the road and went into the field. Balaam hit the donkey to force her back on the road.

Later, the angel of the Lord stood on a narrow path between two vineyards. There were walls on both sides. Again the donkey saw the angel of the Lord. So the donkey walked close to one wall. This crushed Balaam's foot against the wall. So he hit her again.

The angel of the Lord went ahead again. The angel stood at a narrow place. It was too narrow to turn left or right. The donkey saw the angel of the Lord. So she lay down under Balaam. Balaam was very angry and hit her with his stick. Then the Lord made the donkey talk. She said to Balaam, "What have I done to make you hit me three times?"

Balaam answered the donkey, "You have made me look foolish! I wish I had a sword in my hand! I would kill you right now!"

But the donkey said to Balaam, "I am your very own donkey. You have ridden me for years. Have I ever done this to you before?"

"No," Balaam said.

Then the Lord let Balaam see the angel. The angel of the Lord was standing in the road with his sword drawn. Then Balaam bowed facedown on the ground.

The angel of the Lord asked Balaam, "Why have you hit your donkey three times? I have stood here to stop you. What you are doing is wrong. The donkey saw me. She turned away from me three times. If she had not turned away, I would have killed you by now. But I would let her live."

Then Balaam said to the angel of the Lord, "I have sinned. I did not know you were standing in the road to stop me. If I am wrong, I will go back."

The angel of the Lord said to Balaam, "Go with these men. But say only what I tell you." So Balaam went with Balak's leaders.

Balak went out to meet him.

Balak took Balaam to see the edge of the Israelite camp.

Balaam's Messages

Balaam said, "Build me seven altars here. And prepare seven bulls and seven male sheep for me." Balak did what Balaam asked. Then they offered a male sheep and a bull on each of the altars.

Then the Lord told Balaam what he should say.

So Balaam went back to Balak and gave this message: "Balak brought me here from the eastern mountains. Balak said, 'Come, put a curse on the people of Jacob for me. Come, wish evil on the people of Israel.' But God has not wished evil on them. So I cannot wish evil on them."

Then Balaam gave this message: "God is not a man. He will not lie. God is not a human being. He does not change his mind. What he says he will do, he does. What he promises, he keeps. So I cannot change the blessing. He has found no wrong in the people of Israel. The Lord their God is with them. The people are strong like a lion."

Then Balaam gave this message: "I see a vision from the All-Powerful One. Israel's crops will have plenty of water. Their kingdom will be very great. They will defeat their enemies."

Then Balak was angry with Balaam. Balak pounded his fist. He said to Balaam, "I called you here to curse my enemies. But you have blessed them. Now go home!"

Balaam said to Balak, "I am going back. But I will tell you what these people will do to your people in the future."

Then Balaam gave this message: "I see a vision from the All-Powerful One. I see someone who will come some day, but not soon. A star will come from Jacob. A ruler will rise from Israel."

Then Balaam got up and returned home.

Joshua Is the New Leader

Then the Lord said to Moses, "Take Joshua. My Spirit is in him. Put your hand on him. Have him stand before Eleazar the priest and all the people. Then give him his orders as they watch. Let him share your honor. Then all the Israelites will obey him."

Moses did what the Lord told him.

WORTH WONDERING...

■ What good example can you give of someone in this book who did what was right?

■ What example can you give of someone in this book who did what was wrong?

■ What lessons did God's people learn in this book?

■ How was God training and testing His people?

■ How does God train and test you?

GREAT VERSES TO THINK ABOUT AGAIN...

Look back in Numbers to see if you can find these verses:

■ *May the Lord watch over you and give you peace.*

■ *God is not a man. He will not lie.*

■ *We should go up and take the land for ourselves. We can do it.*

AND THERE'S MORE...

When you read Numbers in a full Bible, look especially for...

■ How Miriam, the sister of Moses and Aaron, was punished.

■ A group of people called Nazirites, who lived for God in a special way.

■ How Aaron saved the people from being totally destroyed by a spreading sickness.

The Book of
DEUTERONOMY

Moses' Last Message
to Israel

Looking forward to Deuteronomy...

"Moses' Last Message to Israel "

This book tells us what God expects from His people — and why. Notice how much God loves Israel.

This book is like a group of "goodbye messages" from Moses. These words were his final sermons to the people of Israel before he died. Moses spoke these messages while the people of Israel were camped near the Jordan River. Across that river was Canaan, the Promised Land they would soon enter.

In this book Moses spoke about a special "prophet" who would come someday to Israel. These words came true in the most wonderful way when Jesus Christ came to earth.

This book is the last one about the life and work of Moses. The story of Moses takes up the books of Exodus, Leviticus, Numbers, and Deuteronomy. It is longer than anyone else's story in the Bible, except for that of Jesus Himself.

Moses is nearing the end of his life.

Joshua: Moses' helper. He is the one chosen to be Israel's leader after Moses dies.

Canaan: The land God had promised to Abraham and to the people of Israel. It lies across the Jordan River from where the people are camped when this book takes place.

I wonder what God wants most from His people...

IT WAS NOW 40 years after the Israelites had left Egypt. Moses spoke to the people. He told them everything the Lord had commanded him to tell them. Moses said: The Lord our God spoke to us at Mount Sinai. He said, "You have stayed long enough at this mountain. Get ready."

Look, I have taught you the laws and rules the Lord my God commanded me. Now you can obey the laws in the land you are entering. It is the land you will own. Obey these laws carefully. This will show the other nations that you have wisdom and understanding. They will hear about these laws. And they will say, "This great nation of Israel is wise and under-standing." No other nation is as great as we are. Their gods do not come near them. But the Lord our God comes near when we pray to him. And no other nation has such good teachings and commands.

But be careful! Watch out. Don't forget the things that you have seen. Don't forget them as long as you live. Teach them to your children and grandchil-dren. Remember the day you stood before the Lord your God at Mount Sinai. You came and stood at the bottom of the mountain. It blazed with fire that reached to the sky. Black clouds made it very dark. Then the Lord spoke to you from the fire. You heard the sound of words. But you did not see him.

There was only a voice. The Lord told you about his agreement. It was the Ten Commandments. And he told you to obey them. Then he wrote them on two stone tablets. Then the Lord commanded me to teach you the laws and rules. You must obey them in the land you will own when you cross the Jordan River.

The Lord Is Great

Nothing like this has ever happened before! Look at the past, long before you were even born. Go all the way back to when God made man on the earth. Look from one end of heaven to the other. Nothing like this has ever been heard of! No other people have ever heard God speak from a fire and still lived. But you have. No other god has ever taken for himself one nation out of another. But the Lord your God did this for you in Egypt. He did it right before your own eyes. He did it with tests, signs, miracles, war and great sights. He did it by his great power and strength.

Know and believe today that the Lord is God. He is God in heaven above and on the earth below. There is no other god! Obey his laws and commands, which I am giving you today. Obey them so that things will go well for you and your children.

Then you will live a long time in this land. The Lord your God is giving it to you forever.

The Command to Love God

You, your children and grandchildren must respect the Lord your God. You must do this as long as you live. Obey all his rules and commands I give you. Then you will live a long time. Then all will go well for you. You will become a great nation in a land where much food grows. The Lord, the God of your ancestors, has promised it to you.

Listen, people of Israel! The Lord is our God. He is the only Lord. Love the Lord your God with all your heart, soul and strength. Always remember these commands I give you today. Teach them to your children. Talk about them when you sit at home and walk along the road. Talk about them when you lie down and when you get up. Write them down and tie them to your hands as a sign. Tie them on your forehead to remind you. Write them on your doors and gates.

In the future your son will ask you, "What do the laws, commands and rules the Lord our God gave us mean?" Tell him, "We were slaves to the king of Egypt. But the Lord brought us out of Egypt by his great power. The Lord showed us great and terrible signs and miracles. He led us here. And he will give us the land he promised our ancestors. The Lord ordered us to obey all these commands. And we must respect the Lord our God. Then we will always do well and stay alive as we are today. The right thing for us to do is this: Obey all these rules in the presence of the Lord our God. He has commanded it."

God's People

The Lord your God will bring you into the land. You are entering that land to own it. As you go in, he will force out these nations: the Hittites, Girgashites, Amorites, Canaanites, Perizzites, Hivites and Jebusites. These seven nations are stronger than you. The Lord your God will hand these nations over to you. You will defeat them. You must destroy them completely. Do not make a peace treaty with them. Do not show them any mercy. Do not marry any of them. Don't let your daughters marry their sons. And don't let your sons marry their daughters. Those people will turn your children away from me. Your children will begin serving other gods. The Lord will be very

angry with you. And he will quickly destroy you.

The Lord did not care for you and choose you because there were many of you. You are the smallest nation of all. But the Lord chose you because he loved you. So know that the Lord your God is God. He is the faithful God. He will keep his agreement of love for a thousand lifetimes. He does this for people who love him and obey his commands. But he will pay back those people who hate him. He will destroy them. And he will not be slow to pay back those who hate him. So be careful to obey the commands, rules and laws I give you today.

You might say to yourselves, "These nations are stronger than we are. We can't force them out." But don't be afraid of them. Remember what the Lord your God did to all of Egypt and its king. The Lord your God will do the same thing to all the nations you now fear. The Lord your God will also send hornets to attack them. The Lord will help you defeat their kings. The world will forget who they were. No one will be able to stop you. You will destroy them all. Burn up their idols in the fire. Do not wish for the silver and gold on them. Don't take it for yourselves, or you will be trapped by it. The Lord your God hates it. Do not bring one of those hated things into your house. If you do, you will be completely destroyed along with it. Hate and reject those things. They must be completely destroyed.

Remember the Lord

Remember how the Lord your God has led you in the desert for these 40 years. He took away your pride. He tested you. He wanted to know what was in your heart. He wanted to know if you would obey his commands. He let you get hungry. Then he fed you with manna. Manna was something neither you nor your ancestors had ever seen. This was to teach you that a person does not live only by eating bread. But a person lives by everything the Lord says. During these 40 years, your clothes did not wear out. And your feet did not swell. Know in your heart that the Lord your God corrects you. He corrects you as a father does his son.

The Lord your God is bringing you into a good land. The land has rivers and pools of water. Springs flow in the valleys and hills. The land has wheat and barley, vines, fig trees, pomegranates, olive oil and honey. It is a land where you will have plenty of food. You will have everything you need there. The rocks are iron. You can dig copper out of the hills.

Never forget the Lord your God. Do not follow other gods. Do not worship them. Do not bow down to them. If you do, I warn you today that you will be destroyed. The Lord destroyed the other nations for you. And

PAUSE & WONDER

When Satan tempted Jesus three times in the desert, Jesus answered each time with words from Deuteronomy. These are the words He spoke: "Respect the Lord your God. Serve only him.... Do not test the Lord your God.... A person does not live only by eating bread. But a person lives by everything the Lord says."

God's words are my weapons against the devil. I can use them just as Jesus did to fight against the devil's attacks.

you can be destroyed the same way if you do not obey the Lord your God.

Listen, Israel. You will soon cross the Jordan River. You will go in to force out nations that are bigger and stronger than you. The Lord your God will force those nations out ahead of you. After that, don't say to yourself, "The Lord brought me here. I own this land because I am so good." No! It is because these nations are evil. It is not because you are good. You are a stubborn people. You would not obey the Lord from the day you left Egypt until you arrived here.

What the Lord Wants You To Do

Now, Israel, this is what the Lord wants you to do. Respect the Lord your God. Do what he has told you to do. Love him. Serve the Lord your God with your whole being. And obey the Lord's commands and laws.

The Lord owns the world and everything in it. The heavens, even the highest heavens, are his. Give yourselves to serving the Lord. Do not be stubborn any longer. Be loyal to him. Make your promises in his name. You should praise him. He is your God. He has done great and wonderful things for you. You have seen them with your own eyes. There were only 70 of your ancestors when they went down to Egypt. Now the Lord your God has made you as many as the stars in the sky.

So obey all the commands I am giving you today. Then you will be strong. Then you can go in and take the land you are going to own. The Lord promised to give it to your ancestors and their descendants. It is a land where much food grows. It is a land of hills and valleys. It drinks rain from heaven. It is a land the Lord your God loves. His eyes are on it continually. He watches it from the beginning of the year to the end.

See, today I am letting you choose a blessing or a curse. You will be blessed if you obey the commands of the Lord your God. But you will be cursed if you disobey the commands of the Lord your God.

The Place for Worship

The Lord your God will choose a place among your tribes where he is to be worshiped. Go there. Bring to that place your burnt offerings and sacrifices.

Don't sacrifice your burnt offerings just anywhere you please. Offer them only in the place the Lord will choose.

Giving One-Tenth

Be sure to save one-tenth of all your crops each year. Take it to the place the Lord your God will choose where he is to be worshiped.

Choosing a King

You will enter the land the Lord your God is giving you. You will take it as your own and live in it. Then you will say, "Let's appoint a king over us like the nations all around us." Be sure to appoint over you the king the Lord your God chooses. He must be one of your own people. Do not appoint a foreigner as your king. He is not a fellow Israelite. The king must not have too many horses for himself. He must not send people to Egypt to get more horses. The Lord has told you, "Don't return that way again." The king must not have many wives. If he does, his heart will be led away from God. He must not have too much silver and gold.

When he becomes king, he should write a copy of the teachings on a scroll for himself. He should copy it from the priests and Levites. He should keep it with him all the time. He should read from it every day of his life. Then he will learn to respect the Lord his God. And he will obey all the teachings and commands. He should not think he is better than his brothers. He must not stop obeying the law in any way. Then he and his descendants will rule the kingdom for a long time.

You will enter the land the Lord your God is giving you. But don't learn to do the terrible things the other nations do. Don't let anyone among you offer his son or daughter as a sacrifice in the fire. Don't let anyone use magic or witchcraft. Don't let them try to talk with the spirits of dead people. The Lord hates anyone who does these things. The other nations do these things. That is why the Lord your God will force them out of the land ahead of you. You must be innocent in the presence of the Lord your God.

The Lord's Special Prophet

The Lord your God will give you a prophet like me. He will be one of your own people. Listen to him.

The Lord said to me, "I will give them a prophet like you. He will be one of their own people. I will tell him what to say. And he will tell them everything I command. This prophet will speak for me. Anyone who does not listen when he speaks will answer to me."

Life or Death

You must follow the Lord your God with your whole being. This command I give you today is not too hard for you. It is not beyond what you can do. It is not up in heaven. You do not have to ask, "Who will go up to heaven and get it for us? Then we can obey it and keep it." It is not on the other side of the sea. You do not have to ask, "Who will go across the sea and get it? Who will tell it to us? Then we can keep it." No, the word is very near you. It is in your mouth and in your heart. So, you may obey it.

Today I ask heaven and earth to be witnesses. I am offering you life or death, blessings or curses. Now, choose life! Then you and your children may live. Love the Lord your God. Obey him. Stay close to him. He is your life.

Joshua Takes Moses' Place

Then Moses went and spoke these words to all the Israelites: "I am now 120 years old. I cannot lead you anymore. The Lord told me I would not cross the Jordan River. The Lord your God will lead you across himself. He will destroy those nations for you. You will take over their land. Joshua will also lead you

across. Be strong and brave. Don't be afraid of them. Don't be frightened. The Lord your God will go with you. He will not leave you or forget you."

Then Moses called Joshua and spoke to him in front of the people. Moses said, "Be strong and brave. Lead these people into the land the Lord promised to give their ancestors. Help the people take it as their own. The Lord himself will go before you. He will be with you. He will not leave you or forget you. Don't be afraid. Don't worry."

The Lord Calls Moses and Joshua

The Lord said to Moses, "Soon you will die. Get Joshua and come to the Meeting Tent. I will command him." So Moses and Joshua went to the Meeting Tent.

The Lord appeared at the Meeting Tent in a cloud. And the Lord said to Moses, "You will soon die. Then these people will not be loyal to me. They will worship the foreign gods of the land they are entering. They will leave me. And they will break the agreement I made with them. Then I will become very angry at them. I will leave them. I will turn away from them. And they will be destroyed. Many terrible things will happen to them. Then they will say, 'God is not with us. That is why these terrible things are happening.' I will turn away from them then. They have done wrong. They have turned to other gods."

Then the Lord gave this command to Joshua son of Nun: "Be strong and brave. Lead the people of Israel to the land I promised them. And I will be with you."

Moses wrote all the words of the teachings in a book. Then he gave a command to the Levites. They carried the Box of the Agreement with the Lord. He said, "Take this Book of the Teachings. Put it beside the Box of the Agreement with the Lord your God. It must stay there as a witness against you. I know how stubborn and disobedient you are. You have disobeyed the Lord while I am alive and with you. You will disobey even more after I die! I know that after I die you will become completely evil. You will turn away from the commands I have given you. Then terrible things will happen to you in the future. You will do what the Lord says is evil. You will make him angry with the idols you have made."

When Moses finished speaking these words to all Israel, he said to them: "Pay attention to all the words I have said to you today. Command your children to obey carefully everything in these teachings. These should not be unimportant words for you. They mean life for you! By these words you will live a long time in the land you are crossing the Jordan River to own."

The Lord spoke to Moses again that same day. He said, "Go up to Mount Nebo in the country of Moab. Look at the land of Canaan. I am giving it to the Israelites to own. You will die on that mountain that you climb. You will not enter the land I am giving the people of Israel."

Moses Dies

Then Moses climbed up Mount Nebo. From there the Lord showed him all the land. He could see as far as the Mediterranean Sea. Then the Lord said to Moses, "This is the land I promised to Abraham, Isaac and Jacob. I said to them, 'I will give this land to your descendants.' "

Then Moses, the servant of the Lord, died there in Moab. The Lord buried Moses in Moab. But even today no one knows where his grave is. Moses was 120 years old when he died. And he was still strong. The Israelites cried for Moses for 30 days. They stayed in the plains of Moab until the time of sadness was over.

There has never been another prophet like Moses. The Lord knew Moses face to face.

WORTH WONDERING...

- Notice in Deuteronomy how often God tells His people to remember His command- ments and obey them. What do you think are the most important things God wants you to remember and obey?
- In this book of the Bible, how do you see that God is great? And how do you see that He is good?
- Through Moses, God told the people of Israel that He was offering them a choice between life and death. Is that true for us today as well? If so, in what way?

GREAT VERSES TO THINK ABOUT AGAIN...

Look back in Deuteronomy to see if you can find these verses:

- *The Lord your God is bringing you into a good land.*
- *Always remember these commands I give you today. Teach them to your children. Talk about them when you sit at home and walk along the road.*

Talk about them when you lie down and when you get up.

- *I am offering you life or death, blessings or curses. Now, choose life!*
- *Love the Lord your God with all your heart, soul and strength.*
- *This was to teach you that a person does not live only by eating bread. But a person lives by everything the Lord says.*

AND THERE'S MORE...

When you read Deuteronomy in a full Bible, look especially for...

- How Moses talks again about everything that happened to the people of Israel during the forty years of wandering in the desert.
- How Moses talks again about the Ten Commandments. He tells each one of them again, to help the people of Israel remember them.

INTRODUCING...

JOSHUA • JUDGES • RUTH
1 and 2 SAMUEL • 1 and 2 KINGS
1 and 2 CHRONICLES
EZRA • NEHEMIAH • ESTHER

W e call this second part of God's Word the Old Testament History Books—and what interesting history they tell! Some of the Bible's most exciting stories are here, plus many of our favorite Bible heroes...including Joshua, Deborah,Gideon, Ruth, Samuel, David, Jonathan, Elijah, Elisha, Nehemiah, and Esther.

In the book of Genesis, the nation of Israel had started small, with Abraham, his son Isaac, and Isaac's son Jacob. But soon this family grew to many millions of people, and became a true nation. Now, in these 12 history books, God gives them their first king, and they build the first Temple for God in Jerusalem.

But many sad and terrible things also happen in these books. Very often the people turn away from worshiping God, and disobey Him. Then God has to discipline them. Many times He sends foreign armies to fight against them. The people tell God how sorry they are, and God forgives them — but they turn away from God once more. This happens again and again, and gets worse and worse. It's like a sickness. Finally God allows an enemy army to capture Israel's king, cut out his eyes, and lead him away. The army burns down the Temple and all of Jerusalem. They take away most of Israel's people and force them to live as prisoners in another land. The people of Israel lose their king, their homeland, and their Temple. Eventually, though, God allows the people to return and to rebuild their nation and their Temple.

It's a wonderful story, with many twists and turns...

The Book of
JOSHUA

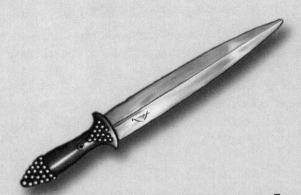

Israel Conquers the
Promised Land

Looking forward to Joshua...

"Israel Conquers the Promised Land"

SIGNS AND WONDERS

With Joshua as their leader, God gives big victories to the people of Israel as they take over the Promised Land. This is a book about being a winner in the Lord!

Joshua's name in the Hebrew language means the same as Jesus' name. Joshua is a great warrior and leader, because He obeys the Lord. And Jesus is the greatest warrior and leader, because He is the Son of God.

FACES AND PLACES

Joshua: Israel's leader did what God told him to do: to be strong and brave!

Canaan: This is the land whose name would change to Israel now that the people of Israel are taking it over. This is the Promised Land.

Jericho: This city was near the Jordan River. It was across from where the people of Israel were camped before they entered the land of Canaan. It was the first city in the land to be defeated by Israel.

Rahab: This woman in Jericho escaped with her life when she showed how much she respected the Lord. She hid spies who came from Joshua's army.

Achan: This man became an example to all of Israel when his secret sin was discovered.

When the time came to take over the land God promised them, I wonder how well God's people will fight...

THE LORD SAID to Joshua: "My servant Moses is dead. Now you and all these people go across the Jordan River. Go into the land I am giving to the people of Israel. I promised Moses I would give you this land. So I will give you every place you go in the land. Just as I was with Moses, so I will be with you. No one will be able to stop you all your life. I will not leave you. I will never leave you alone.

"Joshua, be strong and brave! You must lead these people so they can take their land. This is the land I promised their fathers I would give them. Be strong and brave. Be sure to obey all the teachings my servant Moses gave you. If you follow them exactly, you will be successful in everything you do. Always remember what is written in the Book of the Teachings. Study it day and night. Then you will be sure to obey everything that is written there. If you do this, you will be wise and successful in everything. Remember that I commanded you to be strong and brave. So don't be afraid. The Lord your God will be with you everywhere you go."

Spies Sent to Jericho

Joshua son of Nun secretly sent out two spies. Joshua said to them, "Go and look at the land. Look closely at the city of Jericho."

So the men went to Jericho.

They went to the house of Rahab.

Someone told the king of Jericho, "Some men from Israel have come here tonight. They are spying out the land."

So the king of Jericho sent this message to Rahab: "Bring out the men who came to you and entered your house. They have come to spy out our whole land."

Now the woman had hidden the two men. She said, "They did come here. But I didn't know where they came from. In the evening, when it was time to close the city gate, they left. I don't know where they went. Go quickly. Maybe you can catch them." (But the woman had taken the men up to the roof. She had hidden them there under stalks of flax. She had spread the flax out there to dry.)

The spies were ready to sleep for the night. So Rahab went to the roof and talked to them. She said, "I know the Lord has given this land to your people. You frighten us very much. Everyone living in this land is terribly afraid of you. We are afraid because we have heard how the Lord helped you. This is because the Lord your God rules the heavens above and the earth below! So now, make me a promise before the Lord. Promise that you will show kindness to my family just as I showed you kindness. Promise me you will allow my family to live."

The men agreed. They said, "When the Lord gives us our land, we will be kind to you. You may trust us."

The house Rahab lived in was built on the city wall. So she used a rope to let the men down through a window. She said to them, "Go into the hills. The king's men will not find you there. Hide there for three days. After the king's men return, you may go on your way."

The men said to her, "You are using a red rope to help us escape. Bring all your family into your house. We can keep everyone safe who stays in this house."

Rahab answered, "I agree to this." So she sent them away, and they left. Then she tied the red rope in the window.

The men left and went into the hills. They crossed the river. They went to Joshua son of Nun and told him everything that had happened to them. They said to Joshua, "The Lord surely has given us all of the land. All the people in that land are terribly afraid of us."

Crossing the Jordan

Early the next morning Joshua and all the people of

Israel traveled to the Jordan River and camped there before crossing it.

Joshua said to the priests, "Take the Box of the Agreement. Cross over the river ahead of the people." So the priests lifted the Holy Box and carried it ahead of the people.

The priests came to the edge of the river. And they stepped into the water. Just at that moment, the water stopped flowing. It stood up in a heap. The ground there became dry. The priests carried the Box of the Agreement with the Lord to the middle of the river and stopped. They waited there while all the people of Israel walked across. They crossed the Jordan River on dry land.

Now all the kings of the Amorites west of the Jordan heard about it. And the Canaanite kings living by the Mediterranean Sea heard about it. They were very scared. After that they were too afraid to face the Israelites.

The people of Israel were on the plains of Jericho. It was there they celebrated the Passover Feast. The next day after the Passover, the people ate some of the food grown on that land: bread made without yeast and roasted grain. The day they ate this food, the manna stopped coming. The Israelites no longer got the manna from heaven. They ate the food grown in the land of Canaan that year.

Joshua was near Jericho. He looked up and saw a man standing in front of him. The man had a sword in his hand. Joshua went to him and asked, "Are you a friend or an enemy?"

The man answered, "I am neither one. I have come as the commander of the Lord's army."

Then Joshua bowed face-down on the ground. He asked, "Does my master have a command for me, his servant?"

The commander of the Lord's army answered, "Take off your sandals. The place where you are standing is holy." So Joshua did.

The Fall of Jericho

Now the people of Jericho were afraid because the Israelites were near. So they closed the city gates and guarded them. No one went into the city. And no one came out.

Then the Lord spoke to Joshua. He said, "Look, I have given you Jericho, its king and all its fighting men. March around the city with your army one time every day. Do this for six days. Have seven priests carry trumpets made from horns of male sheep. Tell them to march in front of the Holy

Box. On the seventh day march around the city seven times. On that day tell the priests to blow the trumpets as they march. They will make one long blast on the trumpets. When you hear that sound, have all the people give a loud shout. Then the walls of the city will fall. And the people will go straight into the city."

Then Joshua ordered the people, "Now go! March around the city."

On the seventh day they got up at dawn. They marched just as they had on the days before. But on that day they marched around the city seven times. The seventh time around the priests blew their trumpets. Then Joshua gave the command: "Now, shout! The Lord has given you this city!"

At the sound of the trumpets and the people's shout, the walls fell. And everyone ran straight into the city. So the Israelites defeated that city. They completely destroyed every living thing in the city. They killed men and women, young and old. They killed cattle, sheep and donkeys.

The men brought out Rahab. They also brought out her father, mother, brothers and all those with her. They put all of her family in a safe place outside the camp of Israel.

Then Israel burned the whole city and everything in it. But they did not burn the things made from silver, gold, bronze and iron. These were saved for the Lord.

So the Lord was with Joshua. And Joshua became famous through all the land.

The Sin of Achan

There was a man from the tribe of Judah named Achan. Achan kept some of the things that were to be given to the Lord. So the Lord became very angry at the Israelites.

Joshua sent some men from Jericho to Ai. He told them, "Go to Ai and spy out the area." So the men went to spy on Ai.

Later they came back to Joshua. They said, "There are only a few men in Ai to fight against us. So we will not need all our people to defeat them."

But the people of Ai beat them badly. The people of Ai chased the Israelites. They killed about 36 Israelites as they went down the hill. When the Israelites saw this, they became very afraid.

Then Joshua said, "Lord God, you brought our people across the Jordan River. Why did you bring us this far and then let the Amorites destroy us?"

The Lord said to Joshua, "The Israelites have sinned. They took some of the things I commanded them to destroy. They have stolen from me. They have lied. That is why the Israelites cannot face their enemies.

"'Tomorrow morning you must all stand before the Lord. The Lord will choose one tribe. Then the Lord will choose one family group from that tribe. Then the Lord will choose one family from that family group. Then the Lord will look at that family man by man. The man who is keeping what should have been destroyed will himself be destroyed by fire. And everything he owns will be destroyed with him. He has done a disgraceful thing among the people of Israel!'"

The Lord chose Achan.

Then Joshua said to Achan, "My son, you should tell the truth. Confess to the Lord, the God of Israel. Tell me what you did. Don't try to hide anything from me."

Achan answered, "It is true! I have sinned against the Lord, the God of Israel. I saw a beautiful coat, and I saw silver and gold. I wanted these things very much. So I took them. You will find them buried in the ground under my tent."

Joshua said, "I don't know why you caused so much trouble for us. But now the Lord will bring trouble to you." Then all the people threw stones at Achan until he died. They also killed his family with stones. Then the people burned them. They piled rocks over Achan's body. After this the Lord was no longer angry.

Ai Is Destroyed

Then the Lord said to Joshua, "Don't be afraid. Don't give up. Lead all your fighting men to Ai. I will help you defeat the king of Ai. I am giving you his people, his city and his land. You will do to Ai and its king what you did to Jericho and its king. Only this time you may take all the wealth."

So Joshua led his whole army toward Ai. Then he chose 30,000 of his best fighting men. He sent these men out at night. Joshua gave them these orders: "Listen carefully. You must set up an ambush behind the city. Don't go far from it. Continue to watch and be ready. I and the men who are with me will march toward the city. The men in the city will come out to fight us. Then we will turn and run away from them as we did before. They will chase us away from the city. They will think we are running away from them as we did before. When we run away, come out from your ambush and take the city. The Lord your God will give you the power to win. After you take the city, burn it. See to it! You have your orders."

Now the king of Ai saw the army of Israel. So he and his people got up early the next morning and hurried out to fight them. The king did not know soldiers were waiting in ambush behind the city. Joshua and all the men of Israel let the army of Ai push them back. Then they ran east toward the desert. The men in Ai were called to chase Joshua and his men. So they left the city and went after them. All the men of Ai and Bethel chased the army of Israel. The city was left open. Not a man stayed to protect it.

Then the Lord said to Joshua, "Hold your spear toward Ai. I will give you that city." So Joshua held his spear toward the city of Ai. The men of Israel who were in ambush saw this. They quickly came out of their hiding place and hurried toward the city. They entered the city and took control of it. Then they quickly set it on fire.

The men of Ai were caught between the armies of Israel. The Israelites fought until not one of the men of Ai was left alive. None of the enemy escaped. But the king of Ai was left alive. And Joshua's men brought him to Joshua.

Then Joshua built an altar for the Lord, the God of Israel. Joshua built the altar as it was explained in the Book of the Teachings of Moses. The altar was made from stones that were not cut. No tool was ever used on them. The Israelites offered burnt offerings to the Lord on that altar. They also offered fellowship offerings. There Joshua wrote the teachings of Moses on stones. He did this for all the people of Israel to see.

Then Joshua read all the words of the teachings. He read the blessings and the curses. He read it exactly as it was written in the Book of the Teachings. Joshua read every command that Moses had given.

Joshua captured the kings in the land and killed them. He fought against them for many years. The Lord made those people stubborn so they would fight against Israel. This way he could completely destroy them without mercy. This is what the Lord had commanded Moses to do.

Joshua Says Good-bye

Then Joshua divided the land among the tribes of Israel.

The Lord gave Israel peace from their enemies around them. He made Israel safe. Many years passed, and Joshua became very old. So he called a meeting of all the older leaders, heads of families, judges and officers of the Israelites. He said, "I am now very old. You have seen what the Lord has done to our enemies. He did it to help us. The Lord your God fought for you.

"There are still some people living among us who are not Israelites. They worship their own gods. Don't become friends with them. Don't serve or worship their gods.

"It's almost time for me to die. You know and fully believe that the Lord has done great things for you. You know that he has not failed in any of his promises. He has kept every promise he has given. Every good promise that the Lord your God made has come true. You will lose this land if you go and serve other gods. You must not worship them. If you do, the Lord will become very angry with you. Then none of you will be left in this good land he has given you."

Then Joshua spoke to the people. He said, "You must serve the Lord. But maybe you don't want to serve the Lord. You must choose for yourselves today. You must decide whom you will serve. As for me and my family, we will serve the Lord."

On that day Joshua made an agreement for the people. He made the agreement a law for them to follow. Joshua wrote these things in the Book of the Teachings of God. Then he found a large stone. He put the stone under the oak tree near the Lord's Holy Tent.

Then Joshua said to all the people, "See this stone! It will help you remember what we did today. It will stop you from turning against your God."

After that, Joshua died. He was 110 years old. And they buried him in his own land at Timnath Serah.

WORTH WONDERING...

- How did Joshua find out what God wanted him to do?

- If you could meet Joshua today, what kind of questions would you like to ask him?

- Use your imagination for this one: If you were there when the people of Israel captured the city of Jericho, what kinds of things do you think you would see and hear and smell?

- What good example can you

give of someone in this book who did what was right?

- What example can you give of someone in this book who did what was wrong?

- Is Joshua the kind of leader you would like to follow?

- In the book of Joshua, what does God do to keep His promises made in the book of Genesis to Abraham, Isaac, and Jacob?

- In the book of Joshua, God gives victory to His people. How does God give victory to you?

GREAT VERSES TO THINK ABOUT AGAIN...

Look back in Joshua to see if you can find these verses:

- *Joshua went to him and asked, "Are you a friend or an enemy?" The man answered, "I am neither one. I have come as the commander of the Lord's army."*

- *Always remember what is written in the Book of the Teachings. Study it day and night. Then you will be sure to obey everything that is written there. If you do this, you will be wise and successful in everything.*

- *You must choose for yourselves today. You must decide whom you will serve. As for me and my family, we will serve the Lord.*

- *Every good promise that the Lord your God made has come true.*

AND THERE'S MORE...

When you read Joshua in a full Bible, look especially for...

- More details of the many battles Joshua and the people fought as they took over the Promised Land.

- How Joshua divided up the land among all of the twelve tribes of Israel.

- How land was awarded to Caleb, who by now was an old man.

The Book of
JUDGES

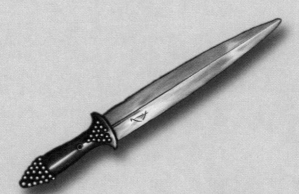

Great Leaders
Rescue Israel

Looking forward to Judges...

WHAT'S IT ABOUT?

"Great Leaders Rescue Israel"

SIGNS AND WONDERS

In Joshua we read happy stories of victory for God's people. But in Judges we watch sadly as the people are turning away from God. The people become weak, and are defeated again and again by their enemies. But the bright spots in this book are when God sends leaders (we sometimes call them "judges") to rescue His people from their misery.

FACES AND PLACES

Deborah: She is the only woman judge included in this book. She was a bold leader.

Gideon: He had a lot of fear at first. But his faith grew, and he became a brave warrior.

Samson: God gave him great physical strength. He killed many of his people's enemies. But he made bad mistakes, too.

I wonder what happens when God's people keep turning away from Him...

The people of Israel continued serving the Lord during the lifetimes of the older leaders who lived on after Joshua.

After those people had died, their children grew up. They did not know the Lord or what he had done for Israel. They did what the Lord said was wrong. They began to worship the gods of the people who lived around them. The Lord was angry with the people of Israel. So he let robbers attack them and take their possessions. He let their enemies who lived around them defeat them. They could not protect themselves from their enemies. When the Israelites went out to fight, they always lost. They lost because the Lord was not on their side.

God Chooses Judges

Then the Lord chose leaders called judges. These leaders saved the people of Israel from the robbers. But the Israelites did not listen to their judges. They were not faithful to God. They followed other gods instead. Many times the enemies of Israel hurt the Israelites. So the Israelites would cry for help. And each time the Lord felt sorry for them. Each time he sent a judge to save them from their enemies. The Lord was with those judges. But when each judge died, the Israelites again sinned and worshiped the false gods. They became worse than their ancestors. The Israelites were very stubborn; they refused to change their evil ways.

So the Lord said, "These people have broken the agreement I made with their ancestors. They have not listened to me. So I will no longer defeat the nations who were left when Joshua died."

He wanted to test the Israelites who had not fought in the wars to take Canaan. He wanted to teach the people who had not fought in those wars how to fight. The Lord wanted to see if Israel would obey the commands he had given to their ancestors by Moses.

Deborah

The Lord let Jabin, a king of Canaan, defeat Israel. Sisera was the commander of Jabin's army. He had 900 iron chariots and was very cruel to the people of Israel for 20 years. So they cried to the Lord for help.

Deborah was judge of Israel at that time. Deborah sent a message to a man named Barak. Deborah said to Barak, "The Lord, the God of Israel, commands you: 'Go and gather 10,000 men of Naphtali and Zebulun. Lead them to Mount Tabor. I will make Sisera, the commander of Jabin's army, come to you. Sisera, his chariots and his army will meet you at the Kishon River. I will help you to defeat Sisera there.'"

Then Barak said to Deborah, "I will go if you will go with me. But if you will not go with me, I won't go."

"Of course I will go with you," Deborah answered. "But you will not get credit for the victory. The Lord will let a woman defeat Sisera."

Then Sisera was told that Barak had gone up to Mount Tabor. So Sisera and all the men with him went to the Kishon River.

Then Deborah said to Barak, "Get up! Today is the day the Lord will help you defeat Sisera. You know the Lord has already cleared the way for you."

So Barak and his men attacked Sisera and his men. During the battle the Lord confused Sisera and his army and chariots. Barak and his men chased Sisera's chariots and army. They used their swords to kill all of Sisera's men. Not one of them was left alive.

But Sisera himself ran away. He came to the tent where Jael lived. She was the wife of Heber. Heber's family was at peace with Jabin king of Hazor. Jael went out to meet Sisera. She said to him, "Come into my tent, master! Come in. Don't be afraid." So Sisera went into Jael's tent, and she covered him with a rug.

Sisera said to Jael, "I am thirsty. Please give me some water to drink." So she opened a leather bag in which she kept milk and gave him a drink.

Jael, the wife of Heber, took a tent peg and a hammer. She quietly went to Sisera. Since he was very tired, he was sleeping. She hammered the tent peg through the side of Sisera's head and into the ground! And so Sisera died.

Then Barak came by Jael's tent, chasing Sisera. Jael went out to meet him and said, "Come. I will show you the man you are looking for." So Barak entered her tent. There Sisera lay dead, with the tent peg in his head.

So there was peace in the land for 40 years.

Gideon

Again the people of Israel did what the Lord said was wrong. So for seven years the Lord let the people of Midian rule Israel. The Midianites were very powerful and were cruel to the Israelites. So the Israelites made hiding places in the mountains. They also hid in caves and safe places. Whenever the Israelites planted crops, the Midianites, Amalekites and other peoples from the east destroyed the crops. They left nothing for Israel to eat. So the Israelites cried out to the Lord for help.

The angel of the Lord appeared to Gideon and said, "The Lord is with you, mighty warrior!"

Then Gideon said, "If the Lord is with us, why are we having so many troubles?"

The Lord turned to Gideon and said, "You have the strength to save the people of Israel. Go and save them from the Midianites. I am the one who is sending you."

Gideon Defeats Midian

All the Midianites, the Amalekites and other peoples from the east joined together. They came across the Jordan River and camped in the Valley of Jezreel. But the Spirit of the Lord entered Gideon. Gideon sent messengers to the people. They also went up to meet Gideon and his men.

Then Gideon said to God, "You said you would help me save Israel. I will put some wool on the threshing floor. Let there be dew only on the wool. But let all of the ground be dry. Then I will know what you said is true. I will know that you will use me to save Israel." And that is just what happened. Gideon got up early the next morning and squeezed the wool. He got a full bowl of water from the wool.

Then Gideon said to God, "Don't be angry with me. Let me ask just one more thing. Please let me make one more test. Let the wool be dry while the ground around it gets wet with dew." That night God did that very thing. Just the wool was dry, but the ground around it was wet with dew.

Early in the morning the Lord said to Gideon, "You have too many men to defeat the Midianites. I don't want the Israelites to brag that they saved themselves. So now, announce to the people, 'Anyone who is afraid may leave. He may go back home.'"

Then the Lord said to Gideon, "There are still too many men. Take the men down to the water."

So Gideon led the men down to the water. There the Lord said to him, "Separate them. Those who drink water by lapping it up like a dog will be in one group. Those who bend down to drink will be in the other group."

Then the Lord said to Gideon, "I will save you, using the 300 men who lapped the water. And I will allow you to defeat Midian. Let all the other men go to their homes." So Gideon sent the rest of Israel to their homes. But he kept 300 men. He took the jars and the trumpets of those who went home.

Now the camp of Midian was in the valley below Gideon. That night the Lord spoke to Gideon. He said, "Get up. Go down and attack the camp of the Midianites. I will allow you to defeat them."

Then Gideon divided the 300 men into three groups. He gave each man a trumpet and an empty jar. A burning torch was inside each jar.

Gideon told the men, "Watch me and do what I do. When I get to the edge of the camp, do what I do. Surround the enemy camp. I and everyone with me will blow our trumpets. When we blow our trumpets, you blow your trumpets, too. Then shout, 'For the Lord and for Gideon!'"

Midian Is Defeated

So Gideon and the 100 men with him came to the edge of the enemy camp. They came just after the enemy had changed guards. It was during the middle watch of the night. Then Gideon and his men blew their trumpets and smashed their jars. They held the torches in their left hands and the trumpets in their right hands. Then they shouted, "A sword for the Lord and for Gideon!" Inside the camp, the men of Midian began shouting and running away.

The men of Israel were called out to chase the Midianites. Gideon said, "Come down and attack the Midianites. Take control of the Jordan River. Do this before the Midianites can get to the river and cross it."

So they took control of the Jordan River. And they continued chasing the Midianites.

Samson

Again the people of Israel did what the Lord said was wrong. So he let the Philistines rule over them for 40 years.

Then the Spirit of the Lord entered Samson and gave him great power. Samson went out and caught 300 foxes. He took 2 foxes at a time and tied their tails together. Then he tied a torch to the tails of each pair of foxes. Samson lit the torches. Then he let the foxes loose in the grainfields of the Philistines. In this way he burned up their standing grain and the piles of grain. He also burned up their vineyards and their olive trees.

Samson attacked the Philistines and killed many of them. Then he went down and stayed in a cave. It was in the rock of Etam.

Then 3,000 men of Judah went to the cave in the rock of Etam. They said to Samson, "What have you done to us? Don't you know that the Philistines rule over us? We have come to tie you up. We will give you to the Philistines."

Samson said to them, "Promise me you will not hurt me yourselves."

The men from Judah said, "We agree. We will just tie you up and give you to the Philistines. We will not kill you." So they tied Samson with two new ropes. Then they led him up from the cave in the rock. When Samson came to the place named Lehi, the Philistines came to meet him. They were shouting for joy. Then the Spirit of the Lord entered Samson and gave him great power. The ropes on him became weak like strings that had been burned. They fell off his hands! Samson found a jawbone of a donkey that had just died. He took it and killed 1,000 men with it!

Samson was very thirsty. So he cried out to the Lord. Then God opened up a hole in the ground at Lehi, and water came out. When Samson drank that water, he felt better. He felt strong again.

Samson and Delilah

After this, Samson fell in love with a woman named Delilah. The kings of the Philistines went to Delilah. They said, "Try to find out what makes Samson so strong. Try to trick him into telling you. Find out how we could capture him and tie him up. If you do this, each one of us will give you 28 pounds of silver."

So Delilah said to Samson, "Tell me why you are so strong. How could someone tie you up and take control of you?"

Samson answered, "Someone would have to tie me up. He would have to use seven new bowstrings that have not been dried. If he did that, I would be as weak as any other man."

Then the kings of the Philistines brought seven new bowstrings to Delilah. They had not been dried. She tied Samson with them. Some men were hiding in another room. Delilah said to Samson, "Samson, the Philistines are about to capture you!" But Samson easily broke the bowstrings. They broke like pieces of string burned in a fire. So the Philistines did not find out the secret of Samson's strength.

Then Delilah said to Samson,

"You've made me look foolish. You lied to me. Please tell me. How could someone tie you up?"

Samson said, "They would have to tie me with new ropes that have not been used before. Then I would become as weak as any other man."

So Delilah took new ropes and tied Samson. Some men were hiding in another room. Then she called out to him, "Samson, the Philistines are about to capture you!" But he broke the ropes as easily as if they were threads.

Then Delilah said to Samson, "You have lied to me. Tell me how someone could tie you up."

He said, "Use the loom. Weave the seven braids of my hair into the cloth. Tighten it with a pin. Then I will become as weak as any other man."

Then Samson went to sleep. So Delilah wove the seven braids of his hair into the cloth. Then she fastened it with a pin.

Again she called out to him, "Samson, the Philistines are about to capture you!" Samson woke up and pulled up the pin and the loom with the cloth.

Then Delilah said to him, "How can you say, 'I love you,' when you don't even trust me? This is the third time you have made me look foolish. You haven't told me the secret of your great strength." She kept bothering Samson about his secret day after day. He became so tired of it he felt he was going to die!

So he told her everything. He said, "I have never had my hair cut. I have been set apart to God since I was born. If someone shaved my head, then I would lose my strength. I would become as weak as any other man."

Delilah saw that he had told her everything sincerely. So she sent a message to the kings of the Philistines. She said, "Come back one more time. He has told me everything." So the kings of the Philistines came back to Delilah. They brought the silver they had promised to give her. Delilah got Samson to go to sleep. He was lying in her lap. Then she called in a man to shave off the seven braids of Samson's hair.

Then she called out to him, "Samson, the Philistines are about to capture you!"

Then the Philistines captured Samson. They tore out his eyes. And they took him down to Gaza. They put bronze chains on him. They put him in prison and made him grind grain. But his hair began to grow again.

Samson Dies

The kings of the Philistines gathered to celebrate. They were going to offer a great sacrifice to their god Dagon. They said, "Our god has given us Samson our enemy."

The people were having a good time at the celebration. They said, "Bring Samson out to perform for us." So they brought Samson from the prison. He performed for them. They made him stand between the pillars of the temple of Dagon. A servant was holding his hand. Samson said to him, "Let me feel the pillars that hold up the temple. I want to lean against them." Now the temple was full of men and women. All the kings of the Philistines were there. There were about 3,000 men and women on the roof. Then Samson prayed to the Lord. He said, "Lord God, remember me. God, please give me strength one more time. Let me pay these Philistines back for putting out my two eyes!" Then Samson held the two center pillars of the temple. Samson said, "Let me die with these Philistines!" Then he pushed as hard as he could. And the temple fell on the kings and all the people in it. So Samson killed more of the Philistines when he died than when he was alive.

In those days the Israelites did not have a king. Everyone did what he thought was right.

WORTH WONDERING...

■ In this book, who are the men or women who seem to have the strongest faith in God?

■ Who is your favorite person in this book of Judges? What do you like about this person?

■ Suppose you were a famous artist. Someone has asked you to paint a picture showing something that happens in this book of Judges. What person or event from this book would you choose to paint?

■ What good example can you give of someone in this book who did what was right?

■ What example can you give of someone in this book who did what was wrong?

■ If you could meet Samson today, what kind of questions would you like to ask him?

■ In this book we see that the people's faith in God is not as strong as it was earlier in the book of Joshua. How about you? Is your faith in God stronger than ever, or is it weaker now than it used to be?

GREAT VERSES TO THINK ABOUT AGAIN...

Look back in Judges to see if you can find these verses:

■ *A sword for the Lord and for Gideon!*

■ *The Lord is with you, mighty warrior!*

■ *You know the Lord has already cleared the way for you.*

■ *They did not know the Lord or what he had done for Israel.*

■ *Lord God, remember me. God, please give me strength one more time.*

■ *Everyone did what he thought was right.*

AND THERE'S MORE...

When you read Judges in a full Bible, look especially for...

■ Ehud, the left-handed judge. He tricked the king of Moab. Then he led the people of Israel in an attack on their enemies.

■ Shamgar, another judge. He killed 600 Philistines with a sharp stick.

■ Jephthah. His brothers forced him to leave home. But later he became the leader of all the people and the commander of their army.

The Book of
RUTH

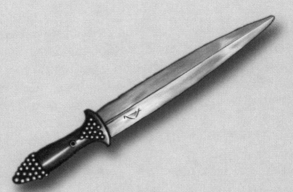

A Story
of Loyalty

Looking forward to Ruth...

"A Story of Loyalty"

Ruth's story is especially bright and beautiful because it happens during the dark years of sadness described in the book of Judges. Ruth was born into a family that was not a part of the people of Israel. But she becomes the great-grandmother of David, Israel's greatest king. And so she is also listed in the family record of Jesus, a descendant of David. This woman is rewarded for being loving and loyal.

Ruth: She chose to return with Naomi to the land of Israel, even though she would be a stranger there. Ruth was from the land of Moab, a nation that was often an enemy to Israel.

Naomi: She was bitter and sad, because her husband and both her sons had died. But Ruth became a great comfort to her.

Boaz: This kind and godly man was happy to marry Ruth.

**I wonder what it means
to be truly loyal to someone...**

Long ago there was a time in the land when there was not enough food to eat. A man named Elimelech left Bethlehem in Judah and moved to the country of Moab. He took his wife and his two sons with him. His wife was named Naomi, and his two sons were named Mahlon and Kilion.

Later, Naomi's husband, Elimelech, died. So only Naomi and her two sons were left. These sons married women from Moab. The name of one wife was Orpah. The name of the other wife was Ruth. Then Mahlon and Kilion also died. So Naomi was left alone without her husband or her two sons.

While Naomi was in Moab, she heard that the Lord had taken care of his people. He had given food to them in Judah. So Naomi got ready to leave Moab and go back home. The wives of Naomi's sons also got ready to go with her. But Naomi said to her two daughters-in-law, "Go back home. Each of you go to your own mother's house. You have been very kind to me and to my sons who are now dead. I hope the Lord will also be kind to you in the same way. I hope the Lord will give you another home and a new husband."

Then Naomi kissed the women. And they began to cry out loud. Orpah kissed Naomi good-bye, but Ruth held on to her.

Naomi said, "Look, your sister-in-law is going back to her

own people and her own gods. Go back with her."

Ruth Stays with Naomi

But Ruth said, "Don't ask me to leave you! Every place you go, I will go. Every place you live, I will live. Your people will be my people. Your God will be my God. And where you die, I will die. And there I will be buried. I ask the Lord to punish me terribly if I do not keep this promise: Only death will separate us."

Naomi saw that Ruth had made up her mind to go with her. So Naomi stopped arguing with her. Naomi and Ruth went on until they came to the town of Bethlehem. When the two women entered Bethlehem, all the people became very excited.

But Naomi told the people, "God All-Powerful has made my life very sad. When I left, I had all I wanted. But now, the Lord has brought me home with nothing."

Naomi and Ruth came to Bethlehem at the beginning of the barley harvest.

Ruth Meets Boaz

Now there was a rich man living in Bethlehem whose name was Boaz. Boaz was one of Naomi's close relatives from Elimelech's family.

One day Ruth said to Naomi, "Let me go to the fields. Maybe someone will be kind and let me gather the grain he leaves in his field."

Naomi said, "Go, my daughter."

So Ruth went to the fields. She followed the workers who were cutting the grain. And she gathered the grain that they had left. The field belonged to Boaz.

When Boaz came from Bethlehem, he spoke to his workers: "The Lord be with you!"

And the workers answered, "May the Lord bless you!"

Then Boaz spoke to his servant who was in charge of the workers. He asked, "Whose girl is that?"

The servant answered, "She is the Moabite woman who came with Naomi from the country of Moab. She said, 'Please let me follow the workers and gather the grain that they leave on the ground.' She came and has remained here. From morning until just now, she has stopped only a few moments to rest in the shelter."

Then Boaz said to Ruth, "Listen, my daughter. Stay here in my field to gather grain for yourself. Do not go to any other person's field. Continue following behind my women workers. When you are thirsty, you may go and drink. Take water from the water jugs that the servants have filled."

Then Ruth bowed low with her face to the ground. She said to Boaz, "I am a stranger. Why have you been so kind to notice me?"

Boaz answered her, "I know about all the help you have given to Naomi, your mother-in-law. You helped her even after your husband died. You left your father and mother and your own country. You came to this nation where you did not know anyone. The Lord will reward you for all you have done. You will be paid in full by the Lord, the God of Israel. You have come to him as a little bird finds shelter under the wings of its mother."

At mealtime Boaz told Ruth, "Come here! Eat some of our bread. Here, dip your bread in our vinegar."

So Ruth sat down with the workers. Boaz gave her some roasted grain. Ruth ate until she was full, and there was some food left over. Ruth rose and went back to work. Then Boaz told his servants, "Let her gather even around the bundles of grain. Don't tell her to go away. Drop some full heads of grain

for her. Let her gather that grain, and don't tell her to stop."

So Ruth gathered grain in the field until evening. Then she separated the grain from the chaff. There was about one-half bushel of barley. Ruth carried the grain into town. And her mother-in-law saw what she had gathered. Ruth also gave her the food that was left over from lunch.

Naomi asked her, "Where did you gather all this grain today? Where did you work? Blessed be the man who noticed you!"

Ruth told her about whose field she had worked in. She said, "The man I worked with today is named Boaz."

Naomi told her daughter-in-law, "The Lord bless him! The Lord still continues to be kind to all people—the living and the dead!" Then Naomi told Ruth, "Boaz is one of our close relatives, one who will take care of us."

Then Naomi said to Ruth, "It is good for you to continue working with his women servants. If you work in another field, someone might hurt you."

So Ruth continued working closely with the women servants of Boaz. She gathered grain until the barley harvest was finished. She also worked there through the end of the wheat harvest. And Ruth continued to live with Naomi, her mother-in-law.

Naomi's Plan

Then Naomi said to her, "My daughter, I must find a suitable home for you. Boaz is our close relative. Tonight he will be working at the threshing floor. Go wash yourself and put on perfume. Change your clothes, and go down to the threshing floor. But don't let him see you until he has finished eating and drinking. He will tell you what you should do."

Then Ruth answered, "I will do everything you say."

So Ruth went down to the threshing floor. She did all her mother-in-law told her to do. She said, "I am Ruth, your servant girl. You are the one who is to take care of me."

Then Boaz said, "The Lord bless you, my daughter. Your kindness to me is greater than the kindness you showed to Naomi in the beginning. You didn't look for a young man to marry, either rich or poor. Now, my daughter, don't be afraid. I will do everything you ask. All the people in our town know you are a very good woman. And it is true, I am a relative who is to take care of you. But there is a man who is a closer relative to you than I. But stay here tonight. In the morning we will see if he will take care of you. If he decides to take care of you, that is fine. If he refuses to take care of you, I myself will marry you. Then I will buy back Elimelech's land for you. As surely as the Lord lives, I promise to do this."

Boaz said to his servants, "Don't tell anyone that the woman came here to the threshing floor." Then Boaz said to Ruth, "Bring me your shawl. Now, hold it open."

So Ruth held her shawl open, and Boaz poured six portions of barley into it. Boaz then put it on her back, and she went to the city.

Ruth told Naomi everything that Boaz did for her. She said, "Boaz gave me these six portions of barley. He said, 'You must not go home without a gift for your mother-in-law.' "

Boaz Marries Ruth

Boaz went to the city gate. He sat there until the close relative he had mentioned passed by. Boaz called to him, "Come here, friend! Sit down here!" So the man came over and sat down. Boaz gathered ten of the old men who were leaders of the city.

Then Boaz spoke to the close relative. He said, "Naomi has

come back from the country of Moab. She wants to sell the piece of land that belonged to our relative Elimelech. If you want to buy back the land, then buy it in front of the leaders. I am the only person after you who can buy back the land. If you don't buy it back, I will."

And the close relative said, "I will buy back the land."

Then Boaz said, "When you buy the land from Naomi, you must marry Ruth, the dead man's wife. She is the woman from Moab. That way, the land will stay in her dead husband's family."

The close relative answered, "Then I can't buy back the land. If I did, I might lose what I can pass on to my own sons."

Long ago in Israel when people traded or bought back something, one person took off his sandal and gave it to the other person. This was their proof of purchase.

So the close relative said, "Buy the land yourself." And then he took off his sandal.

Then Boaz spoke to the older leaders and to all the people. He said, "You are witnesses today of what I am buying from Naomi. I am buying everything that belonged to Elimelech and Kilion and Mahlon. I am also taking Ruth as my wife. She is

the Moabite who was the wife of Mahlon. I am doing this so her dead husband's property will stay with his family. This way, his name will not be separated from his family and his land. You are witnesses this day."

So Boaz took Ruth and married her. And she gave birth to a son. The women told Naomi, "Praise the Lord who gave you this grandson. And may he become famous in Israel. He will give you new life. And he will take care of you in your old age. This happened because of your daughter-in-law. She loves you. And she is better for you than seven sons."

Naomi took the boy, held him in her arms and cared for him. The neighbors gave the boy his name. These women said, "This boy was born for Naomi." The neighbors named him Obed. Obed was Jesse's father. And Jesse was the father of David.

WORTH WONDERING...

- Ruth is a story of love and loyalty. What does the word loyalty mean to you?

- In your life, who are you loyal to?

- If you could meet Ruth today,

what kind of questions would
you like to ask her?

GREAT VERSES TO THINK
ABOUT AGAIN...

Look back in Ruth to see if you
can find these verses:

■ *The Lord will reward you for all
you have done. You will be paid
in full by the Lord, the God of
Israel.*

■ *Every place you go, I will go.
Every place you live, I will live.
Your people will be my people.
Your God will be my God.*

The First Book of
SAMUEL

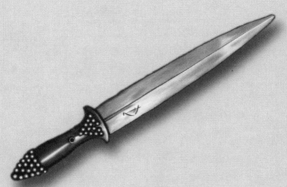

Samuel,
Saul, and David

Looking forward to 1 Samuel...

"Samuel, Saul, and David"

The people of Israel want a king...and now they get one, about 350 years after Joshua led them into the Promised Land. First Samuel is the exciting story of how this happens. (First and Second Samuel were once together in one book.)

Samuel: Samuel's mother Hannah had given him up to serve the Lord when he was just a boy. So Samuel grew up with the priest Eli. For the nation of Israel, the man Samuel is the "link" between the time of the judges, and the time of the kings. Samuel was a prophet, and he was Israel's last judge. He was also the man God sent to choose the first two kings of Israel.

Saul: He was chosen by God to be Israel's first king. But he was not willing to fully trust God.

David: He began as a shepherd boy. He was brave and strong, and he loved God. God made him Israel's greatest king.

The Philistines: These people lived along the western border of the land of Israel, between Jerusalem and the Sea.

Bethlehem: This town was in southern Israel, in the land of the tribe of Judah. This was David's hometown.

I wonder what God wants to see in the leader He chooses for His people...

HANNAH GAVE BIRTH to a son. She named him Samuel. When Samuel was old enough, Hannah took him to the Tent of the Lord at Shiloh. She said, "I prayed for this child. The Lord answered my prayer and gave him to me. Now I give him back to the Lord. He will belong to the Lord all his life."

The Lord was with Samuel as he grew up. He did not let any of Samuel's messages fail to come true. Then all Israel knew Samuel was a prophet of the Lord. And the Lord continued to show himself to Samuel at Shiloh. He also showed himself to Samuel through his word. News about Samuel spread through all of Israel.

Israel Asks for a King

When Samuel became old, all the older leaders came together and met at Ramah. They said to him, "You're old, and your sons don't live as you do. Give us a king to rule over us like all the other nations."

Samuel was not pleased. He prayed to the Lord. The Lord told Samuel, "Listen to whatever the people say to you. But give them a warning. Tell them what the king who rules over them will do."

Samuel said, "If you have a king ruling over you, this is what he will do: He will take your sons, your daughters, your best fields, vineyards, and olive groves. He will take one-tenth of your grain and grapes and give it to his officers and servants. He will take your servants. He will take your best cattle and your donkeys. You yourselves will become his slaves. When that time comes, you will cry out because of the king you chose. The Lord will not answer you then."

But the people would not listen to Samuel. They said, "No! We want a king to rule over us. Then we will be the same as all the other nations. Our king will judge us. He will go with us and fight our battles."

Saul Meets Samuel

Saul was a fine young man. There was no Israelite better than he. Saul stood a head taller than any other man in Israel.

Now the donkeys of Saul's father, Kish, were lost. So Kish said to Saul, his son, "Take one of the servants. Go and look for the donkeys." Saul went through the mountains of Ephraim. But he and the servant could not find the donkeys. They went into the land of Shaalim, but the donkeys were not there. They went through the land of Benjamin. But they still did not find the donkeys. Saul said to his servant, "Let's go back. My father will stop thinking about the donkeys. He will start worrying about us."

But the servant answered, "A man of God is in this town. Maybe he can tell us something."

Saul said to his servant, "That is a good idea. Come, let's go."

The day before Saul came, the Lord had told Samuel: "About this time tomorrow I will send you a man. He will be from Benjamin. You must appoint him as leader over my people Israel. He will save my people from the Philistines. I have seen the suffering of my people. I have listened to their cry."

When Samuel first saw Saul, the Lord spoke to Samuel. He said, "This is the man I told you about. He will rule my people."

Saul came near Samuel at the gate. Saul said, "Please tell me where the seer's house is."

Samuel answered, "I am the seer. Go ahead of me to the place of worship. Today you and your servant are to eat with me. Tomorrow morning I will send you home. And I will answer all your questions. Don't worry about the donkeys you lost three days ago. They have been found. Israel now wants you and all your father's family."

Saul answered, "But I am from the tribe of Benjamin. It's the smallest tribe in Israel. And my family group is the smallest in the tribe of Benjamin. Why do you say Israel wants me?"

Then Samuel took Saul and his servant into a large room. He gave them a chief place at the table. About 30 guests were there.

After they finished eating, they came down from the place of worship. They went to the town. At dawn Samuel called to Saul. "Get up, and I will send you on your way." So Saul got up. He went out of the house with Samuel. Saul, his servant and Samuel were getting near the edge of the city. Samuel said to Saul, "Tell the servant to go on ahead of us. I have a message from God for you."

Samuel took a jar of olive oil. He poured the oil on Saul's head. He kissed Saul and said, "The Lord has appointed you to be leader of his people Israel."

Saul Made King

Samuel called all the people of Israel to meet with the Lord at Mizpah. When Saul stood among the people, he was a head taller than anyone else. Then Samuel said to the people, "See the man the Lord has chosen. There is no one like him among all the people."

Then the people shouted, "Long live the king!"

Then the Philistines gathered to fight Israel. Their soldiers were many in number, like the grains of sand on the seashore. The Israelites saw that they were in trouble. So they went to hide in caves and bushes. They also hid among the rocks and in pits and wells. Some Hebrews even went across the Jordan River.

But Saul stayed at Gilgal. All the men in his army were shaking with fear. Saul waited seven days, because Samuel had said he would meet him then. But Samuel did not come to Gilgal. And the soldiers began to leave.

So Saul said, "Bring me the whole burnt offering and the fellowship offerings." Then Saul offered the whole burnt offering. Just as he finished, Samuel arrived. Saul went to meet him.

Samuel asked, "What have you done?"

Saul answered, "I saw the soldiers leaving me, and you were not here. The Philistines were gathering at Micmash. Then I thought, 'The Philistines will come against me at Gilgal. And I haven't asked for the Lord's approval.' So I forced myself to offer the whole burnt offering."

Samuel said, "You acted foolishly! You haven't obeyed God's command. If you had obeyed him, God would make your kingdom continue in Israel forever. But now your kingdom will not continue. The Lord is doing this because you haven't obeyed his command."

Saul became strong. He fought hard against the Philistines. When he saw strong or brave men, he took them into his army.

Saul Rejected as King

Samuel said to Saul, "This is what the Lord of heaven's armies says: 'The Israelites came out of Egypt. But the Amalekites tried to stop them from going to Canaan. Now go, attack the Amalekites. Destroy everything that belongs to them as an offering to the Lord. Don't let anything live.'"

So Saul called the army together and defeated the Amalekites. But Saul and the army let Agag live. They also let the best sheep, fat cattle and lambs live. They let every good animal live. They did not want to destroy them. But when they found an animal that was weak or useless, they killed it.

Then the Lord spoke his word to Samuel: "Saul has stopped following me. And I am sorry I made him king. He has not obeyed my commands." Samuel was upset, and he cried out to the Lord all night long.

Then Samuel came to Saul. And Saul said, "I have obeyed the Lord's commands."

But Samuel said, "Then why do I hear cattle mooing and sheep bleating? The Lord appointed you to be king over Israel. And he said, 'Go and destroy those evil people, the Amalekites. Make war on them until all of them are dead.' Why didn't you obey the Lord?"

Saul said, "But I destroyed all the Amalekites. And I brought back Agag their king. The soldiers took the best sheep and cattle to sacrifice to the Lord your God at Gilgal."

But Samuel answered, "It is better to obey God than to offer a sacrifice. Being stubborn is as bad as the sin of worshiping idols. You have rejected the Lord's command. For this reason, he now rejects you as king."

Then Samuel left and went to Ramah. But Saul went up to his home in Gibeah. And Samuel never saw Saul again all the rest of his life. But he was sorry for Saul. And the Lord was very sorry he had made Saul king of Israel.

Samuel Goes to Bethlehem

The Lord said to Samuel, "How long will you continue to feel sorry for Saul? I have rejected him as king of Israel. Fill your container with olive oil and go. I am sending you to Jesse who lives in Bethlehem. I have chosen one of his sons to be king."

Samuel did what the Lord told him to do. When he arrived at Bethlehem, he made Jesse and his sons holy for the Lord. And he invited them to come to the sacrifice.

When they arrived, Samuel saw Eliab. Samuel thought, "Surely the Lord has appointed this person standing here before him."

But the Lord said to Samuel, "Don't look at how handsome Eliab is. Don't look at how tall he is. I have not chosen him. God does not see the same way people see. People look at the outside of a person, but the Lord looks at the heart."

Then Jesse had seven of his sons pass by Samuel. But Samuel said to him, "The Lord has not chosen any of these."

Then he asked Jesse, "Are these all the sons you have?"

Jesse answered, "I still have the youngest son. He is out taking care of the sheep."

So Jesse sent and had his youngest son brought in. He was a fine boy, tanned and handsome.

The Lord said to Samuel, "Go! Appoint him. He is the one."

So Samuel took the container of olive oil. Then he poured oil on Jesse's youngest son to appoint him in front of his brothers. From that day on, the Lord's Spirit entered David with power. Samuel then went back to Ramah.

But the Lord's Spirit had gone out of Saul. And an evil spirit troubled him.

PAUSE & WONDER

Samuel said, "God does not see the same way people see. People look at the outside of a person, but the Lord looks at the heart." God can see everything that is going on inside me — my thoughts and attitudes. And He really cares about what I think and how I feel. That's why it's so important for me to keep filling my mind and heart with words from the Bible. Then God's voice will speak to me through those words, giving me courage and happiness.

David and Goliath

The Philistines gathered their armies for war. Saul and the Israelites took their positions to fight the Philistines. The Philistines controlled one hill. The Israelites controlled another. The valley was between them.

The Philistines had a champion fighter named Goliath. He was from Gath. He was about nine feet four inches tall. He had a bronze helmet on his head. And he wore a coat of scale armor. He had a spear of bronze tied on his back.

Goliath stood and shouted to the Israelite soldiers, "Choose a man and send him to fight me. If he can fight and kill me, we will become your servants. But if I defeat and kill him, you will become our servants. Today I stand and dare the army of Israel! Send one of your men to fight me!"

The Philistine Goliath came out every morning and evening. This continued for 40 days.

Jesse said to his son David, "Take this grain and bread. Also take ten pieces of cheese. See how your brothers are. Your brothers are with Saul and the army. They are fighting against the Philistines."

When David arrived at the camp, the Israelites and Philistines were lining up their men to face each other in battle.

Goliath came out. He was the Philistine champion from Gath. He shouted things against Israel, and David heard it. When the Israelites saw Goliath, they were very much afraid and ran away.

David asked the men who stood near him, "Why does he think he can speak against the armies of the living God?"

David's oldest brother Eliab heard David talking with the soldiers. He became angry with David. He asked David, "Why did you come here? Who's taking care of those few sheep of yours in the desert? I know you are proud. Your attitude is very bad. You came down here just to watch the battle!"

David asked, "Now what have I done wrong? Can't I even talk?" He then turned to other people and asked the same questions. Some men heard what David said and told Saul. Then Saul ordered David to be sent to him.

David said to Saul, "Don't let anyone be discouraged. I, your servant, will go and fight this Philistine!"

Saul answered, "You can't go out against this Philistine and fight him. You're only a boy.

Goliath has been a warrior since he was a young man."

But David said to Saul, "I, your servant, have been keeping my father's sheep. When a lion or bear came and took a sheep from the flock, I would chase it. I would attack it and save the sheep from its mouth. When it attacked me, I caught it by its fur. I would hit it and kill it. Goliath the Philistine will be like the lion or bear I killed. He will die because he has stood against the armies of the living God. The Lord saved me from a lion and a bear. He will also save me from this Philistine."

Saul said to David, "Go, and may the Lord be with you." Saul put his own clothes on David. He put a bronze helmet on David's head and armor on his body. David put on Saul's sword and tried to walk around. But he was not used to all the armor Saul had put on him.

He said to Saul, "I can't go in this. I'm not used to it." Then David took it all off. He took his stick in his hand. And he chose five smooth stones from a stream. He put them in his pouch and held his sling in his hand. Then he went to meet Goliath.

At the same time, the Philistine was coming closer to David. Goliath saw that David was only a boy, tanned and handsome. He looked down at David with disgust. He said, "Do you think I am a dog, that you come at me with a stick? Come here. I'll feed your body to the birds of the air and the wild animals!"

But David said to him, "You come to me using a sword, a large spear and a small spear. But I come to you in the name of the Lord of heaven's armies. He's the God of the armies of Israel! You have spoken out against him. Today the Lord will give you to me. I'll kill you, and I'll cut off your head. Today I'll feed the bodies of the Philistine soldiers to the birds of the air and the wild animals. Then all the world will know there is a God in Israel! Everyone gathered here will know the Lord does not need swords or spears to save people. The battle belongs to him! And he will help us defeat all of you."

As Goliath came near to attack him, David ran quickly to meet him. He took a stone from his pouch. He put it into his sling and slung it. The stone hit the Philistine on his forehead and sank into it. Goliath fell facedown on the ground.

David did not even have a sword in his hand. David ran and stood beside the Philistine. He took Goliath's sword out of its holder and killed him. Then he cut off Goliath's head.

When the Philistines saw that their champion was dead, they turned and ran. The men of Israel shouted and started chasing the Philistines. They chased them all the way to the entrance to the city of Gath.

When David came back from killing Goliath, Abner brought him to Saul. David still held Goliath's head.

Saul Fears David

Saul sent David to fight in different battles. And David was very successful. Then Saul put David over the soldiers. When he did this, Saul's officers and all the other people were pleased.

After David had killed the Philistine, he and the men returned home. Women came out from all the towns of Israel to meet King Saul. They sang songs of joy, danced and played tambourines and stringed instruments. As they played, they sang, "Saul has killed thousands of his enemies. But David has killed tens of thousands!"

The women's song upset Saul, and he became very angry. He thought, "The women say David has killed tens of thousands of enemies. But they say I killed only thousands of enemies. The only thing left for him to have is the kingdom!" So

Saul watched David closely from then on. He was jealous of him.

The next day an evil spirit entered Saul with power. David was playing the harp. But Saul had a spear in his hand. He raised the spear and thought, "I'll pin David to the wall." But David got away from him two times.

The Lord was with David but had left Saul. Saul saw that David was very successful. And he became even more afraid of David. But all the people of Israel and Judah loved David. This was because he led them well in battle.

Saul Plans to Kill David

Saul told his son Jonathan and all his servants to kill David. But Jonathan cared very much for David. So he warned David.

Then David left, and went to Nob to see Ahimelech the priest. Ahimelech gave David the bread the priests had taken from the holy table before the Lord.

David asked Ahimelech, "Do you have a spear or sword here?"

The priest answered, "The sword of Goliath the Philistine is here. If you want it, you may take it. There's no other sword here but that one."

David said, "There is no other sword like Goliath's. Give it to me."

Saul Chases David

Someone told Saul that David was now at Keilah. Saul said, "God has given David to me! He has trapped himself because he has entered a town with gates and bars." Saul called all his army together for battle. They prepared to go down to Keilah to attack David and his men.

David prayed, "Lord, God of Israel, I have heard about Saul's plans. Will Saul come to Keilah, as I heard? Lord, God of Israel, tell me, your servant!"

The Lord answered, "Saul will come down."

Again David asked, "Will the people of Keilah give me and my men to Saul?"

The Lord answered, "They will."

So David and his men left Keilah. There were about 600 men who went with him. And they kept moving from place to place.

David was at Horesh in the Desert of Ziph. Saul's son Jonathan went to David at Horesh. He helped David have stronger faith in God. Jonathan told him, "Don't be afraid. My father won't touch you. You will become king of Israel, and I will be second to you. Even my father Saul knows this." The two of them made an agreement before the Lord. Then Jonathan went home. But David stayed at Horesh.

Saul and his men went to look for David. But people warned David that Saul was looking for him.

Saul was going along one side of the mountain. David and his men were on the other side. They were hurrying to get away from Saul. Saul and his soldiers were closing in on David and his men. But a messenger came to Saul. He said, "Come quickly! The Philistines are attacking our land!" So Saul stopped chasing David and went to fight the Philistines. That is why people call this place Rock of Parting. David left and lived in the protected places of En Gedi.

The Death of Saul

Later, the Philistines gathered their armies. The Philistines fought against Israel, and the Israelites ran away from them. Many Israelites were killed at Mount Gilboa. The Philistines fought hard against Saul. They killed his sons Jonathan, Abinadab and Malki-Shua. The fighting became bad around Saul. When the archers shot at him, he was badly wounded. He said to the officer who carried his armor, "Pull out your sword and kill me. Then those uncircumcised men won't make fun of me and kill me." But Saul's officer refused, because he was afraid. So Saul took his own sword and threw himself on it. The officer saw that Saul was dead. So he threw himself on his own sword. And he died with Saul.

So Saul, his three sons and the officer who carried his armor died together that day.

WORTH WONDERING...

■ Why did God decide not to let Saul remain as king of Israel?

■ What would you say are the most important lessons to learn from the life of Saul?

■ What would you say are the most important lessons to learn from the life of David?

■ If you could meet David today, what kind of questions would you like to ask him?

GREAT VERSES TO THINK ABOUT AGAIN...

Look back in First Samuel to see if you can find these verses:

■ *God does not see the same way people see. People look at the outside of a person, but the Lord looks at the heart.*

■ *The Lord was with Samuel as he*

grew up. He did not let any of Samuel's messages fail to come true.

■ *You come to me using a sword, a large spear and a small spear. But I come to you in the name of the Lord of heaven's armies.*

■ *It is better to obey God than to offer a sacrifice.*

AND THERE'S MORE...

When you read First Samuel in a full Bible, look especially for...

■ The story behind the birth of Samuel, after his mother Hannah had been unable to have children.

■ How God called Samuel when he was a boy serving the Lord under Eli the priest.

■ How Eli's evil sons were the cause of much sadness and defeat for Israel.

■ David's marriage to Saul's daughter.

■ Jonathan's plan for warning David about Saul's anger.

■ How Saul did evil by killing an entire city of priests and their families.

■ How a wise woman kept David from responding to a fool with too much anger.

■ David's war with the Amalekites, in which he and his men rescued their captured families.

The Second Book of
SAMUEL

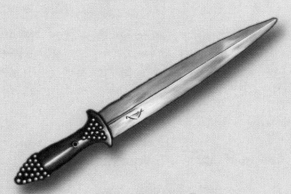

David,
the Greatest King

Looking forward to 2 Samuel...

"David, the Greatest King"

David isn't perfect, but he truly loves God. So God's blessing is on the life of David, and he becomes Israel's greatest king until Jesus came to earth. This book gives us an honest picture of David the hero. We see his weaknesses as well as his strengths.

Jesus was descended from David. And Jesus called Himself "the Son of David." David lived about halfway between the time of Abraham and the time of Jesus.

David: In the New Testament book of Acts, we can read these words from God about David: "I have found David son of Jesse. He is the kind of man I want. He will do all that I want him to do." Can God say that about you as well? Will you do all that God wants you to do?

Bathsheba: David sinned against the Lord by taking Bathsheba from her husband Uriah, and then having Uriah killed. Bathsheba became the mother of Solomon.

Solomon: David has many sons, but only his son Solomon is chosen to be king after David.

Hebron: This town in Judah was where David ruled for his first seven years as king.

Jerusalem: David made this city the new capital of Israel. David ruled in Jerusalem for 33 years.

I wonder what kind of king David will make...

DAVID SANG a funeral song about Saul and his son Jonathan. David ordered that the people of Judah be taught this song. This song is written in the Book of Jashar:

"Israel, your leaders have been killed on the hills. How the mighty men have fallen in battle!

"We loved Saul and Jonathan. We enjoyed them while they lived. Saul and Jonathan are together even in death. They were faster than eagles. They were stronger than lions.

"How the mighty men have fallen in battle! Jonathan is dead on Gilboa's hills. I cry for you, my brother Jonathan. I enjoyed your friendship so much. Your love to me was wonderful, more wonderful than the love of women.

"How the mighty men have fallen in battle! The weapons of war are gone."

David Is Made King

Later, David prayed to the Lord. David said, "Should I go up to any of the cities of Judah?"

The Lord said to David, "Go."

David asked, "Where should I go?"

The Lord answered, "To Hebron." David went up to Hebron. David also brought his men and their families. They all made their homes in the cities of Hebron. Then the men of Judah came to Hebron. They appointed David king over Judah.

Then all the tribes of Israel came to David at Hebron. They said to him, "Look, we are your own family. In the past Saul was king over us. But you were the one leading us in battle for Israel. The Lord said to you, 'You will be like a shepherd for my people, the Israelites. You will become their ruler.'"

David made an agreement with them in Hebron in front of the Lord. Then they poured oil on David to make him king over Israel.

Now the Philistines heard that David had been made king over Israel. So all the Philistines went to look for him. But when David heard the news, he went down to a safe place. So the Philistines came and camped in the Valley of Rephaim. David asked the Lord, "Should I attack the Philistines? Will you help me defeat them?"

The Lord said to David, "Go! I will certainly help you defeat them."

So David went and defeated the Philistines. David said, "Like a flood of water, the Lord has broken through my enemies."

Once again the Philistines came and camped at the Valley of Rephaim. David prayed to the Lord. This time the Lord told David, "Don't attack the Philistines from the front. Instead, go around them. Attack them opposite the balsam trees. You will hear the sound of marching in the tops of the balsam trees. Then you must act quickly. I, the Lord, will have gone ahead of you and defeated the Philistine army." So David did what the Lord commanded. He defeated the Philistines and chased them all the way from Gibeon to Gezer.

David Wants to Build a Temple

King David was living in his palace. And the Lord gave him peace from all his enemies around him. David said to Nathan the prophet, "Look, I am living in a palace made of cedar wood. But the Holy Box of God is still kept in a tent!"

Nathan said to the king, "Go and do what you really want to do. The Lord is with you."

But that night the Lord spoke his word to Nathan. The Lord said, "Go and tell my servant David, 'This is what the Lord says: You are not the person to build a house for me to live in. I did not live in a house when I brought the Israelites out of Egypt. I have been moving around all this time with a tent as my home. I have continued to move with the tribes of Israel. But I have never asked their leaders who take care of them to build me a house of cedar wood.'

"You must tell my servant David, 'This is what the Lord of heaven's armies says: I took you from the pasture when you were following the sheep. I took you to become leader of my people, the Israelites. I have been with you everywhere you have gone. I have defeated your enemies for you. I will make you as famous as any of the great men on the earth. I will give you peace from all your enemies. I also tell you that I will make your descendants kings of Israel after you.

"'Your days will come to an end, and you will die. At that time I will make one of your sons the next king. He will build a temple for me. I will make his kingdom strong forever. I will be his father, and he will be my son. When he sins, I will use other people to punish him. But I will not stop loving him. I took away my love and kindness from Saul. I removed Saul when I turned to you. But your family and your kingdom will continue forever before me. Your rule will last forever.'"

Nathan told David everything he had heard.

Then King David went in the tent and sat in front of the Lord. David said, "Lord God, why have you made me so important to you? Why have you made my family important? But that was not enough for you, Lord God. You have also said these kind things about my future family.

"What more can I say to you? Lord God, you love me, your servant, so much! You have done this wonderful thing because you said you would. You have done it because you wanted to. And you have decided to let me know all these great things. This is why you are great, Lord God! There is no one like you.

"Lord of heaven's armies, the God of Israel, you have shown things to me. You have said, 'I will make your family great.' So I, your servant, am brave enough to pray to you. Lord God, you are God, and your words are true. Please, bless my family. Let it continue before you forever. With your blessing let my family be blessed forever."

David Wins Many Wars

Later, David defeated the Philistines. And he took control of their capital city.

He also defeated the people

of Moab. He forced them to lie on the ground. Then he used a rope to measure them. When two men were measured, David ordered them killed. But every third man was allowed to live. So the people of Moab became servants of David. They gave him the payments he demanded.

David defeated Hadadezer king of Zobah. Then David put groups of soldiers in Damascus in Aram. The Arameans became David's servants and gave him the payments he demanded.

David took the shields of gold that had belonged to Hadadezer's officers. He brought them to Jerusalem. Toi king of Hamath sent his son Joram to greet and congratulate King David. Joram brought things made of silver, gold and bronze. David took these things and gave them to the Lord. He also had given other silver and gold to the Lord. He had taken it from the nations he had defeated.

David put groups of soldiers through all the land of Edom. All the people of Edom became servants for him.

The Lord gave David victory everywhere he went. David was king over all Israel. His decisions were fair and right for all his people.

David Helps Saul's Family

Now there was a servant named Ziba from Saul's family. So David's servants called Ziba to him. King David said to him, "Are you Ziba?"

He answered, "Yes, I am Ziba, your servant."

The king asked, "Is there anyone left in Saul's family? I want to show God's kindness to this person."

Ziba answered the king, "Jonathan has a son still living. He is crippled in both feet."

Then King David had servants bring Jonathan's son. Mephibosheth, Jonathan's son, came before David and bowed facedown on the floor.

Mephibosheth said, "I am your servant."

David said to him, "Don't be afraid. I will be kind to you for your father Jonathan's sake. I will give you back all the land of your grandfather Saul. And you will always be able to eat at my table."

So Mephibosheth ate at David's table as if he were one of the king's sons.

David and Bathsheba

In the spring the kings would go out to war. So in the spring

David sent out Joab, his servants and all the Israelites. They destroyed the Ammonites and attacked the city of Rabbah. But David stayed in Jerusalem. One evening David got up from his bed. He walked around on the roof of his palace. While he was on the roof, he saw a woman bathing. She was very beautiful. So David sent his servants to find out who she was. A servant answered, "That woman is Bathsheba daughter of Eliam. She is the wife of Uriah the Hittite." David sent messengers to bring Bathsheba to him.

So David sent this message to Joab: "Put Uriah on the front lines where the fighting is worst. Then leave him there alone. Let him be killed in battle."

Joab watched the city and saw where its strongest defenders were. He put Uriah there. The men of the city came out to fight against Joab. Some of David's men were killed. And Uriah the Hittite was one of them.

When Bathsheba heard that her husband was dead, she cried for him. After she finished her time of sadness, she became David's wife and gave birth to his son. But the Lord did not like what David had done.

David's Son Dies

The Lord sent Nathan to David. When Nathan came to David, Nathan said, "There were two men in a city. One man was rich, but the other was poor. The rich man had very many sheep and cattle. But the poor man had nothing except one little female lamb he had bought. The poor man fed the lamb. It grew up with him and his children. It shared his food and drank from his cup. It slept in his arms. The lamb was like a daughter to him.

"Then a traveler stopped to visit the rich man. The rich man wanted to give food to the traveler. But he didn't want to take one of his own sheep or cattle to feed the traveler. Instead, he took the lamb from the poor man. The rich man killed the lamb and cooked it for his visitor."

David became very angry at the rich man. He said to Nathan, "As surely as the Lord lives, the man who did this should die! He must pay for the lamb four times for doing such a thing. He had no mercy!"

Then Nathan said to David, "You are the man! This is what the Lord, the God of Israel, says: 'I appointed you king of Israel. I saved you from Saul. I gave you his kingdom and his wives. And I made you king of Israel and Judah. And if that had not been enough, I would have given you even more. So why did you ignore the Lord's command? Why did you do what he says is wrong? You killed Uriah the Hittite with the sword of the Ammonites! And you took his wife to become your wife! So there will always be people in your family who will be killed by a sword. This is because you showed that you did not respect me!'

Then David said to Nathan, "I have sinned against the Lord."

Nathan answered, "The Lord has taken away your sin. You will not die. But what you did caused the Lord's enemies to lose all respect for him. For this reason the son who was born to you will die."

Then Nathan went home. And the Lord caused the son of David and Bathsheba, Uriah's widow, to become very sick. David prayed to God for the baby. David refused to eat or drink. He went into his house and stayed there. He lay on the ground all night. The older leaders of David's family tried to pull him up from the ground. But he refused to get up. And he refused to eat food with them.

On the seventh day the baby died. David's servants were afraid to tell him that the baby was dead. They said, "If we tell him the baby is dead, he may harm himself."

But David saw his servants whispering. So he asked them, "Is the baby dead?"

They answered, "Yes, he is dead."

Then David got up from the floor. He washed himself, put lotions on himself and changed his clothes. Then he went into the Lord's house to worship. After that, he went home and asked for something to eat. His servants gave him some food, and he ate.

David's servants said to him, "Why are you doing this? When the baby was still alive, you refused to eat. You cried. But when the baby died, you got up and ate food."

David said, "While the baby was still alive, I thought, 'Who knows? Maybe the Lord will feel sorry for me and let the baby live.' But now the baby is dead. So why should I go without food? I can't bring him back to life. Some day I will go to him. But he cannot come back to me."

Then David comforted Bathsheba his wife. She had another son. David named the boy Solomon. The Lord loved Solomon.

David Captures Rabbah

Now Joab fought against Rabbah, a city of Ammonites. And he was about to capture the royal city. Joab sent messengers to David and said, "Bring the other soldiers together and attack this city. Capture it before I capture it myself."

So David gathered all the army and went to Rabbah. He fought against Rabbah and captured it. Then David and all his army went back to Jerusalem.

Absalom

Now David had a son named Absalom and a son named Amnon.

Absalom had some men come to Baal Hazor, near Ephraim. Absalom invited all the king's sons to come also. Then Absalom gave a command to his servants. He said, "Watch Amnon. When he is drunk, I will tell you, 'Kill Amnon.' Right then, kill him! I have commanded you!" So Absalom's young men killed Amnon as Absalom commanded. But all of David's other sons got on their mules and escaped.

Absalom ran away to Talmai.

Joab knew that King David missed Absalom very much. The king said to Joab, "Please bring back the young man Absalom." Then Joab brought Absalom back to Jerusalem.

Now Absalom was greatly praised for his handsome appearance. No man in Israel was as handsome as Absalom. No blemish was on him from his head to his foot. At the end of every year, Absalom would cut the hair on his head. He cut it because it became too heavy. He would weigh it, and it would weigh about five pounds by the royal measure.

Absalom got a chariot and horses for himself. He got 50 men to run before him. Absalom would get up early and stand near the city gate. People would come near Absalom to bow to him. When they did, Absalom would reach out his hand and take hold of them. Then he would kiss them. Absalom did that to all the Israelites. In this way, Absalom won the hearts of all Israel.

After four years Absalom went to Hebron. But he sent secret messengers through all the tribes of Israel. They told the people, "When you hear the trumpets, say this: 'Absalom has become the king!'"

Absalom's plans were working very well. More and

more people began to support him.

Then David spoke to all his officers who were with him in Jerusalem. He said, "We must leave quickly! If we don't, we won't be able to get away from Absalom. We must hurry before he catches us. He would destroy us and kill the people of Jerusalem."

The king set out with everyone in his house. The king left with all his people following him. Zadok and all the Levites with him were carrying the Box of the Agreement with God. The king said to Zadok, "Take the Holy Box of God back into the city. If the Lord is pleased with me, he will let me see both it and Jerusalem again."

The king also said to Zadok the priest, "Go back to the city in peace. I will wait near the crossings into the desert until I hear from you." So Zadok and Abiathar took the Holy Box of God back to Jerusalem and stayed there.

David went up the Mount of Olives crying as he went. He covered his head and went barefoot. All the people with David covered their heads also. And they were crying as they went. Someone told David, "Ahithophel is one of the people with Absalom who made secret plans against you."

So David prayed, "Lord, please make Ahithophel's advice foolish."

David came to the top of the mountain. This was where he used to worship God. Hushai came to meet him. Hushai's coat was torn, and there was dirt on his head to show how sad he was. David said to Hushai, "If you go with me, you will be just one more person to take care of. But if you return to the city, you can make Ahithophel's advice useless. The priests Zadok and Abiathar will be with you. You must tell them everything you hear in the king's palace." So David's friend Hushai entered Jerusalem. About that time, Absalom also arrived there.

Shimei Curses David

As King David came to Bahurim, a man came out from there. His name was Shimei son of Gera. Shimei came out, cursing David as he came. He began throwing stones at David and his officers. He said, "Get out, get out, you murderer, you troublemaker. The Lord is punishing you for the people in Saul's family you killed!"

Abishai said to the king, "Why should this dead dog curse you, the king? Let me go over and cut off his head!"

But the king answered, "If he is cursing me because the Lord told him to, who can question him? Leave him alone."

The king and all his people arrived at the Jordan. They were very tired. So they rested there.

Ahithophel's Advice

Absalom said to Ahithophel, "Please tell us what we should do."

At that time people thought Ahithophel's advice was as reliable as God's own word. Both David and Absalom thought it was that reliable.

Ahithophel said to Absalom, "Let me choose 12,000 men. I'll chase David tonight. I'll catch him while he is tired and weak. I'll frighten him so all his people will run away. But I'll kill only King David. Then I'll bring everyone back to you." This plan seemed good to Absalom and to all the leaders of Israel.

But Absalom said, "Now call Hushai. I also want to hear what he says." So Hushai came to Absalom.

Hushai said to Absalom, "Ahithophel's advice is not good this time." Hushai added, "You know your father and his men are strong. They are as angry as a bear that is robbed of its babies. Your father is a skilled fighter.

"This is what I suggest: Gather all the Israelites. There will be as many people as grains of sand by the sea. Then you yourself must go into the battle. We will catch David where he is hiding. We will kill him and all of his men. No one will be left alive."

Absalom and all the Israelites said, "The advice of Hushai is better than that of Ahithophel." They said this because the Lord had planned to destroy the good advice of Ahithophel. In this way the Lord could bring disaster on Absalom.

Hushai told these things to Zadok and Abiathar, the priests. Hushai said, "Quickly! Send a message to David. Tell him to cross over the Jordan River at once. If he crosses the river, he and all his people won't be caught."

So David and all his people crossed the Jordan River. By dawn, everyone had crossed the Jordan.

Now Ahithophel saw that the Israelites did not accept his advice. So he saddled his donkey and went to his hometown. He gave orders for his family and property. Then he hung himself. After Ahithophel died, he was buried in his father's tomb.

Absalom and all his Israelites crossed over the Jordan River.

David counted his men. He chose commanders over groups of 1,000 and commanders over groups of 100. He sent the troops out in three groups. King David said to them, "I will also go with you."

But the men said, "No! You must not go with us! If we run away in the battle, Absalom's men won't care. Even if half of us are killed. But you're worth 10,000 of us! It is better for you to stay. Then, if we need help, you can send it."

The king said to his people, "I will do what you think is best." So the king stood at the side of the gate as the army went out.

The king gave a command to Joab, "Be gentle with young Absalom for my sake." Everyone heard the king's orders about Absalom.

David's army went out into the field against Absalom's Israelites. They fought in the forest of Ephraim. There David's army defeated the Israelites. Many died that day — 20,000 men. The battle spread through all the country. But that day more men died in the forest than in the fighting.

Absalom Dies

Then Absalom happened to meet David's troops. As Absalom was riding his mule, it went under a large oak tree. The branches were thick, and Absalom's head got caught in the tree. His mule ran out from under him. So Absalom was left hanging above the ground.

So Joab took three spears and stabbed him in the heart. Ten young men who carried Joab's armor also gathered around Absalom. They struck him and killed him.

Then Joab blew the trumpet. So the troops stopped chasing Absalom's Israelites. Then Joab's men took Absalom's body. They threw it into a large pit in the forest. Then they filled the pit with many stones. All the Israelites who followed Absalom ran away and went home.

Then Joab said to a man from Cush, "Go. Tell the king what you have seen."

Then the king knew Absalom was dead. He was very upset. He went to the room over the city gate and cried. As he went, he cried out, "My son Absalom, my son Absalom! I wish I had died for you. Absalom, my son, my son!"

Joab Scolds David

David's army had won the battle that day. But it became a very sad day for all the people. This was because they heard, "The king is very sad for his son." The people came into the city quietly. They were like people who had been defeated in battle and had run away.

Then Joab went into the king's house. He said to the king, "Today you have shamed all your men. They saved your life today! Today you've made it clear that your commanders and men mean nothing to you. What if Absalom had lived and all of us were dead? I can see you would be very pleased. Now go out and encourage your servants. I swear by the Lord that if you don't go out, no man will be left with you by tonight! That will be worse than all the troubles you have had from your youth until today."

So the king went to the city gate. The news spread that the king was at the gate. So everyone came to see him.

David Goes Back to Jerusalem

Then the king returned as far as the Jordan River. The men of Judah came to Gilgal to meet him. They wanted to bring the king across the Jordan River.

As the king was about to cross the river, Shimei son of Gera came to him. Shimei bowed facedown on the ground in front of the king. He said to the king, "My master, don't hold me guilty. Don't remember the wrong things I did when you left Jerusalem! Don't hold it against me. I know I have sinned."

But Abishai said, "Shimei should die. He cursed you, the Lord's appointed king!"

David said, "No one will be put to death in Israel today. Today I know I am king over Israel!" Then the king said to Shimei, "You won't die."

All the troops of Judah and half the troops of Israel led David across the river. David came to his palace in Jerusalem.

Wars with the Philistines

Again there was war between the Philistines and Israel. David and his men went out to fight the Philistines. But David became tired and weak.

Then David's men made a promise to David. They said, "Never again will you go out with us to battle. If you were killed, Israel would lose its greatest leader."

David sang this song to the Lord: "The Lord is my rock, my place of safety, my Savior. My God is my rock. I can run to him for safety. He is my shield and my saving strength. The Lord is my high tower and my place of safety. The Lord saves me from those who want to harm me. I will call to the Lord. He is worthy of praise. And I will be saved from my enemies."

WORTH WONDERING...

■ What kind of a man was David? What was especially good about him? And what was not so good?

■ God forgave David. But how did David still suffer for the mistakes he had made?

■ What good example can you give of someone in this book who did what was right?

■ What example can you give of someone in this book who did what was wrong?

■ How well did David know how to learn from his mistakes?

■ Suppose you were a famous artist. Someone has asked you to paint a picture showing something that happens in this book of Second Samuel. What person or event from this book would you choose to paint?

GREAT VERSES TO THINK ABOUT AGAIN...

Look back in Second Samuel to see if you can find these verses:

■ *Lord God, you love me, your servant, so much!*

■ *David was king over all Israel. His decisions were fair and right for all his people.*

■ *Lord God, you are God, and your words are true. Please, bless my family.*

■ *I took you from the pasture when you were following the sheep. I took you to become leader of my people, the Israelites. I have been with you everywhere you have gone. I have defeated your enemies for you. I will make you as famous as any of the great men on the earth.*

■ *You are the man!*

■ *They were faster than eagles. They were stronger than lions.*

■ *The Lord gave David victory everywhere he went.*

AND THERE'S MORE...

When you read Second Samuel in a full Bible, look especially for...

■ The war between the tribes of Israel and the tribe of Judah before David became king over all of them.

■ How Saul's army commander, Abner, was killed.

■ How Saul's son Ish-Bosheth was killed.

■ How the Holy Box of God was moved to Jerusalem, and how David jumped and danced before the Lord.

The First Book of
KINGS

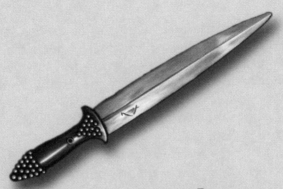

The Kingdom
Is Divided

Looking forward to 1 Kings...

"The Kingdom Is Divided"

SIGNS AND WONDERS

Some of the men who became king of Israel are strong and brave, while others are weak. Some are honest and good, while others are evil. In this book, you'll see how Israel is split into two kingdoms — all because of the disobedience of one king, and the foolishness of another. In First and Second Kings together we read the stories of 39 kings. 30 of them were evil, and 9 were good.

The books of First and Second Kings go back and forth between stories about the two parts of the divided kingdom.

FACES AND PLACES

Solomon: As king, David's son Solomon built the Temple in Jerusalem. Solomon was wise and wealthy.

Rehoboam: Solomon's foolish son.

Judah: The tribe of Judah (along with the smaller tribe of Benjamin) continued to keep kings who were from the family of David. These two tribes came to be known together as Judah.

Israel: After Solomon's son Rehoboam became king, the ten northern tribes pulled away from David and Solomon's kingdom. These northern tribes kept the name Israel.

Jeroboam: One of Solomon's officers. Later he was the first king of the ten northern tribes who broke away from serving King Rehoboam.

Elijah: A bold prophet who spoke out against the wickedness of Israel.

Ahab: One of many evil kings of Israel. His wife was the wicked Jezebel.

After good King David died, I wonder how well Israel's later kings would rule...

KING DAVID was very old. Then King David said, "My son Solomon will sit on my throne and rule in my place. I have chosen him to be the ruler over Israel and Judah."

The Death of David

David talked to Solomon and gave him his last commands. David said, "My time to die is near. Be a good and strong leader. Obey everything that the Lord commands. Follow the commands he has given us. If you do these things, you will be successful in all you do and wherever you go. And if you obey the Lord, he will keep the promise he made to me. He promised: 'Your descendants must live as I tell them. They must have complete faith in me. If they do this, then a man from your family will always be king over the people of Israel.'"

Then David died and was buried with his ancestors in Jerusalem. He had ruled over Israel 40 years. Solomon became king after David, his father.

Solomon Asks for Wisdom

Solomon showed that he loved the Lord. He did this by following the commands his father David had given him. But Solomon still used the many places of worship to offer sacrifices and to burn incense.

The Lord came to him in a dream during the night. God

said, "Ask for anything you want. I will give it to you."

Solomon answered, "You were very kind to your servant, my father David. He obeyed you. He was honest and lived right. And you showed great kindness to him when you allowed his son to be king after him. But I am like a little child. I do not have the wisdom I need to do what I must do. So I ask that you give me wisdom. Then I can rule the people in the right way. Then I will know the difference between right and wrong. Without wisdom, it is impossible to rule this great people of yours."

The Lord was pleased that Solomon had asked him for this. So God said to him, "You did not ask for a long life. And you did not ask for riches for yourself. You did not ask for the death of your enemies. Since you asked for wisdom to make the right decisions, I will give you what you asked. I will give you wisdom and understanding. Your wisdom will be greater than anyone has had in the past. And there will never be anyone in the future like you. Also, I will give you what you did not ask for. You will have riches and honor. During your life no other king will be as great as you. I ask you to follow me

and obey my laws and commands. Do this as your father David did. If you do, I will also give you a long life."

Solomon Makes a Wise Decision

One day two women came to Solomon. One of the women said, "My master, this woman and I live in the same house. I gave birth to a baby while she was there with me. Three days later this woman also gave birth to a baby. No one else was in the house with us. There were only the two of us. One night this woman rolled over on her baby, and it died. So during the night she took my son from my bed while I was asleep. Then she put the dead baby in my bed. The next morning I got up to feed my baby. But I saw that he was dead! Then I looked at him more closely. I saw that he was not my son."

But the other woman said, "No! The living baby is my son. The dead baby is yours!"

But the first woman said, "No! The dead baby is yours, and the living one is mine!" So the two women argued before the king.

Then King Solomon sent his servants to get a sword. When they brought it to him, he said, "Cut the living baby into two pieces. Give each woman half of the baby."

The real mother of the living child was full of love for her son. She said to the king, "Please, my master, don't kill him! Give the baby to her!"

But the other woman said, "Neither of us will have him. Cut him into two pieces!"

Then King Solomon said, "Give the baby to the first woman. Don't kill him. She is the real mother."

When the people of Israel heard about King Solomon's decision, they respected him very much. They saw he had wisdom from God to make the right decisions.

Solomon's Kingdom

There were many people in Judah and Israel. There were as many people as there were grains of sand on the seashore. The people ate, drank and were happy. Solomon ruled over all the kingdoms from the Euphrates River to the land of the Philistine people. His kingdom went as far as the border of Egypt. These countries brought Solomon the payments he demanded. And they obeyed him all his life.

Solomon's Wisdom

God gave great wisdom to Solomon. Solomon could under-stand many things. His wisdom was greater than the wisdom of all the men in the East. And his wisdom was greater than all the wisdom of the men in Egypt. He was wiser than any other man on earth. King Solomon became famous in all the countries around Israel and Judah. During his life King Solomon spoke 3,000 wise teachings. He also knew 1,005 songs. He taught about many different kinds of plants. He taught about everything from the great cedar trees of Lebanon to the hyssop that grows out of the walls. He also taught about animals, birds, crawling things and fish. People from all nations came to listen to King Solomon's wisdom.

Solomon Builds the Temple

King Solomon forced 80,000 men to work in the hill country, cutting stone. And he had 70,000 men to carry the stones. There were also 3,300 men who directed the workers. King Solomon commanded them to cut large blocks of fine stone. These were to be used for the foundation of the Temple.

So Solomon began to build the Temple. This was 480 years after the people of Israel had left Egypt. The Temple was 90 feet long and 30 feet wide. It was 45 feet high.

Solomon put a roof made from beams and cedar boards on the Temple. He prepared the inner room at the back of the Temple to keep the Box of the Agreement with the Lord. Solomon covered this room with pure gold. Also the altar in the Most Holy Place was covered with gold.

Solomon made two creatures with wings from olive wood. Each creature was 15 feet tall. They were put in the Most Holy Place. Each creature had two wings. Their wings were spread out. So one creature's wing touched one wall. The other creature's wing touched the other wall. And their wings touched each other in the middle of the room. The two creatures were covered with gold.

All the walls around the Temple were carved with pictures of creatures with wings, palm trees and flowers. This was true for both the main room and the inner room. The floors of both rooms were covered with gold.

Doors made from olive wood were put at the entrance to the Most Holy Place. Creatures with wings, palm trees and flowers were carved on the two olive wood doors. Then the doors were covered with gold. And the creatures and the palm trees were covered with gold.

The Temple was finished exactly as it was planned. Solomon had worked seven years to build the Temple.

The Holy Box in the Temple

King Solomon called for all the leaders of Israel to come to him in Jerusalem. Then the priests carried the Box of the Agreement with the Lord. Its right place was inside the Most Holy Place in the Temple. The Box of the Agreement was put under the wings of the golden creatures. The only things inside the Holy Box were two stone tablets. Moses had put them in the Holy Box at Mount Sinai. That was where the Lord made his agreement with the Israelites after they came out of Egypt.

When the priests left the Holy Place, the cloud filled the Temple of the Lord. The priests could not continue their work. This was because the Temple was filled with the glory of the Lord.

Solomon's Prayer

Then Solomon stood facing the Lord's altar. All of the people of Israel were standing behind him. He spread out his hands and looked toward the sky. He said:

"Lord, God of Israel, there is no god like you in heaven above or on the earth below. You make agreements with your people because you love them. And you keep your agreements with those who truly follow you. You have kept the promise you made to your servant David, my father. You have made it come true today. Now Lord, God of Israel, keep the other promises you made to your servant David, my father. You said, 'Your sons must be careful to obey me as you have obeyed me. If they do this, there will always be someone from your family ruling Israel.' Please continue to keep that promise you made to my father.

"But, God, can you really live here on the earth? Even the sky and the highest place in heaven cannot contain you. Certainly this house which I have built cannot contain you either. But please listen to my prayer and my request. I am your servant, and you are the Lord my God. So please watch over this Temple night and day. Please hear us when we pray facing this place. Hear us from your home in heaven. And when you hear us, forgive us."

So Solomon finished building everything he wanted to build. Then the Lord appeared to him again. The Lord said to him: "I have heard your prayer. You built this Temple. I will watch over it and protect it always.

"But you and your children must follow me. You must obey the laws and commands I have given you. You must not go off to serve or worship other gods. If you do, I will force Israel to leave the land I have given them. I made the Temple holy for people to worship me there. But if you don't obey me, I will tear it down."

Solomon's Wealth

Every year King Solomon received about 50,000 pounds of gold.

King Solomon made 200 large shields of hammered gold. He also made 300 smaller shields of hammered gold.

Then King Solomon built a large throne of ivory. And he covered it with pure gold. All of Solomon's drinking cups were made of gold. All of the dishes were pure gold.

So Solomon had more riches and wisdom than all the other kings on earth. People everywhere wanted to see King Solomon.

Solomon's Many Wives

But King Solomon loved many women who were not from Israel. He loved the daughter of the king of Egypt. He also loved women of the Moabites, Ammonites, Edomites, Sidonians and Hittites. The Lord had told the Israelites, "You must not marry people of other nations. If you do, they will cause you to follow their gods." But Solomon fell in love with these women. He had 700 wives who were from royal families. He also had 300 slave women who gave birth to his children. His wives caused him to turn away from God. As Solomon grew old, his wives caused him to follow other gods. He did not follow the Lord completely as his father David had done.

So the Lord was angry with him.The Lord said to Solomon, "You have chosen to break your agreement with me. You have not obeyed my commands. So I promise I will tear your kingdom away from you. I will give it to one of your officers. But I will not take it away while you are alive. This is because of my love for your father David. I will tear it away from your son when he becomes king. But I will not tear away all the kingdom from him. I will leave him one tribe to rule. I will do this because of David, my servant. And I will do it because of Jerusalem, the city I have chosen."

Solomon's Enemies

Jeroboam was one of Solomon's officers. Jeroboam was a capable man. Solomon saw that this young man was a good worker. So Solomon put him over all the workers from the tribes of Ephraim and Manasseh.

One day Jeroboam was leaving Jerusalem. Ahijah, the prophet from Shiloh, met him on the road. Ahijah was wearing a new coat. The two men were alone out in the country. Ahijah took his new coat and tore it into 12 pieces. Then he said to Jeroboam, "Take 10 pieces of this coat for yourself. The Lord, the God of Israel, says: 'I will tear the kingdom away from Solomon. Then I will give you 10 tribes. I will do this because Solomon has stopped following me.

"Jeroboam, I will allow you to rule over the 10 tribes. I will always be with you if you do what I say is right. You must obey all my commands. If you obey my laws and commands as David did, I will be with you. I will make your family a family of kings, as I did for David. I will give Israel to you. I will punish David's children because of this. But I will not punish them forever.'"

Solomon tried to kill Jeroboam. But Jeroboam ran away to Egypt. And Jeroboam stayed there until Solomon died.

Solomon ruled in Jerusalem over all Israel for 40 years. Then he died and was buried in Jerusalem, the city of David, his father. And his son Rehoboam became king after him.

Israel Turns Against Rehoboam

When Jeroboam heard about Rehoboam being made king, Jeroboam returned from Egypt. So the people sent for him. Then he and the people went to Rehoboam. They said to Rehoboam, "Your father forced us to work very hard. Now, make it easier for us. Don't make us work as hard as your father did. Then we will serve you."

Rehoboam answered, "Come back to me in three days. Then I will answer you." So the people left.

Some of the older leaders had helped Solomon make decisions during his lifetime. So King Rehoboam asked them what he should do. He said, "How do you think I should answer these people?"

They answered, "You should be like a servant to them today. Serve them, and give them a kind answer. If you do, they will serve you always."

But Rehoboam did not listen to this advice. He asked the young men who had grown up with him. Rehoboam said, "What is your advice?"

The young men answered, "You should tell them, 'My father forced you to work hard. But I will make you work even harder! My father beat you with whips. But I will beat you with whips that have sharp points.'"

So after three days all the people returned to Rehoboam. At that time King Rehoboam spoke cruel words to them.

All the people of Israel saw that the new king refused to listen to them. So they said to the king, "We have no share in David! We have no part in the son of Jesse! People of Israel, let's go to our own homes! Let David's son rule his own people!"

Adoniram was in charge of the people who were forced to work. King Rehoboam sent him to the people. But they threw stones at him until he died. But King Rehoboam ran to his chariot and escaped to Jerusalem.

All the Israelites heard that Jeroboam had returned. And they made him king over all Israel. But the tribe of Judah continued to follow the family of David.

Jeroboam Builds Golden Calves

Jeroboam said to himself, "The people will continue going to the Temple of the Lord in Jerusalem. If they do, they will want to be ruled again by Rehoboam. Then they will kill me and follow Rehoboam king of Judah."

So he made two golden calves. He said to the people, "It is too hard for you to go to Jerusalem to worship. Israel, here are your gods who brought you out of Egypt." King Jeroboam did not stop doing evil things.

Elijah Stops the Rain

Ahab ruled Israel in the town of Samaria for 22 years. Ahab did more evil than any of the kings before him. He married Jezebel daughter of Ethbaal. (Ethbaal was king of the city of Sidon.) Then Ahab began to serve Baal and worship him. He built a temple in Samaria for worshiping Baal.

Now Elijah was a prophet from Gilead. Elijah said to King Ahab, "I serve the Lord, the God of Israel. As surely as the Lord lives, I tell you the truth. No rain or dew will fall during the next few years unless I command it."

Then the Lord spoke his word to Elijah: "Leave this place. Go east and hide near Kerith Ravine. It is east of the Jordan River. You may drink from the brook. And I have commanded ravens to bring you food there." So Elijah did what the Lord told him to do.

After a while the brook dried up because there was no rain. Then the Lord spoke his word to Elijah, "Go to Zarephath in Sidon. Live there. I have commanded a widow there to take care of you."

So Elijah went to Zarephath. When he reached the town gate, he saw a widow there. She was gathering wood for a fire. Elijah asked her, "Would you bring me a little water in a cup? I would like to have a drink." As she was going to get his water, Elijah said, "Please bring me a piece of bread, too."

The woman answered, "As surely as the Lord your God lives, I tell you the truth. I have no bread. I have only a handful of flour in a jar. And I have only a little olive oil in a jug. I came here to gather some wood. I will take it home and cook our last meal. My son and I will eat it and then die from hunger."

Elijah said to her, "Don't worry. Go home and cook your food as you have said. But first make a small loaf of bread from the flour you have. Bring it to me. Then cook something for yourself and your son. The Lord, the God of Israel, says, 'That jar of flour will never become empty. The jug will always have oil in it. This will continue until the day the Lord sends rain to the land.'"

So the woman went home. And she did what Elijah told her to do. So Elijah, the woman and her son had enough food every day. The jar of flour and the jug of oil were never empty. This happened just as the Lord, through Elijah, said it would.

Elijah Brings a Boy Back to Life

Some time later the son of the woman who owned the house became sick. He grew worse and worse. Finally he stopped breathing. So the woman said to Elijah, "You are a man of God. Did you come here to kill my son?"

Elijah said to her, "Give me your son." So Elijah took the boy from her and carried him upstairs. Elijah laid the boy on the bed in the room where he was staying. Then he prayed to the Lord. He said, "Lord my God, this widow is letting me stay in her house. Why have you done this terrible thing to her? Why have you caused her son to die?" Then Elijah lay on top of the boy three times. Elijah prayed to the Lord, "Lord my God, let this boy live again!"

The Lord answered Elijah's prayer. The boy began breathing again, and he was alive. Elijah carried the boy downstairs. He gave the boy to his mother and said, "See! Your son is alive!"

The woman said to Elijah, "Now I know you really are a man from God. I know that the Lord truly speaks through you!"

Elijah and the Prophets of Baal

During the third year without rain, the Lord spoke his word to Elijah. The Lord said, "Go and meet King Ahab. I will soon send rain." So Elijah went to meet Ahab.

By this time there was no food in Samaria. So King Ahab sent for Obadiah. Obadiah was in charge of the king's palace. (Obadiah was a true follower of the Lord. One time Jezebel was killing all the Lord's prophets. So Obadiah took 100 of them and hid them in caves. And he brought them food and water.) King Ahab said to Obadiah, "Let's look at every spring and valley in the land. Maybe we can find enough grass to keep our horses and mules alive. Then we will not have to kill our animals."

While Obadiah was walking along, Elijah met him. Obadiah bowed down to the ground before Elijah. He said, "Elijah? Is it really you, master?"

Elijah answered, "Yes. Go tell your master the king that I am here."

So Obadiah went to Ahab and told him where Elijah was. Then Ahab went to meet Elijah.

When he saw Elijah, he said, "Is it you — the biggest trouble-maker in Israel?"

Elijah answered, "I have not caused trouble in Israel. You and your father's family have caused all this trouble. You have not obeyed the Lord's commands. You have followed the Baals. Now tell all Israel to meet me at Mount Carmel. Also bring the 450 prophets of Baal there."

So Ahab called all the Israelites and those prophets to Mount Carmel. Elijah stood before the people. He said, "How long will you try to serve both Baal and the Lord? If the Lord is the true God, follow him. But if

Baal is the true God, follow him!"

But the people said nothing. Elijah said, "I am the only prophet of the Lord here. But there are 450 prophets of Baal. So bring two bulls. Let the prophets of Baal choose one bull. Let them kill it and cut it into pieces. Then let them put the meat on the wood. But they are not to set fire to it. Then I will do the same with the other bull. And I will put it on the wood. But I will not set fire to it. You prophets of Baal, pray to your god. And I will pray to the Lord. The god who answers the prayer will set fire to his wood. He is the true God."

All the people agreed that this was a good idea.

Then Elijah said to the prophets of Baal, "There are many of you. So you go first. Choose a bull and prepare it. Pray to your god, but don't start the fire."

So they took the bull that was given to them and prepared it. They prayed to Baal from morning until noon. They shouted, "Baal, answer us!" But there was no sound. No one answered. They danced around the altar they had built.

At noon Elijah began to make fun of them. He said, "Pray louder! If Baal really is a god, maybe he is thinking. Or maybe he is busy or traveling! Maybe he is sleeping so you will have to wake him!" So the prophets prayed louder. They cut themselves with swords and spears until their blood flowed. (This was the way they worshiped.) The afternoon passed, and the prophets continued to act wildly. They continued until it was time for the evening sacrifice. But no voice was heard. Baal did not answer. No one paid attention.

Then Elijah said to all the people, "Now come to me." So they gathered around him. Elijah took 12 stones. He took 1 stone for each of the 12 tribes named for the 12 sons of Jacob. Elijah used these stones to rebuild the altar in honor of the Lord. Then he dug a small ditch around it. Elijah put the wood on the altar. He cut the bull into pieces and laid them on the wood. Then he said, "Fill four jars with water. Put the water on the meat and on the wood."

Then Elijah said, "Do it again." And they did it again.

Then he said, "Do it a third time." And they did it the third time. So the water ran off of the altar and filled the ditch.

Elijah went near the altar. He prayed, "Lord, you are the God of Abraham, Isaac and Israel. I ask you now to prove that you are the God of Israel. And prove that I am your servant. Show these people that you commanded me to do all these things. Lord, answer my prayer. Show these people that you, Lord, are God. Then the people will know that you are bringing them back to you."

Then fire from the Lord came down. It burned the sacrifice, the wood, the stones and the ground around the altar. It also dried up the water in the ditch. When all the people saw this, they fell down to the ground. They cried, "The Lord is God! The Lord is God!"

Then Elijah said, "Capture the prophets of Baal! Don't let any of them run away!" So the people captured all the prophets. Then Elijah led them down to Kishon Valley. There he killed all the prophets.

Rain Comes Again

Then Elijah said to Ahab, "Now, go, eat and drink. A heavy rain is coming." So King Ahab went to eat and drink. At the same time Elijah climbed to the top of Mount Carmel. There he bent down to the ground with his head between his knees.

Then Elijah said to his servant, "Go and look toward the sea." The servant went and looked. He said, "I see nothing."

Elijah told him to go and look again. This happened seven times. The seventh time, the servant said, "I see a small cloud. It's the size of a man's fist. It's coming from the sea."

Elijah told the servant, "Go to Ahab. Tell him to get his chariot ready and to go home now. If he doesn't leave now, the rain will stop him."

After a short time the sky was covered with dark clouds. The wind began to blow. Then a heavy rain began to fall. Ahab got in his chariot and started back to Jezreel. The Lord gave his power to Elijah. Elijah tightened his clothes around him. Then he ran ahead of King Ahab all the way to Jezreel.

Elijah at Mount Sinai

King Ahab told Jezebel everything Elijah had done. Ahab told her how Elijah had killed all the prophets with a sword. So Jezebel sent a messenger to Elijah. Jezebel said, "By this time tomorrow I will kill you. I will kill you as you killed those prophets. If I don't succeed, may the gods punish me terribly."

When Elijah heard this, he was afraid. So he ran away to save his life. He took his servant with him. When they came to Beersheba in Judah, Elijah left his servant there. Then Elijah walked for a whole day into the desert. He sat down under a bush and asked to die. Elijah prayed, "I have had enough, Lord. Let me die. I am no better than my ancestors." Then Elijah lay down under the tree and slept.

Suddenly an angel came to him and touched him. The angel said, "Get up and eat." Elijah saw near his head a loaf baked over coals and a jar of water. So he ate and drank. Then he went back to sleep.

Later the Lord's angel came to him a second time. The angel touched him and said, "Get up and eat. If you don't, the journey will be too hard for you." So Elijah got up and ate and drank. The food made him strong enough to walk for 40 days and nights. He walked to Mount Sinai, the mountain of God. There Elijah went into a cave and stayed all night.

Then the Lord spoke his word to him: "Elijah! Why are you here?"

Elijah answered, "Lord, God of heaven's armies, I have always served you the best I could. But the people of Israel have broken their agreement with you. They have destroyed your altars. They have killed your prophets with swords. I am the only prophet left. And now they are trying to kill me, too!"

Then the Lord said to Elijah, "Go. Stand in front of me on the mountain. I will pass by you." Then a very strong wind blew. It caused the mountains to break apart. It broke apart large rocks in front of the Lord. But the Lord was not in the wind. After the wind, there was an earthquake. But the Lord was not in the earthquake. After the earthquake, there was a fire. But the Lord was not in the fire. After the fire, there was a quiet, gentle voice. When Elijah heard it, he covered his face with his coat. He went out and stood at the entrance to the cave.

The Lord said to him, "Go back. Pour oil on Elisha. He will be a prophet in your place. But I have left 7,000 people living in Israel. Those 7,000 have never bowed down before Baal. Their mouths have never kissed his idol."

So Elijah left there and found Elisha. He was plowing a field with a team of oxen. Then Elisha went and followed Elijah and became his helper.

King Ahab

One day Ahab went home, angry and upset. Ahab lay down on his bed. He turned his face to the wall and refused to eat.

His wife, Jezebel, came in.

She asked him, "Why are you upset?"

Ahab answered, "I talked to Naboth, the man from Jezreel. I said, 'Sell me your vineyard. Or, if you prefer, I will give you another vineyard for it.' But Naboth refused."

Jezebel answered, "I will get Naboth's vineyard for you." So the older leaders and important men of Jezreel obeyed Jezebel's command. They carried Naboth out of the city. And they killed him with stones.

At this time the Lord spoke his word to Elijah. "Go to Ahab king of Israel, who rules in Samaria. He is at Naboth's vineyard to take it as his own."

When Ahab saw Elijah, he said, "So you have found me, my enemy!"

Elijah answered, "Yes, I have found you. You have always chosen to do what the Lord says is wrong. So the Lord says to you, 'I will destroy you. You have caused the people of Israel to sin.' "

At this same time Ahab asked his officers, "Remember that the king of Aram took Ramoth in Gilead from us? Why have we done nothing to get it back?" So Ahab king of Israel went to Ramoth in Gilead.

The king of Aram had 32 chariot commanders. A soldier

shot an arrow. He hit Ahab king of Israel. King Ahab said to his chariot driver, "Turn the chariot around. Take me out of the battle. I am hurt!" The battle continued all day. King Ahab was in his chariot, leaning against it to hold himself up. That evening he died. Near sunset a cry went out through the army of Israel: "Each man go back to his own country and city."

So in that way King Ahab died.

WORTH WONDERING...

- The prophet Elijah knew how to "stand up" for God when others would not stand with him. What can help you to be obedient to God when others around you are not?

- If you could meet Elijah today, what kind of questions would you like to ask him?

- What good example can you give of someone in this book who did what was right?

- What example can you give of someone in this book who did what was wrong?

- Use your imagination for this one: Suppose you were there when Elijah and the prophets of Baal met for their contest on the mountain. What kinds of things do you think you would see and hear and smell?

GREAT VERSES TO THINK ABOUT AGAIN...

Look back in First Kings to see if you can find these verses:

- *Hear us from your home in heaven. And when you hear us, forgive us.*

- *I am like a little child. I do not have the wisdom I need to do what I must do. So I ask that you give me wisdom.*

- *Show these people that you, Lord, are God. Then the people will know that you are bringing them back to you.*

- *God, can you really live here on the earth? Even the sky and the highest place in heaven cannot contain you.*

AND THERE'S MORE...

When you read First Kings in a full Bible, you'll read about a total of 14 kings of both Israel, the Northern Kingdom, and Judah, the Southern Kingdom.

The Second Book of
KINGS

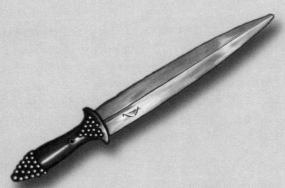

Two Kingdoms
Are Destroyed

Looking forward to 2 Kings...

"Two Kingdoms Are Destroyed"

SIGNS AND WONDERS

In Second Kings we read the long story of how God's people are defeated and led into captivity. But notice how patient God is as He gives His people warnings and "second chances" to do what is right.

Like the book of First Kings, this book goes back and forth from the Northern Kingdom (Israel) to the Southern Kingdom (Judah) as it tells their history.

FACES AND PLACES

Elijah: A bold prophet to the Northern Kingdom, Israel.
Elisha: The man God chose as a prophet to follow in the steps of Elijah.
Jehu: One of the better kings of the Northern Kingdom.
Jezebel: The evil wife of Ahab, king of the Northern Kingdom.
Hezekiah: A good king of Judah, the Southern Kingdom.
Josiah: The last good king of Judah.
Nebuchadnezzar: The king of Babylon, who marched against Jerusalem.
Babylon: The city of Babylon was where the Jewish captives were taken. It was the capital of a great empire. For about 100 years, this was the most powerful empire the world had ever known.

When people won't keep their promises to God, I wonder if He'll keep His promises to them...

ELIJAH AND ELISHA were at Gilgal. Elijah said to Elisha, "Please stay here. The Lord has told me to go to Bethel."

But Elisha said, "As the Lord lives, and as you live, I won't leave you." Elijah and Elisha were by the Jordan. Elijah took off his coat. Then he rolled it up and hit the water. The water divided to the right and to the left. Then Elijah and Elisha crossed over on dry ground.

After they had crossed over, Elijah and Elisha were still walking and talking. Then a chariot and horses of fire appeared. The chariot and horses of fire separated Elijah from Elisha. Then Elijah went up to heaven in a whirlwind. Elisha saw it and shouted, "My father! My father! The chariots of Israel and their horsemen!" Elisha did not see him anymore. Elisha grabbed his own clothes and tore them to show how sad he was.

He picked up Elijah's coat that had fallen from him. Then Elisha returned and stood on the bank of the Jordan. Elisha hit the water with Elijah's coat. He said, "Where is the Lord, the God of Elijah?" When he hit the water, it divided to the right and to the left. Then Elisha crossed over.

A group of the prophets at Jericho were watching. They said, "Elisha now has the spirit Elijah had."

Elisha Makes the Water Pure

The men of the city said to Elisha, "Look, master, this city is a nice place to live. You can see that. But the water is bad. That's why the land cannot grow crops."

Elisha said, "Bring me a new bowl and put salt in it." So they brought it to him.

Then Elisha went out to the spring of water and threw the salt in it. He said, "This is what the Lord says: 'I have healed this water. From now on it won't cause death. And it won't keep the land from growing crops.'" The water was healed. It happened just as Elisha had said.

Elisha and the Poison

Elisha came to Gilgal. There was a time of hunger in the land. A group of prophets was sitting in front of him. He said to his servant, "Put the large pot on the fire. Boil some stew for these men."

One of them went out into the field to gather plants. He found a wild vine. He picked fruit from the vine and filled his robe with it. Then he came and cut up the fruit into the pot. But they did not know what kind of fruit it was. Then they poured out the stew for the men to eat.

But when they began to eat it, they shouted out, "Man of God! There's death in the pot!" They could not eat it.

Elisha told them to bring some flour. Then he threw it into the pot. He said, "Pour it out for the people to eat." And there was nothing harmful in the pot.

Elisha Multiplies Bread

A man came to Elisha. He brought 20 loaves of barley bread from the first harvest to Elisha. He also brought fresh grain in his sack. Then Elisha said, "Give it to the people to eat."

Elisha's servant said, "How can I feed 100 men with so little?"

But Elisha said, "Give the bread to the people to eat. This is what the Lord says: 'They will eat and will have food left over.'" Then he gave it to them. The people ate and had food left over, as the Lord had said.

An Axhead Floats

The group of the prophets said to Elisha, "The place where we meet with you is too small for us. Let's go to the Jordan River. And let's build a place there to live."

Elisha went with them. When they arrived at the Jordan, they cut down some trees. As one man was cutting down a tree, the head of his ax fell into the water. He yelled, "Oh, my master! I borrowed that ax!"

Elisha asked, "Where did it fall?" The man showed Elisha the place. Then Elisha cut down a stick and threw it into the water. It made the iron head float. Elisha said, "Pick up the axhead." Then the man reached out and took it.

Jehu Is Chosen King

Elisha called a man from the group of the prophets. Elisha said, "Tighten your clothes around you. And take this small bottle of olive oil in your hand. Go find Jehu. Take him to an inner room. Take the bottle and pour the oil on Jehu's head. Say, 'This is what the Lord says: I have appointed you king over Israel.' Then open the door and run away. Don't wait!"

So the young man, the prophet, went to Gilead. When he arrived, he poured the olive oil on Jehu's head. He said to Jehu, "This is what the Lord of Israel says: 'I have appointed you king over the Lord's people, Israel. You must destroy the family of Ahab your master. I will punish Jezebel for the deaths of my servants the prophets. And I will punish her for all the Lord's servants who

were murdered. So all Ahab's family will die."

Then the young prophet opened the door and ran away.

Jehu went back to his master's officers. One of them said to Jehu, "Is everything all right? Why did this crazy man come to you?"

Jehu said, "He said, 'This is what the Lord says: I have appointed you to be king over Israel.' "

Then the officers hurried. Each man took off his own coat. They put them on the stairs for Jehu. Then they blew the trumpet. They said, "Jehu is king!"

So Jehu made plans against Joram. Jehu got into his chariot and set out for Jezreel. Joram was resting there. When Joram saw Jehu, he said, "Do you bring good news, Jehu?"

Jehu answered, "There will never be any good news as long as your mother Jezebel worships idols and uses witchcraft."

Then Jehu drew his bow and shot Joram between his shoulders.

Death of Jezebel

When Jehu came to Jezreel, Jezebel heard about it. She put paint on her eyes and fixed her hair. Then she looked out the window. Jehu entered the city gate. And Jezebel said, "Have you come in peace, you who killed your master?"

Jehu looked up at the window. He said, "Who is on my side? Who?" Two or three eunuchs looked out from the window at Jehu. Jehu said to them, "Throw her down!" So they threw Jezebel down. And the horses ran over her body. Some of her blood splashed on the wall and on the horses.

Jehu went into the house and ate and drank. Then he said, "Now see about this cursed woman. Bury her, because she is a king's daughter."

The men went to bury Jezebel. But they could not find her body. They could only find the skull, feet and palms of her hands.

When Jehu came to Samaria, he killed all of Ahab's family. He did this until he had destroyed all of those who were left. Jehu did what the Lord had told Elijah would happen.

Israelites Punished for Sin

Hoshea became king over Israel. He did what the Lord said was wrong.

Shalmaneser king of Assyria came to attack Hoshea. Hoshea had quit giving Shalmaneser the payments he demanded. So the king put Hoshea in prison.

Then the king of Assyria came and attacked all the land of Israel. He surrounded Samaria and attacked it for three years. He defeated Samaria in the ninth year Hoshea was king. He took the Israelites away to Assyria.

All these things happened because the Israelites had sinned against the Lord their God. He had rescued them from the power of the king of Egypt. But the Israelites had honored other gods. They lived like the nations the Lord had forced out of the land ahead of them. They secretly sinned against the Lord their God. They built places in all their cities where false gods were worshiped. They served idols. The Lord used every prophet to warn Israel. He said, "Stop your evil ways. Obey my commands and laws. Follow all the teachings that I commanded your ancestors to obey. I sent you this law through my servants the prophets."

But the people would not listen. They were stubborn, just as their ancestors had been.

They always chose to do what the Lord said was wrong. And this made him angry. So He removed them from his presence. Only Judah was left.

Hezekiah King of Judah

Hezekiah son of Ahaz king of Judah became king. And he ruled 29 years in Jerusalem. Hezekiah did what the Lord said was right. He did just as his ancestor David had done. He removed the places where false gods were worshiped. He broke the stone pillars they worshiped. He cut down the idols. Also the Israelites had been burning incense to the bronze snake made by Moses. But Hezekiah broke it into pieces.

Hezekiah trusted in the Lord, the God of Israel. Hezekiah was loyal to the Lord. He did not stop following the Lord. He obeyed the commands the Lord had given Moses. And the Lord was with Hezekiah. He had success in everything he did. He turned against the king of Assyria and stopped serving him. Hezekiah defeated the Philistines all the way to Gaza and its borders. He defeated them everywhere, from the watchtower to the strong, walled city.

Assyria Attacks Judah

During Hezekiah's fourteenth year as king, Sennacherib king of Assyria attacked Judah. He attacked all the strong, walled cities of Judah and defeated them.

The king of Assyria sent out his supreme commander, his chief officer and his field commander. They went with a large army to Jerusalem. When they came near the waterway from the upper pool, they stopped. They called for the king. So Eliakim, Shebna and Joah went out to meet them. Eliakim son of Hilkiah was the palace manager. Shebna was the royal assistant. And Joah was the recorder.

The field commander said to them, "Tell Hezekiah this:

"'The great king, the king of Assyria, says: You have nothing to trust in to help you. You say you have battle plans and power for war. But your words mean nothing. Whom are you trusting for help so that you turn against me?'"

Then the commander stood and shouted loudly in the Hebrew language. He said, "Listen to the word from the great king, the king of Assyria! The king says you should not let Hezekiah fool you. Hezekiah can't save you from my power. Don't let Hezekiah talk you into trusting the Lord. The god of any other nation has not saved his people from the power of the king of Assyria. Then the Lord cannot save Jerusalem from my power."

Then Eliakim, Shebna and Joah tore their clothes to show how upset they were. The three men went to Hezekiah and told him what the field commander had said.

Jerusalem Will Be Saved

When King Hezekiah heard the message, he tore his clothes. And he put on rough cloth to show how sad he was. Then he went into the Temple of the Lord. Hezekiah sent Eliakim, Shebna and the older priests to Isaiah. He was a prophet, the son of Amoz. These men told Isaiah, "The king of Assyria sent his field commander to make fun of the living God. Maybe the Lord your God will hear what the commander said. Maybe the Lord your God will punish him for what he said. So pray for the few people who are left alive."

Isaiah said to them, "Tell your master this: The Lord says, 'Don't be afraid of what you have heard. Don't be frightened by the words the servants of the king of Assyria said against me. Listen! I am going to put a spirit in the king of Assyria. He will hear a report that will make him return to his own country. And I will cause him to die by the sword there.'"

The king received a report that Tirhakah was coming to attack him. Tirhakah was the king of Egypt. When the king of Assyria heard this, he sent messengers to Hezekiah. The king said: "Say this to Hezekiah king of Judah: Don't be fooled by the god you trust. Don't believe him when he says Jerusalem will not be defeated by the king of Assyria. You have heard what the kings of Assyria have done. They have completely defeated every country. Do not think you will be saved. The gods of those people did not save them."

Hezekiah Prays to the Lord

Hezekiah received the letter from the messengers and read it. Then he went up to the Temple of the Lord. Hezekiah spread the letter out before the Lord. And he prayed to the Lord: "Lord, God of Israel, you are God of all the kingdoms of the earth. You made the heavens and the earth. Listen to the word Sennacherib has said to insult the living God. It is true, Lord. The kings of Assyria have destroyed these countries and their lands. These kings have thrown the gods of these nations into the fire. But they were only wood and rock statues that men made. Now, Lord our God, save us from the king's power. Then all the kingdoms of the earth will know that you, Lord, are the only God."

God Answers Hezekiah

Then Isaiah sent a message to Hezekiah. Isaiah said, "The Lord, the God of Israel, says this: I have heard your prayer to me about Sennacherib king of Assyria. So this is what the Lord has said against Sennacherib: "'King of Assyria, surely you have heard. Long ago I, the Lord, planned these things. Now I have made them happen. I allowed you to turn those strong, walled cities into piles of rocks.

"'I know when you rest and when you come and go. I know how you speak against me. You speak strongly against me. And I have heard your proud words. So I will put my hook in your nose. And I will put my bit in your mouth. Then I will force you to leave my country the same way that you came.'

"Then the Lord said, 'Hezekiah, the strong love of the Lord of heaven's armies will cause this to happen.'

"So this is what the Lord says about the king of Assyria: 'He will not enter this city. He will not even shoot an arrow here.

The Lord says, 'I will defend and save this city. I will do this for myself and for David, my servant.'"

That night the angel of the Lord went out. He killed 185,000 men in the Assyrian camp. The people got up early the next morning. And they saw all the dead bodies! So Sennacherib king of Assyria left. He went back to Nineveh and stayed there.

One day Sennacherib was worshiping in the temple of his god Nisroch. While he was there, his sons killed him with a sword.

Then Hezekiah died. And his son Manasseh became king in his place.

Manasseh King of Judah

Manasseh did what the Lord said was wrong. Manasseh's father, Hezekiah, had destroyed the places where false gods were worshiped. But Manasseh rebuilt them. He built altars for Baal. Manasseh worshiped all the stars of heaven and served them. He built altars to worship the stars in the two courtyards of the Temple of the Lord. He burned his own son as a sacrifice. He practiced magic and told the future by explaining signs and dreams. He got advice from mediums and fortune-tellers. He did many things that the Lord said were wrong. And this made the Lord angry.

The Lord spoke through his servants the prophets. He said, "Manasseh king of Judah has done these hated things. Manasseh also has caused Judah to sin with his idols. So this is what the Lord, the God of Israel, says: 'I will bring much trouble on Jerusalem and Judah. Anyone who hears about it will be shocked. I will wipe out Jerusalem as a man wipes a dish. I will give them to their enemies. They will be robbed by all their enemies. My people did what I said was wrong. They have made me angry from the day their ancestors left Egypt until now.'"

Manasseh also killed many innocent people. He filled Jerusalem from one end to the other with their blood.

Josiah King of Judah

Josiah was eight years old when he became king. He ruled 31 years in Jerusalem. Josiah did what the Lord said was right. He did good things as his ancestor David had done.

In Josiah's eighteenth year as king, he sent Shaphan to the Temple of the Lord. Shaphan was the royal assistant. Josiah said, "Go up to Hilkiah the high priest. Have him empty out the money the gatekeepers have gathered from the people. This is the money they have brought into the Temple of the Lord. Have him give the money to the supervisors of the work on the Temple. They must pay the men who work to repair the Temple of the Lord. Also use the money to buy timber and cut stone to repair the Temple."

The Book of the Law Is Found

Hilkiah the high priest said to Shaphan the royal assistant, "I've found the Book of the Teachings. It was in the Temple of the Lord." He gave it to Shaphan, who read it.

Then Shaphan went to the king and reported to Josiah, "Hilkiah the priest has given me a book." And Shaphan read from the book to the king.

The king heard the words of the Book of the Teachings. Then he tore his clothes to show how upset he was. He gave these orders to Hilkiah and Shaphan: "Go and ask the Lord about the words in the book that has been found. The Lord's anger is burning against us because our ancestors did not obey the words of this book. They did not do all the things written for us to do!"

So they went to talk to Huldah the prophetess.

She said to them, "This is what the Lord, the God of Israel, says: 'I will bring trouble to this place and to the people living here. It is in the words of the book which the king of Judah has read. The people of Judah have left me. My anger burns against this place like a fire. It will not be put out.' Tell the king of Judah, who sent you to ask the Lord, 'This is what the Lord, the God of Israel, says about the words you heard. You became sorry in the Lord's presence for what you had done. Then you tore your clothes to show how upset you were. And you cried in my presence. This is why I have heard you, says the Lord. So I will cause you to die. You will be buried in peace. You won't see all the trouble I will bring to this place.'"

So they took her message back to the king.

The People Hear the Law

Then the king gathered all the older leaders of Judah and Jerusalem together. He went up to the Temple of the Lord. All the men from Judah and Jerusalem went with him. The priests, prophets and all the people — from the least important to the most important — went with him. He read to them all the words of the Book of the Agreement. That book was found in the Temple of the Lord. The king stood by the pillar. He made an agreement in the presence of the Lord. He agreed to follow the Lord and obey his commands, rules and laws with his whole being. He agreed to do what was written in this book. Then all the people promised to obey the agreement.

Josiah Destroys Idols

The king gave a command to the priests. He told them to bring out of the Temple of the Lord everything made for Baal, Asherah and all the stars of heaven. Then Josiah burned them outside Jerusalem in the fields of the Kidron Valley. Josiah removed the Asherah idol from the Temple of the Lord. He took it outside Jerusalem to the Kidron Valley. There he burned it and beat it into dust. And he threw the dust on the graves of the common people. Josiah burned the chariots that were for sun worship.

Josiah broke down the altars Manasseh had made. He smashed them to pieces. Then he threw their dust into the Kidron Valley. Josiah cut down the Asherah idols. And he covered the places with human bones.

The kings of Israel had built temples for worshiping false gods in the cities of Samaria. Josiah removed all those temples. Josiah killed all the priests of those places of worship. He killed them on the altars. And he burned human bones on the altars. Then he went back to Jerusalem.

While Josiah was king, Neco king of Egypt went to help the king of Assyria. King Josiah marched out to fight against Neco. But at Megiddo, Neco faced Josiah and killed him. Josiah's servants carried his body in a chariot from Megiddo. They brought him to Jerusalem and buried him in his own grave.

Jehoiakim King of Judah

While Jehoiakim was king, Nebuchadnezzar king of Babylon attacked the land of Judah. So Jehoiakim became Nebuchadnezzar's servant for three years. Then Jehoiakim turned against Nebuchadnezzar. The Lord sent men from Babylon, Aram, Moab and Ammon against Jehoiakim. He sent them to destroy Judah. This happened the way the Lord had said it would through his servants the prophets.

Jehoiakim died, and his son Jehoiachin became king in his place.

The king of Egypt did not come out of his land again. This was because of the king of Babylon. He had captured all that belonged to the king of Egypt. He took all the land from the brook of Egypt to the Euphrates River.

Jehoiachin King of Judah

Jehoiachin was king three months in Jerusalem. Jehoiachin did what the Lord said was wrong, just as his father had done.

At that time the officers of Nebuchadnezzar king of Babylon came up to Jerusalem. They surrounded the city and attacked it. Nebuchadnezzar himself came to the city while his officers were attacking it. Jehoiachin king of Judah surrendered to the king of Babylon. Then the king of Babylon made Jehoiachin a prisoner. Nebuchadnezzar took away all the people of Jerusalem. This included all the leaders and all the wealthy people. He also took all the craftsmen and metal workers. There were 10,000 prisoners in all. Only the poorest people in the land were left. Nebuchadnezzar carried away Jehoiachin to Babylon. The king of Babylon also took all 7,000 soldiers. These men were all strong and able to fight in war. Nebuchadnezzar took them as prisoners to Babylon. He made Mattaniah king in Jehoiachin's place. Mattaniah was Jehoiachin's uncle. He also changed Mattaniah's name to Zedekiah.

Zedekiah King of Judah

Zedekiah was king in Jerusalem for 11 years. Zedekiah did what the Lord said was wrong, just as Jehoiakim had done. All this happened in Jerusalem and Judah because the Lord was angry with them. Finally, he threw them out of his presence.

Zedekiah turned against the king of Babylon.

Then Nebuchadnezzar king of Babylon marched against Jerusalem with his whole army. He made a camp around the city. Then he built devices all around the city walls to attack it. The hunger was terrible in the city. There was no food for the people to eat. Then the city wall was broken through. Zedekiah's army ran away at night. They went through the gate between the two walls by the king's garden. Zedekiah and his men ran toward the Jordan Valley. But the Babylonian army chased King Zedekiah. They caught up with him in the plains of Jericho. So they captured Zedekiah and took him to the king of Babylon at Riblah. There he passed sentence on Zedekiah. They killed Zedekiah's sons as he watched. Then they put out his eyes. They put bronze chains on him and took him to Babylon.

Nebuzaradan was the commander of the king's special guards. Nebuzaradan set fire to the Temple of the Lord and the palace. He also set fire to all the houses of Jerusalem. Every important building was burned.

The whole Babylonian army broke down the walls around Jerusalem. The rest of the people were also taken away. But the commander left behind some of the poorest people of the land. They were to take care of the vineyards and fields.

So the people of Judah were led away from their country as captives.

Jehoiachin Is Set Free

Jehoiachin king of Judah was held in Babylon for 37 years. In the thirty-seventh year Evil-Merodach became king of Babylon. He let Jehoiakin out of prison. Evil-Merodach spoke kindly to Jehoiachin. He gave Jehoiachin a seat of honor. So Jehoiachin put away his prison clothes. For the rest of his life, he ate at the king's table. This lasted as long as he lived.

WORTH WONDERING...

- In this book, why do you think so many kings and other people in Israel kept disobeying God, and refusing to listen to Him?

- What good example can you give of someone in this book who did what was right?

- What example can you give of someone in this book who did what was wrong?

- Who is your favorite king in this book? What do you like about him?

- In this book of the Bible, how do you see that God is great? And how do you see that He is good?

- Suppose you were a famous artist. Someone has asked you to paint a picture showing something that happens in this book of Second Kings. What person or event from this book would you choose to paint?

GREAT VERSES TO THINK ABOUT AGAIN...

Look back in Second Kings to see if you can find these verses:

- *The Lord used every prophet to warn Israel. He said, "Stop your evil ways. Obey my commands and laws. Follow all the teachings that I commanded your ancestors to obey. I sent you this law through my servants the prophets."*

- *Hezekiah trusted in the Lord, the God of Israel. Hezekiah was loyal to the Lord. He did not stop following the Lord. He obeyed the commands the Lord had given Moses. And the Lord was with Hezekiah. He had success in everything he did.*

- *As the Lord lives, and as you live, I won't leave you.*

AND THERE'S MORE...

When you read Second Kings in a full Bible, you'll read about a total of 28 different kings of both Israel, the Northern Kingdom, and Judah, the Southern Kingdom.

The First Book of
CHRONICLES

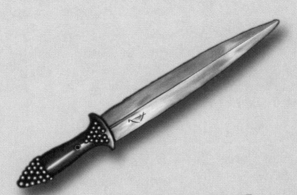

Another Look at David

Looking forward to 1 Chronicles...

"Another Look at David"

First and Second Chronicles were at first only one book. Together they return to the same story that we read in the books of Samuel and Kings. But the writer of Chronicles carefully chooses certain parts of the story to tell us. He wants to help us see them more closely from God's point of view.

David: In First Chronicles, we can especially see David's love for God in David's desire to build the Temple.

Joab: The commander of David's army.

Araunah's threshing floor: A threshing floor was the place where wheat was threshed: the grains of wheat were separated from the husks. Araunah's threshing floor was in a very important place. It was on Mount Moriah. This was the mountain where Abraham had offered his son Isaac as a sacrifice.

I wonder what kind of a man David really was...

DAVID'S WARRIORS helped make David's kingdom strong.

Jashobeam was the leader of the Three, David's most powerful soldiers. He used his spear to fight 300 men at one time. And he killed them all.

Three of the 30 leaders went to David. He was at the rock by the cave near Adullam. At the same time a group from the Philistine army was camped in the Valley of Rephaim.

David was in a protected place at that time. The Philistine army was staying in the town of Bethlehem. David had a strong desire for some water. He said, "Oh, I wish someone would get me water from the well near the city gate of Bethlehem!" So the Three fought their way through the Philistine army. And they took water out of the well near the city gate in Bethlehem. Then they took it back to David. But he refused to drink it. He poured it out before the Lord. David said, "May God keep me from drinking this water! It would be like drinking the blood of the men who risked their lives to bring me this water." So David refused to drink it.

These were the brave things the Three did.

Abishai brother of Joab was the leader of the Three. Abishai fought 300 men with his spear and killed them.

Benaiah son of Jehoiada was a brave fighter from Kabzeel. Benaiah did many brave things.

He killed two of the best warriors from Moab. He also went down into a pit when it was snowing. There he killed a lion. Benaiah also killed an Egyptian who was about seven and a half feet tall. David chose Benaiah to be the leader of his bodyguards.

David's Kingdom Grows

David knew that the Lord really had made him king of Israel. And he knew the Lord had made his kingdom very important. The Lord did this because he loved his people, the Israelites.

David became famous in all the countries. And the Lord made all nations afraid of David. David was king over all of Israel. He did what was right and fair for everyone.

David Counts Israel

Satan was against Israel. He encouraged David to count the people of Israel. So David gave an order to Joab and the commanders of the troops. He said, "Go and count all the Israelites. Then tell me so I will know how many people there are."

But Joab answered, "Why do you want to do this, my master? You will make Israel guilty of sin."

But King David made Joab follow his order. So Joab left and went through all Israel, counting the people.

Then David said to God, "I have done something very foolish. It was a terrible sin. Now, I beg you to forgive me, your servant."

The Lord sent a terrible disease on Israel, and 70,000 people died. God sent an angel to destroy Jerusalem. But when the angel started to destroy it, the Lord saw it and felt sorry. So he said to the angel who was destroying, "That is enough! Stop!" The angel of the Lord was then standing at the threshing floor of Araunah.

David looked up and saw the angel of the Lord in the sky. The angel was holding his sword over Jerusalem. Then David and the older leaders bowed face-down on the ground. They were wearing rough cloth to show their sadness. David said to God, "I am the one who sinned. I gave the order for the people to be counted. I have done wrong. These people are only sheep. Lord my God, punish me and my family. But stop the terrible disease that is killing your people."

Then the angel of the Lord told David to build an altar to worship the Lord. It was to be at the threshing floor of Araunah the Jebusite. Gad told David these things from the Lord. So David went to Araunah's threshing floor.

David said to him, "Sell me your threshing floor. Then I can build an altar to worship the Lord here. Then the terrible disease will be stopped."

So David paid Araunah about 15 pounds of gold for the place. David built an altar to worship the Lord there. He offered burnt offerings and fellowship offerings. David prayed to the Lord. And the Lord answered him by sending down fire from heaven. It came down on the altar of burnt offering. Then the Lord commanded the angel to put his sword back into its holder.

David's Plans for the Temple

David said, "The Temple of the Lord God will be built here. And the altar for burnt offerings for Israel will be built here."

Then David called for his son Solomon. David said to him, "My son, I wanted to build a temple for worshiping the Lord my God. But the Lord spoke his word to me, 'David, you have killed too many people. You have fought too many wars. So you cannot build a temple for worship to me. But, you will have a son. He will be a man of peace and rest. I will give him rest from all his enemies around him. His name will be Solomon. Solomon will build a temple for worship to me. He will be my son, and I will be his father. I will make his kingdom strong. Someone from his family will rule Israel forever.'"

David also said, "Now, my son, may the Lord be with you. May you build a temple for the Lord your God, as he said you would. Be careful to obey the rules and laws the Lord gave Moses for Israel. If you obey them, you will have success. Be strong and brave. Don't be afraid or discouraged.

"Solomon, I have worked hard getting many of the materials for building the Temple of the Lord. I have supplied about seven and a half million pounds of gold. And I have supplied about seventy-five million pounds of silver. I have supplied so much bronze and iron it cannot be weighed. And I have supplied wood and stone. Now begin the work. And may the Lord be with you."

Then David gave his son Solomon the plans for building the Temple. David said, "All these plans were written with the Lord guiding me. He helped me understand everything in the plans."

David's Prayer

David praised the Lord in front of all of the people. He said: "We praise you, Lord. Everything in heaven and on earth belongs to you. You are the ruler over everything. You have the power and strength to make anyone great and strong.

"Please help your people to want to serve you always. And help them to want to obey you always. Give my son Solomon a strong desire to serve you. Help him always obey your commands, laws and rules. Help him build the Temple for which I have prepared."

David died when he was old. He had lived a good, long life. He had received many riches and honors.

WORTH WONDERING...

- Why do you think David wanted to build a Temple for the Lord?
- Remember what you have read before about King Solomon. How well did Solomon follow the advice which David his father gave him in this book?
- Which parts of this book would you most like to know more about?

GREAT VERSES TO THINK ABOUT AGAIN...

Look back in First Chronicles to see if you can find these verses:

- *Be careful to obey the rules and laws the Lord gave Moses for Israel. If you obey them, you will have success. Be strong and brave. Don't be afraid or discouraged.*
- *David knew that the Lord really had made him king of Israel. And he knew the Lord had made his kingdom very important. The Lord did this because he loved his people, the Israelites.*
- *Oh, I wish someone would get me water from the well near the city gate of Bethlehem!*

AND THERE'S MORE...

When you read First Chronicles in a full Bible, look especially for...

- More details about David's mighty warriors.
- Family records of the famous people in Israel's history.

The Second Book of
CHRONICLES

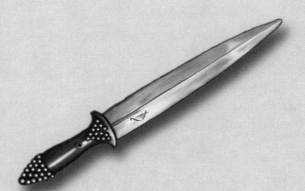

*The Road
to Captivity*

Looking forward to 2 Chronicles...

"The Road to Captivity"

The Temple built by Solomon is very important to the writer of Chronicles, as he helps us see Israel's story from God's point of view. But at the end of this book the Temple (and all of Jerusalem) will be destroyed when the kings and the people refuse to obey God. The time from David to the fall of Jerusalem was about 400 years.

Solomon: The wise king who built the Temple in Jerusalem.
Rehoboam: Solomon's son.
Asa, Jehoshaphat, Uzziah, Hezekiah, Manasseh, and **Zedekiah:** Other kings of Judah.
Nebuchadnezzar: The king of Babylon, who marched against Jerusalem and captured it.
Babylon: The city of Babylon was where the Jewish captives were taken. It was the capital of a great empire. For about 100 years, this was the most powerful empire the world had ever known.

I wonder what lessons God wants us most to learn from the terrible punishment He brought to Jerusalem and His people...

SOLOMON was David's son, and he became a powerful king. This was because the Lord his God was with him. The Lord made Solomon very great.

In Jerusalem, Solomon gathered much silver and gold. He got so much it was as common as rocks.

Solomon began to build the Temple of the Lord. He built it in Jerusalem on Mount Moriah. Then Solomon called for all the leaders of Israel. He asked them to come to him in Jerusalem.

King Solomon and all the Israelites met in front of the Box of the Agreement. They sacrificed so many sheep and bulls no one could count them.

The Lord Appears to Solomon

Solomon had success in doing everything he planned in the Temple of the Lord and his own palace. Then the Lord appeared to Solomon at night. The Lord said, "Solomon, I have heard your prayer. And I have chosen this place for myself to be a Temple for sacrifices.

"I may stop the sky from sending rain. I may command the locusts to destroy the land. I may send sicknesses to my people. Then my people, who are called by my name, will be sorry for what they have done. They will pray and obey me and stop their evil ways. If they do, I will hear them from heaven. I will forgive their sin, and I will heal their land. Now I will see them. And I will listen to the prayers prayed in this place. I have chosen this Temple and made it holy. So I will be worshiped here forever. Yes, I will always watch over it and love it."

Rehoboam King of Judah

Rehoboam became a strong king. He also made his kingdom strong. Then he and the people of Judah stopped obeying the teachings of the Lord. Shishak was the king of Egypt. He attacked Jerusalem. This happened because Rehoboam and the people were unfaithful to the Lord. Shishak had 1,200 chariots and 60,000 horsemen. Shishak captured the strong, walled cities of Judah. And he came as far as Jerusalem.

Then Shemaiah the prophet came to Rehoboam and the leaders of Judah. Shemaiah said to them, "This is what the Lord says: 'You have left me. So now I will leave you to face Shishak alone.'"

Then the leaders of Judah and King Rehoboam were sorry for what they had done. They said, "The Lord does what is right."

The Lord saw that they were sorry for what they had done. So the Lord spoke his word to Shemaiah. The Lord said, "The king and the leaders are sorry. So I will not destroy them but will save them soon."

Asa King of Judah

Asa called out to the Lord his God. He said, "Lord, only you can help weak people against the strong. Help us, Lord our God. We depend on you. We fight against this large army in your name. Lord, you are our God. Don't let anyone win against you."

Then Asa got a disease in his feet. His disease was very bad. But he did not ask for help from the Lord. He only asked for help from the doctors. Then Asa died.

Jehoshaphat King of Judah

Some people came to start a war with Jehoshaphat. They were the Moabites, Ammonites and some Meunites. Jehoshaphat was afraid. So he decided to ask the Lord what to do.

The people of Judah and Jerusalem met in front of the new courtyard in the Temple of the Lord. Then Jehoshaphat stood up before them. He said, "Lord, you are the God of our ancestors. You are the God in heaven. You rule over all the kingdoms of the nations. You have power and strength. No one can stand against you.

"But now here are men from Ammon, Moab and Edom. They have come to force us out of your land. And you gave us this land as our own. Our God, punish those people. We have no power against this large army that is attacking us. We don't know what to do. So we look to you for help."

All the men of Judah stood before the Lord. Their babies, wives and children were with them. Then the Spirit of the Lord entered Jahaziel. He stood up in the meeting. And he said: "Listen to me, King Jehoshaphat! Listen, all you people living in Judah and Jerusalem! The Lord says this to you: 'Don't be afraid or discouraged because of this large army. The battle is not your battle. It is God's battle. You won't need to fight in this battle. Just stand strong in your places. You will see the Lord save you. Judah and Jerusalem, don't be afraid. Don't be discouraged. The Lord is with you. So go out against those people tomorrow!'"

Jehoshaphat's army went out early in the morning. As they were starting out, Jehoshaphat stood and said, "Listen to me, people of Judah and Jerusalem! Have faith in the Lord your God.

Then you will stand strong. Then you will succeed." Then he chose men to be singers to the Lord. They were to praise the Lord because he is holy and wonderful. They marched in front of the army. They said, "Thank the Lord. His love continues forever."

As they began to sing and praise God, the Lord set ambushes. The men of Ammon and Moab started to attack the men from Edom. They killed and destroyed them. After they had killed the men from Edom, they killed each other.

The men from Judah came to a place where they could see the desert. They looked at the enemy's large army. But they only saw dead bodies lying on the ground. No one had escaped.

Uzziah King of Judah

God helped Uzziah fight the Philistines. Uzziah was very powerful.

Uzziah built towers in Jerusalem and made them strong. He also built towers in the desert and dug many wells. He had people who worked his fields and vineyards. Uzziah loved the land.

He had an army of trained soldiers. In Jerusalem Uzziah made devices that were invented by clever men. They were used to shoot arrows and large rocks. So Uzziah became famous in faraway places.

But when Uzziah became strong, his pride caused him to be destroyed. He was unfaithful to the Lord his God. He went into the Temple of the Lord to burn incense on the altar. Azariah and 80 other brave priests who served the Lord followed Uzziah into the Temple. They told Uzziah he was wrong. They said to him, "You don't have the right to burn incense to the Lord. Only the priests, Aaron's descendants, should burn the incense. They have been made holy for the Lord to do this special duty. Leave this holy place. You have been unfaithful to God. The Lord God will not honor you for this."

Uzziah was standing beside the altar for incense in the Temple of the Lord. He had in his hand a pan for burning incense. He was very angry with the priests. As he was standing in front of the priests, a harmful skin disease broke out on his forehead. Azariah the leading priest and all the other priests looked at him. They could see the harmful skin disease on his forehead. So they hurried him out of the Temple. Uzziah rushed out, because the Lord had punished him. So King

Uzziah had the skin disease until the day he died. He had to live in a separate house. He could not enter the Temple of the Lord.

Hezekiah King of Judah

King Hezekiah sent messages to all the people of Israel and Judah. Hezekiah invited all these people to come to the Temple of the Lord in Jerusalem. There they could celebrate the Passover for the Lord, the God of Israel. For a long time most of the people had not celebrated the Passover as the law commanded.

A large crowd came together in Jerusalem. The people ate the feast for seven days. Then all the people agreed to stay seven more days. So they celebrated the Passover with joy for seven more days. There was much joy in Jerusalem. There had not been a celebration like this since Solomon's time.

Manasseh King of Judah

Manasseh did what the Lord said was wrong. Manasseh's father, Hezekiah, had torn down the places where false gods were worshiped. But Manasseh rebuilt them. He bowed down to the stars and worshiped them. Manasseh built altars for false gods in the Temple of the Lord. He burned his sons as sacrifices. He practiced magic and witchcraft. He did many things the Lord said were wrong. And this made the Lord angry.

The Lord spoke to Manasseh and his people, but they did not listen. So the Lord brought the king of Assyria's army commanders to attack Judah. They captured Manasseh and put hooks in him. They put bronze chains on his hands. They made him their prisoner and took him to Babylon. As Manasseh suffered, he begged the Lord his God for help. He became very sorry for what he had done before the God of his ancestors. When Manasseh prayed, the Lord heard him and had pity for him. So the Lord let him return to Jerusalem and to his kingdom. Then Manasseh knew that the Lord is the true God.

Zedekiah King of Judah

King Nebuchadnezzar of Babylon attacked Judah. Then Nebuchadnezzar made Zedekiah the king of Judah and Jerusalem.

Zedekiah did what the Lord his God said was wrong. The prophet Jeremiah spoke messages from the Lord. But Zedekiah did not obey.

Zedekiah turned against King Nebuchadnezzar. Nebuchadnezzar had forced Zedekiah to promise to be loyal to him. And Zedekiah had promised, using God's name. But Zedekiah became stubborn. He refused to obey the Lord, the God of Israel. Also, all the leaders of the priests and the people of Judah became more wicked. They followed the evil example of the other nations. The Lord had made the Temple in Jerusalem holy. But the leaders made the Temple unholy.

The Fall of Jerusalem

The Lord, the God of their ancestors, sent prophets again and again to warn his people. He did this because he had pity for them and for his Temple. But they made fun of God's prophets. They hated God's messages. So they refused to listen to the prophets. Finally God became so angry with his people that he could not be stopped. So God brought the king of Babylon to attack them. The king killed the young men even when they were in the Temple. He did not have mercy on the people. He killed both young men and women. He even killed the old men and those who were sick. God permitted Nebuchadnezzar to punish the people of Judah and Jerusalem. Nebuchadnezzar carried away to Babylon all the things from the Temple of God, both large and small. He took all the treasures from the Temple of the Lord and from the king and his officers. Nebuchadnezzar and his army set fire to God's Temple. They broke down Jerusalem's wall. And they burned all the palaces. They took or destroyed every valuable thing in Jerusalem.

Nebuchadnezzar took captive to Babylon the people who were left alive. And he forced them to be slaves for him and his descendants. They remained there as slaves until the Persian kingdom defeated Babylon. And so what the Lord had told Israel through the prophet Jeremiah happened.

WORTH WONDERING...

- Why did God allow His people to go into captivity? What did He want them to learn?

- Which kings in this book give us the best examples of what is right to do?

- Which kings in this book are the biggest examples of what is not right to do?

- If you could meet Solomon today, what kind of questions would you like to ask him?

GREAT VERSES TO THINK ABOUT AGAIN...

Look back in Second Chronicles to see if you can find these verses:

- *You are the God in heaven. You rule over all the kingdoms of the nations. You have power and strength. No one can stand against you.*

- *I may send sicknesses to my people. Then my people, who are called by my name, will be sorry for what they have done. They will pray and obey me and stop their evil ways. If they do, I will hear them from heaven. I will forgive their sin, and I will heal their land.*

- *Don't be afraid or discouraged because of this large army. The battle is not your battle. It is God's battle.*

- *The Lord made Solomon very great.*

AND THERE'S MORE...

When you read Second Chronicles in a full Bible, you'll read about a total of 21 kings of Judah.

The Book of
EZRA

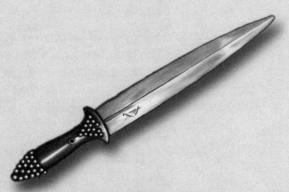

The Return
from Captivity

Looking forward to Ezra...

WHAT'S IT ABOUT?

"The Return from Captivity"

SIGNS AND WONDERS

Now we see God's people as they start returning to Jerusalem from captivity in Babylon. Their punishment as prisoners is over. They come back to a city in ruins. Only a small number of them return at first. And now that small group can begin rebuilding the most important building in Jerusalem — God's Temple.

FACES AND PLACES

Ezra: Ezra was a priest and a teacher of God's Word. He did not come back to Jerusalem with the first group of Jews who returned. He came later. He also appears in the book of Nehemiah, where he reads the Teachings of God to the people.

Cyrus: The King of Persia who wrote an announcement allowing the Jews to return to Jerusalem and Judah.

Persia: While the Jews were captured in Babylon, the Persians defeated the Babylonians and took over their empire.

Haggai and **Zechariah:** These prophets encouraged the people to keep working on rebuilding the Temple in Jerusalem.

Jeshua and **Zerubbabel:** Leaders of the Jews who came back to Jerusalem.

I Wonder

God's people had been prisoners in another country. Now, as they finally return to Jerusalem, I wonder if they'll be better at listening to God...

IT WAS THE FIRST YEAR Cyrus was king of Persia. The Lord caused Cyrus to write an announcement and send it everywhere in his kingdom. The announcement said:

All of you who are God's people are free to go to Jerusalem. May your God be with you. And you may build the Temple of the Lord.

Then the family leaders of Judah and Benjamin got ready to go to Jerusalem. So did the priests and the Levites. They were going to Jerusalem to build the Temple of the Lord.

Rebuilding the Altar

By the seventh month, the Israelites were settled in their hometowns. They met together in Jerusalem. Then Jeshua and his fellow priests began to build the altar of the God of Israel. They built the altar where it had been before. They offered burnt offerings on it to the Lord morning and evening.

Rebuilding the Temple

Then they finished laying the foundation of the Temple of the Lord. The priests, dressed in their robes, got trumpets. And the Levites, the sons of Asaph, had cymbals. They all took their places. They praised the Lord just as David king of Israel had said to do. With praise and thanksgiving, they sang to the

Lord: "He is good; his love for Israel continues forever."

Enemies of the Rebuilding

The people had enemies. The enemies said, "Let us help you build. We are like you. We want to worship your God."

But the leaders of Israel answered, "No. You people will not help us build a Temple to our God. We will build it ourselves. It is for the Lord, the God of Israel. This is what King Cyrus, the king of Persia, commanded us to do."

Then the people around them tried to discourage the people of Judah. They tried to make them afraid to build. Their enemies hired others to delay the building plans.

So the work on the Temple of God in Jerusalem stopped. It stopped until the second year Darius was king of Persia.

Haggai and Zechariah were prophets. They prophesied to the Jews in the name of the God of Israel. Then Zerubbabel and Jeshua started working again. They worked to rebuild the Temple of God in Jerusalem. The prophets of God were there, helping them.

They finished building the Temple as the God of Israel had said. Then the people of Israel celebrated.

WORTH WONDERING...

■ Why was the Temple important to the Jews?

■ Why do you think enemies tried to stop the people from rebuilding the Temple?

GREAT VERSES TO THINK ABOUT AGAIN...

Look back in Ezra to see if you can find this verse:

■ *With praise and thanksgiving, they sang to the Lord: "He is good; his love for Israel continues forever."*

AND THERE'S MORE...

When you read Ezra in a full Bible, look especially for...

■ More details about how the enemies tried to stop the Jews from rebuilding the Temple.

■ What Ezra did when he learned some bad news. He learned that the people who had returned from captivity were now doing some of the same sins that their ancestors had done. These were the same sins that caused God to send them away as prisoners.

The Book of
NEHEMIAH

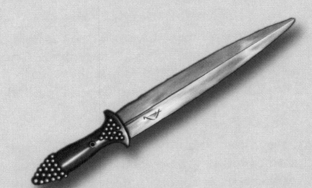

Rebuilding the Walls of Jerusalem

Looking forward to Nehemiah...

WHAT'S IT ABOUT?

"Rebuilding the Walls of Jerusalem"

SIGNS AND WONDERS

Long before Jerusalem was destroyed and the Jewish people were captured and taken away, God had promised that the city and Israel would be restored and rebuilt. Now, in Nehemiah's time, it is truly happening! God is faithful!

FACES AND PLACES

Nehemiah: His name means "comforted by God." He was an important officer in the palace of the king of Persia, where the Jews were taken as prisoners more than a century earlier. Nehemiah left his good job to do something more important — a job that God had prepared him to do.

Sanballat, Tobiah, and **Geshem:** These men were living in Israel when Nehemiah came to Jerusalem (they were not Jews). They led the way in mocking Nehemiah and his workers, and in trying to stop the work Nehemiah was doing.

Susa: Persia's capital. It was strongly protected.

Jerusalem: As this book begins, Jerusalem—God's holy city—was still in ruins from destruction by the army of Babylon more than a hundred years earlier. The city was unprotected; its walls and gates were nothing but rubble.

I wonder what it's like to take on a job bigger than anything I've ever done... and to face evil enemies who try to stop me from doing the work God gave me to do...

I WAS IN the capital city of Susa. One of my brothers named Hanani came from Judah. Some other men were with him. I asked them about the Jews who lived through the captivity. And I also asked about Jerusalem.

They answered, "Nehemiah, those who are left are in much trouble and are full of shame. The wall around Jerusalem is broken down. And its gates have been burned."

When I heard these things, I sat down and cried for several days.

Nehemiah Is Sent to Jerusalem

King Artaxerxes was king. He wanted some wine. So I took some and gave it to the king. The king said, "Why does your face look sad? You are not sick. Your heart must be sad."

Then I said to the king, "My face is sad because the city where my ancestors are buried lies in ruins. And its gates have been destroyed by fire."

The king said to me, "What do you want?"

First I prayed to the God of heaven. Then I answered the king, "Send me to the city in Judah where my ancestors are buried. I will rebuild it. Do this if you are willing and if I have pleased you."

It pleased the king to send me. So I set a time.

Nehemiah Inspects Jerusalem

I went to Jerusalem and stayed there three days. Then at night I started out with a few men. I had not told anyone what God had caused me to do for Jerusalem.

It was night. I went out through the Valley Gate. I rode toward the Dragon Well and the Trash Gate. I was inspecting the walls of Jerusalem. They had been broken down. And the gates had been destroyed by fire. Then I rode on toward the Fountain Gate and the King's Pool. Finally, I turned and went back in through the Valley Gate. The officers did not know where I had gone or what I was doing. I had not yet said anything to the Jews, the priests, or the officers. I had not said anything to any of the others who would do the work.

Then I said to them, "You can see the trouble we have here. Jerusalem is a pile of ruins. And its gates have been burned. Come, let's rebuild the wall of Jerusalem. Then we won't be full of shame any longer." I also told them how God had been kind to me. And I told them what the king had said to me.

Then they answered, "Let's start rebuilding." So they began to work hard.

But Sanballat, Tobiah, and Geshem the Arab heard about it. They made fun of us and laughed at us. They said, "What are you doing? Are you turning against the king?"

But I answered them, "The God of heaven will give us success. We are God's servants. We will start rebuilding. But you have no share in Jerusalem. You have no claim or past right to it."

Those Against the Rebuilding

Sanballat was furious. He made fun of the Jews. He said to his friends and the army of Samaria, "What are these weak Jews doing? They think they can rebuild the wall. They can't bring stones back to life. These are piles of trash and ashes."

Tobiah said, "A fox could climb up on what they are building. Even it could break down their stone wall."

I prayed, "Hear us, our God. We are hated. Turn the insults of Sanballat and Tobiah back on their own heads."

So we rebuilt the wall until all of it went halfway up. The people were willing to work hard.

But Sanballat, Tobiah, the Arabs, the Ammonites and the men from Ashdod were very angry. They all made plans to come and fight and stir up trouble. But we prayed to our God. And we appointed guards to watch for them day and night.

The people of Judah said, "The workers are getting tired. There is too much dirt and trash. We cannot rebuild the wall."

And our enemies said, "The Jews won't know it or see us. But we will come among them and kill them. We will stop the work."

From that day on, half my men worked on the wall. The other half was ready with spears, shields, bows and armor. The officers stood in back of the people who were building the wall. Those who carried materials did their work with one hand. They carried a weapon in the other hand. Each builder wore his sword at his side as he worked. The man who blew the trumpet to warn the people stayed next to me.

We worked from sunrise till the stars came out. At that time I also said to the people, "Let every man and his helper stay inside Jerusalem at night. They can be our guards at night. And they can be workmen during the day." Neither I, my brothers, my men nor the guards with me ever took off our clothes. Each person carried his weapon even when he went for water.

More Problems for Nehemiah

One day I went to the house of Shemaiah. Shemaiah had to stay at home. He said, "Nehemiah, let's meet in the Temple of God. Let's go inside the Temple and close the doors. Men are coming at night to kill you."

But I said, "Should a man like me run away? Should I run into the Temple to save my life? I will not go." I knew that God had not sent him. Tobiah and Sanballat had paid him to frighten me so I would do this and sin. Then they could give me a bad name to shame me.

I prayed, "Remember Tobiah and Sanballat, my God. Remember what they have done. Also remember the others who have been trying to frighten me."

The Wall Is Finished

So the wall of Jerusalem was completed. It took 52 days to rebuild. Then all our enemies heard about it. And all the nations around us saw it. So they were shamed. They understood that the work had been done with the help of our God.

All the people of Israel gathered together. They asked Ezra the teacher to bring out the Book of the Teachings of Moses. So all the people listened carefully to the Book of the Teachings. Then they bowed down and worshiped the Lord with their faces to the ground.

Then Nehemiah and Ezra said to all the people, "This is a holy day to the Lord your God. Don't be sad or cry." All the people had been crying as they listened to the words of the Teachings.

Nehemiah said, "Go and enjoy good food and sweet drinks. Today is a holy day to the Lord. Don't be sad. The joy of the Lord will make you strong."

Then all the people celebrated with great joy.

WORTH WONDERING...

■ When Nehemiah started rebuilding Jerusalem's walls, he was doing what he believed God wanted him to do. When other people tried to stop him, what did he do?

■ How did Nehemiah find out what God wanted him to do?

■ Why do you think Nehemiah cared so much about rebuilding Jerusalem?

■ How did Nehemiah get other people to help him to do the work God gave him to do?

■ Is Nehemiah the kind of leader you would like to follow?

■ In what ways are you a leader...or in what ways would you like to be a leader? In what ways is Nehemiah an example of a good leader?

■ If you could meet Nehemiah today, what kind of questions would you like to ask him?

GREAT VERSES TO THINK ABOUT AGAIN...

Look back in Nehemiah to see if you can find these verses:

■ *The God of heaven will give us success.*

■ *The joy of the Lord will make you strong.*

■ *The people were willing to work hard.*

■ *First I prayed to the God of heaven. Then I answered the king.*

AND THERE'S MORE...

When you read Nehemiah in a full Bible, look especially for...
■ How the people confess their sins.

■ How Nehemiah helps the poor people in Judah.

The Book of
ESTHER

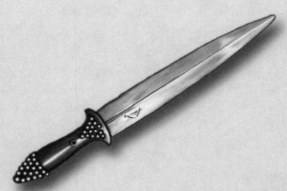

A Brave Woman
Saves Her People

Looking forward to Esther...

"A Brave Woman Saves Her People"

SIGNS AND WONDERS

Queen Esther bravely saves her family and all the Jews in Persia from being killed. Esther's exciting story actually takes place before Ezra and Nehemiah went back to Jerusalem, although her book comes after theirs in the Bible. God's name isn't mentioned in the book of Esther. But as you read, you'll see that it shows how God takes care of His people.

FACES AND PLACES

Xerxes: The powerful king of Persia.

Haman: An officer in the palace of Xerxes.

Esther (also called **Hadassah**): A beautiful Jewish woman whom Xerxes chose to be his queen.

Mordecai: A Jewish man, and the uncle of Esther. They were away from Israel because the king of Babylon had taken the Jews as prisoners many years before.

**When the lives of wise people are in danger,
I wonder how brave they can be...**

KING XERXES was the king who ruled from his capital city of Susa.

Now there was a Jewish man in the palace of Susa. His name was Mordecai. Mordecai had been taken captive from Jerusalem by Nebuchadnezzar king of Babylon. Mordecai was part of the group taken into captivity with Jehoiachin king of Judah. Mordecai had a cousin named Hadassah, who had no father or mother. So Mordecai took care of her. Hadassah was also called Esther, and she had a very pretty figure and face. Mordecai had adopted her as his own daughter when her father and mother died.

Many girls had been brought to the palace in Susa. Esther was also taken to the king's palace. She was put into the care of Hegai, who was in charge of the women. Esther pleased Hegai, and he liked her. So Hegai quickly began giving Esther her beauty treatments and special food. He gave her seven servant girls chosen from the king's palace. Then Hegai moved Esther and her seven servant girls to the best part of the women's quarters.

Esther did not tell anyone about her family or who her people were. Mordecai had told her not to. Every day Mordecai walked back and forth near the courtyard. This was where the king's women lived. He wanted to find out how Esther was and what was happening to her.

The time came for Esther to go to the king. And the king was pleased with Esther more than with any of the other girls. And he liked her more than any of the other virgins. So King Xerxes put a royal crown on Esther's head. And he made her queen.

Haman Plans to Destroy the Jews

King Xerxes gave Haman a new rank that was higher than all the important men. And all the royal officers at the king's gate would bow down and kneel before Haman. But Mordecai would not bow down, and he did not kneel.

Then the royal officers at the king's gate told Haman about it.

Haman became very angry. He had been told who the people of Mordecai were. So he looked for a way to destroy all of Mordecai's people, the Jews, in all of Xerxes' kingdom.

Then Haman said to King Xerxes, "There is a certain group of people in all the areas of your kingdom. And they do not obey the king's laws. Let an order be given to destroy those people."

Then the king said to Haman, "Do with them as you please."

Letters were sent by messengers to all the king's empire. They stated the king's order to destroy, kill and completely wipe out all the Jews. That meant young and old, women and little children, too. The order said to kill all the Jews on a single day. That was to be the thirteenth day of the twelfth month, which was Adar.

The messengers set out, hurried by the king's command. And the king and Haman sat down to drink.

Mordecai Asks Esther to Help

Now Mordecai heard about all that had been done. To show how upset he was, he tore his clothes. Then he put on rough cloth and ashes. And he went out into the city crying loudly and very sadly.

Esther's servant girls and eunuchs came to her and told her about Mordecai. Esther was very upset and afraid. She sent clothes for Mordecai to put on instead of the rough cloth. But he would not wear them. Then Esther called for Hathach. He was one of the king's eunuchs chosen by the king to serve her. Esther ordered him to find out what was bothering Mordecai and why.

So Hathach went to Mordecai. Mordecai was in the city square in front of the king's gate. Then Mordecai told

Hathach everything that had happened to him. And he told Hathach about the amount of money Haman had promised to pay into the king's treasury for the killing of the Jews. Mordecai also gave him a copy of the order to kill the Jews, which had been given in Susa. He wanted Hathach to show it to Esther and to tell her about it. Mordecai told him to order Esther to go into the king's presence. He wanted her to beg for mercy and to plead with him for her people.

Hathach went back and reported to Esther everything Mordecai said. Then Esther told Hathach to say to Mordecai, "No man or woman may go to the king in the inner courtyard without being called. Anyone who enters must be put to death. But if the king holds out his gold scepter, that person may live. And I have not been called to go to the king for 30 days."

Esther's message was given to Mordecai. Then Mordecai gave orders to say to Esther: "Just because you live in the king's palace, don't think that out of all the Jews you alone will escape. You might keep quiet at this time. Then someone else will help and save the Jews. But you and your father's family will all die. And who knows, you may have been chosen queen for just such a time as this."

Then Esther sent this answer to Mordecai: "Then I will go to the king, even though it is against the law. And if I die, I die."

Esther Speaks to the King

Esther put on her royal robes. Then she stood in the inner courtyard of the king's palace, facing the king's hall. The king was sitting on his royal throne in the hall, facing the doorway. The king saw Queen Esther standing in the courtyard. When he saw her, he was very pleased. He held out to her the gold scepter that was in his hand. So Esther went up to him and touched the end of the scepter.

Then the king asked, "What is it, Queen Esther? What do you want to ask me? I will give you as much as half of my kingdom."

Esther answered, "My king, if it pleases you, come today with Haman to a banquet. I have prepared."

Then the king said, "Bring Haman quickly so we may do what Esther asks."

So the king and Haman went to the banquet Esther had

prepared for them. As they were drinking wine, the king said to Esther, "Now, Esther, what are you asking for? I will give it to you. I will give you as much as half of my kingdom."

Esther answered, "This is what I want and ask for. My king, I hope you are pleased with me. If it pleases you, give me what I ask for and do what I want. Come with Haman tomorrow to the banquet I will prepare for you. Then I will answer your question about what I want."

Haman's Plans Against Mordecai

Haman left the king's palace that day happy and content. Then he saw Mordecai at the king's gate. And he saw that Mordecai did not stand up nor did he tremble with fear before him. So Haman became very angry with Mordecai. But he controlled his anger and went home.

Then Haman called his friends and Zeresh, his wife, together. He told them about all the ways the king had honored him. And he told them how the king had placed him higher than his important men and his royal officers. "And that's not all," Haman added. "I'm the only person Queen Esther invited to come with the king to the banquet she gave. And tomorrow also the queen has asked me to be her guest with the king. But I'm not happy as long as I see that Jew Mordecai sitting at the king's gate."

Then Haman's wife Zeresh and all his friends said, "Have a platform built to hang someone. And in the morning ask the king to have Mordecai hanged on it. Then go to the banquet with the king and be happy." Haman liked this suggestion. So he ordered the platform to be built.

Mordecai Is Honored

That same night the king could not sleep. So he gave an order for the daily court record to be brought in and read to him. And it was found recorded that Mordecai had warned the king about Bigthana and Teresh. These men had planned to kill the king. They were two of the king's officers who guarded the doorway.

Then the king asked, "What honor and reward have been given to Mordecai for this?"

The king's personal servants answered, "Nothing has been done for Mordecai."

Now Haman had just entered the outer court of the king's palace. He had come to ask the king about hanging

Mordecai on the platform he had prepared.

The king's personal servants said, "Haman is standing in the courtyard."

So the king said, "Bring him in."

So Haman came in. And the king asked him, "What should be done for a man that the king wants very much to honor?"

And Haman thought to himself, "Who would the king want to honor more than me?" So he answered the king, "This is what you could do for the man you want very much to honor. Have the servants bring a royal robe that the king himself has worn. And also bring a horse with a royal crown on its head. The horse should be one the king himself has ridden. Then let the robe and the horse be given to one of the king's most important men. Let the servants put the robe on the man the king wants very much to honor. And let them lead him on the horse through the city streets. As they are leading him, let them announce: 'This is what is done for the man the king wants very much to honor!'"

The king commanded Haman, "Go quickly. Take the robe and the horse just as you have said. And do all this for Mordecai who sits at the king's gate. Do not leave out anything that you have suggested."

So Haman took the robe and the horse. And he put the robe on Mordecai. Then he led him on horseback through the city streets. Haman announced before Mordecai: "This is what is done for the man the king wants very much to honor!"

Then Mordecai went back to the king's gate. But Haman hurried home with his head covered. He was embarrassed and ashamed. He told his wife Zeresh and all his friends everything that had happened to him.

While they were still talking, the king's eunuchs came to Haman's house. They made Haman hurry to the banquet Esther had prepared.

Haman Is Hanged

So the king and Haman went in to eat with Queen Esther. They were drinking wine. And the king said to Esther on this second day also, "What are you asking for? I will give it to you. I will give you as much as half of my kingdom."

Then Queen Esther answered, "My king, let me live. This is what I ask. And let my people live, too. I ask this because my people and I have been sold to be destroyed. We are to be killed and completely wiped out."

Then King Xerxes asked Queen Esther, "Who has done such a thing?"

Esther said, "Our enemy is this wicked Haman!"

Then Haman was filled with terror before the king and queen. The king was very angry. Servants came in and covered Haman's face. One of the eunuchs there serving the king said, "Look, a platform for hanging people stands near Haman's house. This is the one Haman prepared for Mordecai, who gave the warning that saved the king."

The king said, "Hang Haman on it!" So they hanged Haman on the platform he had prepared for Mordecai. Then the king was not so angry anymore.

The King Helps the Jews

That same day Mordecai came in to see the king. He came because Esther had told the king how he was related to her.

Once again Esther spoke to the king. She fell at the king's feet and cried. She begged the king to stop the evil plan of Haman. She said, "My king, let an order be written to cancel the letters Haman wrote. I could not

stand to see that terrible thing happen to my people. I could not stand to see my family killed."

King Xerxes answered, "Write another order in the king's name. Write it to the Jews as it seems best to you. Then seal the order with the king's signet ring. No letter written in the king's name and sealed with his signet ring can be canceled."

Mordecai wrote orders in the name of King Xerxes. And he sent the king's orders by messengers on horses. The messengers rode fast horses, which were raised just for the king.

These were the king's orders: "The Jews in every city have the right to gather together to protect themselves. The Jews also have the right to take by force the property of the enemies." The one day set for the Jews to do this was the thirteenth day of the twelfth month. They were allowed to do this in all the empire of King Xerxes. This was so the Jews would be ready on that set day. The Jews would be allowed to pay back their enemies.

Victory for the Jews

So the Jews themselves met in order to attack those who wanted to harm them. And no one was strong enough to fight against them. This was because all the other people living in the empire were afraid of the Jews. This happened on the thirteenth day of the month of Adar. And on the fourteenth day the Jews rested. They made it a day of joyful feasting.

have been chosen queen for just such a time as this.

- ◼ *I will go to the king, even though it is against the law. And if I die, I die.*

WORTH WONDERING...

- ◼ What helped Esther to be brave?

- ◼ What good example can you give of someone in this book who did what was right?

- ◼ What example can you give of someone in this book who did what was wrong?

- ◼ If you could meet Esther today, what kind of questions would you like to ask her?

- ◼ Use your imagination for this one: Suppose you were one of the servants when Esther gave her two banquets for the king and for Haman. What kinds of things do you think you would see and hear and smell?

GREAT VERSES TO THINK ABOUT AGAIN...

Look back in Esther to see if you can find these verses:

- ◼ *You might keep quiet at this time. Then someone else will help and save the Jews. But you and your father's family will all die. And who knows, you may*

INTRODUCING...

JOB • PSALMS • PROVERBS
ECCLESIASTES • SONG of SOLOMON

In the very middle of the Bible are five books that we often call "Wisdom and Poetry Books." In these books we can especially see how important *beauty* is to God. These books are written in poetry that people have loved for thousands of years. These are God's special words for special times in everyone's life.

The five books are all quite different from one another.

Job is the story of a good man who had to face terrible trouble. This book gives us a picture of how to face the terrible hurt that sometimes comes into our lives.

The *Psalms* help us love and worship God. In the Psalms we can often find just the right words to help us tell God how we feel. That's true whether we're afraid, or tired, or happy, or worried.

Next come the *Proverbs*. They give us a picture of how to do what is right. They especially help us get along with other people. More than any other part of the Bible, the book of Proverbs was written for boys and girls your age.

The fourth book is *Ecclesiastes*. This book gives us a picture of how to find happiness that doesn't go away.

The last of the five books is the *Song of Solomon*. (It's sometimes called the *Song of Songs*.) This book gives us a picture of the deep love between a husband and wife.

The Book of
JOB

A Good Man
Suffers

Looking forward to Job...

WHAT'S IT ABOUT?

"A Good Man Suffers"

SIGNS AND WONDERS

God allows Satan to attack Job, and to take away his wealth, his children, and his health. Job is upset, but he doesn't lose his trust in God. Job's three friends say that when bad things happen to us, it's always because of our sin. And in an amazing conversation with Job, God shows that these three men are wrong.

God is in control even when bad things happen to good people.

FACES AND PLACES

Job: A wealthy man who lived perhaps about the time of Abraham, Isaac, and Jacob.
Eliphaz, Bildad, and **Zophar:** Three of Job's friends.
Uz: This is the land where Job lived. This land was east of the Jordan River.

I wonder what I should remember most when bad things happen to me, and they aren't my fault...

Job lived in the land of Uz. Job had seven sons and three daughters. He owned 7,000 sheep, 3,000 camels, 500 pairs of oxen and 500 female donkeys. And he had a large number of servants. He was the greatest man among all the people of the East.

Job's sons took turns holding feasts in their homes. And they invited their sisters to eat and drink with them. After a feast was over, Job would send and have them made clean. Early in the morning Job would offer a burnt offering for each of them. He thought, "My children may have sinned and cursed God in their hearts." Job did this every time.

Satan Appears Before God

One day the angels came to show themselves before the Lord. Satan also came with them. The Lord said to Satan, "Where have you come from?"

Satan answered the Lord, "I have been wandering around the earth. I have been going back and forth in it."

Then the Lord said to Satan, "Have you noticed my servant Job? No one else on earth is like him. He is an honest man and innocent of any wrong. He honors God and stays away from evil."

But Satan answered God, "Job honors God for a good reason. You have blessed the things he has done. But reach out your hand and destroy everything he has. Then he will curse you to your face."

The Lord said to Satan, "All right, then. Everything Job has is in your power. But you must not touch Job himself." Then Satan left the Lord's presence.

One day a messenger came to Job and said, "The oxen were plowing. And the donkeys were eating grass nearby. And the Sabeans attacked and carried them away. They killed the servants with swords. And I am the only one who escaped to tell you!"

The messenger was still speaking when another messenger came in. He said, "Lightning from God fell from the sky. It burned up the sheep and the servants. And I am the only one who escaped to tell you!"

The second messenger was still speaking when another messenger came in. He said, "The Babylonians sent three groups of attackers. They swept down and stole your camels. They killed the servants. And I am the only one who escaped to tell you!"

The third messenger was still speaking when another messenger came in. He said, "Your sons and daughters were eating and drinking wine together. They were at the oldest brother's house. Suddenly a great wind came in from the desert. It struck all four corners of the house at once. The house fell in on your sons and daughters. And they are all dead. I am the only one who escaped to tell you!"

When Job heard this, he got up. To show how sad he was he tore his robe and shaved his head. Then he bowed down to the ground to worship God. He said: "The Lord gave these things to me. And he has taken them away. Praise the name of the Lord."

In all this Job did not sin. He did not blame God.

Satan Appears Before God Again

On another day the angels came to show themselves before the Lord. And Satan also came with them. The Lord said to Satan, "Where have you come from?"

Satan answered the Lord, "I have been wandering around the earth. I have been going back and forth in it."

Then the Lord said to Satan, "Have you noticed my servant Job? He continues to be without blame."

"One skin for another!" Satan answered. "Reach out

your hand and destroy his own flesh and bones. Then he will curse you to your face."

The Lord said to Satan, "All right, then. Job is in your power. But you must let him live."

So Satan left the Lord's presence. And he put painful sores all over Job's body. They went from the top of his head to the soles of his feet. Then Job took a piece of broken pottery. And he used it to scrape himself. He sat in ashes to show how upset he was.

Job's wife said to him, "Are you still trying to stay innocent? You should just curse God and die!"

Job answered, "You are talking like a foolish woman. Should we take only good things from God and not trouble?" In all this Job did not sin in what he said.

Job's Three Friends

Now Job had three friends. They were Eliphaz, Bildad, and Zophar. These friends heard about the troubles that had happened to Job. So they agreed to meet and go see Job. They wanted to show him they were upset for him, too. And they wanted to comfort him. They saw Job from far away. But he looked so different they almost didn't recognize him. They began to cry loudly. They tore their robes and put dirt on their heads to show how sad they were. Then they sat on the ground with Job seven days and seven nights. No one said a word to him. This was because they saw how much he was suffering.

Job Speaks

After seven days Job spoke. He said, "Why didn't I die as soon as I was born? I would be lying dead in peace. I would be asleep and at rest.

"My groans pour out like water. I have no peace. I have no quietness. I have no rest. I only have trouble."

Eliphaz Speaks to Job

Then Eliphaz answered: "God does not punish you for respecting him. He does not bring you into court for this. No! It is because your evil is without limits. And your sins have no end.

"Obey God, and then you will be at peace with him. Remove evil from your house."

Bildad Speaks to Job

Then Bildad answered: "Your children sinned against God. And he punished them for their sins. But you should ask God for help.

"The lamp of the wicked person will be put out. The

flame in his lamp will stop burning. Disaster is at his side. Disease eats away parts of his skin. He will be driven from the light into darkness. This is surely what will happen to the home of an evil person. This is the place of one who does not know God."

Zophar Speaks to Job

Then Zophar answered:

"Put away the sin that is in your hand. Let no evil live in your tent. Then you can lift up your face without shame.

"God will send blows of punishment down like rain. This is what God plans for evil people. This is what he has decided they will receive."

Job Answers

Then Job answered:

"How long will you hurt me and crush me with your words? God has made my brothers my enemies. My friends have become complete strangers. My wife hates my breath. All my close friends hate me.

"How I wish my words were carved into stone forever! I know that my Defender lives. And in the end he will come to show that I am right. Even after my skin has been destroyed, in my flesh I will still see God. I will see him myself. I myself will see him with my own eyes. How my heart wants that to happen!"

And Job continued speaking:

"As long as I am alive my lips will not speak evil. And my tongue will not tell a lie. Until I die, I will never stop saying I was innocent.

"How I wish for the months that have passed. I wish for the days when I was at my strongest, when God's close friendship blessed my house. That was when my children were all around me. And God All-Powerful was still with me. Life was so good. It was as if my path were covered with cream. I would go to the city gate and sit in the public square. And the old men would stand up in respect for me. Anyone who heard me said good things about me. And those who saw me praised me. This was because I saved the poor who cried for help. And I saved the orphan who had no one to help him. And I made the widow's heart sing. I put on right living as if it were clothing. I tried to be eyes for the blind. And I tried to be feet for those who were crippled. I was like a father to needy people. And I took the side of strangers when they were in trouble.

"But now men who are younger than I make fun of me.

My name has become a joke among them. They hate me and stay far away from me. But they do not mind spitting in my face. God has taken away my strength and made me suffer.

"Now my life is almost over. My days are full of suffering. At night my bones ache. Gnawing pains never stop. In his great power God grabs hold of my clothing. He chokes me with the collar of my coat. He throws me into the mud. And I become like dirt and ashes.

"I cry out to you, God, but you do not answer. I stand up, but you just look at me.

"I have not been a dishonest person. I have been fair. I have never refused anything the poor wanted. I have not let a needy person go without a coat. I have not put my trust in gold. I have not celebrated my great wealth.

I have not been happy when my enemy was ruined. I have not laughed when he had trouble. No stranger ever had to spend the night in the street. I always let the traveler stay in my home.

"How I wish a court would hear my case! I have told the truth. Now let God All-Powerful answer me. I would explain to God every step I took. I would come near to God like a prince."

The Lord Questions Job

Then the Lord answered Job from the storm. He said:

"Be strong like a man. I will ask you questions, and you must answer me. Where were you when I made the earth's foundation? Tell me, if you understand.

PAUSE & WONDER

God showed Job how big and powerful He was. But He also showed Job His love. God is so vast, so huge, so complete and perfect…that He doesn't *need* anything or anybody. But that doesn't mean He's unfriendly. When He does something for me, it's because He truly loves me and wants to make me happy — and not because He needs something from me.

"Have you ever given orders for morning to begin?

"Have you ever walked in the valleys under the sea?

"Can you bring out the stars at the right times?

"Can you send lightning bolts on their way?

"Job, are you the one who gives the horse his strength?

"Is it through your wisdom that the hawk flies?

"Let the person who accuses God answer him!"

Then Job answered the Lord: "I am not worthy. I cannot answer you anything. I will put my hand over my mouth. I spoke, but I will not answer again. I will say nothing more."

Then the Lord spoke to Job from the storm: "Be strong, like a man. I will ask you questions. And you must answer me. Would you say that I am unfair? Would you blame me to make yourself look right? Are you as strong as God? And can your voice thunder like his?"

Then Job answered the Lord: "I know that you can do all things. No plan of yours can be ruined. Surely I talked about things I did not understand. I spoke of things too wonderful for me to know. I will change my heart and life and sit in the dust and ashes."

End of the Story

After the Lord had said these things to Job, he spoke to Eliphaz. The Lord said to him, "I am angry with you and your two friends. This is because you have not said what is right about me. But my servant Job did. So now take seven bulls and seven male sheep. Go to my servant Job. And offer a burnt offering for yourselves. My servant Job will pray for you. And I will listen to his prayer. Then I will not punish you for being foolish. You have not said what is right about me. But my servant Job did." So Eliphaz the Temanite did as the Lord told him to do.

After Job had prayed for his friends, God gave him success again. God gave Job twice as much as he had owned before. Job's brothers and sisters came to his house. Everyone who had known him before came to his house. And they all ate with him there. They comforted Job and spoke kindly to him. They made him feel better about the trouble the Lord had brought on him. And each one gave Job a piece of silver and a gold ring.

The Lord blessed the last part of Job's life even more than the first part. Job had 14,000 sheep and 6,000 camels. He had 1,000 pairs of oxen and 1,000 female donkeys. Job also had seven sons and three daughters. He named the first daughter Jemimah. The second daughter he named Keziah. And his third daughter he named Keren-Happuch. There were no other women in all the land as beautiful as Job's daughters. And their father Job gave them land to own along with their brothers.

After this, Job lived 140 years. He lived to see his children, grandchildren, great-grandchildren and great-great-grandchildren. Then Job died. He was old and had lived many years.

- The Lord gave these things to me. And he has taken them away. Praise the name of the Lord.

AND THERE'S MORE...

When you read Job in a full Bible, you'll see the long conversations that Job had with his three friends. Another friend, Elihu, was also there. Elihu was younger. He did not agree with Job's other three friends.

WORTH WONDERING...

- What was God trying to help Job understand?
- What was wrong about what Job's three friends said to him?
- Why did Job tell God that he would change his heart and his life? Why did Job need to do this?

GREAT VERSES TO THINK ABOUT AGAIN...

Look back in Job to see if you can find these verses:

- I know that my Defender lives.
- I will change my heart and life and sit in the dust and ashes.

The Book of
PSALMS

The Songbook of Israel

Looking forward to Psalms...

"The Songbook of Israel"

The Psalms are songs. The people of Israel use these songs to worship God, and to tell Him their feelings. Many times the songs also include God's answers to the people.

In the earlier books of the Bible, we saw all the events of the full Old Testament story. But now — from the book of Psalms to the end of the Old Testament — we look more at what God's people were thinking and feeling as these same events took place. Most of these thoughts and feelings are included in the Psalms.

David: Israel's greatest king wrote more of the Psalms than anyone else.

I wonder what God wants us to think about when we worship Him...

Psalm 1 —
Two Ways to Live

Happy is the person who doesn't listen to the wicked. He doesn't go where sinners go. He doesn't do what bad people do. He loves the Lord's teachings. He thinks about those teachings day and night. He is strong, like a tree planted by a river. It produces fruit in season. Its leaves don't die. Everything he does will succeed.

But wicked people are not like that. They are like useless chaff that the wind blows away. So the wicked will not escape God's punishment. Sinners will not worship God with good people. This is because the Lord protects good people. But the wicked will be destroyed.

Psalm 8 —
God's Greatness

A song of David.

Lord our Master, your name is the most wonderful name in all the earth! It brings you praise in heaven above. You have taught children and babies to sing praises to you.

I look at the heavens, which you made with your hands. I see the moon and stars, which you created. But why is man important to you? Why do you take care of human beings? You made man a little lower than the angels. And you crowned him with glory and honor. You put him in charge of everything you made. You put all things under his control: all the sheep, the cattle and the wild animals, the birds in the sky, the fish in the sea, and everything that lives under water.

Lord our Master, your name is the most wonderful name in all the earth!

Psalm 18 — A Song of Victory

David sang this song when the Lord had saved him from all his enemies.

I love you, Lord. You are my strength.

The Lord is my rock, my protection, my Savior. My God is my rock. I can run to him for safety. He is my shield and my saving strength, my high tower. I will call to the Lord. He is worthy of praise. And I will be saved from my enemies.

The deadly rivers overwhelmed me. The ropes of death wrapped around me. The traps of death were before me. In my trouble I called to the Lord. I cried out to my God for help. From his temple he heard my voice. My call for help reached his ears.

The earth trembled and shook. The foundations of the mountains began to shake. The Lord tore open the sky and came down. The Lord thundered from heaven. God Most High raised his voice. And there was hail and lightning. He shot his arrows and scattered his enemies. His many bolts of lightning confused them with fear.

The Lord reached down from above and took me. He pulled me from the deep water. He saved me from my powerful enemies. Those who hated me were too strong for me. They attacked me at my time of trouble. But the Lord supported me. He took me to a safe place. Because he delights in me, he saved me.

My God brightens the darkness around me. With your help I can attack an army. With God's help I can jump over a wall.

The ways of God are without fault. The Lord's words are pure. He is a shield to those who trust him. Who is the Rock? Only our God. God is my protection. He makes my way free from fault. He makes me like a deer, which does not stumble. He helps me stand on the steep mountains. He trains my hands for battle. So my arms can bend a bronze bow. You give me a wide path on which to walk. My feet have not slipped.

I will sing praises to your name. The Lord gives great victories to his king. He is loyal to his appointed king, to David and his descendants forever.

Psalm 19 — God's Works and Word

A song of David.

The heavens tell the glory of God. And the skies announce what his hands have made. Day after day they tell the story. Night after night they tell it again. They don't make any sound to be heard. But their message goes out through all the world.

The sky is like a home for the sun. The sun comes out like a bridegroom from his bedroom. It rejoices like an athlete eager to run a race. The sun rises at one end of the sky, and it follows its path to the other end. Nothing hides from its heat.

The Lord's teachings are perfect. They give new strength. The Lord's rules can be trusted. They make plain people wise.

The Lord's orders are right. They make people happy. The Lord's commands are pure. They light up the way. It is good to respect the Lord. That respect will last forever. The Lord's judgments are true. They are completely right. They are worth more than gold, even the purest gold. They are sweeter than honey, even the finest honey. They tell your servant what to do. Keeping them brings great reward.

No one can see all his own mistakes. Forgive me for my secret sins. Keep me from the sins that I want to do. Don't let them rule me. Then I can be pure and free from the greatest of sins.

I hope my words and thoughts please you. Lord, you are my Rock, the one who saves me.

PAUSE & WONDER

In Psalm 19 I read that God's teachings are perfect. God's Word is worth more than gold. And it is sweeter than honey. The Bible is a wonderful book because it's God's book, and God is wonderful. It is a wonderful book because it tells me wonderful things. It tells me about Jesus! And the Bible is a wonderful book because it's written in a wonderful way. It is full of beauty and power! Yes, God's Book is great and wonderful!

Psalm 23 —The Lord the Shepherd

A song of David.

The Lord is my shepherd. I have everything I need. He gives me rest in green pastures. He leads me to calm water. He gives me new strength. For the good of his name, he leads me on paths that are right. Even if I walk through a very dark valley, I will not be afraid because you are with me. Your rod and your walking stick comfort me.

You prepare a meal for me in front of my enemies. You pour oil on my head. You give me more than I can hold. Surely your goodness and love will be with me all my life. And I will live in the house of the Lord forever.

Psalm 25 — A Prayer for God to Guide

Of David.

Lord, I give myself to you. My God, I trust you. Do not let me be disgraced.

Lord, tell me your ways. Show me how to live. Guide me in your truth. Teach me, my God, my Savior. Do not remember the sins and wrong things I did when I was young. But remember to love me always because you are good, Lord.

The Lord is good and right.

He points sinners to the right way. All the Lord's ways are loving and true for those who follow the demands of his agreement. The Lord tells his secrets to those who respect him. He tells them about his agreement. My eyes are always looking to the Lord for help. He will keep me from any traps.

Psalm 42 — Wishing to Be near God

A maskil of the sons of Korah.

A deer thirsts for a stream of water. In the same way, I thirst for you, God. Day and night, my tears have been my food. People are always saying, "Where is your God?" When I remember these things, I speak with a broken heart. I used to walk with the happy crowd to God's Temple, with songs of praise.

Why am I so sad? Why am I so upset? I should put my hope in God. I should keep praising him, my Savior and my God.

I am very sad. So I remember you while I am in the land where the Jordan River begins. Troubles have come again and again. They sound like waterfalls. Your waves are crashing all around me.

The Lord shows his true love every day. At night I have a song, and I pray to my living God.

Psalm 46 — God Protects His People

A song of the sons of Korah.

God is our protection and our strength. He always helps in times of trouble. So we will not be afraid if the earth shakes, or if the mountains fall into the sea.

The Lord of heaven's armies is with us. The God of Jacob is our protection.

Come and see what the Lord has done. He has done amazing things on the earth. He stops wars everywhere on the earth. He breaks all bows and spears and burns up the chariots with fire. God says, "Be quiet and know that I am God. I will be supreme over all the nations. I will be supreme in the earth."

Psalm 51 — A Prayer for Forgiveness

A song of David when the prophet Nathan came to David after David's sin with Bathsheba.

God, be merciful to me because you are loving. Because you are always ready to be merciful, wipe out all my wrongs. Wash away all my guilt and make me clean again.

I know about my wrongs. I can't forget my sin. You are the one I have sinned against. I have done what you say is wrong. So you are right when you judge me.

You want me to be completely truthful. So teach me wisdom. Take away my sin, and I will be clean. Wash me, and I will be whiter than snow. Make me hear sounds of joy and gladness. Let the bones you crushed be happy again. Wipe out all my guilt.

Create in me a pure heart, God. Make my spirit right again. Do not send me away from you. Do not take your Holy Spirit away from me. Give me back the joy that comes when you save me. Keep me strong by giving me a willing spirit. Then I will teach your ways to those who do wrong. And sinners will turn back to you.

God, save me from the guilt of murder. God, you are the one who saves me. I will sing about your goodness. God, you will not reject a heart that is broken and sorry for its sin.

Psalm 63 — Wishing to Be near God

A song of David when he was in the desert of Judah.

God, you are my God. I want to follow you. My whole being thirsts for you, like a man in a dry, empty land where there is no water. Your love is better than life. I will praise you. I will praise you as long as I live. I will lift up my hands in prayer to your name. I will be content as if I had eaten the best foods. My lips will sing. My mouth will praise you.

I remember you while I'm lying in bed. I think about you through the night. You are my help. Because of your protection, I sing. I stay close to you. You support me with your right hand.

Psalm 73 — Should the Wicked Be Rich?

A song of Asaph.

God is truly good to Israel, to those who have pure hearts. But I had almost stopped believing this truth. I had almost lost my faith because I was jealous of proud people. I saw wicked people doing well.

They don't have troubles like the rest of us. They don't have problems like other people. So they wear pride like a necklace. They make fun of others and speak evil. They brag to the sky. These people are wicked, always at ease and getting richer.

So why have I kept my heart pure? Why have I kept my hands from doing wrong? I have suffered all day long. I have been punished every morning.

God, I tried to understand all this. But it was too hard for me to see until I went to the Temple. Then I understood what will happen to them. You have put them in danger. You cause them to be destroyed. They are destroyed in a moment. They are swept away by terrors. Lord, when you come, they will disappear.

When my heart was sad and I was angry, I was senseless and stupid. I acted like an animal toward you. But I am always with you. You have held my hand. You guide me with your advice. And later you will receive me in honor. I have no one in heaven but you. I want nothing on earth besides you. My mind and my body may become weak. But God is my strength. He is mine forever.

Those who are far from God will die. But I am close to God, and that is good. The Lord God is my protection. I will tell all that you have done.

Psalm 90 — God Is Eternal, We Are Not

A prayer of Moses, the man of God.

Lord, before you created the earth and the world, you are God. You have always been, and you will always be.

To you, a thousand years is

like the passing of a day. It passes like an hour in the night.

Our lifetime is 70 years. If we are strong, we may live to be 80. But the years are full of hard work and pain. They pass quickly, and then we are gone.

Teach us how short our lives really are so that we may be wise.

Fill us with your love every morning. Then we will sing and rejoice all our lives. We have seen years of trouble. Now give us joy as you gave us sorrow. Show your servants the wonderful things you do. Show your greatness to their children. Lord our God, be pleased with us. Give us success in what we do. Yes, give us success in what we do.

Psalm 91 — Safe in the Lord

Those who go to God Most High for safety will be protected by God All-Powerful. I will say to the Lord, "You are my place of safety and protection. You are my God, and I trust you."

God will save you from hidden traps and from deadly diseases. He will protect you like a bird spreading its wings over its young. His truth will be like your armor and shield. You will not fear any danger by night or an arrow during the day. You will not be afraid of diseases that come in the dark or sickness that strikes at noon. At your side 1,000 people may die, or even 10,000 right beside you. But you will not be hurt. You will only watch what happens. You will see the wicked punished.

The Lord is your protection. You have made God Most High your place of safety. Nothing bad will happen to you. No disaster will come to your home. He has put his angels in charge of you. They will watch over you wherever you go. They will catch you with their hands. And you will not hit your foot on a rock. You will walk on lions and cobras. You will step on strong lions and snakes.

The Lord says, "If someone loves me, I will save him. I will protect those who know me. They will call to me, and I will answer them. I will be with them in trouble. I will rescue them and honor them. I will give them a long, full life. They will see how I can save."

Psalm 100 — A Call to Praise God

A song of thanks.
Shout to the Lord, all the earth. Serve the Lord with joy. Come before him with singing. Know that the Lord is God. He made us, and we belong to him.

We are his people, the sheep he tends.

Come into his city with songs of thanksgiving. Come into his courtyards with songs of praise. Thank him, and praise his name. The Lord is good. His love continues forever. His loyalty continues from now on.

Psalm 119 — The Word of God

Happy are the people who live pure lives. They follow the Lord's teachings. Happy are the people who keep his rules. When I learned that your laws are fair, I praised you with an honest heart.

How can a young person live a pure life? He can do it by obeying your word. I have taken your words to heart so I would not sin against you. I enjoy living by your rules as people enjoy great riches. I think about your orders and study your ways. I enjoy obeying your demands. And I will not forget your word.

Open my eyes to see the wonderful things in your teachings. Keep me from looking at worthless things. Let me live by your word.

How I love your teachings! I think about them all day long. Your commands make me wiser than my enemies because they are mine forever.

Your word is like a lamp for my feet and a light for my way. I love your teachings. You are my hiding place and my shield. I trust your word.

Lord, I call to you with all my heart. I wake up early in the morning and cry out.

I am as happy over your promises as if I had found a great treasure.

PAUSE & WONDER

For many people, the world has a lot of darkness. But Psalm 119 tells me that God's Word is like a lamp for my feet and a light for my way. I never have to stay in darkness. I can choose light if I want to. And I find that light in the Bible. God gives me this light because He loves me. Yes, God's Word comes straight from God's heart!

Psalm 139 — God Knows Everything

A song of David.

Lord, you have examined me. You know all about me. You know when I sit down and when I get up. You know my thoughts before I think them. You know where I go and where I lie down. You know well everything I do. Lord, even before I say a word, you already know what I am going to say. You are all around me — in front and in back. You have put your hand on me. Your knowledge is amazing to me. It is more than I can understand.

You made my whole being. You formed me in my mother's body. I praise you because you made me in an amazing and wonderful way. What you have done is wonderful. I know this very well. You saw my bones being formed as I took shape in my mother's body. When I was put together there, you saw my body as it was formed. All the days planned for me were written in your book before I was one day old.

God, examine me and know my heart. Test me and know my thoughts. See if there is any bad thing in me. Lead me in the way you set long ago.

Psalm 145 — Praise to God the King

A song of praise. Of David.

I praise your greatness, my God the King. I will praise you forever and ever. I will praise you every day.

Parents will tell their children what you have done. They will retell your mighty acts, wonderful majesty and glory. They will remember your great goodness. They will sing about your fairness.

The Lord is kind and shows mercy. He does not become angry quickly but is full of love. The Lord is good to everyone. He is merciful to all he has made.

The Lord will keep his promises. With love he takes care of all he has made. The Lord takes care of those who are in trouble. All living things look to you for food. And you give it to them at the right time. You open your hand, and you satisfy all living things.

Everything the Lord does is right. With love he takes care of all he has made. The Lord is close to everyone who prays to him, to all who truly pray to him. He gives those who fear him what they want. He listens when they cry, and he saves them. The Lord protects everyone who loves him. But he will destroy the wicked.

Psalm 148 — Praise the Lord

Praise the Lord from the heavens. Praise him high above the earth. Praise him, all you angels. Praise him, all you armies of heaven. Praise him, sun and moon. Praise him, all you shining stars. Praise him, highest heavens and you waters above the sky. Let them praise the Lord because they were created by his command. He set them in place forever and ever.

Praise the Lord from the earth. Praise him, you sea animals and all the oceans. Praise him, lightning and hail, snow and clouds, and stormy winds that obey him. Praise him, mountains and all hills, fruit trees and cedar trees. Praise him, you wild animals and all cattle and birds. Praise him, you kings of the earth and all nations, princes and all rulers of the earth. Praise him, you young men and women, old people and children.

Praise the Lord. He alone is great. He is greater than heaven and earth.

WORTH WONDERING...

■ Which of these Psalms would you say give the best words for praising God?

■ Which of these Psalms would you say give the most helpful words for telling God about your needs?

■ Which of these Psalms would you say give the best words for understanding how God wants you to live?

GREAT VERSES TO THINK ABOUT AGAIN...

Look back in the Psalms to see if you can find these verses:

■ *My God is my rock. I can run to him for safety.*

■ *Even if I walk through a very dark valley, I will not be afraid because you are with me. Your rod and your walking stick comfort me.*

■ *I praise you because you made me in an amazing and wonderful way. What you have done is wonderful.*

■ *Create in me a pure heart, God.*

■ *How can a young person live a pure life? He can do it by obeying your word.*

AND THERE'S MORE...

When you read the Psalms in a full Bible, you'll see a total of 150 Psalms. Each one is different from the others. Each one is beautiful in its own way.

The Book of
PROVERBS

Wise Teachings
for God's People

Looking forward to Proverbs...

WHAT'S IT ABOUT?

"Wise Teachings for God's People"

SIGNS AND WONDERS

What's big in Proverbs? Wisdom! Wisdom begins with having true respect for God. And wisdom goes on to know and do what is right toward other people. This book is like a textbook for knowing how to live everyday life in a way that pleases God.

What is a proverb? A proverb is a short, wise saying. Very often it compares one thing with another. This gives us a picture about a wise truth that makes it easier to remember.

FACES AND PLACES

Solomon wrote most of these Proverbs. He probably wrote them in the early years after he became king.

I wonder what are the best rules to remember when I want to do what is right...

These are the wise words of Solomon son of David. They will teach you how to be wise and self-controlled. They will teach you what is honest and fair and right. They give knowledge and good sense to the young. Even smart people will find wise advice in these words.

Knowledge begins with respect for the Lord. But foolish people hate wisdom and self-control.

Warnings Against Evil

My child, listen to your father's teaching. And do not forget your mother's advice. Their teaching will be like flowers in your hair or a chain around your neck.

My child, sinners will try to lead you into sin. But do not follow them. They might say, "Come with us. Let's attack some harmless person just for fun. We will take all kinds of valuable things. Come join us, and we will share with you what we steal." My child, do not go along with them. Do not do what they do. They are setting their own trap. They will only catch themselves! All greedy people end up this way. Greed takes away the life of the greedy person.

Advice to Children

My child, do not forget my teaching. Keep my commands in mind. Then you will live a long time. And your life will be successful.

Don't ever stop being kind and truthful. Let kindness and truth show in all you do. Write them down in your mind as if on a tablet. Then you will be respected and pleasing to both God and men.

Trust the Lord with all your heart. Don't depend on your own understanding. Remember the Lord in everything you do. And he will give you success.

Don't depend on your own wisdom. Respect the Lord and refuse to do wrong. Then your body will be healthy. And your bones will be strong.

Honor the Lord by giving him part of your wealth.

My child, do not reject the Lord's discipline. And don't become angry when he corrects you. The Lord corrects those he loves, just as a father corrects the child that he likes.

Happy is the person who finds wisdom. Wisdom is worth more than silver. It brings more profit than gold. Nothing you want is equal to it. Wisdom will make your life pleasant. Everyone who uses wisdom will be happy.

Using his wisdom, the Lord made the earth. Using his understanding, he set the sky in place. Using his knowledge, he made rivers flow from underground springs. And he made the clouds drop rain on the earth.

My child, hold on to wisdom and reason. Don't let them out of your sight! Then you will go on your way in safety. And you will not get hurt. You won't need to be afraid when you lie down. You won't need to be afraid of trouble coming suddenly. The Lord will keep you safe. He will keep you from being trapped.

Whenever you are able, do good to people who need help. If you have what your neighbor asks for, don't say to him, "Come back later. I will give it to you tomorrow."

Wisdom Is Important

I was once a young boy in my father's house. I was like an only child. And my father taught me and said, "Hold on to my words with all your heart. Keep my commands and you will live. Get wisdom and understanding. Use wisdom, and it will take care of you. Love wisdom, and it will keep you safe. Wisdom is the most important thing. So get wisdom. If it costs everything you have, get understanding. Believe in the value of wisdom, and it will make you great. Use it, and it will bring honor to you. Like a crown, it will make you look beautiful."

Always remember what you have been taught. Don't let go of it. Keep safe all that you have learned. It is the most important thing in your life. Don't do what evil people do. Avoid their ways. Stay away from them and keep on going. They cannot sleep until they do evil. They cannot rest until they hurt someone.

The way of the good person is like the light of dawn. It grows brighter and brighter until it is full daylight. But the wicked are like those who stumble in the dark. They can't even see what has hurt them.

Keep your eyes focused on what is right. Keep looking straight ahead to what is good.

Proverbs of Solomon

These are the wise words of Solomon:

A wise son makes his father happy. But a foolish son makes his mother sad.

Riches gotten by doing wrong have no value. But right living will save you from death.

The honest person will live safely. But the one who is dishonest will be caught.

Hatred stirs up trouble. But love forgives all wrongs.

Wise people don't tell everything they know. But a foolish person talks too much and is ruined.

If you talk a lot, you are sure to sin. If you are wise, you will keep quiet.

A lazy person brings trouble to the one he works for. He bothers others like vinegar on the teeth or smoke in the eyes.

The Lord will protect good people. But he will ruin those who do evil.

Pride leads only to shame. It is wise not to be proud.

A person who gossips can't keep secrets. But a trustworthy person can keep a secret.

Whoever guarantees to pay what somebody else owes will suffer. It is safer to avoid such promises.

A kind person is doing himself a favor. But a cruel person brings trouble on himself.

Anyone who loves learning accepts being corrected. But a person who hates being corrected is stupid.

A good wife is like a crown for her husband. But a disgraceful wife is like a disease in his bones.

A wise person is praised. But a stupid person is not respected.

A good man takes care of his animals. But even the kindest acts of the wicked are cruel.

Careless words stab like a sword. But wise words bring healing.

Hard workers will become leaders. But those who are lazy will be slaves.

Worry makes a person feel as if he is carrying a heavy load. But a kind word cheers up a person.

A wise son takes his father's advice. But a person who makes fun of wisdom won't listen to correction.

Whoever is careful about what he says protects his life. But anyone who speaks without thinking will be ruined.

Pride leads to arguments. But those who take advice are wise.

Money that comes easily disappears quickly. But money that is gathered little by little will slowly grow.

It is sad when you don't get what you hoped for. But when wishes come true, it's like eating fruit from the tree of life.

Whoever spends time with wise people will become wise. But whoever makes friends with fools will suffer.

If a person does not punish his children, he does not love them. But the person who loves his children is careful to correct them.

Stay away from a foolish person. You won't learn anything from him.

What makes a person wise is understanding what to do. But what makes a person foolish is dishonesty.

When someone is laughing, he may be sad inside. And when the laughter is over, there is sorrow.

A wise person is careful and stays out of trouble. But a foolish person is careless.

A person who quickly loses his temper does foolish things. But a person with understanding remains calm.

It is a sin to hate your neighbor. But being kind to the needy brings happiness.

Those who work hard make a profit. But those who only talk will be poor.

Whoever is cruel to the poor insults their Maker. But anyone who is kind to the needy honors God.

More Proverbs of Solomon

A gentle answer will calm a person's anger. But an unkind answer will cause more anger.

The Lord's eyes see everything that happens. He watches both evil and good people.

As a tree gives us fruit,

healing words give us life. But evil words crush the spirit.

It is better to be poor and respect the Lord than to be wealthy and have much trouble.

A wise son makes his father happy. But a foolish person hates his mother.

A wise person does things that will make his life better. He avoids whatever would cause his death.

Good news makes you feel better. Your happiness will show in your eyes.

A wise person pays attention to correction that will improve his life.

Respect for the Lord will teach you wisdom. If you want to be honored, you must not be proud.

A person may believe he is doing right. But the Lord will judge his reasons.

Depend on the Lord in whatever you do. Then your plans will succeed.

The Lord makes everything work the way he wants it. He even has a day of disaster for evil people.

The Lord hates those who are proud. You can be sure that they will be punished.

Kings are pleased with those who speak honest words. They value a person who speaks the truth.

Pride will destroy a person. A proud attitude leads to ruin.

It is better not to be proud and to be with those who suffer than to share stolen property with proud people.

Whoever pays attention to what he is taught will succeed. And whoever trusts the Lord will be happy.

Pleasant words are like a honeycomb. They make a person happy and healthy.

Some people think they are

PAUSE & WONDER

The wisdom that is taught in Proverbs has been built into this world by God. If I go against this wisdom, I will only be sorry for it later. But if I learn this wisdom and live by it, my happiness can never be taken away.

doing what's right. But in the end it causes them to die.

An evil person makes evil plans. And his words are like a burning fire.

If you make fun of the poor, you insult God, who made them. If you laugh at someone's trouble, you will be punished.

Grandchildren are the reward of old people. And children are proud of their parents.

Whoever forgives someone's sin makes a friend. But the one who tells about the sin breaks up friendships.

A wise man will learn more from a warning than a foolish person will learn from 100 lashings.

Starting a quarrel is like a leak in a dam. So stop the quarrel before a fight breaks out.

The Lord hates both these things: letting guilty people go free and punishing those who are not guilty.

More Proverbs of Solomon

A friend loves you all the time. A brother is always there to help you.

Whoever loves to quarrel loves to sin. Whoever is proud is asking for trouble.

It is sad to have a foolish son.

There is no joy in being the father of a fool.

A happy heart is like good medicine. But a broken spirit drains your strength.

A foolish son makes his father sad. And he causes his mother great sorrow.

A person who doesn't work hard is just like a person who destroys things.

The Lord is like a strong tower. Those who do what is right can run to him for safety.

People who are proud will be ruined. But those who are not proud will be honored.

A person who answers without listening is foolish and disgraceful.

The mind of a smart person is ready to get knowledge. The wise person listens to learn more.

Taking a gift to an important person will help get you in to see him.

The first person to tell his side of a story seems right. But that may change when somebody comes and asks him questions.

A man who finds a wife finds something good. She shows that the Lord is pleased with him.

Some friends may ruin you. But a real friend will be more loyal than a brother.

A wise person is patient. He

will be honored if he ignores a wrong done against him.

Lazy people sleep a lot. Idle people will go hungry.

Being kind to the poor is like lending to the Lord. The Lord will reward you for what you have done.

Listen to advice and accept correction. Then in the end you will be wise.

Wine and beer make people loud and uncontrolled. It is not wise to get drunk on them.

A lazy farmer doesn't plow when he should. So at harvest time he has no crop.

Many people claim to be loyal. But it is hard to find someone who really can be trusted.

Gossips can't keep secrets. So avoid people who talk too much.

Whoever curses his father or mother will die like a light going out in darkness.

It's dangerous to promise something to God too quickly. After you've thought about it, it may be too late.

The Lord looks into a person's feelings. He searches through a person's thoughts.

The Lord can control a king's mind as easily as he controls a river. He can direct it as he pleases.

If you ignore the poor when they cry for help, you also will cry for help and not be answered.

A person who tries to live right and be loyal finds life, success and honor.

You can get the horses ready for battle. But it is the Lord who gives the victory.

Being respected is more important than having great riches. To be well thought of is better than owning silver or gold.

The rich and the poor are alike in that the Lord made them all.

When a wise person sees danger ahead, he avoids it. But a foolish person keeps going and gets into trouble.

Respecting the Lord and not being proud will bring you wealth, honor and life.

Train a child how to live the right way. Then even when he is old, he will still live that way.

A generous person will be blessed because he shares his food with the poor.

A person who loves innocent thoughts and kind words will have even the king as a friend.

Other Wise Sayings

Pay attention and listen to what wise people say.

God gave me a conscience. That's why I can tell that some things are good and others are evil. He made me able to choose between right and wrong.

Remember what I am teaching you. It will be good to keep these things in mind. Be prepared to repeat them. I am teaching you true and reliable words. Then you can give true answers to anyone who asks.

Do not abuse poor people because they are poor.

Don't make friends with someone who easily gets angry. Don't spend time with someone who has a bad temper. If you do, you may learn to be like him. Then you will be in real danger.

Don't promise to pay what someone else owes.

Do you see a man skilled in his work? That man will work for kings. He won't have to work for ordinary people.

Don't wear yourself out trying to get rich. Be wise enough to control yourself. Wealth can vanish in the wink of an eye. It seems to grow wings and fly away like an eagle in the sky.

Don't speak to a foolish person. He will only ignore your wise words.

Remember what you are taught. And listen carefully to words of knowledge.

Don't fail to punish a child. If you spank him, you will keep him from dying. If you punish him with a spanking, you will save him from a fool's death.

My child, if you are wise, then I will be happy. I will be so pleased if you speak what is right.

Listen, my child, and be wise. Keep your mind on what is right. Don't be one of those who drink too much wine or who eat too much food. Those who drink too much and eat too much become poor. They sleep too much and end up wearing rags.

Listen to your father, who gave you life. And do not forget

your mother when she is old. Make your father and mother happy. Give your mother a reason to be glad.

Some people drink too much wine. They try out all the different kinds of drinks. So they have trouble. They are sad. They fight. They complain. They have unnecessary bruises. They have bloodshot eyes. Don't stare at the wine's pretty red color. It may sparkle in the cup. It may go down your throat smoothly. But later it bites like a snake. Like a snake, it poisons you. Your eyes will see strange sights. And your mind will be confused. You will feel dizzy, as if you're out on the stormy ocean.

It takes wisdom to have a good family. It takes understanding to make it strong. It takes knowledge to fill a home with rare and beautiful treasures.

A wise man has great power. And a man who has knowledge is very strong.

If you give up when trouble comes, it shows that you have very little strength.

Save those who are being led to their death. Rescue those who are about to be killed. You may say, "We don't know anything about this." But God knows what is in your mind, and he will notice. He is watching you,

and he will know. He will pay each person back for what he has done.

My child, eat honey because it is good. Honey from the honeycomb tastes sweet. In the same way, wisdom is pleasing to you. If you find it, you have hope for the future. Your wishes will come true.

Don't envy evil people. And don't be jealous of the wicked. An evil person has nothing to hope for. The wicked will die like a flame that is put out.

More Words of Wisdom

These are also wise sayings:

An honest answer is as pleasing as a kiss on the lips.

Don't testify against your neighbor for no good reason. Don't say things that are false. Don't say, "I'll get even with that man. I'll do to him what he did to me."

I passed by a lazy person's field. Thorns had grown up everywhere. The ground was covered with weeds. And the stone walls had fallen down. I thought about what I had seen. I learned this lesson from what I saw. You sleep a little; you take a nap. You fold your hands and rest. Soon you will be poor, as if you had been robbed. You will have as little as if you had been held up.

More Wise Sayings of Solomon

These are more wise sayings of Solomon. They were copied by the men of Hezekiah king of Judah.

If you have an argument with your neighbor, don't tell other people what was said. Whoever hears it might say bad things about you. And you might not ever be respected again.

The right word spoken at the right time is as beautiful as gold apples in a silver bowl.

People who brag about gifts they never give are like clouds and wind that give no rain.

If you find honey, don't eat too much. Too much of it will make you sick. Don't go to your neighbor's house too often. Too much of you will make him hate you.

Anyone who lies about his neighbor hurts him as a club, a sword or a sharp arrow would.

Don't trust unfaithful people when you are in trouble. It's like eating with a broken tooth or walking with a crippled foot.

If your enemy is hungry, feed him. If he is thirsty, give him a drink. Doing this will be like pouring burning coals on his head. And the Lord will reward you.

Hearing good news from a faraway place is like having a cool drink when you are tired.

A good person who gives in to evil is like a muddy spring or a dirty well.

It is not good to eat too much honey. In the same way, it is not good to brag about yourself.

A person who does not control himself is like a city whose walls have been broken down.

A dog eats what it throws up. And a foolish person repeats his foolishness.

The lazy person is like a door that turns back and forth on its hinges. He stays in bed and turns over and over.

To grab a dog by the ears is asking for trouble. So is interfering in someone else's quarrel if you're just passing by.

A person shouldn't trick his neighbor and then say, "I was just joking!" That is like a madman shooting deadly, burning arrows.

A person who hates you may fool you with his words. His words are kind, but don't believe him. His mind is full of evil thoughts. He hides his hate with lies.

A liar hates the people he hurts. And false praise can ruin others.

Don't brag about what will happen tomorrow. You don't really know what will happen then.

Don't praise yourself. Let someone else do it. Let the praise come from a stranger and not from your own mouth.

It is better to correct someone openly than to love him and not show it.

The slap of a friend can be trusted to help you. But the kisses of an enemy are nothing but lies.

Iron can sharpen iron. In the same way, people can help each other.

The person who tends a fig tree will eat its fruit. And the person who takes care of his master will be honored.

People will never stop dying and being destroyed. In the same way, people will never stop wanting more than they have.

More Proverbs from Solomon

Evil people run even though no one is chasing them. But good people are as brave as a lion.

Evil people do not understand fairness. But those who follow the Lord understand it completely.

If you refuse to obey what you have been taught, your prayers will not be heard.

When good people win, there is great happiness. But when the wicked get power, everybody hides.

If you hide your sins, you will not succeed. If you confess and reject them, you will receive mercy.

Those who always respect the Lord will be happy. But those who are stubborn will get into trouble.

The person who works his land will have plenty of food. But the one who chases useless dreams instead will end up very poor.

A selfish person is in a hurry to get rich. He does not realize his selfishness will make him poor.

Those who correct others will later be liked more than those who give false praise.

Some people rob their fathers or mothers and say, "It's not wrong." Such people are just like those who destroy things.

Some people are still stubborn after they have been corrected many times. But they will suddenly be hurt beyond cure.

If a king is fair, he makes his country strong. But if he takes money dishonestly, he tears his country down.

An evil person is trapped by his own sin. But a good person can sing and be happy.

Punishment and correction make a child wise. If he is left to do as he pleases, he will disgrace his mother.

Correct your child, and you will be proud of him. He will give you pleasure.

Where there is no word from God, people are uncontrolled. But those who obey what they have been taught are happy.

A man's pride will ruin him. But a person who is humble will be honored.

WORTH WONDERING...

■ When is it easiest for you to tell what is right and what is wrong?

■ When is it hardest for you to tell what is right and what is wrong?

■ When you think of the word wisdom, what comes to your mind?

■ What do you think are the most helpful things this book tells you about how to get along with other people?

GREAT VERSES TO THINK ABOUT AGAIN...

Look back in Proverbs to see if you can find these verses:

■ *Knowledge begins with respect for the Lord.*

■ *Trust the Lord with all your heart. Don't depend on your own understanding.*

■ *The Lord is like a strong tower. Those who do what is right can run to him for safety.*

■ *A person who does not control himself is like a city whose walls have been broken down.*

■ *It takes wisdom to have a good family. It takes understanding to make it strong. It takes knowledge to fill a home with rare and beautiful treasures.*

■ *The Lord's eyes see everything that happens. He watches both evil and good people.*

■ *The Lord corrects those he loves, just as a father corrects the child that he likes.*

■ *The way of the good person is like the light of dawn. It grows brighter and brighter until it is full daylight.*

AND THERE'S MORE...

When you read Proverbs in a full Bible, you'll find hundreds of wise sayings. They are all full of good advice.

The Book of
ECCLESIASTES

A Wise Man
Believes in God

Looking forward to Ecclesiastes...

"A Wise Man Believes in God"

The writer of this book calls himself "the Teacher." He says he is "a son of David" and that he was "king over Israel in Jerusalem." Solomon fits this description best.

Solomon says he has tried many different ways to find true happiness. He tried wisdom. He tried being famous. He tried "having fun." He tried money. He tried hard work.

Now he writes down what he discovered. He passes it on to us so we can learn the same lessons, just by reading them here.

Solomon was the richest and the wisest man on earth. He knew what he was talking about in the book of Ecclesiastes.

I wonder if it's possible to find lasting happiness here on earth — without God...

I DID GREAT THINGS. I built houses, and I planted gardens, and I made parks. I bought men and women slaves. I had large herds of cattle and flocks of sheep. I had more than anyone in Jerusalem before me. I also gathered silver and gold for myself. I took treasures from kings. I became very famous. I was greater than anyone who had lived in Jerusalem before me. My wisdom helped me in all this.

Anything I saw and wanted, I got for myself. I did not miss any pleasure I desired. And this pleasure was the reward for all my hard work. But then I looked at what I had done. Suddenly I realized it was just a waste of time, like chasing the wind!

There Is a Time for Everything

There is a right time for everything. Everything on earth has its special season. There is a time to be born and a time to die. There is a time to plant and a time to pull up plants. There is a time to kill and a time to heal. There is a time to destroy and a time to build. There is a time to cry and a time to laugh. There is a time to be sad and a time to dance. There is a time to throw away stones and a time to gather them. There is a time to hug and a time not to hug. There is a time to look for something and a time to stop looking for it. There is a time to keep things and a time to throw things away. There is a time to tear apart and a time to sew together. There is a time to be silent and a time to speak. There is a time to love and a time to hate. There is a time for war and a time for peace.

God Controls His World

God certainly does everything at just the right time. But we can never completely understand what he is doing. So I realize that the best thing for people is to be happy. They should enjoy themselves as long as they live. God wants everyone to eat and drink and be happy in his work. These are gifts from God. I know anything God does will continue forever.

Friends and Family Give Strength

Two people are better than one. They get more done by working together. If one person falls, the other can help him up. But it is bad for the person who is alone when he falls. No one is there to help him. If two lie down together, they will be warm. But a person alone will not be warm. An enemy might defeat one person, but two people together can defend themselves. A rope that has three parts wrapped together is hard to break.

Conclusion

Here is my final advice: Honor God and obey his commands. This is the most important thing people can do. God knows everything people do, even the things done in secret. He knows all the good and all the bad. He will judge everything people do.

WORTH WONDERING...

- When people don't depend on God for their happiness, where else do they look for it?
- What makes you happiest?

GREAT VERSES TO THINK ABOUT AGAIN...

Look back in Ecclesiastes to see if you can find these verses:

- *There is a right time for everything. Everything on earth has its special season.*
- *Honor God and obey his commands. This is the most important thing people can do.*

AND THERE'S MORE...

When you read Ecclesiastes in a full Bible, look especially for...

- More details of what the Teacher learned as he searched for happiness.

The Song of
SOLOMON

A Love Song

Looking forward to Song of Solomon...

"A Love Song"

This is a book of heavenly love. That's true because the love between a husband and wife is pleasing to God in heaven. And it's also true because this book is like a picture of the love Jesus Christ has for His bride.

And who is His bride? The New Testament tells us that the bride of Christ is the Church. That means everyone who believes in Jesus, for we are all part of His Church. We are His bride!

Solomon wrote this book, and it is also called "the Song of Songs" or "Solomon's Greatest Song."

I wonder how God wants husbands and wives to love each other...

The Bride Speaks to the Man She Loves

Your love is better than wine. The smell of your perfume is pleasant. Your name is pleasant like expensive perfume!

You are so handsome. You are so pleasant, like an apple tree among the trees in the woods!

He's the best of 10,000 men. His head is like the finest gold. His eyes are like doves by springs of water. He is tall like a cedar of Lebanon — like the best cedar trees. This is my friend.

The Man Speaks to His Bride

You are the most beautiful of women. Your cheeks are beautiful with ornaments. Your neck is beautiful with jewels. My darling, you are beautiful! Oh, you are beautiful! Your eyes are like doves!

Your voice is very sweet, and your face is lovely. My bride, you have thrilled my heart with a glance of your eyes. Your love is so sweet, my bride!

WORTH WONDERING...

■ How can you tell from this book that the love between a husband and wife is a good thing in God's eyes?

AND THERE'S MORE...

When you read Song of Solomon in a full Bible, look for more clues of how the man and his bride feel about each other.

INTRODUCING...

ISAIAH • JEREMIAH • LAMENTATIONS
EZEKIEL • DANIEL

Back in the Old Testament Law and History books (the books from Genesis to Esther), we learned how God's people kept sinning in big ways. Over and over again they did evil. Finally God sent armies to destroy their towns and to burn the city of Jerusalem and God's Temple there. Then these armies took God's people away as prisoners.

You may be wondering: Did God warn them enough? Yes, He did! He warned them again and again through His messengers. His messengers were called *prophets.*

The prophets spoke God's words to the people. Because God loved His people, He gave them both warnings and promises. He gave these warnings and promises to the prophets. Then the prophets passed them along to the people.

The words of these prophets make up the final books in the Old Testament. Since they were written by the prophets, we call them the "Prophecy" books. The Old Testament Prophecy books are divided into two groups.

The longer books — Isaiah, Jeremiah, Ezekiel, and Daniel — are grouped together first. Since the word *major* can mean "larger," we call these books the Major Prophets. Lamentations is a smaller book, but it is placed next to Jeremiah because it was written by Jeremiah.

(The other smaller Prophecy books — which come later — are called the Minor Prophets, since the word *minor* means "smaller.")

Except for Lamentations, the Prophecy books are named for the person who wrote them. Isaiah and Jeremiah wrote their books before the nation of Israel went into captivity in the land of Babylon. Ezekiel and Daniel were written while the Jews were still captives in Babylon.

The Book of
ISAIAH

God's Message
in Troubled Times

Looking forward to Isaiah...

"God's Message in Troubled Times"

Isaiah lived 700 years before Jesus came to earth. But God let Isaiah look ahead to the time when Jesus would come. Many of the promises in Isaiah's book are all about the coming Son of God.

Isaiah calls Him names like these: "Wonderful Counselor, Powerful God, Prince of Peace." And near the end of his book he gives us a picture of Jesus as God's Suffering Servant. Isaiah sees how this Servant will suffer and be killed for our sins. He will receive the punishment for all the wrong things that we have done. He will carry our sin and sadness in His own body.

The book of Isaiah tells us more about Jesus Christ than any other Old Testament book.

Isaiah prophesied mostly in Jerusalem. He spoke to the people of Judah, the Southern Kingdom. Isaiah's name means "salvation of the Lord."

When God allowed Old Testament prophets to look into the future and see Jesus, I wonder what they saw...

GOD SHOWED ISAIAH what would happen to Judah and Jerusalem. Isaiah saw these things while Uzziah, Jotham, Ahaz and Hezekiah were kings of Judah.

Heaven and earth, listen, because the Lord is speaking: "I raised my children and helped them grow. But they have turned against me. An ox knows its master. And a donkey knows where its owner feeds it. But the people of Israel do not know me. My people do not understand."

Terrible times are coming for Israel, a nation of sin. The people are loaded down with guilt. They are like a group of children doing evil. They have left the Lord. They hate God, the Holy One of Israel.

The Lord says, "I do not want all these sacrifices you give me. Even if you say many prayers, I will not listen to you. It's because your hands are full of blood. Wash yourselves and make yourselves clean. Stop doing wrong! Learn to do good. Be fair to other people. Punish those who hurt others. Help the orphans. Stand up for the rights of widows."

The Lord says, "Come, we will talk these things over. Your sins are red like deep red cloth. But they can be as white as snow. If you will obey me, you will eat good crops from the land. But if you refuse to obey and you turn against me, you will be destroyed by your enemies' swords."

The Message About Jerusalem

Isaiah saw this message about Judah and Jerusalem.

In the last days the mountain on which the Lord's Temple stands will become the most important of all mountains. It will be raised above the hills. And people from all nations will come streaming to it. Many nations will come and say, "Come, let us go up to the mountain of the Lord. Let us go to the Temple of the God of Jacob. Then God will teach us his ways. And we will obey his teachings." The Lord's teachings will go out from Jerusalem. The Lord's message will go out from Jerusalem. Then the Lord will settle arguments among many nations. He will make decisions for strong nations that are far away. Then the nations will make their swords into plows. They will make their spears into hooks for trimming trees. Nations will no longer fight other nations. They will not even train for war anymore.

A Terrible Day Is Coming

The Lord of heaven's armies has a certain day planned. On that day he will punish the proud and those who brag. They will no longer be important. He will destroy all the tall mountains and the high hills. He will knock down every tall tower and every high, strong wall. He will sink all the trading ships. At that time proud people will stop being proud. They will bow low with shame. And at that time only the Lord will be praised. But all the idols will be gone.

People will run to caves in the rocky cliffs. They will dig holes and hide in the ground. They will hide from the anger of the Lord and his great power. They will do this when the Lord stands to shake the earth. At that time people will throw away their gold and silver idols. They made these idols for themselves to worship. But they will throw them away to the bats and moles.

Israel, God's Special Field

Now I will sing a song to my friend. This song is about his vineyard. My friend had a vineyard on a hill with very rich soil. He dug and cleared the field of stones. He planted the best grapevines there. And he built a tower in the middle of it. He cut out a winepress as well. He hoped good grapes would grow there. But only bad grapes grew.

The vineyard belonging to the Lord of heaven's armies is

the nation of Israel. The garden that the Lord loves is the men of Judah. The Lord looked for justice, but there was only killing. The Lord hoped for right living, but there were only cries of pain.

How terrible it will be for people who rise early in the morning to look for strong drink. They stay awake late at night, becoming drunk with wine.

How terrible it will be for people who call good things bad and bad things good. They think darkness is light and light is darkness. They think sour is sweet and sweet is sour.

How terrible it will be for people who think they are wise. They think they are clever.

They have refused to obey the teachings of the Lord of heaven's armies. They hated the message from the Holy God of Israel. So the Lord has become very angry with his people. And he has raised his hand to punish them.

The enemy comes quickly! Not one of them becomes tired or falls down. Not one of them gets sleepy and falls asleep. Their weapons are close at hand. Their arrows are sharp. All of their bows are ready to shoot. The horses' hoofs are hard as rock. Their chariot wheels move like a whirlwind. Their shout is like the roar of a lion.

Isaiah Becomes a Prophet

In the year that King Uzziah died, I saw the Lord. He was sitting on a very high throne. His long robe filled the Temple. Burning heavenly creatures stood above him. Each creature had six wings. They used two wings to cover their faces. They used two wings to cover their feet. And they used two wings for flying. Each creature was calling to the others: "Holy, holy, holy is the Lord of heaven's armies. His glory fills the whole earth."

Their voices caused the frame around the door to shake. The Temple filled with smoke.

I said, "Oh, no! I will be destroyed. I am not pure. And I live among people who are not pure. But I have seen the King, the Lord of heaven's armies."

On the altar there was a fire. One of the burning heavenly creatures used a pair of tongs to take a hot coal from the fire. Then he flew to me with the hot coal in his hand. The creature touched my mouth with the hot coal. Then he said, "Look. Your guilt is taken away because this hot coal has touched your lips. Your sin is taken away."

Then I heard the Lord's voice. He said, "Whom can I send? Who will go for us?"

So I said, "Here I am. Send me!"

Warnings to Isaiah

The Lord spoke to me with his great power. He warned me not to follow the lead of the rest of the people. The Lord said, "People are saying that others make plans against them. You should not believe those things. Don't be afraid of the things they fear. Do not dread those things. But remember that the Lord of heaven's armies is holy. He is the one you should fear. He is the one you should dread."

People will wander through the land troubled and hungry. When they become hungry, they will become angry. Then they will look up and curse their king and their God. They will look around them at their land. And they will see only trouble and darkness and awful gloom.

A New Day Is Coming

But suddenly there will be no more gloom for the land that suffered.

Now those people live in darkness. But they will see a great light. A light will shine on them. God, you will cause the nation to grow. You will make the people happy. You will take away the heavy pole from their backs. You will take away the rod the enemy uses to punish your people. Every boot that marched in battle will be destroyed. Every uniform stained with blood will be destroyed. They will be thrown into the fire.

A child will be born to us. God will give a son to us. He will be responsible for leading the people. His name will be Wonderful Counselor, Powerful God, Father Who Lives Forever, Prince of Peace. Power and peace will be in his kingdom. It will continue to grow. He will rule as king on David's throne and over David's kingdom. He will make it strong, by ruling with goodness and fair judgment. He will rule it forever and ever. The Lord of heaven's armies will do this because of his strong love for his people.

The King of Peace Is Coming

A branch will grow from a stump of a tree that was cut down. So a new king will come from the family of Jesse. The Spirit of the Lord will rest upon that king. The Spirit gives him wisdom, understanding, guidance and power. And the Spirit teaches him to know and respect the Lord. This king will be glad to obey the Lord. He will not judge by the way things look. He will not judge by what people say. He will judge the poor honestly. He will be fair. At his command evil people will be punished. By his words the wicked will be put to death. Goodness and fairness will give him strength. They will be like a belt around his waist.

Then wolves will live in peace with lambs. And leopards will lie down to rest with goats. Calves, lions and young bulls will eat together. And a little child will lead them. Cows and bears will eat together in peace. Their young will lie down together. Lions will eat hay as oxen do. A baby will be able to play near a cobra's hole. They will not hurt or destroy each other on all my holy mountain. The earth will be full of the knowledge of the Lord, as the sea is full of water.

At that time the new king from the family of Jesse will stand as a banner for the people. The nations will come together around him. And the place where he lives will be filled with glory. At that time the Lord will again reach out and take his people who are left alive.

A Song of Praise to God

At that time you will say: "I praise you, Lord! You were angry with me. But you are not angry with me now! You have comforted me. God is the one who saves me. I trust him. I am not afraid. The Lord gives me strength and makes me sing." You will receive your salvation with joy. You will take it as you would draw water from a well.

At that time you will say, "Praise the Lord, and worship him. Tell everyone what he has done. Tell them how great he is. Sing praise to the Lord, because he has done great things. Shout and sing for joy, you people of Jerusalem. The Holy One of Israel does great things before your eyes."

God Will Punish the World

Look! The Lord will destroy the earth and leave it empty. He will ruin the surface of the land and scatter its people. The earth will be completely empty. The wealth will all be taken. This will happen because the Lord commanded it. The earth will dry up and die. The people of the earth have ruined it. They do not follow God's teachings. They break their agreement with God that was to last forever. The people of the world are guilty. So they will be burned up. Only a few will be left.

A Song of Praise to God

Lord, you are my God. I honor you and praise you. You have done amazing things. You have always done what you said you would.

The Lord of heaven's armies will give a feast. It will be on this mountain for all people. It will be a feast with the best food and wine. On this mountain God will destroy the veil that covers all nations. This veil, called "death," covers all peoples. But God will destroy death forever. The Lord God will wipe away every tear from every face. God will take away the shame of his people from the earth.

At that time people will say, "Our God is doing this! We have trusted in him, and he has come to save us. So we will rejoice and be happy."

At that time people will sing this song in Judah: We have a strong city. God protects us with its strong walls and defenses. Open the gates, and the good people will enter. They follow God's good way of living. You, Lord, give true peace to those who depend on you. You give peace to those who trust you.

Lord, all our success is because of what you have done. So give us peace.

Judgment: Reward or Punishment

In the days to come, the people of Jacob will be like a plant with good roots. Israel will grow like a plant beginning to bloom. Then the world will be filled with their children.

At that time the Lord will begin gathering all his people. He will separate them from others as grain is separated from chaff. Many of my people are now lost in Assyria. Some of my people have run away to Egypt. But at that time a great trumpet will be blown. And all those people will come back to Jerusalem. They will bow down before the Lord on that holy mountain.

At that time the Lord of heaven's armies will be like a beautiful crown. He will be like a wonderful crown of flowers for his people who are left alive.

The Lord is trying to teach the people a lesson. He is trying to make them understand his teachings. But the people are like little babies. They make fun of the Lord's prophet. They will fall back and will be defeated. They will be trapped and captured.

Because of these things, this is what the Lord God says: "I will put a stone in the ground in Jerusalem. This will be a tested stone. Everything will be built on this important and precious rock. Anyone who trusts in it will never be disappointed."

Warnings to Jerusalem

How terrible it will be for you, Jerusalem. That city will be filled with sadness and crying. I will put armies all around you, Jerusalem.

The Lord of heaven's armies will come. He will come with thunder, earthquakes and great noises. He will come with storms, strong winds and a fire that destroys. Then all the nations that fight against Jerusalem will be like a dream. They will be like a hungry man who dreams he is eating. But when he wakes up, he is still hungry. They will be like a thirsty man who dreams he is drinking. But when he wakes up, he is still weak and thirsty.

The Lord says: "These people say they love me. They show honor to me with words. But their hearts are far from me. The honor they show me is nothing but human rules they have memorized. So I will continue to amaze these people by doing more and more miracles. Their wise men will lose their wisdom. Their wise men will not be able to understand."

God Will Help His People

The Lord will hear your crying, and he will comfort you. The Lord will hear you, and he will help you. The Lord has given you sorrow and hurt. But he is your teacher, and he will not continue to hide from you. If you go the wrong way — to the right or to the left — you will hear a voice behind you. It will say, "This is the right way. You should go this way."

At that time the Lord will send rain for you. You will plant seeds in the ground, and the ground will grow food for you. The harvest will be very great. Every mountain and hill will have streams filled with water. These things will happen when the Lord bandages his broken people and heals the hurts he gave them.

A Good Kingdom Is Coming

A king will rule in a way that brings justice. Leaders will make fair decisions. Each ruler will be like a safe place in a storm. He will be like streams of water in a dry land.

People will look to the king

for help. And they will truly listen to what he says. Fools will not be called great men. People will not respect wicked men. But a good leader plans good things to do. And those good things make him a good leader.

God Will Punish His Enemies

All you nations, come near and listen. Pay attention, you peoples! The Lord is angry with all the nations. He is angry with their armies. He will destroy them and kill them all. Their bodies will be thrown outside. The sun, moon and stars will dissolve. The sky will be rolled up like a scroll. The stars will fall like dead leaves from a vine or dried-up figs from a fig tree. The Lord's sword in the sky is covered with blood.

The Lord has chosen a time for punishment. He has chosen a year when people must pay for the wrongs they did to Jerusalem.

God Will Comfort His People

The desert and dry land will become happy. The desert will be glad and will produce flowers. It will show its happiness, as if it is shouting with joy. It will be beautiful. All people will see the glory of the Lord. They will see the splendor of our God.

Then the blind people will see again. Then the deaf will hear. Crippled people will jump like deer. And those who can't talk now will shout with joy.

The people the Lord has freed will return. They will enter Jerusalem with joy. Their happiness will last forever. Their gladness and joy will fill them completely. Sorrow and sadness will go far away.

God Is Supreme

God, the Holy One, says, "Can you compare me to anyone? Is anyone equal to me? Look up to the skies. Who created all these stars? He leads out all the army of heaven one by one. He calls all the stars by name. He is very strong and full of power. So not one of them is missing."

Surely you you have heard. The Lord is the God who lives forever. He created all the world. He does not become tired or need to rest. No one can understand how great his wisdom is. The Lord gives strength to those who are tired. The people who trust the Lord will become strong again. They will be able to rise up as an eagle in the sky. They will run without needing rest. They will walk without becoming tired.

The Lord's Special Servant

The Lord says, "Here is my servant, the one I support. He is the one I chose, and I am pleased with him. I will put my Spirit in him. And he will bring justice to all nations. He will not cry out or yell. He will not speak loudly in the streets. He will not break a crushed blade of grass. He will not put out even a weak flame. He will bring justice and find what is true. He will not lose hope or give up until he brings justice to the world. And people far away will trust his teachings."

God, the Lord, said these things. The Lord says, "I called you to do right. And I will hold your hand. I will protect you. You will be the sign of my agreement with the people. You will be a light to shine for all people. You will help the blind to see. You will lead those who live in darkness out of their prison."

God Is Always with His People

Now this is what the Lord says. He created you, people of Jacob. He formed you, people of Israel. He says, "Don't be afraid, because I have saved you. I have called you by name, and you are mine. When you cross rivers, you will not drown. When you walk through fire, you will not be burned. This is because I, the Lord, am your God. I, the Holy One of Israel, am your Savior. You are precious to me. I give you honor, and I love you. So don't be afraid. I am with you."

The Lord Is the Only God

The Lord says, "I am the beginning and the end. I am the only God. There is no other God like me. I know of no other Rock. I am the only One."

Some people make idols, but they are worth nothing. People love them, but they are useless. Who made these false gods? Who made these useless idols? The workmen who made those gods will be ashamed!

One workman uses tools to heat iron. He works over hot coals. He uses his hammer to beat the metal and make a statue. He uses his powerful arms. But when he becomes hungry, he loses his power. If he does not drink water, he becomes tired.

Another workman cuts down cedar or gets cypress or oak trees. He uses some of the wood for a fire to keep himself warm. He also starts a fire to bake his bread. But he uses part of the wood to make a god. Then he worships it! He makes the idol and bows down to it! He prays to it and says, "You are my god. Save me!" Those people don't know what they are doing. It is as if their eyes are covered so they can't see. They have never thought to themselves, "I am worshiping a block of wood!"

God Will Destroy Babylon

The Lord says, "Babylon, sit in darkness and say nothing. I was angry with my people. So I rejected those people who belonged to me. I gave them to you, but you showed them no mercy. You even made the old people work very hard.

"Now, listen, you lover of pleasure. You think you are safe. You do evil things, but you feel safe. But troubles will come to you. You will not know how to stop them. Disaster will fall on you. And you will not be able to keep it away. You will be destroyed quickly. You will not even see it coming.

"Keep on using your tricks. Continue doing all your magic. But they will not be able to help you. And there will be no one left to save you."

Jerusalem Will Be Saved

Wake up, Jerusalem! Become strong! Be beautiful again, holy city of Jerusalem. Jerusalem, you once were a prisoner. But now free yourself from the chains around your neck.

How beautiful is the person who comes over the mountains to bring good news. How beautiful is the one who announces peace. He brings good news and announces salvation. How beautiful are the feet of the one who says to Jerusalem, "Your God is king." Listen! Your guards are shouting. They are all shouting for joy! They all will see with their own eyes when the Lord returns to Jerusalem. Jerusalem, your buildings are destroyed now. But shout and rejoice together. You can rejoice because the Lord has comforted his people. He has saved Jerusalem. The Lord will show his holy power to all the nations. Then everyone on earth will see the salvation of our God.

You people, leave, leave; get out of Babylon! Touch nothing that is unclean. You men who carry the things used in worship, leave there and make yourselves pure. The Lord will go before you. And the God of Israel will guard you from behind.

God's Suffering Servant

The Lord says, "See, my servant will act wisely. People

will greatly honor and respect him. Kings will be amazed and shut their mouths. They will see the things they had not been told about my servant."

He grew up like a small plant before the Lord. He was like a root growing in a dry land. He had no special beauty or form to make us notice him. There was nothing in his appearance to make us desire him. He was hated and rejected by people. He had much pain and suffering. People would not even look at him. He was hated, and we didn't even notice him.

But he took our suffering on him and felt our pain for us. We saw his suffering. We thought God was punishing him. But he was wounded for the wrong things we did. He was crushed for the evil things we did. The punishment, which made us well, was given to him. And we are healed because of his wounds. We all have wandered away like sheep. Each of us has gone his own way. But the Lord has put on him the punishment for all the evil we have done.

He was beaten down and punished. But he didn't say a word. He was like a lamb being led to be killed. He never opened his mouth. Men took him away roughly and unfairly. He died without children to continue his family. He was put to death. He was punished for the sins of my people. He had done nothing wrong. He had never lied.

But it was the Lord who decided to crush him and make him suffer. So the Lord made his life a penalty offering. But he will see his descendants and live a long life. He will complete the things the Lord wants him to do. He will suffer many things in his soul. But then he will see life and be satisfied. My good servant will make many people right with God. He carried away their sins. For this reason I will make him a great man among people. He will share in all things with those who are strong. He willingly gave his life. He was treated like a criminal. But he carried away the sins of many people. And he asked forgiveness for those who sinned.

God Gives What Is Good

The Lord says, "All you who are thirsty, come and drink. Those of you who do not have money, come, buy and eat! Come buy wine and milk. You don't need money; it will cost you nothing. Why spend your money on something that is not real food? Why work for something that doesn't really satisfy you? Listen closely to me, and you will eat what is good. You will enjoy the food that satisfies your soul. Come to me and listen. Listen to me so you may live. I will make an agreement with you that will last forever. I will give you the blessings I promised to David. I made David a witness of my power for all nations. I made him a ruler and commander of many nations. You will call for nations that you don't yet know. And these nations will run to you. This will happen because of the Lord your God. The Holy One of Israel honors you."

So you should look for the Lord before it is too late. You should call to him while he is near. Evil people should stop being evil. They should stop thinking bad thoughts. They should return to the Lord, and he will have mercy on them. They should come to our God, because he will freely forgive them.

The Lord says, "Your thoughts are not like my thoughts. Your ways are not like my ways. Just as the heavens are higher than the earth, so are my ways higher than your ways. And my thoughts are higher than your thoughts. Rain and snow fall from the sky. They don't return without watering the ground. They cause the plants to sprout and grow. And the plants make seeds for the farmer. And from these seeds people have bread to eat. The words I say do the same thing. They will not return to me empty. They make the things happen that I want to happen. They succeed in doing what I send them to do.

PAUSE & WONDER

God says in Isaiah that His ways are higher than my ways, just as the heavens are higher than the earth. When I'm truly honest with myself, I know that there has to be Someone greater and higher than any human being. There has to be Someone who is so much stronger and wiser and better than we could ever be. I know there's a God! And why do I know? Because God Himself put those true feelings inside my heart.

"So you will go out with joy. You will be led out in peace. The mountains and hills will burst into song before you. All the trees in the fields will clap their hands. Large cypress trees will grow where thornbushes were. Myrtle trees will grow where weeds were. These things will be a reminder of the Lord's promise. And this reminder will never be destroyed."

A Prayer for Help

Lord, look down at us from your wonderful holy home in heaven. For our sake come back to us. We are your servants, and we belong to you. Your people had your Temple for a while. But now our enemies have walked on your holy place and crushed it.

Tear open the skies and come down to earth. The mountains would tremble before you. Be like a fire that makes water boil. Do this so that your enemies will know who you are. Then all nations will shake with fear when they see you. You have done amazing things that we did not expect. You came down, and the mountains trembled before you. From long ago no one has ever heard of a God like you. No one has ever seen a God besides you. You help the people who trust you. You help those who enjoy doing good. You help those who remember how you want them to live. But you were angry because we sinned. For a long time we disobeyed. How will we be saved? All of us are dirty with sin. All the right things we have done are like filthy pieces of cloth. All of us are like dead leaves. Like the wind our sins have carried us away. No one worships you. No one even asks you to help us. So you have turned away from us. And we are destroyed because of our sins.

But Lord, you are our father. We are like clay, and you are the potter. Your hands made us all. Lord, don't continue to be angry with us. Don't remember our sins forever.

A New Time Is Coming

This is what the Lord says: "Look, I will make new heavens and a new earth. And people will not remember the past. My people will be happy forever because of the things I will make. I will make a Jerusalem that is full of joy. There will never again be crying and sadness in that city. All my people will be blessed by the Lord. My people and their children will be blessed. I will provide for their needs before they ask. I will help them while they are still asking for help. Wolves and lambs will eat together in peace. Lions will eat hay like oxen. A snake on the ground will not hurt anyone. They will not hurt or destroy each other on all my holy mountain."

WORTH WONDERING...

- In this book of the Bible, how do you see that God is great? And how do you see that He is good?
- What verses in this book remind you of Jesus?
- Which parts of this book would you most like to know more about?
- Think about some friends you have who might know very little about Jesus or the Bible. What parts of this book do you think would be most interesting to them?

GREAT VERSES TO THINK ABOUT AGAIN...

Look back in Isaiah to see if you can find these verses:

- *So you will go out with joy. You will be led out in peace. The mountains and hills will burst into song before you. All the trees in the fields will clap their hands.*
- *Come, we will talk these things over. Your sins are red like deep red cloth. But they can be as white as snow.*
- *A child will be born to us. God will give a son to us. He will be responsible for leading the people. His name will be Wonderful Counselor, Powerful God, Father Who Lives Forever, Prince of Peace.*
- *So a new king will come from the family of Jesse. The Spirit of the Lord will rest upon that king. The Spirit gives him wisdom, understanding, guidance and power.*
- *We all have wandered away like sheep. Each of us has gone his own way. But the Lord has put on him the punishment for all the evil we have done.*

AND THERE'S MORE...

When you read Isaiah in a full Bible, look especially for...

- Isaiah's words about Ahaz, a king who rebelled against God.
- The story of Hezekiah. He depended on God, and God gave him a miraculous victory over the invading Assyrians.
- God's words of judgment upon other nations, including Babylon.

The Book of
JEREMIAH

A Warning
about Captivity

Looking forward to Jeremiah...

"A Warning about Captivity"

SIGNS AND WONDERS

Jeremiah warns about the disaster that is coming soon to God's people. He said an enemy army was coming to destroy Jerusalem and take the people as prisoners. This disaster was coming as punishment for their sins.

It was a sad message Jeremiah gave, and the people wouldn't listen to him. But Jeremiah stayed strong and brave.

Like other prophets, Jeremiah also had words of hope to speak. He talked about a New Israel. He spoke about a New Agreement that God would make with His new people. He said God would write His teachings in the minds and hearts of His people. Jeremiah was looking ahead to a future time. It was the time after Jesus had lived on earth, when the Holy Spirit came to live inside all those who believe in Jesus. Jeremiah spoke of Jesus as the "Good Descendant" of David. This was a new king who would rule in a wise way. Jeremiah also spoke of Jesus as a righteous "branch" sprouting up from David's family. So God gave Jeremiah words of encouragement to speak, as well as words of warning!

FACES AND PLACES

Jeremiah prophesied mostly in **Jerusalem.** He spoke to each of the last five kings of Judah, the Southern Kingdom. Then he watched as Jerusalem was destroyed. Jeremiah's name means "chosen by the Lord."

Baruch: Jeremiah's helper and secretary.

**If a man gave God's warnings
to His people, but they kept ignoring him...
I wonder how long he could keep going...**

JEREMIAH BELONGED to the family of priests who lived in the town of Anathoth. The Lord spoke his word to Jeremiah. This happened during the thirteenth year that Josiah was king of Judah. The Lord also spoke to Jeremiah while Jehoiakim was king of Judah. And the Lord spoke to Jeremiah during the years Zedekiah was king of Judah. After that, the people who lived in Jerusalem were taken away as captives out of their country.

God Calls Jeremiah

The Lord spoke these words to me: "Before I made you in your mother's womb, I chose you. Before you were born, I set you apart for a special work. I appointed you as a prophet to the nations."

Then I said, "But Lord God, I don't know how to speak. I am only a boy."

But the Lord said to me, "Don't say, 'I am only a boy.' You must go everywhere that I send you. You must say everything I tell you to say. Don't be afraid of anyone, because I am with you. I will protect you."

Then the Lord reached out with his hand and touched my mouth. He said to me, "See, I am putting my words in your mouth.

"Jeremiah, get ready. Stand up and speak to the people. Tell them everything I tell you to say. Don't be afraid of them. Today I am going to make you an iron pillar, a bronze wall. You will be able to stand against everyone in the land: Judah's kings, officers, priests and the people of the land. They will fight against you. But they will not defeat you. This is because I am with you, and I will save you!"

Israel Turns from God

The Lord spoke this word to me: "Go and speak to the people of Jerusalem. Say to them: This is what the Lord says: 'When you were a young nation, you were faithful to me. You loved me like a young bride. You followed me through the desert. It was a land that had never been planted. The people of Israel were holy to the Lord. They were like the first fruits from his harvest. Those who tried to hurt Israel were judged guilty. Disasters happened to them.'

"I was fair to your ancestors. Why did they turn away from me? Your ancestors worshiped useless idols. And they became useless themselves. I brought you into a fertile land. I did this so you could eat its fruit and produce. But you came and made my land unclean. You made it a hated place.

"If you will come back, Israel, then come back to me. Throw away your idols that I hate.

Don't wander away from me. Then the nations will be blessed by the Lord. And they will praise the Lord for what he has done."

No One Is Right

The Lord says, "Walk up and down the streets of Jerusalem. Look around and think about these things. Search the public squares of the city. See if you can find one person who does honest things. Find just one who searches for the truth. If you can, I will forgive this city.

"Announce this message to the family of Jacob. And tell it to the nation of Judah: Hear this message, you foolish people who have no sense. You have eyes, but you don't really see. You have ears, but you don't really listen. The people of Judah are stubborn and have turned against me. Like cages full of birds, their houses are full of lies. They have become rich and powerful. They have grown big and fat. There is no end to the evil things they do. They won't plead the case of the orphan. They won't help the poor be judged fairly."

Jerusalem Is Surrounded

This is what the Lord says: "Look, an army is coming from the land of the north. A great nation is coming from the far sides of the earth. The soldiers carry bows and spears. They are cruel and show no mercy. They sound like the roaring ocean when they ride their horses. That army is coming lined up for battle. It is coming to attack you, Jerusalem.

"I will pour out my anger on this place. I will pour it out on man and animal. I will pour out my anger on the trees in the field. And I will pour it out on the crops in the ground. My anger will be like a hot fire. And no one will be able to put it out.

Sin and Punishment

"Say to the people of Judah: 'This is what the Lord says: When a man falls down, doesn't he get up again? And when a man goes the wrong way, doesn't he come back again? Why, then, do the people of Jerusalem not turn back? They refuse to turn around and come back. They do not feel sorry about their wicked ways. Each person goes his own way. He is like a horse charging into a battle. Even the birds in the sky know the right times to do things.

"'Even the prophets and priests all tell lies. They try to heal my people's serious injuries as if they were small wounds. They say, "It's all right, it's all right!" But really, it is not all right. So they will fall, along with everyone else. I will take away what I gave them!'"

The Lord and Idols

Family of Israel, listen to what the Lord says to you. This is what he says: "Don't live like the people from other nations. Their idols are nothing but wood from the forest. They are made by a worker with his chisel. They decorate their idols with silver and gold. With hammers and nails they fasten them down. That keeps them from falling over. Their idols are like scarecrows in melon fields. They cannot talk. They cannot walk. They must be carried. Do not be afraid of those idols. They can't hurt you. And they can't help you either!"

Lord, there is no one like you. You are great and powerful. Everyone should respect you, King of all nations. There are many wise men among the nations. And there are wise men in all the kingdoms. But none of them are as wise as you.

God is not like the idols. God made everything. And he made Israel to be his special people. The Lord of heaven's armies is his name.

Trusting in God

This is what the Lord says: "A curse will be placed on those who have stopped trusting the Lord. They are like a bush in a desert. It grows in a hot and dry land with bad soil. They don't know about the good things that God can give.

"But the person who trusts in the Lord will be blessed. The Lord will show him that he can be trusted. He will be strong, like a tree planted near water. That tree has large roots that find the water. It is not afraid when the days are hot. Its leaves are always green. It does not worry in a year when no rain comes. That tree always produces fruit."

The Potter and the Clay

This is the word the Lord spoke to Jeremiah: "Go down to the potter's house. I will give you my message there." So I went down to the potter's house. I saw him working at the potter's wheel. He was making a pot from clay. But something went wrong with it. So the potter used that clay to make another pot. He used his hands to shape the pot the way that he wanted it to be.

Then the Lord spoke his word to me: "Family of Israel, can't I do the same thing with you? You are like the clay in the potter's hands. There may come a time when I will speak about a nation or a kingdom. I might say I will pull that nation up by its roots. Or I might say I will pull that nation down and destroy it. But if the people of that nation are sorry for the evil they have done, I would change my mind. I would not carry out my plans to bring disaster to them. There may come another time when I will speak about a nation. I might say that I will build up and plant that nation. But if I see it doing evil by not obeying me, I would change my mind. I would not carry out my plans to do good for them.

"So, say this to the people of Judah and those who live in Jerusalem: 'This is what the Lord says: I am preparing disaster for you right now. I am making plans against you. So stop doing the evil you are doing. Change your ways and do what is right.' But the people of Judah will answer, 'It won't do any good to try! We will continue to do what we want. Each of us will do what his stubborn, evil heart wants!'"

So this is what the Lord says: "Ask the people in other nations this question: 'Have you ever heard anything like this?' The people of Israel have done a horrible thing. The snow on the mountains of Lebanon never melts from the rocks. Its cool, flowing streams do not dry up.

But my people have forgotten me. They make offerings to worthless idols. This makes them stumble in what they do. They stumble about in the old ways of their ancestors. They walk along back roads and on poor highways. So Judah's country will become an empty desert. I will scatter them before their enemies as a strong east wind blows things away. At that awful time they will not see me coming to help them. They will see me leaving."

Zedekiah's Request

This is the word that the Lord spoke to Jeremiah. It came when Zedekiah king of Judah sent Pashhur to Jeremiah. He also sent the priest Zephaniah. They said, "Ask the Lord for us what will happen. We want to know because Nebuchadnezzar king of Babylon is attacking us. Maybe the Lord will do miracles for us as he did in the past. Maybe he will make Nebuchadnezzar stop attacking us and leave."

But Jeremiah answered them, "Tell King Zedekiah this: 'Here is what the Lord, the God of Israel, says: You have weapons of war in your hands. You are using them to defend yourselves against the king of Babylon and the Babylonians. But I will make those weapons useless. The army from Babylon is all around the outside of the city wall. Soon I will bring that army into the center of the city. I myself will fight against you with my great power and strength. I am very angry with you. I will fight very hard against you in my very great anger. I will let those win who want to kill the people of Judah. So the people of Judah and Jerusalem will be killed in war. Nebuchadnezzar will not show any mercy or pity or feel sorry for them!'

"Also tell this to the people of Jerusalem: 'This is what the Lord says: I will let you choose to live or die. Anyone who stays in Jerusalem will die. He will die in war or from hunger or from a terrible disease. But anyone who goes out of Jerusalem and surrenders to the Babylonians who are around the city will live. I have decided to make trouble for this city and not to help it, says the Lord. I will give it to the king of Babylon. He will burn it with fire.'"

The Good Descendant

"The days are coming," says the Lord, "when I will raise up a good descendant in David's family. This descendant will be a king who will rule in a wise way.

And he will do what is fair and right in the land. In his time Judah will be saved. Israel will live in safety. This will be his name: The Lord Does What Is Right."

Both Near and Far

"I am a God who is near," says the Lord. "I am also a God who is far away. No one can hide where I cannot see him. I fill all of heaven and earth.

"Let the person who hears my message speak it truthfully! My message is like a fire. It is like a hammer that smashes a rock!"

This is what the Lord of heaven's armies says: "You have not listened to my messages. So I will soon send for all the peoples of the north. I will soon send for my servant Nebuchadnezzar king of Babylon. I will bring them all against Judah and all the nations around you, too. I will completely destroy all those countries. I will leave them in ruins forever. People will be shocked when they see how badly they will be destroyed. I will bring an end to the sounds of joy and happiness. That whole area will be an empty desert. And these nations will be slaves of the king of Babylon for 70 years.

"But when the 70 years have passed, I will punish the king of Babylon and his nation. I will punish the Babylonians for their evil. I will make that land a desert forever. I have said many terrible things will happen to Babylonia. All of them will happen. Jeremiah prophesied about those foreign nations. The Babylonians will have to serve many nations and many great kings. I will give them the punishment they deserve. They

PAUSE & WONDER

The Lord told Jeremiah that His words were like fire, and like a hammer that smashes a rock. Like no other book, the Bible — God's Word — has power. The Bible can burn away my wrong attitudes. And it can smash the wrong thoughts in my mind. The Bible can change me!

will be punished for all the things they do."

Promises of Hope

These are the words that the Lord spoke to Jeremiah. The Lord, the God of Israel, said: "Jeremiah, write in a book all the words I have spoken to you. The days will come when I will make everything as good as it was before. I will bring Israel and Judah back from captivity. I will return them to the land I gave their ancestors. Then my people will own that land again!

"At that time I will be God of all Israel's family groups. And they will be my people."

And from far away the Lord appeared to his people. He said, "I love you people with a love that will last forever. I became your friend because of my love and kindness. People of Israel, I will build you up again, and you will be rebuilt. You will pick up your tambourines again. You will dance with those who are joyful. You will plant vineyards again on the hills around Samaria. The farmers will plant them and enjoy their fruit. There will be a time when watchmen in the mountains of Ephraim shout this message: 'Come, let's go up to Jerusalem to worship the Lord our God!'"

This is what the Lord says: "Be happy and sing for the people of Jacob. Look, I will bring Israel from the country in the north. I will gather them from the faraway places on earth. Some of the people are blind and crippled. Some of the women will be pregnant and ready to give birth. A great many people will come back. Those people will be crying as they come back. But they will pray as I bring them back. I will lead those people by streams of water. I will lead them on an even road where they will not stumble. This is because I am Israel's father. And Israel is my firstborn son."

The New Agreement

"Look, the time is coming," says the Lord, "when I will make a new agreement. It will be with the people of Israel and the people of Judah. It will not be like the agreement I made with their ancestors. That was when I took them by the hand to bring them out of Egypt. I was a husband to them, but they broke that agreement. I will make this agreement with the people of Israel. I will put my teachings in their minds. And I will write them on their hearts. I will be their God, and they will be my people. People will no longer have to teach their neighbors and relatives to know the Lord. This is because all people will know me, from the least to the most important. I will forgive them for the wicked things they did. I will not remember their sins anymore."

The Good Branch

The Lord says, "The time is coming when I will do the things I promised. I made a special promise to the people of Israel and Judah. In those days and at that time, I will make a righteous branch sprout from David's family. He will do what is fair and right in the land. At this time Judah will be saved. The people of Jerusalem will live in safety. The branch will be named: The Lord Does What Is Right."

Jehoiakim Burns Jeremiah's Scroll

The Lord spoke his word to Jeremiah. This was during the fourth year that Jehoiakim son of Josiah was king of Judah. This was his message: "Jeremiah, get a scroll. Write on it all the words I have spoken to you about Israel and Judah and all the nations. Write everything I have spoken to you since Josiah was king until now. Maybe the family of Judah will hear what disasters I am planning to bring on them. And maybe they will stop doing wicked things. Then I would forgive them for the sins and the evil things they have done."

So Jeremiah called for Baruch. Jeremiah spoke the messages the Lord had given him. And Baruch wrote those messages on the scroll. Then Jeremiah said to Baruch, "I cannot go to the Temple of the Lord. I must stay here. So I want you to go to the Temple of the Lord. Go there on a day when the people are giving up eating. Read to all the people of Judah from the scroll. These people come into Jerusalem from the towns where they live. Read the messages from the Lord. Read the words that you wrote on the scroll as I spoke them to you. Perhaps they will ask the Lord to help them. Perhaps each one will stop doing wicked things. The Lord has announced that he is very angry with them." So Baruch did everything Jeremiah the prophet told him to do. He read aloud the scroll that had the Lord's messages written on it. He read it in the Lord's Temple.

A man named Micaiah heard all the messages from the Lord. Micaiah went down to the royal assistant's room in the king's palace. All of the officers were sitting there. Micaiah told those officers everything he had heard Baruch read from the scroll.

Then the officers went to the king in the courtyard and told him all about the scroll. So King Jehoiakim sent Jehudi to get the scroll. King Jehoiakim was sitting in the winter apartment. There was a fire burning in a small firepot in front of him. Jehudi began to read from the scroll. But after he had read three or four columns, the king cut those columns off of the scroll with a pen knife. And he threw them into the firepot. Finally, the whole scroll was burned in the fire. The king ordered some men to arrest Baruch the secretary and Jeremiah the prophet. But the Lord had hidden Baruch and Jeremiah.

The Lord spoke his word to Jeremiah. The Lord said: "Jeremiah, get another scroll. Write all the words on it that were on the first scroll. That was the scroll that Jehoiakim king of Judah burned up. Also say this to Jehoiakim king of Judah: 'This is what the Lord says: You burned up that scroll. So the Lord says this about Jehoiakim king of Judah: Jehoiakim's descendants will not sit on David's throne. When Jehoiakim dies, his body will be thrown out on the ground. It

will be left out in the heat of the day. And it will also be left in the cold frost of the night. I, the Lord, will punish Jehoiakim and his children. This is because they have not listened to me.'"

So Jeremiah took another scroll and gave it to Baruch. As Jeremiah spoke, Baruch wrote on the scroll. He wrote the same words that were on the scroll Jehoiakim king of Judah had burned in the fire. And many other words like those words were added to the second scroll.

Jeremiah in Prison

Nebuchadnezzar was king of Babylon. He appointed Zedekiah son of Josiah as king of Judah. Zedekiah took the place of Jehoiachin son of Jehoiakim. But Zedekiah, his servants and the people of Judah did not listen to the words of the Lord. The Lord had spoken his words through Jeremiah the prophet.

Now King Zedekiah sent a message to Jeremiah the prophet. This was the message: "Jeremiah, pray to the Lord our God for us."

At that time the Babylonian army had surrounded the city of Jerusalem so they could attack it. Then they had heard about the Egyptian army marching toward them. So the Babylonian army left Jerusalem to fight the Egyptian army.

The Lord spoke his word to Jeremiah the prophet: "This is what the Lord, the God of Israel, says: The Babylonian army will go back to Egypt. After that, the Babylonian army will come back here. And they will attack Jerusalem."

Now Jeremiah wanted to travel from Jerusalem to his home in the land of Benjamin. He was going there to get his share of the property that belonged to his family. Jeremiah got to the Benjamin Gate of Jerusalem. But then the captain in charge of the guards arrested him. The captain's name was Irijah. Irijah said, "You are leaving us to join the Babylonian side!"

Jeremiah said to Irijah, "That's not true! I am not leaving to join the Babylonians." But Irijah refused to listen to Jeremiah. So he arrested Jeremiah and took him to the officers of Jerusalem. Those rulers were very angry with Jeremiah. They gave an order for him to be beaten. Then they put him in prison. And Jeremiah was there for a long time.

The Fall of Jerusalem

This is how Jerusalem was captured:

Nebuchadnezzar king of Babylon marched against Jerusalem with his whole army. He surrounded the city to attack it. Then the city wall was broken through. And all the officers of the king of Babylon came into Jerusalem.

When Zedekiah king of Judah and all his soldiers saw them, they ran away. They left Jerusalem at night and went out from the king's garden. They went through the gate that was between the two walls. Then they headed toward the Jordan Valley. But the Babylonian army chased them. They caught up with Zedekiah in the plains of Jericho. They captured him and took him to Nebuchadnezzar king of Babylon. Nebuchadnezzar was at Riblah in the land of Hamath. There Nebuchadnezzar passed his sentence on Zedekiah. There at Riblah the king of Babylon killed Zedekiah's sons as he watched. And Nebuchadnezzar killed all the important officers of Judah as Zedekiah watched. Then he put out Zedekiah's eyes. He put bronze chains on Zedekiah and took him to Babylon.

The Babylonians set fire to the palace. And they set fire to the houses of the people of Jerusalem. And they broke down the walls around Jerusalem. Nebuzaradan was commander of the king's special guards. He took the people left in Jerusalem as captives. He also took those captives who had surrendered to him earlier. And he took the rest of the people of Jerusalem. He carried them all away to Babylon. But Nebuzaradan, commander of the guard, left some of the poor people of Judah behind. They were the people who owned nothing. So on that day he gave them vineyards and fields.

Nebuchadnezzar had given these orders about Jeremiah through Nebuzaradan, commander of the guard: "Find Jeremiah and take care of him. Do not hurt him. Give him whatever he asks for."

Jeremiah Is Set Free

When commander Nebuzaradan found Jeremiah, Nebuzaradan said to him, "The Lord your God announced this disaster would come to this place. And now the Lord has done everything he said he would do. This disaster happened because the people of Judah sinned against the Lord. You people did not obey the Lord. But now I will set you free. I am taking the chains off your wrists. If you want to, come with me to Babylon. And I will take good care of you. But if you don't want to come, then don't.

Look, the whole country is open to you." Before Jeremiah turned to leave, Nebuzaradan said, "Or go back to Gedaliah. The king of Babylon has chosen Gedaliah to be governor over the towns of Judah. Go and live with Gedaliah among the people. Or go anywhere you want."

Then Nebuzaradan gave Jeremiah some food and a present and let him go. So Jeremiah went to Gedaliah at Mizpah. And Jeremiah stayed with him there. He lived among the people who were left behind in Judah.

There were some officers and their men from the army of Judah. These men were still out in the open country. They heard that the king of Babylon had put Gedaliah in charge of the people who were left in the land: the men, women and children who were very poor. So these soldiers came to Gedaliah at Mizpah. They killed Gedaliah with a sword.

The Escape to Egypt

The other army officers were afraid that the Babylonians would be angry. They decided to run away to Egypt. All the people, from the least important to the greatest, went along, too. They also took Jeremiah the prophet and Baruch. So they all went to Egypt to the town of Tahpanhes.

Disaster in Egypt

Jeremiah received a message from the Lord. It was for all the Jews living in Egypt. This was the message: "The Lord of heaven's armies, the God of Israel, says: You saw the terrible things I brought on Jerusalem and the towns of Judah. There were a few left alive from Judah. They were determined to go to Egypt and settle there. But they will all die in Egypt. They will be killed in war or die from hunger. None of them will return to Judah, except a few people who escape."

WORTH WONDERING...

- What trouble did Jeremiah say was coming to God's people? And why was it coming?

- How did God's people treat Jeremiah?

- If you could meet Jeremiah today, what kind of questions would you like to ask him?

- Use your imagination for this one: Suppose you were one of the king's servants. And you were with him when he burned the scroll of Jeremiah. What kinds of things do you think you would see and hear and smell?

GREAT VERSES TO THINK ABOUT AGAIN...

Look back in Jeremiah to see if you can find these verses:

- *The person who trusts in the Lord will be blessed. The Lord will show him that he can be trusted. He will be strong, like a tree planted near water.*

- *I will make a righteous branch sprout from David's family. He will do what is fair and right in the land.*

- *I will lead those people by streams of water. I will lead them on an even road where they will not stumble. This is because I am Israel's father. And Israel is my firstborn son.*

AND THERE'S MORE...

When you read Jeremiah in a full Bible, look especially for...

- More words about false prophets, and about the sins of God's people.

- All the things that happened when Jerusalem finally was taken over by the Babylonian army.

The Book of
LAMENTATIONS

*Sad Songs
about Jerusalem*

Looking forward to Lamentations...

WHAT'S IT ABOUT?

"Sad Songs about Jerusalem"

SIGNS AND WONDERS

In this book we see tears of sorrow for the horrible punishment that came to Jerusalem. By including this book in the Bible, God tells us clearly that He does not enjoy having to punish His people.

Yes, Lamentations is a book of tears. But without great love, there can be no great sorrow. People who love God are sad when they know they have hurt Him. When He must punish them, they know that it doesn't make Him happy. But He loves us enough to punish us when we need it.

FACES AND PLACES

Jeremiah may be the writer of this book, but we don't know for sure.

Jerusalem was totally destroyed by the enemy army that took her people away. It happened that way only because the people of God kept on sinning against the Lord, even after He warned them again and again.

After God has punished us, I wonder how He wants us to feel — and I wonder how He feels ...

JERUSALEM ONCE was full of people. But now the city is empty. Jerusalem once was a great city among the nations. But now she has become like a widow. She was like a queen of all the other cities. But now she is a slave.

Jerusalem made herself dirty by her sins. She did not think about what would happen to her.

All of Jerusalem's people are groaning. They are looking for bread. They are giving away their precious things for food so they can stay alive.

Jerusalem reaches out her hands, but there is no one to comfort her.

The Lord Destroyed Jerusalem

Look how the Lord in his anger has brought Jerusalem to shame. He has thrown down the greatness of Israel from the sky to the earth.

The Lord has become like an enemy. He has swallowed up Israel. He has swallowed up all her palaces. He has destroyed all her strong places. He has caused more moaning and groaning for Judah.

He has destroyed his Temple as if it were a garden tent. He has destroyed the place where he met with his people. The enemy shouted in the Lord's Temple as if it were a feast day.

The Meaning of Suffering

I am a man who has seen the suffering that comes from the rod of the Lord's anger. He caused my flesh and skin to wear out. He broke my bones. He surrounded me and attacked me with sadness and grief.

Lord, remember my suffering and how I have no home. Remember the misery and suffering. I remember them well. And I am very sad. But I have hope when I think of this:

The Lord's love never ends. His mercies never stop. They are new every morning. Lord, your loyalty is great. I say to myself, "The Lord is what I have left. So I have hope."

The Lord is good to those who put their hope in him. He is good to those who look to him for help. It is good to wait quietly for the Lord to save.

The Lord will not reject his people forever. Although the Lord brings sorrow, he also has mercy. His love is great. The Lord does not like to punish people or make them sad.

Let us examine and look at what we have done. Then let us return to the Lord. Let us lift up our hands and pray from our hearts.

WORTH WONDERING...

■ What is the reason for the sadness in this book?

■ What do you do when you feel sad?

■ How do you think God can best help you when you feel sad?

■ Is it wrong to feel sad? Why or why not?

GREAT VERSES TO THINK ABOUT AGAIN...

Look back in Lamentations to see if you can find these verses:

■ *The Lord is good to those who put their hope in him. He is good to those who look to him for help. It is good to wait quietly for the Lord to save.*

■ *The Lord's love never ends. His mercies never stop. They are new every morning.*

AND THERE'S MORE...

When you read Lamentations in a full Bible, look especially for...

■ More words of sorrow because of the disaster in Jerusalem.

The Book of
EZEKIEL

God's Message
to the Captives

Looking forward to Ezekiel...

"God's Message to the Captives"

Ezekiel was in an early group of prisoners taken away from Israel to Babylon. The city of Jerusalem had not yet been destroyed. But God told Ezekiel it was surely going to happen. And in a vision God showed Ezekiel why it would happen. God also showed Ezekiel the picture of a brighter future.

Ezekiel also tells of a time when God will do something amazing inside each of His people. He will take out their hearts that are hard like stone. Then He will give them each a new heart of flesh. And He will give them His Spirit to live inside them. This promise points to Jesus in the New Testament, and to His Holy Spirit. His Spirit lives inside all who believe in Jesus.

Ezekiel was a young man, and a priest. His name means "strength of God."

Babylon: This was the capital of the great Babylonian empire. Ezekiel was speaking to the Jews who had already been taken to this city as prisoners before Jerusalem was destroyed. While Ezekiel talked to them, Jeremiah was talking to the people who were living in Jerusalem.

Kebar River: This was actually a canal that flowed into the big Euphrates River near Babylon. Many of the Jewish captives lived near it, and they met together on its banks.

As God punished His people, I wonder what He wanted them to know about healing and forgiveness...

IT WAS THE THIRTIETH YEAR of our captivity. I, Ezekiel, was by the Kebar River in Babylon. I was among the people who had been carried away as captives from the land of Judah. The sky opened, and I saw visions of God.

Ezekiel's Vision

When I looked, I saw a stormy wind coming from the north. There was a great cloud with a bright light around it. Fire was flashing out of it. And there was something that looked like glowing metal in the center of the fire. Inside the cloud were what looked like four living creatures. They were shaped like men. Each of them had four faces. And each of them had four wings. Their legs were straight. Their feet were like a calf's hoofs. And they sparkled like polished bronze. The living creatures had men's hands. They were under their wings on their four sides.

Their faces looked like this: In front each living creature had the face of a man. Each one had the face of a lion on the right side. Each one had the face of an ox on the left side. And in back each one had the face of an eagle. The living creatures looked like burning coals of fire. They were like torches. Fire went back and forth among the living creatures. It was bright, and lightning flashed from it. The living creatures ran back and forth like bolts of lightning.

And I saw a wheel on the ground by each of the living creatures with its four faces. The wheels looked like one wheel crossways inside another wheel. I saw the rims of the wheels. The rims were full of eyes all around.

When the living creatures moved, the wheels moved beside them. When the living creatures were lifted up from the ground, the wheels also were lifted up. Wherever the spirit would go, the living creatures would go. And the wheels were lifted up beside them. This is because the spirit of the living creatures was in the wheels. When the living creatures moved, the wheels moved. When the living creatures stopped, the wheels stopped. And when the living creatures were lifted from the ground, the wheels were lifted beside them.

Now there was something like a dome over the heads of the living creatures. It sparkled like ice and was frightening. And under the dome the wings of the living creatures were stretched out straight toward one another. I heard the sound of their wings as they moved. It was like the roaring sound of the sea. It was like the voice of God All-Powerful. It was a roaring sound like a noisy army.

And a voice came from above the dome over the heads of the living creatures. When the living creatures stood still, they lowered their wings. Now above the dome there was something that looked like a throne. It looked like a sapphire gem. And on the throne was a shape like a man. Then I noticed what he looked like from the waist up. He looked like glowing metal with fire inside it. And from his waist down he looked like fire. I saw a bright light all around him. The glow around him looked like the rainbow in the clouds on a rainy day. It seemed to look like the glory of the Lord. So when I saw it, I bowed face-down on the ground. And I heard a voice speaking.

The Lord Speaks to Ezekiel

He said to me, "Human being, stand up on your feet. Then I will speak with you." While he spoke to me, the Spirit entered me and put me on my feet. Then I heard the Lord speaking to me.

He said, "Human being, I am sending you to the people of Israel. They are a nation of people who turned against me. I am sending you to people who are stubborn. They do not obey. You will say this to them, 'This is what the Lord God says.' The people may listen, or they may not. But whatever they do, they will know that a prophet has been among them. You, human being, don't be afraid of the people or their words. Thorny branches and thorns may be all around you. And you may live with insects that sting with poison. Don't be afraid of their words. Don't be afraid of their looks. But speak my words to them. Open your mouth and eat what I am giving you."

I looked and saw a hand stretched out to me. A scroll was in the hand. The Lord opened the scroll in front of me. The scroll was written on the front and back. Funeral songs, sad writings and troubles were written on the scroll.

Then the Lord said to me, "Human being, eat what you find. Eat this scroll. Then go and speak to the people of Israel." So I opened my mouth, and the Lord gave me the scroll. Then I ate it. And it was sweet like honey in my mouth.

Then the Spirit lifted me up. And I heard a loud rumbling sound behind me. A voice said, "Praise God in heaven." I felt the great power of the Lord. I came to the captives from Judah. They lived by the Kebar River. I sat there seven days

where these people lived. I was shocked.

Israel's Warning

After seven days the Lord spoke his word to me again. He said, "Human being, I have made you a watchman for Israel. Any time you hear a word from my mouth, warn them for me. When I say to an evil person, 'You will surely die,' you must warn him. If you don't speak out to warn the evil person to leave his evil way, he will die in his sin. But I will hold you responsible for his death. You must warn the evil person."

A Vision of Jerusalem

I was sitting in my house with the older leaders of Judah before me. There I felt the power of the Lord God. I looked and saw something that looked like a man. From his waist down he looked like fire. From his waist up he looked like bright glowing metal. He stretched out the shape of a hand. And he caught me by the hair on my head. The Spirit lifted me up between the earth and the sky. He took me in the visions of God to Jerusalem. He took me to the Temple.

Then the Lord brought me to the entry of the courtyard. When I looked, I saw a hole in the wall. The Lord said to me, "Human being, dig through the wall." So I dug through the wall and saw an entrance.

Then the Lord said to me, "Go in and see the terrible, evil things they are doing here." So I entered and looked. And I saw pictures of every kind of crawling thing. I saw awful beasts and all the idols of the people of Israel. They were carved on the wall all around. Seventy of the older leaders of Israel were standing there. Each man had his pan for burning incense in his hand.

Then the Lord said to me, "Human being, have you seen what the older leaders of Israel are doing in the dark? They say, 'The Lord doesn't see us. The Lord has left the land.'" And he said to me, "You will see even more terrible things that they are doing."

Then the Lord brought me into the inner courtyard of the Temple. And I saw about 25 men. They faced east. They were worshiping the sun in the east.

The Lord said to me, "Do you see, human being? Look, they are insulting me every way they can. So I will act in anger. I will have no pity. I will not show mercy. Even if they shout in my ears, I won't listen to them."

Then the glory of the Lord left the Temple, and went up from inside Jerusalem. It stopped on the mountain on the east side of the city. The Spirit lifted me up. And he brought me to the captives who had been taken from Judah to Babylonia. He did this in a vision given by the Spirit of God. Then the vision I had seen ended. And I told the things that the Lord had shown me. I told it to the captives from Judah.

The Lord's Kindness to Jerusalem

The Lord spoke his word to me. He said: "Human being, tell Jerusalem about her hated actions. Say, 'This is what the Lord God says to Jerusalem: On the day you were born, you were not washed with water for cleansing. You were not wrapped in cloths. No one felt sorry for you. No one would do any of these things for you. No, you were thrown out into the open field. This is because you were hated on the day you were born.

"'Then I passed by and saw you kicking about in your blood. I said to you, "Live!" I made you grow like a plant in the field. You grew up and became tall. You grew up and became like a beautiful jewel. You became mine.

"'Then I put beautiful clothes on you. I put sandals of fine leather on your feet. I wrapped you in fine linen and covered you with silk. I put jewelry on you. I put bracelets on your arms and a necklace around your neck. And I put a beautiful crown on your head. So you wore gold and silver. You ate fine flour, honey and olive oil. You were very beautiful and became a queen. Then you became famous among the nations because you were so beautiful. Your beauty was perfect, because of the glory I gave you.

"'But you trusted in your beauty. You took your beautiful jewelry. It was made from gold and silver I had given you. Then you made for yourselves idols. You gave my oil and incense as an offering to them. You took the fine flour, oil and honey I gave you to eat. And you offered them before the false gods as a pleasing smell. This is what happened.

"'How terrible! How terrible it will be for you. This is what you did after all these evil things. You built yourself a place to worship false gods.

"'So, hear the word of the Lord. I will punish you as murderers are punished. I will put you to death because I am angry and jealous. Then I will rest from my anger against you.

I will stop being jealous. I will be quiet and not angry anymore.

"'This is what the Lord God says: I will give you what you should have. You hated and broke the agreement. But I will remember my agreement I made with you when you were young. And you will know that I am the Lord. You will remember and be ashamed. This is because I will forgive you for all the things you have done.'"

The Lord Acts for Himself

The Lord spoke his word to me again. He said: "Human being, the nation of Israel was living in their own land. But they made it unclean by their ways and the things they did. So I poured out my anger against them. I scattered them among the nations. And they dishonored my holy name in the nations where they went. The nations said about them: 'These are the people of the Lord. But they had to leave the land which he gave them.' But I felt bad about my holy name. The nation of Israel had dishonored it among the nations where they went.

"So say to the people of Israel, 'This is what the Lord God says: Israel, I am going to act, but not for your sake. Israel, I will do something to help my holy name. You have dishonored it among the nations where you went. I will prove the holiness of my great name.

"'I will take you from the nations. I will gather you out of all the lands. And I will bring you back into your own land. Then I will sprinkle clean water on you, and you will be clean. I will cleanse you from all your uncleanness and your idols. Also, I will teach you to respect me completely. I will put a new way to think inside you. I will take out the stubborn heart like stone from your bodies. And I will give you an obedient heart of flesh. I will put my Spirit inside you. And I will help you live by my rules. You will be careful to obey my laws. Then you will live in the land I gave to your ancestors. So you will be my people, and I will be your God.'"

The Vision of Dry Bones

I felt the power of the Lord was on me. He brought me out by the Spirit of the Lord. And he put me down in the middle of a valley. It was full of bones. The Lord led me around among the bones. I saw the bones were very dry. Then he asked me, "Human being, can these bones live?"

I answered, "Lord God, only you know."

The Lord said to me, "Prophesy to these bones. Say to them, 'Dry bones, hear the word of the Lord. This is what the Lord God says to the bones: I will put muscles on you. I will put flesh on you. I will cover you with skin. Then I will put breath in you, and you will live. Then you will know that I am the Lord.'"

So I prophesied as I was commanded. While I prophesied, there was a noise and a rattling. The bones came together, bone to bone. I looked and saw muscles come on the bones. Flesh grew, and skin covered the bones. But there was no breath in them.

Then the Lord said to me, "Prophesy to the wind. Prophesy, human being, and say to the wind: 'This is what the Lord God says: Wind, come from the four winds. Breathe on these people who were killed so they can live again.'" So I prophesied as the Lord commanded me. And the breath came into them, and they came to life. They stood on their feet. They were a very large army.

Then the Lord said to me: "Human being, these bones are like all the people of Israel. They say, 'Our bones are dried up, and our hope has gone. We are destroyed.' So, prophesy, and say to them: 'This is what the Lord God says: My people, I will open your graves. And I will cause you to come up out of your graves. Then I will bring you into the land of Israel. This is how you, my people, will know that I am the Lord. I will open your graves and cause you to come up from them. And I will put my Spirit inside you. You will come to life. Then I will put you in your own land. And you will know that I, the Lord, have spoken and done it, says the Lord.'"

The New Temple

It was the twenty-fifth year of our captivity. It was at the beginning of the year, on the tenth day of the month. On that same day I felt the power of the Lord. He brought me to Jerusalem. In the visions of God he brought me into the land of Israel. He put me on a very high mountain. On the south of the mountain there were some buildings that looked like a city. The Lord took me closer to the buildings. I saw a man who looked as if he were made of bronze. He was standing in the gateway. He had a cord made of linen and a stick in his hand, both for measuring. The man said to me, "Human being, look with your eyes and hear with your ears. And pay attention to all that I will show you. That's why you have been brought here. Tell the people of Israel all that you see."

The man finished measuring inside the Temple. Then he brought me out through the east gate. He measured the Temple on all four sides. The Temple had a wall all around it. It was 875 feet long and 875 feet wide.

The Lord Among His People

The man led me to the outer east gate. And I saw the greatness of the God of Israel coming from the east. God's voice was like the roar of rushing water. His greatness made the earth shine. I saw a vision. It was like the vision I had seen by the Kebar River. I bowed facedown on the ground. The greatness of the Lord came into the Temple through the east gate.

Then the Spirit picked me up. And he brought me into the inner courtyard. There the Lord's greatness filled the Temple. The man stood at my side. I heard someone speaking to me from inside the Temple. The voice from the Temple said to me, "Human being, this is my throne. And this is the place my feet rest. I will live here among the Israelites forever. The people of Israel will not make my holy name unclean again.

"Human being, tell the people of Israel about the Temple. Then they will be ashamed of their sins. Let them know the design of the Temple. Let them know how it is built."

WORTH WONDERING...

- How would you describe in your own words the vision of wheels and creatures that Ezekiel saw at the beginning of this book?

- What did Ezekiel see inside the Temple in Jerusalem, when the Lord first took him there in a vision?

- What did God want Ezekiel to understand when He showed him the valley of dry bones?

- What did God want Ezekiel to understand when He showed him the new Temple?

GREAT VERSES TO THINK ABOUT AGAIN...

Look back in Ezekiel to see if you can find these verses:

- *I will put a new way to think inside you. I will take out the stubborn heart like stone from your bodies. And I will give you an obedient heart of flesh. I will put my Spirit inside you.*

- *I will open your graves and cause you to come up from them. And I will put my Spirit inside you. You will come to life.*

- *I have made you a watchman for Israel. Any time you hear a word from my mouth, warn them for me.*

AND THERE'S MORE...

When you read Ezekiel in a full Bible, look especially for...

- The many strange things God asked Ezekiel to do. Ezekiel did these to get the attention of God's people so they would listen to His message.

- More amazing details from the visions that God gave Ezekiel.

- Ezekiel's message about the final battle at the end of the world.

- All the details about the new Temple that Ezekiel sees in a vision.

The Book of
DANIEL

A Man
of Adventure

Looking forward to Daniel...

"A Man of Adventure"

As a young man, Daniel had been taken captive from Jerusalem to Babylon. He was a man of courage. Like Joseph in Egypt many centuries earlier, Daniel became a leader in the land where he was taken captive.

Daniel: His name means "God is my judge." His Babylonian name was Belteshazzar.

Shadrach, Meshach, and **Abednego:** Like Daniel, these were young Hebrew men who were brought as prisoners from Jerusalem to serve the king in Babylon. Their Hebrew names were Hananiah, Mishael, and Azariah.

Nebuchadnezzar: The greatest king of the Babylonian Empire.

Belshazzar: A Babylonian king who followed Nebuchadnezzar.

Darius: A king from the land of the Medes. He took over the Babylonian Empire.

Cyrus: A later Persian king who took over Babylon. He is also mentioned in the books of 2 Chronicles and Ezra.

Ashpenaz: The chief officer of King Nebuchadnezzar. He was in charge of Daniel and the other young Hebrew men.

I wonder what God can do for someone who is fully loyal to Him...

NEBUCHADNEZZAR king of Babylon came to Jerusalem and surrounded it with his army.

Then King Nebuchadnezzar gave an order to Ashpenaz, his chief officer. He told Ashpenaz to bring some of the Israelite men into his house. He wanted them to be from important families. And he wanted those who were from the family of the king of Judah. King Nebuchadnezzar wanted only healthy, young, Israelite men. These men were not to have anything wrong with their bodies. They were to be handsome and well educated. They were to be able to learn and understand things. He wanted those who were able to serve in his palace. Ashpenaz was to teach them the language and writings of the Babylonians. The king gave the young men a certain amount of food and wine every day. That was the same kind of food that the king ate. They were to be trained for three years. Then the young men would become servants of the king of Babylon. Among those young men were some from the people of Judah. These were Daniel, Hananiah, Mishael and Azariah.

Then Ashpenaz, the chief officer, gave them Babylonian names. Daniel's new name was Belteshazzar. Hananiah's was Shadrach. Mishael's was Meshach. And Azariah's new name was Abednego.

Daniel decided not to eat the

king's food and wine because that would make him unclean. So he asked Ashpenaz for permission not to make himself unclean in this way.

God made Ashpenaz want to be kind and merciful to Daniel. But Ashpenaz said to Daniel, "I am afraid of my master, the king. He ordered me to give you this food and drink. If you don't eat this food, you will begin to look worse than other young men your age. The king will see this. And he will cut off my head because of you."

Ashpenaz had ordered a guard to watch Daniel, Hananiah, Mishael and Azariah. Daniel said to the guard, "Please give us this test for ten days: Don't give us anything but vegetables to eat and water to drink. Then after ten days compare us with the other young men who eat the king's food. See for yourself who looks healthier. Then you judge for yourself how you want to treat us, your servants."

So the guard agreed to test them for ten days. After ten days they looked very healthy. They looked better than all of the young men who ate the king's food. So the guard took away the king's special food and wine. He gave Daniel, Hananiah,

Mishael and Azariah vegetables instead.

God gave these four men wisdom and the ability to learn. They learned many kinds of things people had written and studied. Daniel could also understand all kinds of visions and dreams.

The end of the three years came. And Ashpenaz brought all of the young men to King Nebuchadnezzar. The king talked to them. He found that none of the young men were as good as Daniel, Hananiah, Mishael and Azariah. So those four young men became the king's servants. Every time the king asked them about something important, they showed much wisdom and understanding. He found they were ten times better than all the fortune-tellers and magicians in his kingdom.

The Gold Idol and Blazing Furnace

Now King Nebuchadnezzar had a gold statue made. That statue was 90 feet high and 9 feet wide. He set up the statue on the plain of Dura in the area of Babylon. Then the king called the important leaders and all officers in his kingdom. He wanted these men to come to the special service for the statue he had set up. So they all came for the special service. And they stood in front of the statue that King Nebuchadnezzar had set up. Then the man who made announcements for the king spoke in a loud voice. He said, "People, nations and men of every language, this is what you are commanded to do: You will hear the sound of musical instruments. When this happens, you must bow down and worship the gold statue. Anyone who doesn't will be quickly thrown into a blazing furnace."

Now people, nations and men who spoke every language were there. And they heard the sound of the musical instruments. So they bowed down and worshiped the gold statue that King Nebuchadnezzar had set up.

Then some Babylonians came up to the king. They began speaking against the men of Judah. They said to King Nebuchadnezzar, "Our king, there are some men of Judah who did not pay attention to your order. Their names are Shadrach, Meshach and Abednego. They do not worship the gold statue you have set up."

So those men were brought to the king. And Nebuchadnezzar said, "Shadrach, Meshach and Abednego, is it true that you do not serve my gods? And is it true that you did not worship the gold statue I have set up? If you do not worship it, you will be thrown quickly into the blazing furnace. Then no god will be able to save you from my power!"

Shadrach, Meshach and Abednego answered the king. They said, "Nebuchadnezzar, we do not need to defend ourselves to you. You can throw us into the blazing furnace. The God we serve is able to save us from the furnace and your power. If he does this, it is good. But even if God does not save us, we want you, our king, to know this: We will not serve your gods. We will not worship the gold statue you have set up."

Then Nebuchadnezzar was furious with Shadrach, Meshach and Abednego. He ordered the furnace to be heated seven times hotter than usual. Then he commanded some of the strongest soldiers in his army to tie up Shadrach, Meshach and Abednego. The king told the soldiers to throw them into the blazing furnace.

So Shadrach, Meshach and Abednego were tied up and thrown into the blazing furnace. The fire was so hot that the flames killed the strong soldiers who took Shadrach, Meshach and Abednego there. Firmly tied, Shadrach, Meshach and Abednego fell into the blazing furnace.

Then King Nebuchadnezzar was very surprised and jumped to his feet. He asked the men who advised him, "Didn't we tie up only three men? Didn't we throw them into the fire?"

They answered, "Yes, our king."

The king said, "Look! I see four men. They are walking around in the fire. They are not tied up, and they are not burned. The fourth man looks like a son of the gods."

Then Nebuchadnezzar went to the opening of the blazing furnace. He shouted, "Shadrach, Meshach and Abednego, come out! Servants of the Most High God, come here!"

So Shadrach, Meshach and Abednego came out of the fire. When they came out, the princes, assistant governors, governors and royal advisers crowded around them. They saw that the fire had not harmed their bodies. Their hair was not burned. Their robes were not burned. And they didn't even smell like smoke.

Then Nebuchadnezzar said, "Praise the God of Shadrach, Meshach and Abednego. Their

God has sent his angel and saved his servants from the fire! These three men trusted their God. They refused to obey my command. And they were willing to die rather than serve or worship any god other than their own. So I now make this law: The people of any nation or language must not say anything against the God of Shadrach, Meshach and Abednego. Anyone who does will be torn apart. And his house will be turned into a pile of stones. No other god can save his people like this." Then the king promoted Shadrach, Meshach and Abednego in the area of Babylon.

Belshazzar and the Writing on the Wall

King Belshazzar gave a big banquet for 1,000 royal guests. And he drank wine with them. As Belshazzar was drinking his wine, he gave an order to his servants. He told them to bring the gold and silver cups that his ancestor Nebuchadnezzar had taken from the Temple in Jerusalem. King Belshazzar wanted his royal guests to drink from those cups. So they brought the gold cups. As they were drinking, they praised their gods. Those gods were made from gold, silver, bronze, iron, wood and stone.

Then suddenly a person's hand appeared. The fingers wrote words on the plaster on the wall. This was near the lampstand in the royal palace. The king watched the hand as it wrote.

King Belshazzar was very frightened. His face turned white, and his knees knocked together. He could not stand up because his legs were too weak. The king called for the magicians and wise men to be brought to him. He said to the wise men of Babylon, "I will give a reward to anyone who can read this writing and explain it. I will give him purple clothes fit for a king. I will put a gold chain around his neck. And I will make him the third highest ruler in the kingdom."

So all the king's wise men came in. But they could not read the writing. And they could not tell the king what it meant. King Belshazzar became even more afraid. His face became even whiter. His royal guests were confused.

Then the king's mother came into the banquet room. She had heard the voices of the king and his royal guests. She said, "My king, there is a man in your kingdom who has under-standing, knowledge and wisdom. Your father, King Nebuchadnezzar, put this man in charge of all the wise men. The man I am talking about is named Daniel. The king gave him the name Belteshazzar. He could explain dreams and secrets. He could answer very hard problems. Call for Daniel. He will tell you what the writing on the wall means."

So they brought Daniel to the king. The king said to him, "I have heard that you are very smart and have knowledge and understanding. Read this writing on the wall and explain it to me. If you can, I will give you purple clothes fit for a king. And I will put a gold chain around your neck. And you will become the third highest ruler in the kingdom."

Then Daniel answered the king, "You may keep your gifts for yourself. I will read the writing on the wall for you. And I will explain to you what it means.

"My king, the Most High God made your father Nebuchad-nezzar a great, important and powerful king. If he wanted a person to die, he put that person to death. And if he wanted a person to live, he let that person live.

"But Nebuchadnezzar

became too proud and stubborn. So he was taken off his royal throne. His glory was taken away. Then Nebuchadnezzar was forced away from people. His mind became like the mind of an animal. He lived with the wild donkeys and was fed grass like an ox. He became wet with dew. These things happened to him until he learned his lesson: The Most High God rules over the kingdoms of men. And the Most High God sets anyone he wants over those kingdoms.

"But, Belshazzar, you have turned against the Lord of heaven. You ordered the drinking cups from the Temple of the Lord to be brought to you. Then you and your royal guests drank wine from them. You praised the gods of silver, gold, bronze, iron, wood and stone. They are not really gods. They cannot see or hear or understand anything. But you did not honor God. He is the One who has power over your life and everything you do. So God sent the hand that wrote on the wall.

"These are the words that were written on the wall: 'Mene, mene, tekel, parsin.'

"This is what these words mean: Mene: God has counted the days until your kingdom will end. Tekel: You have been weighed on the scales and found not good enough. Parsin: Your kingdom is being divided. It will be given to the Medes and the Persians."

That very same night Belshazzar, king of the Babylonian people, was killed. A man named Darius the Mede became the new king.

Daniel and the Lions

Darius thought it would be a good idea to choose 120 governors. They would rule through all of his kingdom. And he chose three men as supervisors over those 120 governors. Daniel was one of these three supervisors. The king set up these men so that he would not be cheated. Daniel showed that he could do the work better than the other supervisors and the governors. Because of this, the king planned to put Daniel in charge of the whole kingdom. So the other supervisors and the governors tried to find reasons to accuse Daniel. But he went on doing the business of the government. And they could not find anything wrong with him. So they could not accuse him of doing anything wrong. Daniel was trustworthy. He was not lazy and did not cheat the king. Finally these men said, "We will never find any reason to accuse Daniel. But we must find something to complain about. It will have to be about the law of his God."

So the supervisors and the governors went as a group to the king. They said: "King Darius, the people who advise you and the captains of the soldiers have all agreed on something. We think the king should make this law that everyone would have to obey: No one should pray to any god or man except to you, our king. This should be done for the next 30 days. Anyone who doesn't obey will be thrown into the lions' den. Now, our king, make the law. Write it down so it cannot be changed. The laws of the Medes and Persians cannot be canceled." So King Darius made the law and had it written.

When Daniel heard that the new law had been written, he went to his house. He went to his upstairs room. The windows of that room opened toward Jerusalem. Three times each day Daniel got down on his knees and prayed. He prayed and thanked God, just as he always had done.

Then those men went as a group and found Daniel. They saw him praying and asking God for help. So they went to the king. They said, "Didn't you write a law that says no one may pray to any god or man except you, our king? Doesn't it say that anyone who disobeys during the next 30 days will be thrown into the lions' den?"

The king answered, "Yes, I wrote that law. And the laws of the Medes and Persians cannot be canceled."

Then those men spoke to the king. They said, "Daniel is not paying attention to the law you wrote. Daniel still prays to his God three times every day." The king became very upset when he heard this. He decided he had to save Daniel. He worked until sunset trying to think of a way to save him.

Then those men went as a group to the king. They said, "Remember, our king, the law of the Medes and Persians. It says that no law or command given by the king can be changed."

So King Darius gave the order. They brought Daniel and threw him into the lions' den. The king said to Daniel, "May the God you serve all the time save you!" A big stone was brought. It was put over the opening of the lions' den. Then the king used his signet ring to put his special seal on the rock. And he used the rings of his royal officers to put their seals on the rock also. This showed that no one could move that rock and bring Daniel out. Then King Darius went back to his palace. He did not eat that night. He did not have any entertainment brought to entertain him. And he could not sleep.

The next morning King Darius got up at dawn. He hurried to the lions' den. As he came near the den, he was worried. He called out to Daniel. He said, "Daniel, servant of the living God! Has your God that you always worship been able to save you from the lions?"

Daniel answered, "My king, live forever! My God sent his angel to close the lions' mouths. They have not hurt me, because my God knows I am innocent. I never did anything wrong to you, my king."

King Darius was very happy. He told his servants to lift Daniel out of the lions' den. So they lifted him out and did not find any injury on him. This was because Daniel had trusted in his God.

Then the king gave a command. The men who had accused Daniel were brought to the lions' den and thrown into it. Their wives and children were also thrown into it. The lions grabbed them before they hit the floor of the den. And the lions crushed their bones.

Then King Darius wrote a letter. It was to all people and all nations, to those who spoke every language in the world:

All of you must fear and respect the God of Daniel.

Daniel's God is the living God. He lives forever. His kingdom will never be destroyed. His rule will never end. God rescues and saves people. God does mighty miracles in heaven and on earth. God saved Daniel from the power of the lions.

So Daniel was successful during the time that Darius was king. This was also the time that Cyrus the Persian was king.

A Vision of a Man

During Cyrus' third year as king of Persia, I was standing beside the great Tigris River. I looked up. And I saw a man. His face was bright like lightning, and his eyes were like fire.

He said, "Daniel, don't be afraid. God loves you very much. Peace be with you. Be strong now, be strong"

"Daniel, there will be a time of much trouble. It will be the worst time since nations have been on earth. But everyone whose name is written in God's book will be saved. The wise people will shine like the brightness of the sky. Those who teach others to live right will shine like stars forever and ever.

"As for you, Daniel, go your way till the end. You will get your rest when you die. And at the end you will rise from the dead to get your reward."

WORTH WONDERING...

- Use your imagination for this one: If you were there when Daniel was thrown in with the lions, what kinds of things do you think you would see and hear and smell?

- Why do you think Daniel was so brave? What makes a person brave?

- In this book of Daniel, how do you see that God is great? And how do you see that He is good?

- Which parts of this book would you most like to know more about?

- If you could meet Daniel today, what kind of questions would you like to ask him?

- Think about some friends you have who might know very little about Jesus or the Bible. What parts of this book do you think would be most interesting to them?

GREAT VERSES TO THINK ABOUT AGAIN...

Look back in Daniel to see if you can find these verses:

- *But you did not honor God. He is the One who has power over your life and everything you do.*

- *God rescues and saves people. God does mighty miracles in heaven and on earth.*

- *The God we serve is able to save us from the furnace and your power. If he does this, it is good. But even if God does not save us, we want you, our king, to know this: We will not serve your gods.*

- *God gave these four men wisdom and the ability to learn.*

AND THERE'S MORE...

When you read Daniel in a full Bible, look especially for...

- Nebuchadnezzar's amazing dreams, and how Daniel was able to interpret them.

- More of Daniel's amazing visions about the future — including the end of the world.

INTRODUCING...

HOSEA • JOEL • AMOS • OBADIAH • JONAH
MICAH • NAHUM • HABAKKUK • ZEPHANIAH
HAGGAI • ZECHARIAH • MALACHI

T hese last twelve books of the Old Testament are Prophecy Books. We sometimes call them the Minor Prophets, because they are shorter than the books we call the Major Prophets (the books from Isaiah to Daniel).

The Lord often allowed these prophets to look into the future. It was as if they were looking through a huge telescope across all time. God's people were facing terrible destruction and captivity at the hands of their enemies. But the prophets could see beyond that. Looking far into the future, the prophets saw some amazingly good things for God's people. And God gave them great and wonderful promises of these good things to come.

We can read about these promises and good things here in the Prophets, more than in any other part of the Old Testament. Many of these promises were about a special man. That man was Jesus. Hundreds of years before Jesus actually came to live on the earth, God let the prophets see it happening. They saw that Jesus would be born in the town of Bethlehem. They saw that He would suffer and die for the sins of the world. They saw that He would then be alive and would someday come back to rule the earth's people as a mighty King.

The Book of
HOSEA

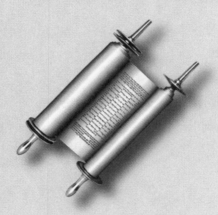

God's
Faithfulness

Looking forward to Hosea...

WHAT'S IT ABOUT?

"God's Faithfulness"

SIGNS AND WONDERS

God is faithful to love His people, even when His people are not faithful to Him.

FACES AND PLACES

Hosea was a prophet to Israel, the Northern Kingdom. His name means "salvation" in the Hebrew language.

I wonder what it means that God is faithful...

WHEN ISRAEL was a child, I loved him. And I called my son out of Egypt.

But the more I called to the people of Israel, the further they went from me. They burned incense to the idols. But it was I who taught Israel to walk. I took them by the arms. I led them with cords of human kindness, with ties of love. I lifted the yoke from their neck. I bent down and fed them.

Israel, I don't want to give you up. I don't want to go away and leave you. My heart beats for you. My love for you stirs up my pity. I won't punish you in my anger. I won't destroy Israel again. I am God and not man. I am the Holy One, and I am among you. I will not come against you in anger. I will call for my people like a lion calling for its young. My children will come and follow me. I will settle them again in their homes, says the Lord.

Israel Returns to God

Israel, return to the Lord your God. Your sins have caused your ruin. Come back to the Lord and say these words to him: "Take away all our sin and kindly receive us."

The Lord says, "I will forgive them for leaving me. I will love them freely. I am not angry with them anymore. I will be like the dew to Israel. It will blossom like a lily. Like the cedar trees in Lebanon, its roots will be firm.

The people will be like spreading branches. They will be like the beautiful olive trees. They will be like the sweet-smelling cedars in Lebanon.

The people of Israel will again live under my protection. They will grow like the grain. They will bloom like a vine. They will be as famous as the wine of Lebanon. Israel, have nothing to do with idols. I, the Lord, am the one who answers your prayers. I am the one who watches over you. I am like a green pine tree. Your blessings come from me."

A wise person will know these things. An understanding person will take them to heart. The Lord's ways are right. Good people live by following them, but those who turn against God die because of them.

WORTH WONDERING...

- What does this book show about God's feelings for His people Israel?
- What does this book show us about God's forgiveness?

GREAT VERSES TO THINK ABOUT AGAIN...

Look back in Hosea to see if you can find these verses:

- *It was I who taught Israel to*

walk. I took them by the arms. I led them with cords of human kindness, with ties of love.

- *I will call for my people like a lion calling for its young.*

AND THERE'S MORE...

When you read Hosea in a full Bible, look especially for...

- How God told Hosea to marry Gomer, an unfaithful woman. Even after she was unfaithful to him, Hosea took her back into his home.
- Hosea's children. Two of them have names that mean "Not Pitied" and "Not My People" in the Hebrew language

The Book of
JOEL

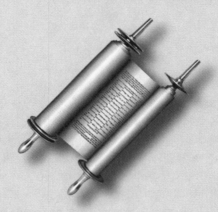

*God Punishes
and Restores*

Looking forward to Joel...

"God Punishes and Restores"

The prophet Joel spoke about the coming "day of the Lord" when God would judge all sin.

He also spoke of a swarm of locusts that would eat up all the crops in the land. This plague of locusts was a good picture for God's people of His coming punishment for them.

Joel also spoke of good things in the future. He spoke of a time when God will give His Spirit freely to all kinds of people. This promise is fulfilled in a big way in the book of Acts. That book tells of the day when the Holy Spirit came down to fill the followers of Jesus. In a sermon that day, Peter spoke words from the book of Joel to explain to everyone what was happening.

Joel was a prophet in Judah, the Southern Kingdom. Joel's name means "The Lord is strong."

I wonder what punishment God has planned for the world...and what will follow the punishment...

THE LORD SPOKE his word to Joel: "Listen to me, all you people who live in the land. What the cutting locusts have not eaten, the swarming locusts have eaten. And what the swarming locusts have left, the hopping locusts have eaten. And what the hopping locusts have left, the destroying locusts have eaten."

Our food is taken away while we watch. Joy and happiness are gone from the Temple of our God. We planted seeds, but they lie dry and dead in the dirt. Our barns are empty and falling down. The storerooms for grain have been broken down. This is because the grain has dried up. The animals are hungry and groaning! The herds of cattle wander around confused. They have no grass to eat. Even the flocks of sheep suffer. Lord, I am calling to you for help. Fire has burned up the open pastures. Flames have burned all the trees in the field. Wild animals also need your help. The water in the streams has dried up. Fire has burned up the open pastures.

Change Your Hearts

The Lord says, "Now, come back to me with all your heart. Go without food, and cry and be sad."

Tearing your clothes is not enough to show you are sad. Let your heart be broken. Come back to the Lord your God. He is kind and shows mercy. He doesn't become angry quickly.

He has great love. He would rather forgive than punish. Who knows? Maybe the Lord will change his mind and leave behind a blessing for you. Then you may give grain and drink offerings to the Lord your God.

The Lord Restores the Land

Then the Lord became concerned about his land. He felt sorry for his people. The Lord said to them: "I will send you grain, wine and olive oil. You will have plenty. No more will I shame you among the nations.

"After this, I will give my Spirit freely to all kinds of people. Your sons and daughters will prophesy. Your old men will dream dreams. Your young men will see visions. At that time I will give my Spirit even to servants, both men and women. I will show miracles in the sky and on the earth: blood, fire and thick smoke. The sun will become dark. The moon will become red as blood. And then the Lord's overwhelming and terrible day of judging will come."

WORTH WONDERING...

■ From what you see in this book, what would it be like to be invaded by an army of locusts?

■ What would you say is the most important thing God says in this book?

A GREAT VERSE TO THINK ABOUT AGAIN...

Look back in Joel to see if you can find this verse:

■ *Come back to the Lord your God. He is kind and shows mercy. He doesn't become angry quickly. He has great love. He would rather forgive than punish.*

AND THERE'S MORE...

When you read Joel in a full Bible, look especially for...

■ More details about the plague of locusts upon the land.

■ God's words about punishment for the enemies of God's people.

The Book of
AMOS

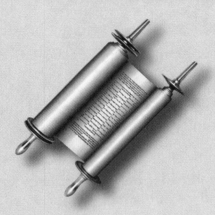

Warnings to
Stop Sinning

Looking forward to Amos...

WHAT'S IT ABOUT?

"Warnings to Stop Sinning"

SIGNS AND WONDERS

Sin must bring punishment. Why? Because God is right and fair. He never gives punishment when it isn't deserved.

Amos was a prophet at a time when Israel was rich and safe. But God saw that the rich leaders and people were dishonest and cruel to the poor.

FACES AND PLACES

Amos was a prophet in Israel, the Northern Kingdom. Amos was a farmer, and his name means "burdened" or "loaded down."

I wonder how important it is to God for me to be fair and kind to others...

THE LORD WILL ROAR like a lion from Jerusalem. His loud voice will sound like a growl from Jerusalem.

Israel Is Punished

This is what the Lord says: "For the many crimes Israel is doing, I will punish them. They walk on poor people as if they were dirt. They refuse to be fair to those who are suffering.

"So get ready to meet your God, Israel."

He is the one who makes the mountains. He creates the wind. He makes his thoughts known to man. He changes the dawn into darkness. He walks over the mountains of the earth. His name is the Lord God of heaven's armies.

Israel Needs to Repent

You hate those who tell the truth. You walk on poor people. You force them to give you grain. You hurt people who do right. You accept money to do wrong. You keep the poor from getting justice in court.

Try to do good, not evil. Then you will live. And the Lord God of heaven's armies will be with you just as you say he is. Hate evil and love good.

The Lord says, "Let justice flow like a river. Let goodness flow like a stream that never stops."

The Vision of Locusts

This is what the Lord God showed me: He was forming a

329

swarm of locusts. The locusts ate all the crops in the country. After that I said, "Lord God, forgive us, I beg you! No one in Israel could live through this. Israel is too small already!"

So the Lord felt sorry about this. "This will not happen," said the Lord.

The Vision of Fire

This is what the Lord God showed me: The Lord God was calling for fire. The fire dried up the deep water and destroyed the land. Then I cried out, "Lord God, stop, I beg you! No one in Israel could live through this. Israel is too small already."

So the Lord felt sorry about this. "This will not happen either," said the Lord God.

The Lord Promises to Restore Israel

The Lord says, "The time is coming when there will be plenty of food. A person will still be harvesting his crops when it's time to plow again. A person will still be taking the juice from his grapes when it's time to plant again. Sweet wine will drip from the mountains. And it will pour from the hills. I will bring my people Israel back from captivity. And they will not be pulled out again from the land which I have given them."

WORTH WONDERING...

■ What do you think God was trying to teach Amos when He showed him the vision of locusts and the vision of fire?

■ How can you see God's great power in this book?

■ How can you see God's great love in this book?

GREAT VERSES TO THINK ABOUT AGAIN...

Look back in Amos to see if you can find these verses:

■ *Let justice flow like a river. Let goodness flow like a stream that never stops.*

■ *Get ready to meet your God.*

AND THERE'S MORE...

When you read Amos in a full Bible, look especially for...

■ Amos's words about the Lord's punishment for Israel's neighbors.

■ Amos's vision of a "plumb line." God wanted to use this straight line to show the people how crooked they were.

The Book of
OBADIAH

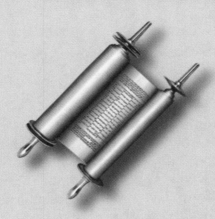

God Will
Punish Edom

Looking forward to Obadiah...

WHAT'S IT ABOUT?

"God Will Punish Edom"

SIGNS AND WONDERS

Obadiah spoke of God's judgment upon a proud and ungodly nation — the land of Edom.

FACES AND PLACES

Obadiah: His name means "servant."

Edom: In the book of Genesis we read about the twin brothers Jacob and Esau. The people of Israel were descended from Jacob. And the nation of Edom was descended from Esau. The people of Edom lived across the Dead Sea from the land of Israel. Edom and Israel had been enemies since the time of King David.

**I wonder what God will say
to a nation that has been an enemy
to His people Israel…**

THIS IS WHAT the Lord God says about Edom: "Look, I have made you only a small nation. But your pride has fooled you. Your home is up high. And you say to yourself, 'No one can bring me down to the ground.' You fly high like the eagle. You make your nest among the stars. But I will bring you down from there," says the Lord.

A Trap for Edom

"You will really be ruined! It would be better if thieves come to you, if robbers come by night. They would steal only enough for themselves. Workers come and pick the grapes from your vines. But they would leave a few grapes behind. But you, Edom, will really lose everything! People will find even your hidden treasures! All the people who are your friends will force you out of the land. The people who are at peace with you will trick you and defeat you. They eat your bread with you now. But they are planning a trap for you. And you will not notice it."

The Lord says, "On that day you will be covered with shame. You will be destroyed forever. You stood aside without helping while strangers carried Israel's treasures away.

"The Lord's day of judging is coming soon. Because you joined the nations in robbing my Temple, you drank my anger. All the nations will drink my anger. They will be punished so much that they will disappear. The people of Jacob will take back their land. They will take it from those who took it from them. The people of Jacob, the Israelites, will be like a fire. They will burn up the Edomites."

And the kingdom will belong to the Lord.

WORTH WONDERING...

- What did God say that the nation of Edom had done wrong to Israel?

- In your own words, what would you say pride is? What does God think about pride?

GREAT VERSES TO THINK ABOUT AGAIN...

Look back in Obadiah to see if you can find these verses:

- *The people of Jacob, the Israelites, will be like a fire.*

- *The Lord's day of judging is coming soon.*

The Book of
JONAH

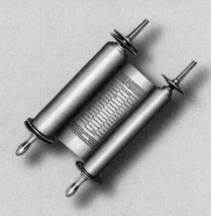

A Prophet
Runs from God

Looking forward to Jonah...

"A Prophet Runs from God"

God cares for everyone — even people we don't like. That's a message that Jonah had to learn the hard way.

Unlike the other Old Testament prophets, the book of Jonah is more a story about him, rather than a collection of what he said and wrote.

Jonah: His name means "dove."

Nineveh was the capital city of Assyria, which at this time was the most powerful nation on earth.

Joppa: A city on the shore of the Mediterranean Sea.

Tarshish: A city in what is today the country of Spain. For Jonah, this city was in the opposite direction from Nineveh, where God told him to go. Tarshish was far on the other side of the Mediterranean Sea.

**If someone has the wrong attitude
toward people that God loves,
I wonder how God could teach that person
the right attitude...**

THE LORD SPOKE his word to Jonah: "Get up, go to the great city of Nineveh and preach against it. I see the evil things they do."

But Jonah got up to run away from the Lord. He went to the city of Joppa. There he found a ship that was going to the city of Tarshish. Jonah paid for the trip and went aboard. He wanted to go to Tarshish to run away from the Lord.

But the Lord sent a great wind on the sea. This wind made the sea very rough. So the ship was in danger of breaking apart. The sailors were afraid. Each man cried to his own god. The men began throwing the cargo into the sea. This would make the ship lighter so it would not sink.

But Jonah had gone down into the ship to lie down. He fell fast asleep. The captain of the ship came and said, "Why are you sleeping? Get up! Pray to your God! Maybe your God will pay attention to us. Maybe he will save us!"

Then the men said to each other, "Let's throw lots to see who caused these troubles to happen to us."

So the men threw lots. The lot showed that the trouble had happened because of Jonah. Then the men said to Jonah, "Tell us what you have done. Why has this terrible thing happened to us? What is your job? Where do you come from?

What is your country? Who are your people?"

Then Jonah said to them, "I am a Hebrew. I fear the Lord, the God of heaven. He is the God who made the sea and the land."

Then the men were very afraid. They knew Jonah was running away from the Lord because Jonah had told them.

The wind and the waves of the sea were becoming much stronger. So the men said to Jonah, "What should we do to you to make the sea calm down?"

Jonah said to them, "Pick me up, and throw me into the sea. Then it will calm down. I know it is my fault that this great storm has come on you."

Instead, the men tried to row the ship back to the land. But they could not. The wind and the waves of the sea were becoming much stronger.

Jonah's Punishment

So the men cried to the Lord, "Lord, please don't let us die because of taking this man's life. Please don't think we are guilty of killing an innocent man. Lord, you have caused all this to happen. You wanted it this way." Then the men picked up Jonah and threw him into the sea. So the sea became calm. Then they began to fear the Lord very much. They offered a sacrifice to the Lord. They also made promises to him.

And the Lord caused a very big fish to swallow Jonah. Jonah was in the stomach of the fish three days and three nights.

Jonah's Prayer

While Jonah was in the stomach of the fish, he prayed to the Lord his God. Jonah said, "I was in danger. You threw me into the sea. I went down, down into the deep sea. The water was all around me. Your powerful waves flowed over me. I was about to die. Seaweed wrapped around my head. I thought I was locked in this prison forever. But you saved me from death, Lord my God.

"When my life had almost gone, I remembered the Lord. Lord, I prayed to you. And you heard my prayers.

"Lord, I will praise and thank you. I will make promises to you. And I will do what I promise. Salvation comes from the Lord!"

Then the Lord spoke to the fish. And the fish spit Jonah out of its stomach onto the dry land.

God Calls and Jonah Obeys

Then the Lord spoke his word to Jonah again. The Lord said, "Get up. Go to the great city

Nineveh. Preach against it what I tell you."

So Jonah obeyed the Lord. He got up and went to Nineveh. It was a very large city. It took a person three days just to walk across it. Jonah entered the city. When he had walked for one day, he preached to the people. He said, "After 40 days, Nineveh will be destroyed!"

The people of Nineveh believed in God. They announced they would stop eating for a while. They put on rough cloth to show how sad they were. All the people in the city wore the cloth. People from the most important to the least important did this.

When the king of Nineveh heard this news, he got up from his throne. He took off his robe. He covered himself with rough cloth and sat in ashes to show how upset he was.

God saw what the people did. He saw that they stopped doing evil things. So God changed his mind and did not do what he had warned. He did not punish them.

God's Mercy Makes Jonah Angry

But Jonah was very unhappy that God did not destroy the city. He was angry. He complained to the Lord and said, "I knew this would happen. I knew it when I was still in my own country. It is why I quickly ran away to Tarshish. I knew that you are a God who is kind and shows mercy. You don't become angry quickly. You have great love. I knew you would rather forgive than punish them. So now I ask you, Lord, please kill me. It is better for me to die than to live."

Then the Lord said, "Do you think it is right for you to be angry?"

Jonah went out and sat down east of the city. There he made a shelter for himself. And he sat there in the shade. He was waiting to see what would happen to the city. The Lord made a plant grow quickly up over Jonah. This made a cool place for him to sit. And it helped him to be more comfortable. Jonah was very pleased to have the plant for shade. The next day the sun rose. And God sent a worm to attack the plant. Then the plant died.

God's Concern

When the sun was high in the sky, God sent a hot east wind to blow. The sun became very hot on Jonah's head. And he became very weak. He wished he were dead. Jonah said, "It is better for me to die than to live."

But God said this to Jonah: "Do you think it is right for you to be angry because of the plant?"

Jonah answered, "It is right for me to be angry! I will stay angry until I die!"

And the Lord said, "You showed concern for that plant. But you did not plant it or make it grow. It appeared in the night, and the next day it died. Then surely I can show concern for the great city Nineveh."

■ *I can show concern for the great city Nineveh.*

■ *God saw what the people did. He saw that they stopped doing evil things. So God changed his mind and did not do what he had warned. He did not punish them.*

WORTH WONDERING...

■ How does this book show that God is in control of nature?

■ What did Jonah pray when he was inside the big fish?

■ Why was Jonah upset when the people of Nineveh were sorry for their sins?

■ What does this book teach us about God?

■ If you could meet Jonah today, what kind of questions would you like to ask him?

GREAT VERSES TO THINK ABOUT AGAIN...

Look back in Jonah to see if you can find these verses:

■ *I thought I was locked in this prison forever. But you saved me from death, Lord my God.*

■ *Lord, you have caused all this to happen. You wanted it this way.*

The Book of
MICAH

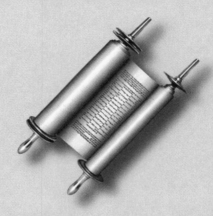

Punishment and Kindness
for God's People

Looking forward to Micah...

WHAT'S IT ABOUT?

"Punishment and Kindness for God's People"

SIGNS AND WONDERS

God hates sin, but He loves sinners. Look for that message from Micah.

Micah also said that a great ruler would come from Bethlehem. This ruler, Micah said, would be "from days long ago." Jesus was with His Father in heaven even before the beginning of time. But He was born as a baby in Bethlehem more than 700 years after Micah spoke these words.

FACES AND PLACES

Micah: His name means "Who is like the Lord?" Micah was a prophet at the same time as Isaiah and Amos.
Bethlehem: This small town is only a few miles south of Jerusalem.

I wonder how God can show His punishment and kindness at the same time...

THE LORD GOD will come from his Holy Temple. He will come as a witness against you. See, the Lord is coming out of his place in heaven. He is coming down to walk on the tops of the mountains. The mountains will melt under him like wax in a fire. The valleys will crack open as if split by water raging down a mountain. This is because of Jacob's sin. It is because of the sins of the nation of Israel.

The Evil Plans of People

How terrible it will be for people who plan wickedness. They lie on their beds and make evil plans. When the morning light comes, they do the things they planned. They do them just because they have the power to do so. They want fields; so they take them. They want houses; so they take them. They cheat a man and take his house. They cheat a man and take his property.

That is why the Lord says: "Look, I am planning trouble against such people. You won't be able to save yourselves. You will no longer walk proudly, because it will be a terrible time. At that time people will make fun of you. They will sing this sad song about you: 'We are completely ruined. The Lord has taken away our land. Yes, he has taken our land away from us. He has divided our fields among our enemies!'"

Micah Is Asked Not to Prophesy

People say, "Don't prophesy to us! Don't say those bad things about us! Nothing like that will happen to us!" But I must say this, people of Jacob. The Lord is becoming angry about what you have done. If you lived right, I could say nice words to you. But you people want a false prophet who will tell you nothing but lies. You want one who promises to prophesy good things for you if you give him wine and beer. He's just the prophet for you.

The Ruler Born in Bethlehem

"You, Bethlehem, are one of the smallest towns in Judah. But from you will come one who will rule Israel for me. He comes from very old times, from days long ago."

The ruler of Israel will stand and take care of his people. He will lead them with the Lord's power. He will lead them in the wonderful name of the Lord his God. They will live in safety. And his greatness will be known all over the earth. He will bring peace.

A Prayer to God

Lord our God, there is no God like you. You forgive people who are guilty of sin. You don't look at the sins of your people who are left alive. You, Lord, will not stay angry forever. You enjoy being kind. Lord, you will have mercy on us again. You will conquer our sins. You will throw away all our sins into the deepest sea. You will be true to the people of Jacob! You will be kind to the people of Abraham. You will do what you promised to our ancestors long ago.

WORTH WONDERING...

■ What does this book teach us about God?

A GREAT VERSE TO THINK ABOUT AGAIN...

Look back in Micah for this verse (it's a prophecy about Jesus):

■ *The ruler of Israel will stand and take care of his people. He will lead them with the Lord's power. He will lead them in the wonderful name of the Lord his God.*

AND THERE'S MORE...

When you read Micah in a full Bible, look especially for...

■ More of God's complaints against His people, as He speaks in the presence of the mountains and the hills.

The Book of
NAHUM

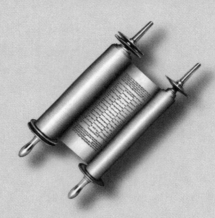

*God Will
Punish Assyria*

Looking forward to Nahum...

WHAT'S IT ABOUT?

"God Will Punish Assyria"

SIGNS AND WONDERS

In the book of Jonah, the people of the great city of Nineveh had turned away from their sin because of Jonah's preaching. But now, 100 years later, they were more wicked than ever. So God gave them punishment.

FACES AND PLACES

Nahum: His name means "helper" or "comforter" in the Hebrew language.
Nineveh was the capital city of Assyria, the most powerful nation on earth.

I wonder what God's message is for a powerful and wicked city...

THIS IS THE MESSAGE for the city of Nineveh: The Lord punishes those who are against him.

The Lord does not become angry quickly. The Lord will not let the guilty go unpunished. Where the Lord goes, whirlwinds and storms show his power. The clouds are the dust that his feet kick up. The Lord speaks to the sea and makes it dry. He dries up all the rivers. He shakes the mountains and makes the hills melt away.

The earth trembles when he comes. No one can stay alive when the Lord is angry with him. No one can survive his strong anger. His anger is poured out like fire. He smashes rocks that are in his path.

It Will Be Terrible for Nineveh

How terrible it will be for the city which has killed so many. It is full of lies. It is full of stolen things from other countries. It is always hurting or killing somebody.

Hear the sound of whips. Listen to the wheels. Hear horses galloping and chariots bouncing along! Soldiers on horses are charging. Their swords are shining. Their spears are gleaming!

"I am against you, Nineveh," says the Lord of heaven's armies. "I will throw dirt on you. I will make a fool of you. People will see you and make fun of you. Everyone who sees you will run away and say, 'Nineveh is

in ruins. Who will cry for her?'
Nineveh, I cannot find anyone
to comfort you."

WORTH WONDERING...

- What does this book tell us about God?
- What did the people of Nineveh do that was wrong in God's eyes?
- What kind of punishment was coming to Nineveh?

GREAT VERSES TO THINK ABOUT AGAIN...

Look back in Nahum to see if you can find these verses:

- *The Lord does not become angry quickly. The Lord will not let the guilty go unpunished.*
- *No one can stay alive when the Lord is angry with him. No one can survive his strong anger.*

The Book of
HABAKKUK

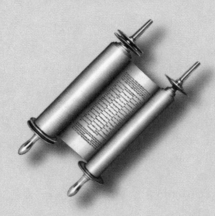

Learning How to Trust God

Looking forward to Habakkuk...

"Learning How to Trust God"

In this book we see God and Habakkuk speaking back and forth to one another. Habakkuk cannot understand why God is allowing the cruel Babylonians to bring punishment to God's people. He asks God about this.

He learns that God brings punishment to all who sin, whether they are God's people or not. In time, God will give victory and salvation to the people who believe in Him. But it might take a while!

God is still in control of the world, even when evil people seem to be winning.

Habakkuk: His name means "embrace." He was a prophet in Judah, the Southern Kingdom.

If I thought God was allowing something wrong and unfair to happen, I wonder how I could talk with Him about it...

Lord, I continue to ask for help. Why do you let me see wrong things? Why do you put up with evil?

The Lord Answers

"You and your people, look at the nations! Watch them and be amazed. I will do something in your lifetime that will amaze you. You won't believe it even when you are told about it. I will use the Babylonian people to punish the evil people. The Babylonians are cruel and powerful fighters. They march across the earth. They take lands that don't belong to them. The Babylonians frighten other people. Their soldiers attack quickly, like an eagle swooping down for food. The Babylonian soldiers laugh at all the strong, walled cities. They capture the cities. Then they leave like the wind and move on. They are guilty of worshiping their own strength."

Habakkuk Complains Again

Lord, you have chosen the Babylonians to punish people. Your eyes are too good to look at evil. So how can you put up with those evil people? How can you be quiet when wicked people defeat people who are better than they are?

The Lord Answers

The Lord answered me: "Write down what I show you. It is not yet time for the message to

351

come true. But that time is coming soon. It may seem like a long time before it happens. But be patient and wait for it. These things will happen. They will not be delayed. See, the nation that is evil and trusts in itself will fail. But those who do right because they trust in God will live.

"How terrible for the nation that becomes angry and makes others suffer. You Babylonians will receive the Lord's anger, not respect. This anger will be like a cup of poison in the Lord's right hand. You will taste this anger and fall to the ground like a drunk person.

"The Lord is in his Holy Temple. So all the earth should be silent in his presence."

Habakkuk's Prayer

Lord, do great things once again in our time. Even when you are angry, remember to be gentle with us.

The Lord stands and shakes the earth. He looks, and the nations shake with fear. The mountains, which stood for ages, break into pieces. I tremble when I hear the sound. My bones feel weak. My legs shake.

But I will wait patiently for the day of disaster. That day is coming to the people who attack us. There may be no food growing in the fields. There may be no sheep in the pens. There may be no cattle in the barns. But I will still be glad in the Lord. I will rejoice in God my Savior. The Lord God gives me my strength. He makes me like a deer, which does not stumble. He leads me safely on the steep mountains.

WORTH WONDERING...

- What does Habakkuk want to know from God?
- What are the most important things God wants Habakkuk to understand?
- When do you feel like complaining to God?

GREAT VERSES TO THINK ABOUT AGAIN...

Look back in Habakkuk to see if you can find these verses:

- *The Lord is in his Holy Temple. So all the earth should be silent in his presence.*
- *The Lord God gives me my strength. He makes me like a deer, which does not stumble.*

AND THERE'S MORE...

When you read Habakkuk in a full Bible, look especially for...

- Habakkuk's words about the foolishness of worshiping idols.

The Book of
ZEPHANIAH

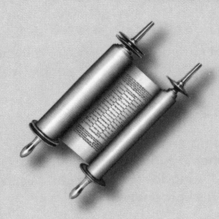

God Will Judge
the World

Looking forward to Zephaniah...

"God Will Judge the World"

The Lord's day of judgment is coming for all who are proud and sinful. But there is happiness for people who are rescued by the Lord.

Zephaniah: His name means "hidden by the Lord." Zephaniah was a prophet in Judah, the Southern Kingdom. This was at the time of King Josiah. Jeremiah, Micah, and Habakkuk were also prophets at that time.

**Even when there is trouble coming,
I wonder what can help God's people
to be happy...**

THE LORD'S DAY of judging is coming soon. That great day is near and coming fast. The cry will be very sad on that day. Even soldiers will cry. That day will be a day of terror and trouble. It will be a day of darkness. It will be a day of alarms and battle cries. The Lord's anger will be like fire. And the whole world will be burned up. Suddenly he will bring an end to everyone on earth.

God Asks People to Change

Gather together, you unwanted people. Do it before it's too late. Do it before you are blown away like chaff. Do it before the Lord's terrible anger reaches you. Do it before the day of the Lord's anger comes to you. All you who are not proud, come to the Lord. You who obey his laws, come to him. Do what is right. Learn to be humble. Maybe you will escape on the day the Lord shows his anger.

How terrible it will be for Jerusalem that hurts its own people. It's a wicked, stubborn city. Her people don't listen. They can't be taught to do right. They don't trust the Lord. They don't worship their God. Their officers are like roaring lions. Their rulers are like hungry wolves that attack in the evening. In the morning nothing is left of those they attacked. Their prophets are proud. They cannot be trusted.

Their priests don't respect holy things.

A New Day for God's People

"Then I will make the people of all nations speak a pure language. All of them will speak the name of the Lord. And they will worship me together. I will remove from this city those who like to brag. There will never be any more proud people on my holy mountain in Jerusalem. Only the meek and humble will stay in my city. And they will trust in the Lord. No one will bother them."

A Happy Song

Sing, Jerusalem. Israel, shout for joy! Rejoice with all your heart. The Lord has stopped punishing you. He has sent your enemies away. The King of Israel, the Lord, is with you. You will never again be afraid of being harmed. The Lord your God is with you. The mighty One will save you. The Lord will be happy with you. You will rest in his love. He will sing and be joyful about you.

WORTH WONDERING...

■ What are the wrong things that God says the people of Jerusalem are doing?

■ Since God says He must punish Jerusalem, why does He also tell Jerusalem to be happy?

■ What promises does God make to His people in this book?

GREAT VERSES TO THINK ABOUT AGAIN...

Look back in Zephaniah to see if you can find these verses:

■ *The Lord's anger will be like fire. And the whole world will be burned up. Suddenly he will bring an end to everyone on earth.*

■ *Do what is right. Learn to be humble.*

■ *The Lord will be happy with you. You will rest in his love. He will sing and be joyful about you.*

AND THERE'S MORE...

When you read Zephaniah in a full Bible, look especially for...

■ God's plans to punish Israel's neighbors.

The Book of
HAGGAI

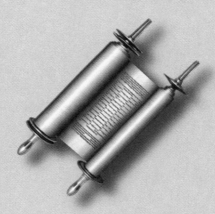

*Rebuilding
the Temple*

Looking forward to Haggai...

WHAT'S IT ABOUT?

"Rebuilding the Temple"

SIGNS AND WONDERS

The last three prophets in the Old Testament (Haggai, Zechariah, and Malachi) all lived in Judah after God's people had come back from being prisoners in Babylon. Haggai gave these people God's message about rebuilding the Temple in Jerusalem.

FACES AND PLACES

Haggai: His name means "celebration."
Zerubbabel: He had been appointed governor of Judah by Cyrus. Cyrus was the king of Persia who let the Jews come back to Jerusalem.
Joshua: This high priest is also mentioned in the books of Ezra and Nehemiah.

In God's eyes, I wonder how important it was for His people to rebuild the Temple after they returned to the ruins of Jerusalem...

THE PROPHET HAGGAI spoke the word of the Lord to Zerubbabel and to Joshua. Zerubbabel was governor of Judah. Joshua was high priest.

This is what the Lord of heaven's armies says: "The people say the right time has not come to rebuild the Temple of the Lord."

Then Haggai the prophet spoke the word of the Lord: "The Temple is still in ruins. Is it right for you to be living in fancy houses?"

This is why the Lord of heaven's armies says: "Think about what you have done. You have planted much, but you harvest little. You eat, but you do not become full. You drink, but you are still thirsty. You put on clothes, but you are not warm enough. You earn money, but then you lose it all. It is as if you put it into a purse full of holes."

This is what the Lord of heaven's armies says: "Go up to the mountains. Bring back wood and build the Temple. Then I will be pleased with it and be honored," says the Lord. The Lord of heaven's armies says: "You look for much, but you find little. When you bring it home, I destroy it. Why? Because you are busy working on your own houses. But my house is still in ruins! Because of what you have done, the sky holds back its rain. And the ground holds back its crops. I have called for a dry time in the land. There will be no rain in the mountains for the grain, new wine and olive oil. It will be a dry time for the plants which the earth produces. It will be a dry time for men and farm animals. The dry time will make your hard work useless."

The Lord made Zerubbabel and Joshua excited about building the Temple. The Lord made all the rest of the people who were left alive excited, too. They came and worked on the Temple of their God, the Lord of heaven's armies.

The Beauty of the Temple

"This is what the Lord of heaven's armies says: 'In a short time I will shake the heavens and earth once again. And I will shake the sea and the dry land. I will shake all the nations. All the nations will bring their wealth. Then I will fill this Temple with glory. The new Temple will be more beautiful than the one that was destroyed,' says the Lord of heaven's armies. 'And in this place I will give peace to the people,' says the Lord of heaven's armies."

WORTH WONDERING...

■ Because the people in Jerusalem were not building God's Temple, what was happening to them?

■ Haggai tells the people to put God first in their lives. How can you put God first in your life?

A GREAT VERSE TO THINK ABOUT AGAIN...

Look back in Haggai to find this verse:

■ *The Lord made Zerubbabel and Joshua excited about building the Temple. The Lord made all the rest of the people who were left alive excited, too. They came and worked on the Temple of their God.*

The Book of
ZECHARIAH

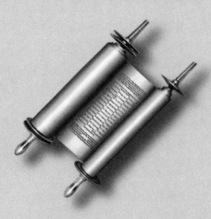

Visions and
a Coming King

Looking forward to Zechariah...

"Visions and a Coming King"

The Lord never forgets His people. That is the message of the prophet Zechariah. Zechariah had many visions. They are filled with powerful pictures to tell the people about the future.

As he looks ahead, Zechariah speaks much about the coming Christ.

Zechariah: His name means "one whom the Lord remembers."

I wonder what God wanted His people to remember as they waited for Jesus to come...

THE LORD'S ANGEL told me, "Announce this: This is what the Lord of heaven's armies says: 'I have a strong love for Jerusalem. And I am very angry with the nations that feel so safe. I was only a little angry, but they made things worse for my people.'

"So this is what the Lord says: 'I will return to Jerusalem with mercy. My Temple will be rebuilt,' says the Lord of heaven's armies. 'And the measuring line will be used to rebuild Jerusalem.'

"Also announce: This is what the Lord of heaven's armies says: 'My towns will be rich again. I will comfort Jerusalem again. I will still choose Jerusalem.'"

The Lord Will Bless Jerusalem

The Lord of heaven's armies spoke his word to me again. This is what the Lord of heaven's armies says: "I have a very strong love for Jerusalem. My strong love for her is like a fire burning in me."

This is what the Lord says: "I will return to Jerusalem. I will live in Jerusalem. Then it will be called the City of Truth. And the mountain of the Lord of heaven's armies will be called the Holy Mountain."

This is what the Lord of heaven's armies says: "Old men and old women will again sit along Jerusalem's streets. And the streets will be filled with boys and girls playing."

The King Is Coming

"Rejoice, people of Jerusalem. Shout for joy, people of Jerusalem. Your king is coming to you. He does what is right, and he saves. He is gentle and riding on a donkey. He is on the colt of a donkey. The king will talk to the nations about peace. His kingdom will go from sea to sea, and to the ends of the earth.

"And the family of David will be like God. They will be like an angel of the Lord leading the people.

"I will give David's family and people in Jerusalem a spirit of kindness and mercy. They will look at me, the one they have stabbed. And they will cry like someone crying over the death of an only child.

"At that time a fountain will be opened. It will be for David's descendants and for the people of Jerusalem. It will cleanse them of their sins and wrongs.

"I will bring all the nations together to fight Jerusalem. Then the Lord will go to war against those nations. He will fight as in a day of battle. On that day he will stand on the Mount of Olives, east of Jerusalem. The Mount of Olives will split in two. A deep valley will run east and west. You will run through this mountain valley to the other side. Then the Lord my God will come. And all the holy ones will be with him.

"On that day there will be no light, cold or frost. There will be no other day like it. The Lord knows when it will come. There will be no day or night. Even at evening it will still be light.

"Then the Lord will be king over the whole world. At that time there will be only one Lord. And his name will be the only name."

WORTH WONDERING...

■ What does Zechariah say about the coming king?

GREAT VERSES TO THINK ABOUT AGAIN...

Look back in Zechariah to see if you can find these verses:

■ Your king is coming to you. He does what is right, and he saves.

■ I have a very strong love for Jerusalem.

AND THERE'S MORE...

When you read Zechariah in a full Bible, look especially for these visions:

■ A flying scroll
■ Four chariots pulled by powerful horses.
■ A high priest in filthy clothes, being accused by Satan.

The Book of
MALACHI

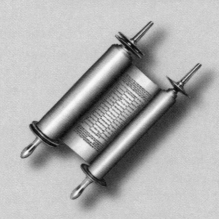

God Tells Israel to Be Loyal

Looking forward to Malachi...

"God Tells Israel to Be Loyal"

This book is a final warning to God's people: Judgment is coming! God's people had come back to Israel after the terrible punishment of being prisoners in another country. This punishment was because of their sins. But Malachi showed them that there were still some sins that the people needed to get rid of.

Malachi is the last book of the Old Testament. After this there will be 400 years of silence before the New Testament begins. This time is sometimes called the "400 Silent Years." God's Spirit did not cause any more books to be added to the Scriptures until after Jesus Christ came.

Malachi: His name means "messenger of the Lord."

I wonder what God's "last words" will be to His people, while they wait for the time when He sends His Son to the earth...

THE LORD of heaven's armies says, "I am a father. So why don't you honor me? I am a master. So why don't you respect me? You bring blind animals as sacrifices, and that is wrong. You bring crippled and sick animals. That is wrong.

"Now ask God to be kind to you. But he won't accept you with such offerings," says the Lord of heaven's armies.

"Priests, this command is for you. Pay attention to what I say. A priest should teach what he knows. People should learn the teachings from him because he is the messenger of the Lord of heaven's armies. But you priests have stopped obeying me. With your teachings you have caused many people to do wrong," says the Lord of heaven's armies.

Judah Was Not Loyal to God

This is another thing you do. You cover the Lord's altar with your tears. You cry and moan because the Lord does not accept your offerings. He is not pleased with what you bring. You ask, "Why?" It is because the Lord sees how you treated the wife you married when you were young. You broke your promise with her.

The Lord God of Israel says, "I hate divorce. And I hate people who do cruel things as easily as they put on clothes." So be careful. And do not break your trust.

The Special Day of Judging

The Lord of heaven's armies says, "I will send my messenger. He will prepare the way for me to come. Suddenly, the Lord you are looking for will come to his Temple. The messenger of the agreement, whom you want, will come." No one can live through that time. No one can survive when he comes. He will be like a purifying fire. He will be like laundry soap. He will be like someone who heats and purifies silver.

The Lord of heaven's armies says, "Then I will come to you and judge you. I will testify against those who take part in evil magic and lying. I will testify against those who cheat workers of their pay and who cheat widows and orphans. And I will testify against those who are unfair. These people do not respect me

Stealing from God

"I am the Lord. Should a man rob God? But you rob me. You have robbed me in your offerings and the tenth of your crops. So a curse is on you because the whole nation has robbed me. Bring to the storehouse a tenth of what you gain. Then there will be food in my house. Test me in this," says the Lord of heaven's armies. "I will open the windows of heaven for you. I will pour out more blessings than you have room for. I will stop the insects so they won't eat your crops. The grapes won't fall from your vines before they are ready to pick," says the Lord of heaven's armies.

The Lord's Promise of Mercy

The Lord says, "You have said terrible things about me.

"But you ask, 'What have we said about you?'

"You have said, 'It is useless to serve God. It did no good to obey his laws. And it did no good to show the Lord of heaven's armies that we are sorry for what we did..'"

Then those who honored the Lord spoke with each other. The Lord listened and heard them. The names of those who honored the Lord and respected him were written in a book. The Lord will remember them.

The Lord of heaven's armies says, "They belong to me. On that day they will be my very own. A father shows mercy to his son who serves him. In the same way I will show mercy to my people. You will again see the difference between good and evil people. You will see the difference between those who serve God and those who don't.

The Day of the Lord's Judging

"There is a day coming that will be like a hot furnace. All the proud and evil people will be like straw. On that day they will be completely burned up. Not a root or branch will be left," says the Lord of heaven's armies. "But for you who honor me, goodness will shine on you like the sun. There will be healing in its rays. You will jump around, like calves freed from their stalls. I will do this on that day," says the Lord of heaven's armies.

"Remember the teaching of Moses my servant. I gave those laws and rules to him at Mount Sinai. They are for all the Israelites.

"But I will send Elijah the prophet to you. He will come before that great and terrible day of the Lord's judging. Elijah will help fathers love their children. And he will help the children love their fathers. Otherwise, I will come and put a curse on the land."

WORTH WONDERING...

- What things does God say His people are doing wrong?
- What promises does God

make to His people in this book?
- Now that you've come to the end of the Old Testament, which books in the Old Testament would you say have been your favorites?

GREAT VERSES TO THINK ABOUT AGAIN...

Look back in Malachi to see if you can find these verses:

- *For you who honor me, goodness will shine on you like the sun. There will be healing in its rays. You will jump around, like calves freed from their stalls.*
- *The names of those who honored the Lord and respected him were written in a book. The Lord will remember them.*

AND THERE'S MORE...

When you read Malachi in a full Bible, look especially for...

- More about God's rules for worship in the Temple, and how His people were not doing right.

INTRODUCING...

MATTHEW • MARK • LUKE • JOHN

The world was lost and dying. Every man and woman and boy and girl on earth had become a slave to sin and death.

*Then...the Lord Jesus Christ, the Son of God, left His home in heaven. He came to earth as a newborn baby. When He became a man, He showed us what God is really like. He showed us by His words and by His actions. He never did or said anything wrong. He was living a perfect life.

But suddenly, while He was still a young man, Jesus was put to death as a criminal.

And that was exactly the way God planned it!

Jesus came here to die. He came to die for men and women and boys and girls, to take *their* sin and death upon Himself. He knew there was no other way that we could live forever with God. He did this for all people, for all time.

What a story! And that's the story that is told in the four books of the Bible that we call the Gospels.

The four Gospels are the most amazing and exciting part of the Bible. Here we see the mighty God Himself coming down to earth. In each Gospel, someone different tells the story of Jesus' life, His death, and His rising up from the dead. All of these writers — Matthew, Mark, Luke, and John — were close to Jesus when He lived on earth, or else learned about Him from others who were very close to Him.

These four Gospels are the start of what is almost a new Bible. So from the Gospels on, all the books of the Bible are called the *New Testament*. That word "Testament" means "Agreement." God is offering a new *agreement* with us. Because of our sins, we deserve the punishment of death. But God put that punishment on His Son Jesus. If we truly believe in Jesus and belong to Him, we can have never-ending life with God in heaven, instead of never-ending death in hell.

It's an offer worth accepting...*don't you agree?*

The Gospel of
MATTHEW

Jesus,
the True King

Looking forward to Matthew...

"Jesus, the True King"

Long ago, God promised to send His people a great and wonderful King. Now, the time for this King to come to earth is finally here!

Jesus: The Son of God, the Savior of the world, and the King who is coming back to us.

Matthew: The one who wrote this gospel. He was one of the 12 followers whom Jesus called apostles. Matthew was a tax collector when he met Jesus. Matthew's other name is "Levi."

Mary: Mother of Jesus. Her husband was **Joseph.**

The Wise Men: They are also called Magi.

Herod: He was made king over the Jewish people. The land of Israel at this time was part of the Roman Empire. The ruler of this empire was called **Caesar,** and he lived in Rome.

John the Baptist: He prepared the way for Jesus by preaching for people to turn away from their sins.

Peter was another one of the 12 apostles.

Judas Iscariot: Another of the 12 apostles. But Judas turned Jesus over to His enemies.

Pharisees: A Jewish religious group. They were very strict.

Pontius Pilate: He was the governor of Judea.

Bethlehem: The town in Judea where David had lived a thousand years before Jesus.

Judea: The New Testament name for the land of Judah.

Galilee: The land near the Sea of Galilee.

Nazareth: The town in Galilee where Jesus grew up.

I wonder what it really means that Jesus is my King...

THE MOTHER of Jesus Christ was Mary. And this is how the birth of Jesus came about. Mary was engaged to marry Joseph. But before they married, she learned that she was going to have a baby. She was pregnant by the power of the Holy Spirit. Mary's husband, Joseph, was a good man. He did not want to disgrace her in public, so he planned to divorce her secretly.

While Joseph thought about this, an angel of the Lord came to him in a dream. The angel said, "Joseph, descendant of David, don't be afraid to take Mary as your wife. The baby in her is from the Holy Spirit. She will give birth to a son. You will name the son Jesus. Give him that name because he will save his people from their sins."

All this happened to make clear the full meaning of what the Lord had said through the prophet: "The virgin will be pregnant. She will have a son, and they will name him Immanuel." This name means "God is with us."

When Joseph woke up, he did what the Lord's angel had told him to do. Joseph married Mary. She gave birth to the son. And Joseph named the son Jesus.

Wise Men Come to Visit Jesus

Jesus was born in the town of Bethlehem in Judea during the time when Herod was king.

After Jesus was born, some wise men from the east came to Jerusalem. They asked, "Where is the baby who was born to be the king of the Jews? We saw his star in the east. We came to worship him."

When King Herod heard about this new king of the Jews, he was troubled. And all the people in Jerusalem were worried too. Herod called a meeting of all the leading priests and teachers of the law. He asked them where the Christ would be born. They answered, "In the town of Bethlehem in Judea. The prophet wrote about this in the Scriptures: 'But you, Bethlehem, in the land of Judah, you are important among the rulers of Judah. A ruler will come from you. He will be like a shepherd for my people, the Israelites.'"

Then Herod had a secret meeting with the wise men from the east. He learned from them the exact time they first saw the star. Then Herod sent the wise men to Bethlehem. He said to them, "Go and look carefully to find the child. When you find him, come tell me. Then I can go worship him too."

The wise men heard the king and then left. They saw the same star they had seen in the east. It went before them until it stopped above the place where the child was. When the wise men saw the star, they were filled with joy. They went to the house where the child was and saw him with his mother, Mary. They bowed down and worshiped the child. They opened the gifts they brought for him. They gave him treasures of gold, frankincense, and myrrh. But God warned the wise men in a dream not to go back to Herod. So they went home to their own country by a different way.

Jesus' Parents Take Him to Egypt

After they left, an angel of the Lord came to Joseph in a dream. The angel said, "Get up! Take the child and his mother and escape to Egypt. Herod will start looking for the child to kill him. Stay in Egypt until I tell you to return."

So Joseph got up and left for Egypt during the night with the child and his mother. Joseph stayed in Egypt until Herod died. This was to make clear the full meaning of what the Lord had said through the prophet. The Lord said, "I called my son out of Egypt."

Herod Kills the Baby Boys

When Herod saw that the

wise men had tricked him, he was very angry. So he gave an order to kill all the baby boys in Bethlehem and in all the area around Bethlehem who were two years old or younger. This was in keeping with the time he learned from the wise men.

Joseph and Mary Return

After Herod died, an angel of the Lord came to Joseph in a dream. This happened while Joseph was in Egypt. The angel said, "Get up! Take the child and his mother and go to Israel. The people who were trying to kill the child are now dead."

So Joseph took the child and his mother and went to Israel. After being warned in a dream, he went to the area of Galilee. He went to a town called Nazareth and lived there.

The Work of John the Baptist

John the Baptist came and began preaching in the desert area of Judea. John said, "Change your hearts and lives because the kingdom of heaven is coming soon." John the Baptist is the one Isaiah the prophet was talking about. Isaiah said: "This is a voice of a man who calls out in the desert: 'Prepare the way for the Lord. Make the road straight for him.'"

John's clothes were made from camel's hair. He wore a leather belt around his waist. For food, he ate locusts and wild honey. Many people went to hear John preach. They told of the sins they had done, and John baptized them in the Jordan River.

Jesus Is Baptized by John

At that time Jesus came from Galilee to the Jordan River. He came to John and wanted John to baptize him. But John tried to stop him. John said, "Why do you come to me to be baptized? I should be baptized by you!"

Jesus answered, "Let it be this way for now. We should do all things that are right." So John agreed to baptize Jesus.

The Temptation of Jesus

Then the Spirit led Jesus into the desert to be tempted by the devil. Jesus ate nothing for 40 days and nights. After this, he was very hungry. The devil came to Jesus to tempt him. The devil said, "If you are the Son of God, tell these rocks to become bread."

Jesus answered, "It is written in the Scriptures, 'A person does not live only by eating bread.

But a person lives by everything the Lord says.'"

Then the devil led Jesus to the holy city of Jerusalem. He put Jesus on a very high place of the Temple. The devil said, "If you are the Son of God, jump off. It is written in the Scriptures, 'He has put his angels in charge of you. They will catch you with their hands. And you will not hit your foot on a rock.'"

Jesus answered him, "It also says in the Scriptures, 'Do not test the Lord your God.'"

Then the devil led Jesus to the top of a very high mountain. He showed Jesus all the kingdoms of the world and all the great things that are in those kingdoms. The devil said, "If you will bow down and worship me, I will give you all these things."

Jesus said to the devil, "Go away from me, Satan! It is written in the Scriptures, 'You must worship the Lord your God. Serve only him!'"

So the devil left Jesus. And then some angels came to Jesus and helped him.

Jesus Chooses Some Followers

From that time Jesus began to preach, saying, "Change your hearts and lives, because the kingdom of heaven is coming soon."

Jesus was walking by Lake Galilee. He saw two brothers, Simon (called Peter) and Simon's brother Andrew. The brothers were fishermen, and they were fishing in the lake with a net. Jesus said, "Come follow me. I will make you fishermen for men." At once Simon and Andrew left their nets and followed him.

Jesus continued walking by Lake Galilee. He saw two other brothers, James and John, the sons of Zebedee. They were in a boat with their father Zebedee, preparing their nets to catch fish. Jesus told them to come with him. At once they left the boat and their father, and they followed Jesus.

Jesus Teaches and Heals People

Jesus went everywhere in Galilee. He taught in the synagogues and preached the Good News about the kingdom of heaven. And he healed all the people's diseases and sicknesses. Many people followed him. They came from Galilee, Jerusalem, Judea, and the land across the Jordan River.

Jesus Teaches the People

Jesus saw the crowds who were there. He went up on a hill and sat down. His followers came to him. Jesus taught the people and said: "Those people who know they have great spiritual needs are happy. The kingdom of heaven belongs to them. Those who are sad now are happy. God will comfort them. Those who are humble are happy. The earth will belong to them. Those who want to do right more than anything else are happy. God will fully satisfy them. Those who give mercy to others are happy. Mercy will be given to them. Those who are pure in their thinking are happy. They will be with God. Those who work to bring peace are happy. God will call them his sons. Those who are treated badly for doing good are happy. The kingdom of heaven belongs to them.

"People will say bad things about you and hurt you. They will lie and say all kinds of evil things about you because you follow me. But when they do these things to you, you are happy. Rejoice and be glad. You have a great reward waiting for you in heaven. People did the same evil things to the prophets who lived before you.

You Are Like Salt and Light

"You are the salt of the earth. But if the salt loses its salty taste, it cannot be made salty again. It is good for nothing. It must be thrown out for people to walk on.

"You are the light that gives light to the world. A city that is built on a hill cannot be hidden. And people don't hide a light under a bowl. They put the light on a lampstand. Then the light shines for all the people in the house. In the same way, you should be a light for other people. Live so that they will see the good things you do. Live so that they will praise your Father in heaven.

Love All People

"You have heard that it was said, 'Love your neighbor and hate your enemies.' But I tell you, love your enemies. Pray for those who hurt you. If you do this, then you will be true sons of your Father in heaven. Your Father causes the sun to rise on good people and on bad people. Your Father sends rain to those who do good and to those who do wrong. Even people without God are nice to their friends. So you must be perfect, just as your Father in heaven is perfect.

Don't Worry

"Don't worry about the food you need to live. And don't worry about the clothes you need for your body. Life is more important than food. And the body is more important than clothes. Look at the birds in the air. They don't plant or harvest or store food in barns. But your heavenly Father feeds the birds. And you know that you are worth much more than the birds. You cannot add any time to your life by worrying about it.

"And why do you worry about clothes? Look at the flowers in the field. See how they grow. They don't work or make clothes for themselves. But I tell you that even Solomon with his riches was not dressed as beautifully as one of these flowers.

"The thing you should want most is God's kingdom and doing what God wants. Then all these other things you need will be given to you. So don't worry about tomorrow. Each day has enough trouble of its own. Tomorrow will have its own worries.

Ask God for What You Need

"Continue to ask, and God will give to you. Continue to search, and you will find. Continue to knock, and the door will open for you. Yes, everyone who continues asking will receive. He who continues searching will find. And he who continues knocking will have the door opened for him.

The Most Important Rule

"Do for other people the same things you want them to do for you. This is the meaning of the law of Moses and the teaching of the prophets.

The Way to Heaven Is Hard

"Enter through the narrow gate. The road that leads to hell is a very easy road. And the gate to hell is very wide. Many people enter through that gate. But the gate that opens the way to true life is very small. And the road to true life is very hard. Only a few people find that road.

Two Kinds of People

"Everyone who hears these things I say and obeys them is like a wise man. The wise man built his house on rock. It rained hard and the water rose. The winds blew and hit that house. But the house did not fall, because the house was built on rock. But the person who hears the things I teach and does not obey them is like a foolish man. The foolish man built his house on sand. It rained hard, the water rose, and the winds blew and hit that house. And the house fell with a big crash."

When Jesus finished saying these things, the people were amazed at his teaching. Jesus did not teach like their teachers of the law. He taught like a person who had authority.

Jesus Chooses Matthew

Jesus saw a man named Matthew. Matthew was sitting in the tax office. Jesus said to him, "Follow me." And Matthew stood up and followed Jesus.

Jesus had dinner at Matthew's house. Many tax collectors and "sinners" came and ate with Jesus and his followers. The Pharisees saw this and asked Jesus' followers, "Why does your teacher eat with tax collectors and 'sinners'?"

Jesus heard the Pharisees ask this. So he said, "Healthy people don't need a doctor. Only the sick need a doctor. Go and learn what this means: 'I want faithful love more than I want animal sacrifices.' I did not come to invite good people. I came to invite sinners."

Jesus traveled through all the towns and villages. He taught in their synagogues and told people the Good News about the kingdom. And he healed all kinds of diseases and sicknesses. He saw the crowds of people and felt sorry for them because they were worried and helpless. They were like sheep without a shepherd. Jesus said to his followers, "There are many people to harvest, but there are only a few workers to help harvest them. God owns the harvest. Pray to him that he will send more workers to help gather his harvest."

Jesus Offers Rest to People

Then Jesus said, "My Father has given me all things. Come to me, all of you who are tired and have heavy loads. I will give you rest. Accept my work and learn from me. I am gentle and humble in spirit. And you will find rest for your souls. The work that I ask you to accept is easy. The load I give you to carry is not heavy."

Stories of a Treasure and a Pearl

Jesus used stories to teach them many things. He said: "The kingdom of heaven is like a treasure hidden in a field. One day a man found the treasure, and then he hid it in the field again. The man was very happy to find the treasure. He went and sold everything that he owned to buy that field.

"Also, the kingdom of heaven is like a man looking for fine pearls. One day he found a very valuable pearl. The man went and sold everything he had to buy that pearl."

More than 5,000 People Fed

Jesus left in a boat. He went to a lonely place by himself. But when the crowds heard about it, they followed him on foot from the towns. When Jesus arrived, he saw a large crowd. He felt sorry for them and healed those who were sick.

Late that afternoon, his followers came to Jesus and said,

"No one lives in this place. And it is already late. Send the people away so they can go to the towns and buy food for themselves."

Jesus answered, "They don't need to go away. You give them some food to eat."

The followers answered, "But we have only five loaves of bread and two fish."

Jesus said, "Bring the bread and the fish to me." Then he told the people to sit down on the grass. He took the five loaves of bread and the two fish. Then he looked to heaven and thanked God for the food. Jesus divided the loaves of bread. He gave them to his followers, and they gave the bread to the people. All the people ate and were satisfied. After they finished eating, the followers filled 12 baskets with the pieces of food that were not eaten. There were about 5,000 men there who ate, as well as women and children.

Jesus Walks on the Water

Then Jesus made his followers get into the boat. He told them to go ahead of him to the other side of the lake. Jesus stayed there to tell the people they could go home. After he said good-bye to them, he went alone up into the hills to pray. It was late, and Jesus was there alone. By this time, the boat was already far away on the lake. The boat was having trouble because of the waves, and the wind was blowing against it.

Between three and six o'clock in the morning, Jesus' followers were still in the boat. Jesus came to them. He was walking on the water. When the followers saw him walking on the water, they were afraid. They said, "It's a ghost!" and cried out in fear.

But Jesus quickly spoke to them. He said, "Have courage! It is I! Don't be afraid."

Peter said, "Lord, if that is really you, then tell me to come to you on the water."

Jesus said, "Come."

And Peter left the boat and walked on the water to Jesus. But when Peter saw the wind and the waves, he became afraid and began to sink. He shouted, "Lord, save me!"

Then Jesus reached out his hand and caught Peter. Jesus said, "Your faith is small. Why did you doubt?"

After Peter and Jesus were in the boat, the wind became calm. Then those who were in the boat worshiped Jesus and said, "Truly you are the Son of God!"

After they crossed the lake, they came to the shore at Gennesaret. The people there saw Jesus and knew who he was. So they told people all around there that Jesus had come. They brought all their sick to him. They begged Jesus to let them just touch the edge of his coat to be healed. And all the sick people who touched it were healed.

Peter Says Jesus Is the Christ

Jesus went to the area of Caesarea Philippi. He said to his followers, "Who do the people say I am?"

They answered, "Some people say you are John the Baptist. Others say you are Elijah. And others say that you are Jeremiah or one of the prophets."

Then Jesus asked them, "And who do you say I am?"

Simon Peter answered, "You are the Christ, the Son of the living God."

Jesus answered, "You are blessed, Simon son of Jonah. No person taught you that. My Father in heaven showed you who I am. So I tell you, you are Peter. And I will build my church on this rock. The power of death will not be able to defeat my church. I will give you the keys of the kingdom of heaven. The things you don't allow on earth will be the things that God does not allow. The things you allow on earth will be the things that God allows."

Jesus Says that He Must Die

From that time on Jesus began telling his followers that he must go to Jerusalem. He explained that the older Jewish leaders, the leading priests, and the teachers of the law would make him suffer many things. And he told them that he must be killed. Then, on the third day, he would be raised from death.

Peter took Jesus aside and began to criticize him. Peter said, "God save you from those things, Lord! Those things will never happen to you!"

Then Jesus said to Peter, "Go away from me, Satan! You are not helping me! You don't care about the things of God. You care only about things that men think are important."

Then Jesus said to his followers, "If anyone wants to follow me, he must say 'no' to the things he wants. He must be willing even to die on a cross, and he must follow me. Whoever wants to save his life will give up true life. And whoever gives up his life for me will have true life. It is worth nothing for a man to have the whole world if he loses his soul. He could never pay enough to buy back his soul. The Son of Man will come again with his Father's glory and with his angels. At that time, he will reward everyone for what he has done. I tell you the truth. There are some people standing here who, before they die, will see the Son of Man coming with his kingdom."

Jesus with Moses and Elijah

Six days later, Jesus took Peter, James, and John the brother of James up on a high

PAUSE & WONDER

When Jesus came to earth, it was God Himself coming down. When Jesus said something, it is God Himself saying it. When Jesus did something, it was God Himself doing it.

mountain. They were all alone there. While they watched, Jesus was changed. His face became bright like the sun. And his clothes became white as light. Then two men were there, talking with him. The men were Moses and Elijah.

Peter said to Jesus, "Lord, it is good that we are here. If you want, I will put three tents here — one for you, one for Moses, and one for Elijah."

While Peter was talking, a bright cloud covered them. A voice came from the cloud. The voice said, "This is my Son and I love him. I am very pleased with him. Obey him!"

The followers with Jesus heard the voice. They were so frightened that they fell to the ground. But Jesus went to them and touched them. He said, "Stand up. Don't be afraid." When the followers looked up, they saw Jesus was now alone.

When Jesus and the followers were coming down the mountain, Jesus commanded them, "Don't tell anyone about the things you saw on the mountain. Wait until the Son of Man has been raised from death. Then you may tell."

Jesus Talks About Paying Taxes

Jesus and his followers went to Capernaum. There some men came to Peter. They were the men who collected the Temple tax. They asked, "Does your teacher pay the Temple tax?"

Peter answered, "Yes, Jesus pays the tax."

Peter went into the house where Jesus was. Before Peter could speak, Jesus said to him, "The kings on the earth collect different kinds of taxes. But who are the people who pay the taxes? Are they the king's children? Or do others pay the taxes? What do you think?"

Peter answered, "Other people pay the taxes."

Jesus said to Peter, "Then the children of the king don't have to pay taxes. But we don't want to make these tax collectors angry. So go to the lake and fish. After you catch the first fish, open its mouth. Inside its mouth you will find a coin. Take that coin and give it to the tax collectors. That will pay the tax for you and me."

Who Is the Greatest?

At that time the followers came to Jesus and asked, "Who is greatest in the kingdom of heaven?"

Jesus called a little child to him. He stood the child before the followers. Then he said, "I tell you the truth. You must change and become like little children. If you don't do this, you will never enter the kingdom of heaven. The greatest person in the kingdom of heaven is the one who makes himself humble like this child."

Jesus Enters Jerusalem as a King

Jesus and his followers were coming to Jerusalem. But first they stopped at the hill called the Mount of Olives. From there Jesus sent two of his followers into the town. He said to them, "Go to the town you can see there. When you enter it, you will find a donkey tied there with its colt. Untie them and bring them to me. If anyone asks you why you are taking the donkeys, tell him, 'The Master needs them. He will send them back soon.'"

This was to make clear the full meaning of what the prophet said: "Tell the people of Jerusalem, 'Your king is coming to you. He is gentle and riding on a donkey. He is on the colt of a donkey.'"

The followers went and did what Jesus told them to do. They brought the donkey and the colt to Jesus. They laid their coats on the donkeys, and Jesus sat on them. Many people spread their coats on the road before Jesus. Others cut branches from the trees and spread them on the road. Some of the people were walking ahead of Jesus. Others were walking behind him. All the people were shouting, "Praise to the Son of David! God bless the One who comes in the name of the Lord! Praise to God in heaven!"

Then Jesus went into Jerusalem. The city was filled with excitement. The people asked, "Who is this man?"

The crowd answered, "This man is Jesus. He is the prophet from the town of Nazareth in Galilee."

In the Temple

Jesus went into the Temple. He threw out all the people who were buying and selling there. He turned over the tables that belonged to the men who were exchanging different kinds of money. And he upset the benches of those who were selling doves. Jesus said to all the people there, "It is written in the Scriptures, 'My Temple will be a house where people will pray.' But you are changing God's house into a 'hideout for robbers.'"

The blind and crippled people came to Jesus in the Temple, and Jesus healed them. The leading priests and the teachers of the law saw that Jesus was doing wonderful things. They saw the children praising him in the Temple. The children were saying, "Praise to the Son of David." All these things made the priests and the teachers of the law very angry.

Jewish Leaders Try to Trap Jesus

Then the Pharisees made plans to trap Jesus with a question. They sent some of their own followers. These men said, "Teacher, tell us what you think. Is it right to pay taxes to Caesar or not?"

But Jesus knew that these men were trying to trick him. So he said, "You hypocrites! Why are you trying to trap me? Show me a coin used for paying the tax." The men showed him a silver coin. Then Jesus asked, "Whose picture is on the coin? And whose name is written on the coin?"

The men answered, "Caesar's."

Then Jesus said to them, "Give to Caesar the things that are Caesar's. And give to God the things that are God's."

The men heard what Jesus said, and they were amazed. They left him and went away.

The Most Important Command

The Pharisees met together. One Pharisee was an expert in the law of Moses. That Pharisee asked Jesus a question to test him. The Pharisee asked, "Teacher, which command in the law is the most important?"

Jesus answered, "'Love the Lord your God with all your heart, soul and mind.' This is the first and most important command. And the second command is like the first: 'Love your neighbor as you love yourself.' All the law and the writings of the prophets depend on these two commands."

Jesus Accuses Jewish Leaders

Then Jesus spoke to the crowds and to his followers. Jesus said, "The teachers of the law and the Pharisees tell you to do things, but they don't do the things themselves. They make strict rules and try to force people to obey them. But they themselves will not try to follow any of those rules.

"How terrible for you, teachers of the law and Pharisees. You are like tombs that are painted white. Outside, those tombs look fine. But inside, they are full of the bones of dead people.

"You are snakes! A family of poisonous snakes! You will not escape God. You will all be judged guilty and be sent to hell!"

The King Will Judge All People

Later, Jesus was sitting on the Mount of Olives. His followers came to be alone with him. They said, "What will happen to show us that it is time for you to come again and for the world to end?"

Jesus answered: "No one knows when that day or time will be. Even the Son and the angels in heaven don't know. Only the Father knows. So always be ready. The Son of Man will come at a time you don't expect him.

"The Son of Man will come again in his great glory. All his angels will come with him. He will be King and sit on his great throne. All the people of the world will be gathered before him. Then he will separate them into two groups as a shepherd separates the sheep from the goats. The Son of Man will put the sheep, the good people, on his right and the goats, the bad people, on his left.

"Then the King will say to the good people on his right, 'Come. My Father has given you his blessing. Come and receive the kingdom God has prepared for you since the world was made. I was hungry, and you gave me food. I was thirsty, and you gave me something to drink. I was alone and away from home, and you invited me into your house. I was without clothes, and you gave me something to wear. I was sick, and you cared for me. I was in prison, and you visited me.'

"Then the good people will answer, 'Lord, when did we see you hungry and give you food? When did we see you thirsty and give you something to drink? When did we see you alone and away from home and invite you into our house? When did we see you without clothes and give you something to wear? When did we see you sick or in prison and care for you?'

"Then the King will answer, 'I tell you the truth. Anything you did for any of my people here, you also did for me.'

"Then the King will say to those on his left, 'Go away from me. God has said that you will be punished. Go into the fire that burns forever. That fire was prepared for the devil and his helpers. I was hungry, and you gave me nothing to eat. I was thirsty, and you gave me nothing to drink. I was alone and away from home, and you did not invite me into your house. I was without clothes, and you gave me nothing to wear. I was sick and in prison, and you did not care for me.'

"Then those people will answer, 'Lord, when did we see you hungry or thirsty? When did we see you alone and away from home? Or when did we see you without clothes or sick or in prison? When did we see these things and not help you?'

"Then the King will answer, 'I tell you the truth. Anything you refused to do for any of my people here, you refused to do for me.'

"These people will go off to be punished forever. But the good people will go to live forever."

The Plan to Kill Jesus

After Jesus finished saying all these things, he told his followers, "You know that the day after tomorrow is the day of the Passover Feast. On that day the Son of Man will be given to his enemies to be killed on a cross."

Then the leading priests and the older Jewish leaders had a meeting at the palace of the high priest. At the meeting, they planned to set a trap to arrest Jesus and kill him.

Judas Becomes an Enemy of Jesus

Then 1 of the 12 followers went to talk to the leading priests. This was the follower named Judas Iscariot. He said, "I will give Jesus to you. What will you pay me for doing this?" The priests gave Judas 30 silver coins. After that, Judas waited for the best time to give Jesus to the priests.

Jesus Eats the Passover Feast

On the first day of the Feast of Unleavened Bread, the followers came to Jesus. They said, "We will prepare everything for you to eat the Passover Feast."

Jesus answered, "Go into the city to a certain man. Tell him that the Teacher says, 'The chosen time is near. I will have the Passover Feast with my followers at your house.'"

In the evening Jesus was sitting at the table with his 12 followers. They were all eating. Then Jesus said, "I tell you the truth. One of you 12 will turn against me."

The Lord's Supper

While they were eating, Jesus took some bread. He thanked God for it and broke it. Then he gave it to his followers and said, "Take this bread and eat it. This bread is my body."

Then Jesus took a cup. He thanked God for it and gave it to

the followers. He said, "Every one of you drink this. This is my blood which begins the new agreement that God makes with his people. This blood is poured out for many to forgive their sins."

They sang a hymn. Then they went out to the Mount of Olives.

Jesus' Followers Will All Leave Him

Jesus told the followers, "Tonight you will lose your faith because of me. It is written in the Scriptures: 'I will kill the shepherd, and the sheep will scatter.'

"But after I rise from death, I will go ahead of you into Galilee."

Peter said, "All the other followers may lose their faith because of you. But I will never lose my faith."

Jesus said, "I tell you the truth. Tonight you will say you don't know me. You will say this three times before the rooster crows."

But Peter said, "I will never say that I don't know you! I will even die with you!" And all the other followers said the same thing.

Jesus Prays Alone

Then Jesus went with his followers to a place called Geth-semane. He said to them, "Sit here while I go over there and pray." He told Peter and the two sons of Zebedee to come with him. Then Jesus began to be very sad and troubled. He said to Peter and the two sons of Zebedee, "My heart is full of sorrow and breaking with sadness. Stay here with me and watch."

Then Jesus walked a little farther away from them. He fell to the ground and prayed, "My Father, if it is possible, do not give me this cup of suffering. But do what you want, not what I want." Then Jesus went back to his followers and found them asleep. Jesus said to Peter, "You men could not stay awake with me for one hour? Stay awake and pray for strength against temptation. Your spirit wants to do what is right. But your body is weak."

Then Jesus went away a second time. He prayed, "My Father, if it is not possible for this painful thing to be taken from me, and if I must do it, then I pray that what you want will be done."

Then Jesus went back to the followers. Again he found them asleep, because their eyes were heavy. So Jesus left them and went away one more time and prayed. This third time he prayed, he said the same thing.

Then Jesus went back to the followers and said, "You are still sleeping and resting? The time has come for the Son of Man to be given to sinful people. Get up. We must go. Here comes the man who has turned against me."

Jesus Is Arrested

While Jesus was still speaking, Judas came up. Judas was 1 of the 12 followers. He had many people with him. They had been sent from the leading priests and the older leaders of the people. They carried swords and clubs. Judas had planned to give them a signal. He had said, "The man I kiss is Jesus. Arrest him." At once Judas went to Jesus and said, "Greetings, Teacher!" Then Judas kissed him.

Jesus answered, "Friend, do the thing you came to do."

Then the men came and grabbed Jesus and arrested him. Jesus said, "Surely you know I could ask my Father, and he would give me more than 12 armies of angels. But this thing must happen this way so that it will be as the Scriptures say."

Then all of Jesus' followers left him and ran away.

Jesus Before the Jewish Leaders

Those men who arrested Jesus led him to the house of the high priest. The teachers of the law and the older Jewish leaders were gathered there. Peter followed Jesus but did not go near him. He followed Jesus to the courtyard of the high priest's house. He sat down with the guards to see what would happen to Jesus.

The leading priests and the Jewish council tried to find something false against Jesus so that they could kill him. Many people came and told lies about him. But the council could find no real reason to kill Jesus. Then two people came and said, "This man said, 'I can destroy the Temple of God and build it again in three days.'"

Then the high priest stood up and said to Jesus, "Aren't you going to answer? Don't you have something to say about their charges against you?" But Jesus said nothing.

Again the high priest said to Jesus, "You must swear to this. I command you by the power of the living God to tell us the truth. Tell us, are you the Christ, the Son of God?"

Jesus answered, "Yes, I am. But I tell you, in the future you will see the Son of Man sitting at the right hand of God, the Powerful One. And you will see him coming in clouds in the sky."

When the high priest heard this, he was very angry. He tore his clothes and said, "This man has said things that are against God! We don't need any more witnesses. You all heard him say these things against God. What do you think?"

The people answered, "He is guilty, and he must die."

Then the people there spit in Jesus' face and beat him with their fists. Others slapped Jesus. They said, "Prove to us that you are a prophet, you Christ! Tell us who hit you!"

Peter Says He Doesn't Know Jesus

At that time, Peter was sitting in the courtyard. A servant girl came to him and said, "You were with Jesus, that man from Galilee."

But Peter said that he was never with Jesus. He said this to all the people there. Peter said, "I don't know what you are talking about."

Then he left the courtyard. At the gate, another girl saw him. She said to the people there, "This man was with Jesus of Nazareth."

Again, Peter said that he was never with Jesus. Peter said, "I swear that I don't know this man Jesus!"

A short time later, some people standing there went to Peter. They said, "We know you are one of those men who followed Jesus. We know this because of the way you talk."

Then Peter began to curse. He said, "May a curse fall on me if I'm not telling the truth. I don't know the man." After Peter said this, a rooster crowed. Then he remembered what Jesus had told him: "Before the rooster crows, you will say three times that you don't know me." Then Peter went outside and cried painfully.

Jesus Is Taken to Pilate

Early the next morning, all the leading priests and older leaders of the people decided to kill Jesus. They tied him, led him away, and turned him over to Pilate, the governor.

Judas Kills Himself

Judas saw that they had decided to kill Jesus. Judas was the one who gave Jesus to his enemies. When Judas saw what happened, he was very sorry for what he had done. So he took the 30 silver coins back to the priests and the leaders. Judas said, "I sinned. I gave you an innocent man to be killed."

The leaders answered, "What is that to us? That's your problem, not ours."

So Judas threw the money into the Temple. Then he went off and hanged himself.

Pilate Questions Jesus

Jesus stood before Pilate the governor. Pilate asked him, "Are you the King of the Jews?"

Jesus answered, "Yes, I am."

When the leading priests and the older leaders accused Jesus, he said nothing.

So Pilate said to Jesus, "Don't you hear these people accusing you of all these things?"

But Jesus said nothing in answer to Pilate. Pilate was very surprised at this.

Pilate Tries to Free Jesus

Every year at the time of Passover the governor would free one person from prison. This was always a person the people wanted to be set free. At that time there was a man in prison who was known to be very bad. His name was Barabbas. All the people gathered at Pilate's house. Pilate said, "Which man do you want me to free: Barabbas, or Jesus who is called the Christ?" Pilate knew that the people gave Jesus to him because they were jealous.

Pilate said these things while he was sitting on the judge's seat. While he was sitting there, his wife sent a message to him. The message said, "Don't do anything to that man. He is not guilty. Today I had a dream about him, and it troubled me very much."

But the leading priests and older leaders told the crowd to ask for Barabbas to be freed and for Jesus to be killed.

Pilate said, "I have Barabbas and Jesus. Which do you want me to set free for you?"

The people answered, "Barabbas!"

Pilate asked, "What should I do with Jesus, the one called the Christ?"

They all answered, "Kill him on a cross!"

Pilate asked, "Why do you want me to kill him? What wrong has he done?"

But they shouted louder, "Kill him on a cross!"

Pilate saw that he could do nothing about this, and a riot was starting. So he took some water and washed his hands in front of the crowd. Then he said, "I am not guilty of this man's death. You are the ones who are causing it!"

All the people answered, "We will be responsible. We accept for ourselves and for our children any punishment for his death."

Then Pilate freed Barabbas. Pilate told some of the soldiers to beat Jesus with whips. Then he gave Jesus to the soldiers to be killed on a cross.

Pilate's soldiers took Jesus into the governor's palace. All the soldiers gathered around Jesus. They took off his clothes and put a red robe on him. Then the soldiers used thorny branches to make a crown. They put this crown of thorns on Jesus' head. They put a stick in his right hand. Then the soldiers bowed before Jesus and made fun of him. They said, "Hail, King of the Jews!" They spit on Jesus. Then they took his stick and hit him on the head many times. After they finished making fun of Jesus, the soldiers took off the robe and put his own clothes on him again. Then they led Jesus away to be killed on a cross.

Jesus Is Killed on a Cross

The soldiers were going out of the city with Jesus. They forced another man to carry the cross to be used for Jesus. This man was Simon, from Cyrene.

They all came to the place called Golgotha. (Golgotha means the Place of the Skull.) At Golgotha, the soldiers gave Jesus wine to drink. This wine was mixed with gall. He tasted the wine but refused to drink it. The soldiers nailed Jesus to a cross. They threw lots to decide who would get his clothes. The soldiers sat there and continued watching him. They put a sign above Jesus' head with the charge against him written on it. The sign read: "THIS IS JESUS, THE KING OF THE JEWS." Two robbers were nailed to crosses beside Jesus, one on the right and the other on the left. People walked by and insulted Jesus. They shook their heads, saying, "You said you could destroy the Temple and build it again in three days. So save yourself! Come down from that cross, if you are really the Son of God!"

The leading priests, the teachers of the law, and the older Jewish leaders were also there. These men made fun of Jesus and said, "He saved other people, but he can't save himself! People say he is the King of Israel! If he is the King, then let him come down now from the cross. Then we will believe in him. He trusts in God. So let God save him now, if God really wants him. He himself

said, 'I am the Son of God.'"
And in the same way, the
robbers who were being killed
on crosses beside Jesus also
insulted him.

Jesus Dies

At noon the whole country
became dark. This darkness
lasted for three hours. About
three o'clock Jesus cried out in a
loud voice, "Eli, Eli, lema
sabachthani?" This means, "My
God, my God, why have you left
me alone?"

Some of the people standing
there heard this. They said, "He
is calling Elijah."

Quickly one of them ran and
got a sponge. He filled the
sponge with vinegar and tied it
to a stick. Then he used the stick
to give the sponge to Jesus to
drink from it. But the others
said, "Don't bother him. We
want to see if Elijah will come to
save him."

Again Jesus cried out in a
loud voice. Then he died.

Then the curtain in the
Temple split into two pieces. The
tear started at the top and tore
all the way down to the bottom.
Also, the earth shook and rocks
broke apart. The graves opened,
and many of God's people who
had died were raised from
death. They came out of the
graves after Jesus was raised
from death. They went into the
holy city, and many people saw
them.

The army officer and the
soldiers guarding Jesus saw this
earthquake and everything else
that happened. They were very
frightened and said, "He really
was the Son of God!"

Many women were standing
at a distance from the cross,
watching. These were women
who had followed Jesus from
Galilee to care for him. Mary
Magdalene, and Mary the
mother of James and Joseph,
and the mother of James and
John were there.

Jesus Is Buried

That evening a rich man
named Joseph came to
Jerusalem. He was a follower of
Jesus from the town of
Arimathea. Joseph went to
Pilate and asked to have Jesus'
body. Pilate gave orders for the
soldiers to give it to Joseph. Then
Joseph took the body and
wrapped it in a clean linen
cloth.

He put Jesus' body in a new
tomb that he had cut in a wall
of rock. He rolled a very large
stone to block the entrance of
the tomb. Then Joseph went
away. Mary Magdalene and the
other woman named Mary were
sitting near the tomb.

The Tomb Is Guarded

That day was the day called Preparation Day. The next day, the leading priests and the Pharisees went to Pilate. They said, "Sir, we remember that while that liar was still alive he said, 'After three days I will rise from death.' So give the order for the tomb to be guarded closely till the third day. His followers might come and steal the body. Then they could tell the people that he has risen from death. That lie would be even worse than the first one."

Pilate said, "Take some soldiers and go guard the tomb the best way you know." So they all went to the tomb and made it safe from thieves. They did this by sealing the stone in the entrance and then putting soldiers there to guard it.

Jesus Rises from Death

The day after the Sabbath day was the first day of the week. At dawn on the first day, Mary Magdalene and another woman named Mary went to look at the tomb.

At that time there was a strong earthquake. An angel of the Lord came down from heaven. The angel went to the tomb and rolled the stone away from the entrance. Then he sat on the stone. He was shining as bright as lightning. His clothes were white as snow. The soldiers guarding the tomb were very frightened of the angel. They shook with fear and then became like dead men.

The angel said to the women, "Don't be afraid. I know that you are looking for

---

P A U S E & W O N D E R

The Bible is like a rose. In the Old Testament the flower is only a bud. It is opening very slowly. In the New Testament that same flower opens into a full bloom, beautiful in color and smell. Both the Old and New Testaments give us the same message. In the Old Testament, this message about Jesus becomes clear only slowly. But in the New Testament the message is open all the way. All the rich beauty is there for me to know and enjoy.

Jesus, the one who was killed on the cross. But he is not here. He has risen from death as he said he would. Come and see the place where his body was. And go quickly and tell his followers. Say to them: 'Jesus has risen from death. He is going into Galilee. He will be there before you. You will see him there.'" Then the angel said, "Now I have told you."

The women left the tomb quickly. They were afraid, but they were also very happy. They ran to tell Jesus' followers what had happened. Suddenly, Jesus met them and said, "Greetings." The women came up to Jesus, took hold of his feet, and worshiped him. Then Jesus said to them, "Don't be afraid. Go and tell my brothers to go on to Galilee. They will see me there."

The Soldiers Report to the Jewish Leaders

The women went to tell Jesus' followers. At the same time, some of the soldiers who had been guarding the tomb went into the city. They went to tell the leading priests everything that had happened. Then the priests met with the older Jewish leaders and made a plan. They paid the soldiers a large amount of money. They said to the soldiers, "Tell the people that Jesus' followers came during the night and stole the body while you were asleep. If the governor hears about this, we will satisfy him and save you from trouble." So the soldiers kept the money and obeyed the priests.

Jesus Talks to His Followers

The 11 followers went to Galilee. They went to the mountain where Jesus told them to go. On the mountain they saw Jesus and worshiped him. But some of them did not believe that it was really Jesus. Then Jesus came to them and said, "All power in heaven and on earth is given to me. So go and make followers of all people in the world. Baptize them in the name of the Father and the Son and the Holy Spirit. Teach them to obey everything that I have told you. You can be sure that I will be with you always. I will continue with you until the end of the world."

WORTH WONDERING...

■ Why can we learn so much about God by learning about Jesus Christ?

■ Why did Jesus Christ come down to this world?

■ Suppose you were a famous artist. Someone has asked you to paint a picture showing something that happens in this book of Matthew. What person or event from this book would you choose to paint?

■ What good example can you give of someone in this book who did what was right?

■ What example can you give of someone in this book who did what was wrong?

■ What promises do you remember seeing Jesus make to us in this book?

■ What commands do you remember seeing in this book — things that God tells us to do or to be?

■ Here in Matthew, Jesus says that everyone who hears His words and obeys them is like a wise man who built his house on rock. Which words in this book do you think are the most important for you to obey right now?

■ Suppose a friend asked you this question: Why did Jesus have to die? As you remember what you read in the book of Matthew, how would you answer your friend?

■ If you could meet Simon Peter today, what kind of questions would you like to ask him?

GREAT VERSES TO THINK ABOUT AGAIN...

Look back in Matthew to see if you can find these verses:

■ *The thing you should want most is God's kingdom and doing what God wants. Then all these other things you need will be given to you.*

■ *The work that I ask you to accept is easy. The load I give you to carry is not heavy.*

■ *Always be ready. The Son of Man will come at a time you don't expect him.*

■ *You are the light that gives light to the world.*

AND THERE'S MORE...

When you read Matthew in a full Bible, look especially for...

■ What Jesus teaches about anger.

■ What Jesus says about prayer.

■ A story about a fishing net.

■ A story about a man who wouldn't forgive.

■ What Jesus told His followers about the coming destruction of the Temple.

■ A story about ten girls — five who were wise, and five who were foolish.

The Gospel of
MARK

Jesus,
the Servant of All

Looking forward to Mark...

WHAT'S IT ABOUT?

"Jesus, the Servant of All"

SIGNS AND WONDERS

In the book of Mark we see more miracles of Jesus than teachings of Jesus. Yes, Jesus was a Man of action and power.

FACES AND PLACES

Jesus: The Savior of the world, and the obedient servant of God, His Father.

Mark, who wrote this book, is also known as John Mark. He was not one of the twelve disciples, but he traveled with the apostle Paul. He was also a friend of the apostle Peter.

The 12 Apostles: Jesus chose 12 men and called them apostles, and their names are listed in Mark. They followed Jesus closely, and He also sent them out to preach. These are the 12 men he chose: Peter (also called Simon) and his brother Andrew, James and his brother John (Jesus called them "Sons of Thunder"), Philip, Bartholomew (also called Nathanael), Matthew (also called Levi), Thomas, James the son of Alphaeus, Thaddaeus (also called Judas son of James), Simon the Zealot, and Judas Iscariot. Judas is the one who gave Jesus to his enemies.

(Look also at the list of "Faces and Places" on page 374)

I wonder what it really means that Jesus is the Servant of God...

JESUS WENT into Galilee and preached the Good News from God. Jesus said, "The right time has come. The kingdom of God is near. Change your hearts and lives and believe the Good News!"

Jesus Heals a Sick Man

A man who had a harmful skin disease came to Jesus. The man fell to his knees and begged Jesus, "I know that you can heal me if you will."

Jesus felt sorry for the man. So he touched him and said, "I want to heal you. Be healed!" At once the disease left the man, and he was healed.

Jesus Heals a Paralyzed Man

A few days later, Jesus came back to Capernaum. The news spread that he was home. So many people gathered to hear him preach that the house was full. There was no place to stand, not even outside the door. Jesus was teaching them. Some people came, bringing a paralyzed man to Jesus. Four of them were carrying the paralyzed man. But they could not get to Jesus because of the crowd. So they went to the roof above Jesus and made a hole in the roof. Then they lowered the mat with the paralyzed man on it. Jesus saw that these men had great faith. So he said to the paralyzed man, "Young man, your sins are forgiven."

Some of the teachers of the law were sitting there. They saw what Jesus did, and they said to themselves, "Why does this man say things like that? He is saying things that are against God. Only God can forgive sins."

At once Jesus knew what these teachers of the law were thinking. So he said to them, "Why are you thinking these things? Which is easier: to tell this paralyzed man, 'Your sins are forgiven,' or to tell him, 'Stand up. Take your mat and walk'? But I will prove to you that the Son of Man has authority on earth to forgive sins." So Jesus said to the paralyzed man, "I tell you, stand up. Take your mat and go home." Immediately the paralyzed man stood up. He took his mat and walked out while everyone was watching him.

The people were amazed and praised God. They said, "We have never seen anything like this!"

Jesus Chooses His 12 Apostles

Then Jesus went up on a hill and called some men to come to him. These were the men Jesus wanted, and they went up to him. Jesus chose 12 men and called them apostles. He wanted these 12 to be with him, and he wanted to send them to other places to preach. He also wanted them to have the power to force demons out of people. These are the 12 men he chose: Simon (Jesus gave him the name Peter); James and John, the sons of Zebedee (Jesus gave them the name Boanerges, which means "Sons of Thunder"); Andrew, Philip, Bartholomew, Matthew, Thomas, James the son of Alphaeus, Thaddaeus, Simon the Zealot, and Judas Iscariot. Judas is the one who gave Jesus to his enemies.

A Story About Planting Seed

Another time Jesus began teaching by the lake. A great crowd gathered around him. So he got into a boat and went out on the lake. All the people stayed on the shore close to the water. Jesus used many stories to teach them. He said, "Listen! A farmer went out to plant his seed. While the farmer was planting, some seed fell by the road. The birds came and ate all that seed. Some seed fell on rocky ground where there wasn't much dirt. The seed grew very fast there because the ground was not deep. But when the sun rose, the plants withered. The plants died because they did not have deep roots. Some other seed fell among thorny weeds. The weeds grew and choked the good plants. So those plants did not make grain. Some other seed fell on good ground. In the good ground, the seed began to grow. It grew and made a crop of grain. Some plants made 30 times more grain, some 60 times more grain, and some 100 times more grain."

Then Jesus said, "You people who hear me, listen!"

Jesus Tells Why He Used Stories

Later, when Jesus was alone, the 12 apostles and others around him asked him about the stories.

Jesus said, "Only you can know the secret truth about the kingdom of God. But to other people I tell everything by using stories."

Jesus Explains the Seed Story

Then Jesus said to the followers, "Do you understand this story? If you don't, then how will you understand any story? The farmer is like a person who plants God's teaching in people. Sometimes the teaching falls on the road. This is like some people. They hear the teaching of God. But Satan quickly comes and takes away the teaching that was planted in them.

"Others are like the seed planted on rocky ground. They hear the teaching and quickly accept it with joy. But they don't allow the teaching to go deep into their lives. They keep it only a short time. When trouble or persecution comes because of

PAUSE & WONDER

God's teaching — the Bible — is the seed in the story Jesus told. Is my heart good soil for God's teaching to grow in? Am I listening carefully to it? Am I asking questions in my heart about the true meaning of it? And do I want to do what God teaches me to do?

the teaching, they quickly give up.

"Others are like the seed planted among the thorny weeds. They hear the teaching. But then other things come into their lives: worries, the love of money, and wanting all kinds of other things. These things stop the teaching from growing. So that teaching does not produce fruit in their lives.

"Others are like the seed planted in the good ground. They hear the teaching and accept it. Then they grow and produce fruit — sometimes 30 times more, sometimes 60 times more, and sometimes 100 times more."

Jesus used many stories like these to teach them. He taught them all that they could understand. He always used stories to teach them. But when he and his followers were alone together, Jesus explained everything to them.

Jesus Stops a Storm

That evening, Jesus said to his followers, "Come with me across the lake." He and the followers left the people there. They went in the boat that Jesus was already sitting in. There were also other boats with them. A very strong wind came up on the lake. The waves began coming over the sides and into the boat. It was almost full of water. Jesus was at the back of the boat, sleeping with his head on a pillow. The followers went to him and woke him. They said, "Teacher, do you care about us? We will drown!"

Jesus stood up and commanded the wind and the waves to stop. He said, "Quiet! Be still!" Then the wind stopped, and the lake became calm.

Jesus said to his followers, "Why are you afraid? Do you still have no faith?"

The followers were very afraid and asked each other, "What kind of man is this? Even the wind and the waves obey him!"

Jesus Gives Healing and Life

Jesus went in the boat back to the other side of the lake. There, a large crowd gathered around him. A ruler from the synagogue, named Jairus, came to that place. Jairus saw Jesus and bowed before him. The ruler begged Jesus again and again. He said, "My little daughter is dying. Please come and put your hands on her. Then she will be healed and will live." So Jesus went with the ruler, and many people followed Jesus. They were pushing very close around him.

A woman was there who had been bleeding for the past 12 years. She had suffered very much. Many doctors had tried to help her. She had spent all the money she had, but she was not improving. She was getting worse. When the woman heard about Jesus, she followed him with the people and touched his coat. The woman thought, "If I can even touch his coat, that will be enough to heal me." When she touched his coat, her bleeding stopped. She could feel in her body that she was healed.

At once Jesus felt power go out from him. So he stopped and turned around. Then he asked, "Who touched my clothes?"

The followers said, "There are so many people pushing against you! And you ask, 'Who touched me?'"

But Jesus continued looking around to see who had touched him. The woman knew that she was healed. So she came and bowed at Jesus' feet. Shaking with fear, she told him the whole story. Jesus said to the woman, "Dear woman, you are made well because you believed. Go in peace. You will have no more suffering."

Jesus was still speaking to her when some men came from the house of Jairus, the synagogue ruler. The men said, "Your daughter is dead. There is now no need to bother the teacher."

But Jesus paid no attention to what the men said. He said to the synagogue ruler, "Don't be afraid; only believe."

Jesus let only Peter, James, and John the brother of James go with him to Jairus's house. They came to the house of the synagogue ruler, and Jesus found many people there crying loudly. There was much confusion. Jesus entered the house and said to the people, "Why are you crying and making so much noise? This child is not dead. She is only asleep." But they only laughed at Jesus. He told all the people to leave. Then he went into the room where the child was. He took the child's father and mother and his three followers into the room with him. Then he took hold of the girl's hand and said to her, "Talitha, koum!" (This means, "Little girl, I tell you to stand up!") The girl stood right up and began walking. (She was 12 years old.) The father and mother and the followers were amazed. Jesus gave the father and mother strict orders not to tell people about this. Then he told them to give the girl some food.

Jesus Heals a Deaf Man

Jesus went to Lake Galilee, to the area of the Ten Towns. While he was there, some people brought a man to him. This man was deaf and could not talk. The people begged Jesus to put his hand on the man to heal him.

Jesus led the man away from the crowd, to be alone with him. Jesus put his fingers in the man's ears. Then Jesus spit and touched the man's tongue. Jesus looked up to heaven and took a deep breath. He said to the man, "Ephphatha!" (This means, "Be opened.") When Jesus did this, the man was able to hear. He was also able to use his tongue, and he spoke clearly.

Jesus commanded the people not to tell anyone about what happened. But the more he commanded them, the more they told about it. They were really amazed. They said, "Jesus does everything well. He makes the deaf hear! And those who can't talk — Jesus makes them able to speak."

Jesus Heals a Blind Man

Jesus and his followers came to Bethsaida. Some people brought a blind man to Jesus and begged him to touch the man. So Jesus took the blind man's hand and led him out of the village. Then he spit on the man's eyes. He put his hands on the blind man and asked, "Can you see now?"

The man looked up and said, "Yes, I see people, but they look like trees walking around."

Again Jesus put his hands on the man's eyes. Then the man opened his eyes wide. His eyes were healed, and he was able to see everything clearly.

Then Jesus began to teach them that the Son of Man must suffer many things. He taught that the Son of Man would not be accepted by the older Jewish leaders, the leading priests, and the teachers of the law. He taught that the Son of Man must be killed and then rise from death after three days. Jesus told them plainly what would happen.

Who Is the Greatest?

Jesus and his followers went to Capernaum and went into a house there. Then Jesus said to them, "What were you arguing about on the road?" But the followers did not answer, because their argument on the road was about which one of them was the greatest.

Jesus sat down and called the 12 apostles to him. He said, "If anyone wants to be the most important, then he must be last of all and servant of all."

Then Jesus took a small child and had him stand among them. He took the child in his arms and said, "If anyone accepts children like these in my name, then he is also accepting me. And if he accepts me, then he is also accepting the One who sent me."

Two Followers Ask Jesus a Favor

Then James and John, sons of Zebedee, came to Jesus. They said, "Teacher, we want to ask you to do something for us."

Jesus asked, "What do you want me to do for you?"

They answered, "You will have glory in your kingdom. Let one of us sit at your right, and let one of us sit at your left."

Jesus said to them, "I cannot choose who will sit at my right or my left. These places are for those for whom they are prepared."

The ten followers heard this. They began to be angry with James and John.

Jesus called all the followers together. He said, "The non-Jewish people have men they call rulers. You know that those rulers love to show their power over the people. And their important leaders love to use all their authority. But it should not be that way among you. If one of you wants to become great, then he must serve you like a servant. If one of you wants to become the most important, then he must serve all of you like a slave. In the same way, the Son of Man did not come to be served. He came to serve. The Son of Man came to give his life to save many people."

True Giving

Jesus entered Jerusalem and went into the Temple. Jesus sat near the Temple money box where people put their gifts. He watched the people put in their money. Many rich people gave large sums of money. Then a poor widow came and gave two very small copper coins. These coins were not worth even a penny.

Jesus called his followers to him. He said, "I tell you the truth. This poor widow gave only two small coins. But she really gave more than all those rich people. The rich have plenty; they gave only what they did not need. This woman is very poor. But she gave all she had. And she needed that money to help her live."

WORTH WONDERING...

■ Use your imagination for this one: Suppose you were there when the paralyzed man was lowered through the roof so Jesus could heal him. What kinds of things do you think you would see and hear and smell?

■ What commands can you find in this book — things that God tells us to do or to be?

■ Jesus said (in the book of Matthew) that everyone who hears His words and obeys them is like a wise man who built his house on rock. Which words in this book do you think are the most important for you to obey right now?

■ What do you think are the most important things this book tells us about Jesus?

■ Think about some friends you have who might know very little about Jesus or the Bible. What parts of this book do you think would be most interesting to them?

GREAT VERSES TO THINK ABOUT AGAIN...

Look back in Mark to see if you can find these verses:

■ *The Son of Man did not come to be served. He came to serve. The Son of Man came to give his life to save many people.*

■ *The right time has come. The kingdom of God is near. Change your hearts and lives and believe the Good News!*

■ *What kind of man is this? Even the wind and the waves obey him!*

AND THERE'S MORE...

Mark also tells in his own way many of the things about Jesus which are in Matthew's gospel. When you read Mark in a full Bible, look also for...

■ Many more people whom Jesus healed.

■ What Jesus said about His true family.

■ Another story Jesus told about seed.

■ A rich young man and his questions for Jesus.

The Gospel of
LUKE

*Jesus, the Man
of Compassion*

Looking forward to Luke...

"Jesus, the Man of Compassion"

Especially in the gospel of Luke we see the love and friendship Jesus had for many different kinds of people. He offers this same love and friendship today to anyone who will believe and obey Him.

Jesus: The Son of God, the Savior of the world, and the perfect Man.

Luke, who wrote this book, was a doctor and friend of the apostle Paul. He went along on some of Paul's missionary trips. He also wrote the book of Acts. To write this gospel, he talked with the people who are mentioned in this book. Then he wrote down what they told him.

Simeon: A good man living in Jerusalem. God had told Simeon that before he died, he would see the Messiah whom God had promised in the Old Testament.

Anna: An old woman who loved to worship God in the Temple in Jerusalem.

Samaritans: People who lived in Samaria. Samaria was the area between Galilee and Judea, the land where the Jews lived. Jews looked down on Samaritans.

Mary and **Martha:** Sisters who lived in the town of Bethany near Jerusalem.

Zacchaeus: A rich tax collector in the city of Jericho.

(Look also at the list of "Faces and Places" on page 374)

I wonder what it really means that Jesus was a perfect Man...

DURING THE TIME Herod ruled Judea, there was a priest named Zechariah. Zechariah's wife was Elizabeth. Zechariah and Elizabeth truly did what God said was good. But Zechariah and Elizabeth had no children. Elizabeth could not have a baby; and both of them were very old.

Zechariah was serving as a priest before God. According to the custom of the priests, he was chosen to go into the Temple of the Lord and burn incense. There were a great many people outside praying at the time the incense was offered. Then, on the right side of the incense table, an angel of the Lord came and stood before Zechariah. When he saw the angel, Zechariah was confused and frightened. But the angel said to him, "Zechariah, don't be afraid. Your prayer has been heard by God. Your wife, Elizabeth, will give birth to a son. You will name him John. You will be very happy. Many people will be happy because of his birth. John will be a great man for the Lord. He will never drink wine or beer. Even at the time John is born, he will be filled with the Holy Spirit. He will help many people of Israel return to the Lord their God. He himself will go first before the Lord. John will be powerful in spirit like Elijah. He will make peace between fathers and their children. He will bring those who are not obeying God back to the right way of thinking. He will make people ready for the coming of the Lord."

Zechariah said to the angel, "How can I know that what you say is true? I am an old man, and my wife is old, too."

The angel answered him, "I am Gabriel. I stand before God. God sent me to talk to you and to tell you this good news. Now, listen! You will not be able to talk until the day these things happen. You will lose your speech because you did not believe what I told you. But these things will really happen."

Outside, the people were still waiting for Zechariah. They were surprised that he was staying so long in the Temple. Then Zechariah came outside, but he could not speak to them. So they knew that he had seen a vision in the Temple. Zechariah could not speak. He could only make signs to them. When his time of service as a priest was finished, he went home.

Later, Zechariah's wife, Elizabeth, became pregnant. Elizabeth said, "Look what the Lord has done for me! My people were ashamed of me, but now the Lord has taken away that shame."

The Virgin Mary

God sent the angel Gabriel to a virgin who lived in Nazareth, a town in Galilee. She was engaged to marry a man named Joseph from the family of David. Her name was Mary. The angel came to her and said, "Greetings! The Lord has blessed you and is with you."

But Mary was very confused by what the angel said. Mary wondered, "What does this mean?"

The angel said to her, "Don't be afraid, Mary, because God is pleased with you. Listen! You will become pregnant. You will give birth to a son, and you will name him Jesus. He will be great, and people will call him the Son of the Most High. The Lord God will give him the throne of King David, his ancestor. He will rule over the people of Jacob forever. His kingdom will never end."

Mary said to the angel, "How will this happen? I am a virgin!"

The angel said to Mary, "The Holy Spirit will come upon you, and the power of the Most High will cover you. The baby will be holy. He will be called the Son of God. Now listen! Elizabeth, your relative, is very old. But she is also pregnant with a son. Everyone thought she could not have a baby, but she has been pregnant for six months. God can do everything!"

Mary said, "I am the servant

girl of the Lord. Let this happen to me as you say!" Then the angel went away.

Mary's Visit

Mary got up and went quickly to a town in the mountains of Judea. She went to Zechariah's house and greeted Elizabeth. When Elizabeth heard Mary's greeting, the unborn baby inside Elizabeth jumped. Then Elizabeth was filled with the Holy Spirit. She cried out in a loud voice, "God has blessed you more than any other woman. And God has blessed the baby which you will give birth to. You are the mother of my Lord, and you have come to me! Why has something so good happened to me? When I heard your voice, the baby inside me jumped with joy. You are blessed because you believed what the Lord said to you would really happen."

Mary stayed with Elizabeth for about three months and then returned home.

The Birth of John

When it was time for Elizabeth to give birth, she had a boy. Her neighbors and relatives heard how good the Lord was to her, and they rejoiced.

When the baby was eight days old, they came to circumcise him. They wanted to name him Zechariah because this was his father's name. But his mother said, "No! He will be named John."

The people said to Elizabeth, "But no one in your family has this name!" Then they made signs to his father, "What would you like to name him?"

Zechariah asked for something to write on. Then he wrote, "His name is John." Everyone was surprised. Then Zechariah could talk again. He began to praise God. And all their neighbors became alarmed. In all the mountains of Judea people continued talking about all these things. The people who heard about these things wondered about them. They thought, "What will this child be?" They said this because the Lord was with him.

And so the child grew up and became strong in spirit. John lived away from other people until the time when he came out to preach to Israel.

The Birth of Jesus

At that time, Augustus Caesar sent an order to all people in the countries that were under Roman rule. The order said that they must list their names in a register. And everyone went to their own towns to be registered.

So Joseph left Nazareth, a town in Galilee. He went to the

town of Bethlehem in Judea. This town was known as the town of David. Joseph went there because he was from the family of David. Joseph registered with Mary because she was engaged to marry him. (Mary was now pregnant.) While Joseph and Mary were in Bethlehem, the time came for her to have the baby. She gave birth to her first son. There were no rooms left in the inn. So she wrapped the baby with cloths and laid him in a box where animals are fed.

Some Shepherds Hear About Jesus

That night, some shepherds were in the fields nearby watching their sheep. An angel of the Lord stood before them. The glory of the Lord was shining around them, and suddenly they became very frightened. The angel said to them, "Don't be afraid, because I am bringing you some good news. It will be a joy to all the people. Today your Savior was born in David's town. He is Christ, the Lord. This is how you will know him: You will find a baby wrapped in cloths and lying in a feeding box."

Then a very large group of angels from heaven joined the first angel. All the angels were praising God, saying: "Give glory to God in heaven, and on earth let there be peace to the people who please God."

Then the angels left the shepherds and went back to heaven. The shepherds said to each other, "Let us go to Bethlehem and see this thing that has happened. We will see this thing the Lord told us about."

So the shepherds went quickly and found Mary and Joseph. And the shepherds saw the baby lying in a feeding box. Then they told what the angels had said about this child. Everyone was amazed when they heard what the shepherds said to them. Mary hid these things in her heart; she continued to think about them. Then the shepherds went back to their sheep, praising God and thanking him for everything that they had seen and heard. It was just as the angel had told them.

When the baby was eight days old, he was circumcised, and he was named Jesus. This name had been given by the angel before the baby began to grow inside Mary.

Jesus Is Presented in the Temple

The time came for Mary and Joseph to do what the law of

Moses taught about being made pure. They took Jesus to Jerusalem to present him to the Lord. It is written in the law of the Lord: "Give every firstborn male to the Lord." Mary and Joseph also went to offer a sacrifice, as the law of the Lord says: "You must sacrifice two doves or two young pigeons."

Simeon Sees Jesus

A man named Simeon lived in Jerusalem. He was a good man and very religious. He was waiting for the time when God would help Israel. The Holy Spirit was in him. The Holy Spirit told Simeon that he would not die before he saw the Christ promised by the Lord. The Spirit led Simeon to the Temple. Mary and Joseph brought the baby Jesus to the Temple to do what the law said they must do. Then Simeon took the baby in his arms and thanked God: "Now, Lord, you can let me, your servant, die in peace as you said. I have seen your Salvation with my own eyes. You prepared him before all people. He is a light for the non-Jewish people to see. He will bring honor to your people, the Israelites." Jesus' father and mother were amazed at what Simeon had said about him. Then Simeon blessed them and said to Mary, "Many in Israel will fall and many will rise because of this child. He will be a sign from God that many people will not accept. The things they think in secret will be made known. And the things that will happen will make your heart sad, too."

Anna Sees Jesus

Anna, a prophetess, was there at the Temple. She was very old. She had once been married for seven years. Then her husband died and she lived alone. She was now 84 years old. Anna never left the Temple. She worshiped God by going without food and praying day and night. She was standing there at that time, thanking God. She talked about Jesus to all who were waiting for God to free Jerusalem.

Joseph and Mary Return Home

Joseph and Mary finished doing everything that the law of the Lord commanded. Then they went home to Nazareth, their own town in Galilee. The little child began to grow up. He became stronger and wiser, and God's blessings were with him.

Jesus As a Boy

Every year Jesus' parents went to Jerusalem for the Passover Feast. When Jesus was 12 years old, they went to the feast as they always did. When the feast days were over, they went home. The boy Jesus stayed behind in Jerusalem, but his parents did not know it. Joseph and Mary traveled for a whole day. They thought that Jesus was with them in the group. Then they began to look for him among their family and friends, but they did not find him. So they went back to Jerusalem to look for him there. After three days they found him. Jesus was sitting in the Temple with the religious teachers, listening to them and asking them questions. All who heard him were amazed at his understanding and wise answers. When Jesus' parents saw him, they were amazed. His mother said to him, "Son, why did you do this to us? Your father and I were very worried about you. We have been looking for you."

Jesus asked, "Why did you have to look for me? You should have known that I must be where my Father's work is!" But they did not understand the meaning of what he said.

Jesus went with them to Nazareth and obeyed them. His mother was still thinking about all that had happened. Jesus continued to learn more and more and to grow physically.

People liked him, and he pleased God.

Jesus' First Followers

One day Jesus was standing beside Lake Galilee. Many people were pressing all around him. They wanted to hear the word of God. Jesus saw two boats at the shore of the lake. The fishermen had left them and were washing their nets. Jesus got into one of the boats, the one which belonged to Simon. Jesus asked Simon to push off a little from the land. Then Jesus sat down in the boat and continued to teach the people on the shore.

When Jesus had finished speaking, he said to Simon, "Take the boat into deep water. If you will put your nets in the water, you will catch some fish."

Simon answered, "Master, we worked hard all night trying to catch fish, but we caught nothing. But you say to put the nets in the water; so I will." The fishermen did as Jesus told them. And they caught so many fish that the nets began to break. They called to their friends in the other boat to come and help them. The friends came, and both boats were filled so full that they were almost sinking.

The fishermen were all amazed at the many fish they

caught. When Simon Peter saw what had happened, he bowed down before Jesus and said, "Go away from me, Lord. I am a sinful man!" James and John, the sons of Zebedee, were amazed too. (James and John were Simon's partners.)

Jesus said to Simon, "Don't be afraid. From now on you will be fishermen for men." When the men brought their boats to the shore, they left everything and followed Jesus.

Jesus Heals a Soldier's Servant

Jesus went to Capernaum. In Capernaum there was an army officer. He had a servant who was so sick he was nearly dead. The officer loved the servant very much. When the officer heard about Jesus, he sent some older Jewish leaders to him. The officer wanted the leaders to ask Jesus to come and heal his servant. The men went to Jesus and begged him saying, "This officer is worthy of your help. He loves our people, and he built us a synagogue."

So Jesus went with the men. He was getting near the officer's house when the officer sent friends to say, "Lord, you don't need to come into my house. I am not good enough for you to be under my roof. That is why I did not come to you myself. You only need to say the word, and my servant will be healed. I, too, am a man under the authority of other men. And I have soldiers under my command. I tell one soldier, 'Go,' and he goes. And I tell another soldier, 'Come,' and he comes. And I say to my servant, 'Do this,' and my servant obeys me."

When Jesus heard this, he was amazed. He turned to the crowd following him and said, "I tell you, this is the greatest faith I have seen anywhere, even in Israel."

The men who had been sent to Jesus went back to the house. There they found that the servant was healed.

Jesus Brings a Man Back to Life

The next day Jesus went to a town called Nain. His followers and a large crowd were traveling with him. When he came near the town gate, he saw a funeral. A mother, who was a widow, had lost her only son. A large crowd from the town was with the mother while her son was being carried out. When the Lord saw her, he felt very sorry for her. Jesus said to her, "Don't cry." He went up to the coffin and touched it. The men who were carrying it stopped. Jesus said, "Young man, I tell you, get up!" And the son sat up and began to talk. Then Jesus gave him back to his mother.

All the people were amazed. They began praising God. They said, "A great prophet has come to us! God is taking care of his people."

This news about Jesus spread through all Judea and into all the places around there.

A Man with Demons Inside Him

Jesus and his followers sailed across the lake from Galilee to the area where the Gerasene people live. When Jesus got out of the boat, a man from the town came to Jesus. This man had demons inside him. For a long time he had worn no clothes. He lived in the burial caves, not in a house. When he saw Jesus, he cried out and fell down before him. The man said with a loud voice, "What do you want with me, Jesus, Son of the Most High God? Please don't punish me!" He said this because Jesus had commanded the evil spirit to come out of him. Many times it had taken hold of him. He had been kept under guard and chained hand and foot. But he had broken his chains and had been driven by the demon out into the desert.

On the hill there was a large herd of pigs eating. The demons begged Jesus to allow them to go into the pigs. So Jesus allowed them to do this. Then the demons came out of the man and went into the pigs. The herd of pigs ran down the hill and into the lake. All the pigs drowned.

The men who took care of the pigs ran away. They told about this in the town and the countryside. And people went to see what had happened. They came to Jesus and found the man sitting there at Jesus' feet. The man was clothed and in his right mind because the demons were gone. But the people were frightened. The men who saw these things happen told the others all about how Jesus had made the man well. All the people of the Gerasene country asked Jesus to go away. They were all very afraid. So Jesus got into the boat and went back to Galilee.

The man that Jesus had healed begged to go with him. But Jesus sent him away, saying, "Go back home and tell people what God did for you." So the man went all over town telling how much Jesus had done for him.

The Good Samaritan

A teacher of the law was

trying to test Jesus. He said, "Teacher, what must I do to get life forever?"

Jesus said to him, "What is written in the law? What do you read there?"

The man answered, "Love the Lord your God. Love him with all your heart, all your soul, all your strength, and all your mind." Also, "You must love your neighbor as you love yourself."

Jesus said to him, "Your answer is right. Do this and you will have life forever."

But the man wanted to show that the way he was living was right. So he said to Jesus, "And who is my neighbor?"

To answer this question, Jesus said, "A man was going down the road from Jerusalem to Jericho. Some robbers attacked him. They tore off his clothes and beat him. Then they left him lying there, almost dead. It happened that a Jewish priest was going down that road. When the priest saw the man, he walked by on the other side of the road. Next, a Levite came there. He went over and looked at the man. Then he walked by on the other side of the road. Then a Samaritan traveling down the road came to where the hurt man was lying. He saw the man and felt very sorry for

him. The Samaritan went to him and poured olive oil and wine on his wounds and bandaged them. He put the hurt man on his own donkey and took him to an inn. At the inn, the Samaritan took care of him. The next day, the Samaritan brought out two silver coins and gave them to the innkeeper. The Samaritan said, 'Take care of this man. If you spend more money on him, I will pay it back to you when I come again.'"

Then Jesus said, "Which one of these three men do you think was a neighbor to the man who was attacked by the robbers?"

The teacher of the law answered, "The one who helped him."

Jesus said to him, "Then go and do the same thing he did!"

Mary and Martha

While Jesus and his followers were traveling, Jesus went into a town. A woman named Martha let Jesus stay at her house. Martha had a sister named Mary. Mary was sitting at Jesus' feet and listening to him teach. Martha became angry because she had so much work to do. She went in and said, "Lord, don't you care that my sister has left me alone to do all the work? Tell her to help me!"

But the Lord answered her, "Martha, Martha, you are

getting worried and upset about too many things. Only one thing is important. Mary has chosen the right thing, and it will never be taken away from her."

A Lost Sheep and a Lost Coin

Many tax collectors and "sinners" came to listen to Jesus. The Pharisees and the teachers of the law began to complain: "Look! This man welcomes sinners and even eats with them!"

Then Jesus told them this story: "Suppose one of you has 100 sheep, but he loses 1 of them. Then he will leave the other 99 sheep alone and go out and look for the lost sheep. The man will keep on searching for the lost sheep until he finds it. And when he finds it, the man is very happy. He puts it on his shoulders and goes home. He calls to his friends and neighbors and says, 'Be happy with me because I found my lost sheep!' In the same way, I tell you there is much joy in heaven when 1 sinner changes his heart. There is more joy for that 1 sinner than there is for 99 good people who don't need to change.

"Suppose a woman has ten silver coins, but she loses one of them. She will light a lamp and clean the house. She will look carefully for the coin until she finds it. And when she finds it, she will call her friends and neighbors and say, 'Be happy with me because I have found the coin that I lost!' In the same way, there is joy before the angels of God when 1 sinner changes his heart."

The Son Who Left Home

Then Jesus said, "A man had two sons. The younger son said to his father, 'Give me my share of the property.' So the father divided the property between his two sons. Then the younger son gathered up all that was his and left. He traveled far away to another country. There he wasted his money in foolish living. He spent everything that he had. Soon after that, the land became very dry, and there was no rain. There was not enough food to eat anywhere in the country. The son was hungry and needed money. So he got a job with one of the citizens there. The man sent the son into the fields to feed pigs. The son was so hungry that he was willing to eat the food the pigs were eating. But no one gave him anything. The son realized that he had been very foolish.

He thought, 'All of my father's servants have plenty of food. But I am here, almost dying with hunger. I will leave and return to my father. I'll say to him: Father, I have sinned against God and have done wrong to you. I am not good enough to be called your son. But let me be like one of your servants.' So the son left and went to his father.

"While the son was still a long way off, his father saw him coming. He felt sorry for his son. So the father ran to him, and hugged and kissed him. The son said, 'Father, I have sinned against God and have done wrong to you. I am not good enough to be called your son.' But the father said to his servants, 'Hurry! Bring the best clothes and put them on him. Also, put a ring on his finger and sandals on his feet. And get our fat calf and kill it. Then we can have a feast and celebrate! My son was dead, but now he is alive again! He was lost, but now he is found!' So they began to celebrate.

"The older son was in the field. As he came closer to the house, he heard the sound of music and dancing. So he called to one of the servants and asked, 'What does all this mean?' The servant said, 'Your brother has come back. Your father killed the fat calf to eat because your brother came home safely!' The older son was angry and would not go in to the feast. So his father went out and begged him to come in. The son said to his father, 'I have served you like a slave for many years! I have always obeyed your commands. But you never even killed a young goat for me to have a feast with my friends. But your other son has wasted all your money. Then he comes home, and you kill the fat calf for him!' The father said to him, 'Son, you are always with me. All that I have is yours. We had to celebrate and be happy because your brother was dead, but now he is alive. He was lost, but now he is found.'"

The Rich Man and Lazarus

Jesus said, "There was a rich man who always dressed in the finest clothes. He lived in luxury every day. There was also a very poor man named Lazarus, whose body was covered with sores. Lazarus was often placed at the rich man's gate. He wanted to eat only the small pieces of food that fell from the rich man's table. And the dogs would come and lick his sores! Later, Lazarus died. The angels took Lazarus and placed him in the arms of Abraham. The rich man died, too, and was buried. But he was sent to where the dead are and had much pain. The rich man saw Abraham far away with Lazarus in his arms. He called, 'Father Abraham, have mercy on me! Send Lazarus to me so that he can dip his finger in water and cool my tongue. I am suffering in this fire!'

"But Abraham said, 'My child, remember when you lived? You had all the good things in life, but all the bad things happened to Lazarus. Now Lazarus is comforted here, and you are suffering. Also, there is a big pit between you and us. No one can cross over to help you. And no one can leave there and come here.' The rich man said, 'Then please send Lazarus to my father's house on earth! I have five brothers. Lazarus could warn my brothers so that they will not come to this place of pain.' But Abraham said, 'They have the law of Moses and the writings of the prophets to read; let them learn from them!' The rich man said, 'No, father Abraham! If someone came to them from the dead, they would believe and change their hearts and lives.' But Abraham said to him, 'No!

If your brothers won't listen to Moses and the prophets, then they won't listen to someone who comes back from death.'"

Sin and Forgiveness

Jesus said to his followers, "If your brother sins, tell him he is wrong. But if he is sorry and stops sinning, forgive him. If your brother sins against you seven times in one day, but he says that he is sorry each time, then forgive him."

Be Thankful

Jesus was on his way to Jerusalem. Traveling from Galilee to Samaria, he came into a small town. Ten men met him there. These men did not come close to Jesus, because they all had a harmful skin disease. But they called to him, "Jesus! Master! Please help us!"

When Jesus saw the men, he said, "Go and show yourselves to the priests."

While the ten men were going, they were healed. When one of them saw that he was healed, he went back to Jesus. He praised God in a loud voice. Then he bowed down at Jesus' feet and thanked him. (This man was a Samaritan.) Jesus asked, "Ten men were healed; where are the other nine? Is this Samaritan the only one who came back to thank God?" Then

Jesus said to him, "Stand up and go on your way. You were healed because you believed."

Being Right with God

There were some people who thought that they were very good and looked down on everyone else. Jesus used this story to teach them: "One day there was a Pharisee and a tax collector. Both went to the Temple to pray. The Pharisee stood alone, away from the tax collector. When the Pharisee prayed, he said, 'God, I thank you that I am not as bad as other people. I am not like men who steal, cheat, or take part in adultery. I thank you that I am better than this tax collector. I give up eating twice a week, and I give one-tenth of everything I earn!'

"The tax collector stood at a distance. When he prayed, he would not even look up to heaven. He beat on his chest because he was so sad. He said, 'God, have mercy on me. I am a sinner!' I tell you, when this man went home, he was right with God. But the Pharisee was not right with God. Everyone who makes himself great will be made humble. But everyone who makes himself humble will be made great."

Who Will Enter God's Kingdom?

Some people brought their small children to Jesus so that he could touch them. When the followers saw this, they told the people not to do this. But Jesus called the little children to him and said to his followers, "Let the little children come to me. Don't stop them, because the kingdom of God belongs to people who are like these little children. I tell you the truth. You must accept God's kingdom like a little child, or you will never enter it!"

Zacchaeus

Jesus was going through the city of Jericho. In Jericho there was a man named Zacchaeus. He was a wealthy, very important tax collector. He wanted to see who Jesus was, but he was too short to see above the crowd. He ran ahead to a place where he knew Jesus would come. He climbed a sycamore tree so he could see Jesus. When Jesus came to that place, he looked up and saw Zacchaeus in the tree. He said to him, "Zacchaeus, hurry and come down! I must stay at your house today."

Zacchaeus came down quickly. He was pleased to have Jesus in his house. All the people saw this and began to complain, "Look at the kind of man Jesus stays with. Zacchaeus is a sinner!"

But Zacchaeus said to the Lord, "I will give half of my money to the poor. If I have cheated anyone, I will pay that person back four times more!"

Jesus said, "Salvation has come to this house today. This man truly belongs to the family of Abraham. The Son of Man came to find lost people and save them."

After Jesus said this, he went on toward Jerusalem.

Jesus Cries for Jerusalem

Jesus came near Jerusalem. He saw the city and began to cry for it. Jesus said to Jerusalem, "I wish you knew today what would bring you peace! But you can't know it, because it is hidden from you. A time is coming when your enemies will build a wall around you and will hold you in on all sides. They will destroy you and all your people. Not one stone of your buildings will be left on another. All this will happen because you did not know the time when God came to save you."

During the day, Jesus taught the people in the Temple. At night he went out of the city and stayed on the Mount of Olives. Every morning all the people got up early to go to the Temple to listen to him.

Jesus Is Killed

When the time came, the leading priests, the soldiers who guarded the Temple, and the older Jewish leaders arrested Jesus and took him away. Then the whole group led Jesus to Pilate.

PAUSE & WONDER

Jesus lived the best life the world has ever seen. He had more love for other people, more patience, more forgiveness, more kindness, and more wisdom than anyone in history. In fact, He is the only person who never did a single thing wrong. He could do this because He was God's own Son.

Pilate wanted to let Jesus go free. So he told this to the crowd. But they shouted again, "Kill him! Kill him on a cross!" Their yelling became so loud that Pilate decided to give them what they wanted.

The soldiers led Jesus away.

There were also two criminals led out with Jesus to be killed. Jesus and the two criminals were taken to a place called the Skull. There the soldiers nailed Jesus to his cross. They also nailed the criminals to their crosses, one beside Jesus on the right and the other beside Jesus on the left. Jesus said, "Father, forgive them. They don't know what they are doing."

One of the criminals began to shout insults at Jesus: "Aren't you the Christ? Then save yourself! And save us too!"

But the other criminal stopped him. He said, "You should fear God! You are getting the same punishment as he is. We are punished justly; we should die. But this man has done nothing wrong!" Then this criminal said to Jesus, "Jesus, remember me when you come into your kingdom!"

Then Jesus said to him, "Listen! What I say is true: Today you will be with me in paradise!"

The whole land became dark until three o'clock in the afternoon. Jesus cried out in a loud voice, "Father, I give you my life." After Jesus said this, he died.

A man from the Jewish town of Arimathea was there, too. His name was Joseph. He was a good, religious man. He wanted the kingdom of God to come. Joseph was a member of the Jewish council, but he had not agreed when the other leaders decided to kill Jesus. Joseph went to Pilate to ask for the body of Jesus. So Joseph took the body down from the cross and wrapped it in cloth. Then he put Jesus' body in a tomb that was cut in a wall of rock. This tomb had never been used before. This was late on Preparation Day. When the sun went down, the Sabbath day would begin.

The women who had come from Galilee with Jesus followed Joseph. They saw the tomb and saw inside where the body of Jesus was laid. Then the women left to prepare perfumes and spices.

On the Sabbath day they rested, as the law of Moses commanded.

Jesus Rises from Death

Very early on the first day of the week, the women came to

the tomb where Jesus' body was laid. They brought the spices they had prepared. They found that the stone had been rolled away from the entrance of the tomb. They went in, but they did not find the body of the Lord Jesus. While they were wondering about this, two men in shining clothes suddenly stood beside them. The women were very afraid; they bowed their heads to the ground. The men said to the women, "Why are you looking for a living person here? This is a place for the dead. Jesus is not here. He has risen from death! Do you remember what he said in Galilee? He said that the Son of Man must be given to evil men, be killed on a cross, and rise from death on the third day." Then the women remembered what Jesus had said.

The women left the tomb and told all these things to the 11 apostles and the other followers. Peter got up and ran to the tomb. He looked in, but he saw only the cloth that Jesus' body had been wrapped in. Peter went away to be alone, wondering about what had happened.

On the Road to Emmaus

That same day two of Jesus' followers were going to a town named Emmaus. It is about seven miles from Jerusalem. They were talking about everything that had happened. While they were discussing these things, Jesus himself came near and began walking with them. (They were not allowed to recognize Jesus.) Then he said, "What are these things you are talking about while you walk?"

The two followers stopped. Their faces were very sad. The one named Cleopas answered, "You must be the only one in Jerusalem who does not know what just happened there."

Jesus said to them, "What are you talking about?"

The followers said, "It is about Jesus of Nazareth. He was a prophet from God to all the people. He said and did many powerful things. Our leaders and the leading priests gave him up to be judged and killed. They nailed him to a cross. But we were hoping that he would free the Jews. It is now the third day since this happened. And today some women among us told us some amazing things. Early this morning they went to the tomb, but they did not find his body there. They came and told us that they had seen a vision of angels. The angels said that Jesus was alive! So some of our group went to the tomb, too. They found it just as the women said, but they did not see Jesus."

Then Jesus said to them, "You are foolish and slow to realize what is true. You should believe everything the prophets said. They said that the Christ must suffer these things before he enters his glory." Then Jesus began to explain everything that had been written about himself in the Scriptures. He started with Moses, and then he talked about what all the prophets had said about him.

They came near the town of Emmaus, and Jesus acted as if he did not plan to stop there. But they begged him, "Stay with us. It is late; it is almost night." So he went in to stay with them.

Jesus sat down with them and took some bread. He gave thanks for the food and divided it. Then he gave it to them. And then, they were allowed to recognize Jesus. But when they saw who he was, he disappeared. They said to each other, "When Jesus talked to us on the road, it felt like a fire burning in us. It was exciting when he explained the true meaning of the Scriptures."

So the two followers got up at once and went back to Jerusalem. There they found the 11 apostles and others gathered.

They were saying, "The Lord really has risen from death! He showed himself to Simon."

Then the two followers told what had happened on the road. They talked about how they recognized Jesus when he divided the bread.

Jesus Appears to His Followers

While the two followers were telling this, Jesus himself stood among those gathered. He said to them, "Peace be with you."

They were fearful and terrified. They thought they were seeing a ghost. But Jesus said, "Why are you troubled? Why do you doubt what you see? Look at my hands and my feet. It is I myself! Touch me. You can see that I have a living body; a ghost does not have a body like this."

After Jesus said this, he showed them his hands and feet. The followers were amazed and very happy. They still could not believe it. Jesus said to them, "Do you have any food here?" They gave him a piece of cooked fish. While the followers watched, Jesus took the fish and ate it.

He said to them, "Remember when I was with you before? I said that everything written about me must happen —

everything in the law of Moses, the books of the prophets, and the Psalms."

Then Jesus opened their minds so they could understand the Scriptures. He said to them, "It is written that the Christ would be killed and rise from death on the third day. You saw these things happen — you are witnesses. You must tell people to change their hearts and lives. If they do this, their sins will be forgiven. You must start at Jerusalem and preach these things in my name to all nations. Listen! My Father has promised you something; I will send it to you. But you must stay in Jerusalem until you have received that power from heaven."

WORTH WONDERING...

- What good example can you give of someone in this book who did what was right?

- What example can you give of someone in this book who did what was wrong?

- What do you think are the most important things this book tells us about Jesus?

- Suppose a friend asked you this question: Why did Jesus have to die? As you remember what you read in the book of Luke, how would you answer your friend?

- Which parts of this book do you think the devil would most like you NOT to remember?

GREAT VERSES TO THINK ABOUT AGAIN...

Look back in Luke to see if you can find these verses:

- *I tell you there is much joy in heaven when 1 sinner changes his heart. There is more joy for that 1 sinner than there is for 99 good people who don't need to change.*

- *If your brother sins against you seven times in one day, but he says that he is sorry each time, then forgive him.*

AND THERE'S MORE...

Luke also tells in his own way many of the things about Jesus which are in the gospels of Matthew and Mark. When you read Luke in a full Bible, look also for...

- Many more people whom Jesus healed.

- How Jesus made people angry in his hometown of Nazareth.

- How Jesus gave a Pharisee a lesson on forgiveness, while a woman showed Jesus her love.

- What Jesus taught about prayer.

The Gospel of
JOHN

Jesus,
the Son of God

Looking forward to John...

WHAT'S IT ABOUT?

"Jesus, the Son of God"

SIGNS AND WONDERS

Look especially in this gospel for the times when Jesus was speaking only with one person. And remember that He speaks one-to-one like this with you too!

FACES AND PLACES

Jesus: The Word of God, the Messiah, the Bread of Life, the Light of the World, the Good Shepherd, the Resurrection and the Life, the Way and the Truth, the True Vine, the Son of God, the Savior of the World.

John, who wrote this book, was one of the twelve disciples. He also wrote the three letters of John which are near the end of the New Testament. And he also wrote the Bible's last book, Revelation. John's name means "God is gracious."

Nicodemus: An important Jewish leader in Jerusalem.

Samaria: The area between Galilee and Judea, the land where the Jews lived. Jews looked down on Samaritans.

Lazarus, Mary, and **Martha:** This was a brother and his two sisters. Jesus was their friend, and He liked to stay in their home.

Bethany: A town near Jerusalem. Lazarus and his sisters lived there.

(Look also at the list of "Faces and Places" on page 374)

I wonder what it really means that Jesus is the Son of God...

BEFORE THE WORLD began, there was the Word. The Word was with God, and the Word was God. He was with God in the beginning. All things were made through him. Nothing was made without him. In him there was life. That life was light for the people of the world. The Light shines in the darkness. And the darkness has not overpowered the Light.

The Word was in the world. The world was made through him, but the world did not know him. He came to the world that was his own. But his own people did not accept him. But some people did accept him. They believed in him. To them he gave the right to become children of God. They did not become his children in the human way. They were born of God.

The Word became a man and lived among us. We saw his glory — the glory that belongs to the only Son of the Father. The Word was full of grace and truth. The law was given through Moses, but grace and truth came through Jesus Christ. No man has ever seen God. But God the only Son is very close to the Father. And the Son has shown us what God is like.

Jesus and Nicodemus

There was a man named Nicodemus who was one of the Pharisees. He was an important Jewish leader. One night Nicodemus came to Jesus. He

Jesus is the "Word." That's what I read at the start of John's gospel. When Jesus came to earth, it was God's very best way of telling me about Himself. Jesus is a personal message from God— because Jesus Himself is God!

said, "Teacher, we know that you are a teacher sent from God. No one can do the miracles you do, unless God is with him."

Jesus answered, "I tell you the truth. Unless one is born again, he cannot be in God's kingdom."

Nicodemus said, "But if a man is already old, how can he be born again? He cannot enter his mother's body again. So how can he be born a second time?"

But Jesus answered, "I tell you the truth. Unless one is born from water and the Spirit, he cannot enter God's kingdom. A person's body is born from his human parents. But a person's spiritual life is born from the Spirit.

"Don't be surprised when I tell you, 'You must all be born again.' The wind blows where it wants to go. You hear the wind blow. But you don't know where the wind comes from or where it is going. It is the same with

every person who is born from the Spirit."

Nicodemus asked, "How can all this be possible?"

Jesus said, "You are an important teacher in Israel. But you still don't understand these things? I tell you the truth. We talk about what we know. We tell about what we have seen. But you don't accept what we tell you. I have told you about things here on earth, but you do not believe me. So surely you will not believe me if I tell you about the things of heaven! The only one who has ever gone up to heaven is the One who came down from heaven — the Son of Man.

"For God loved the world so much that he gave his only Son. God gave his Son so that whoever believes in him may not be lost, but have eternal life. God did not send his Son into the world to judge the world guilty, but to save the world through him.

"He who believes in God's Son is not judged guilty. He who does not believe has already been judged guilty, because he has not believed in God's only Son. People are judged by this fact: I am the Light from God that has come into the world. But men did not want light. They wanted darkness because they were doing evil things. Everyone who does evil hates the light. He will not come to the light because it will show all the evil things he has done. But he who follows the true way comes to the light. Then the light will show that the things he has done were done through God."

Jesus and a Samaritan Woman

Jesus left Judea and went back to Galilee. On the way he had to go through the country of Samaria.

In Samaria Jesus came to the town called Sychar. This town is near the field that Jacob gave to his son Joseph. Jacob's well was there. Jesus was tired from his long trip. So he sat down beside the well. It was about six o'clock in the evening. A Samaritan woman came to the well to get some water. Jesus said to her, "Please give me a drink." (This happened while Jesus' followers were in town buying some food.)

The woman said, "I am surprised that you ask me for a drink. You are a Jew and I am a Samaritan." (Jews are not friends with Samaritans.)

Jesus said, "You don't know what God gives. And you don't know who asked you for a drink. If you knew, you would have asked me, and I would have given you living water."

The woman said, "Sir, where will you get that living water? The well is very deep, and you have nothing to get water with. Are you greater than Jacob, our father? Jacob is the one who gave us this well. He drank from it himself. Also, his sons and flocks drank from this well."

Jesus answered, "Every person who drinks this water will be thirsty again. But whoever drinks the water I give will never be thirsty again. The water I give will become a spring of water flowing inside him. It will give him eternal life."

The woman said to him, "Sir, give me this water. Then I will never be thirsty again. And I will not have to come back here to get more water."

Jesus told her, "Go get your husband and come back here."

The woman answered, "But I have no husband."

Jesus said to her, "You are right to say you have no husband. Really you have had five husbands. But the man you live with now is not your husband. You told the truth."

The woman said, "Sir, I can see that you are a prophet. Our fathers worshiped on this mountain. But you Jews say that Jerusalem is the place where people must worship."

Jesus said, "Believe me, woman. The time is coming when you will not have to be in Jerusalem or on this mountain to worship the Father. The time is coming when the true worshipers will worship the Father in spirit and truth. That time is now here. And these are the kinds of worshipers the Father wants. God is spirit. Those who worship God must worship in spirit and truth."

The woman said, "I know that the Messiah is coming." (Messiah is the One called Christ.) "When the Messiah comes, he will explain everything to us."

Then Jesus said, "He is talking to you now. I am he."

Just then his followers came back from town. They were surprised because they saw Jesus talking with a woman. But none of them asked, "What do you want?" or "Why are you talking with her?"

Then the woman left her water jar and went back to town. She said to the people, "A man told me everything I have ever done. Come see him. Maybe he is the Christ!" So the people left the town and went to see Jesus.

While the woman was away, the followers were begging him, "Teacher, eat something!"

But Jesus answered, "I have food to eat that you know nothing about."

PAUSE & WONDER

Jesus told the woman at the well that God is spirit. God isn't wrapped up in a body like me. I get sick or tired or cold or hot, and I will grow old. But none of that ever happens to God.

So the followers asked them-selves, "Did somebody already bring Jesus some food?"

Jesus said, "My food is to do what the One who sent me wants me to do. My food is to finish the work that he gave me to do. You say, 'Four more months to wait before we gather the grain.' But I tell you, open your eyes. Look at the fields that are ready for harvesting now. Even now, the one who harvests the crop is being paid. He is gathering crops for eternal life. So now the one who plants can be happy along with the one who harvests. It is true when we say, 'One person plants, but another harvests the crop.' I sent you to harvest a crop that you did not work for. Others did the work, and you get the profit from their work."

Many of the Samaritans in that town believed in Jesus. They believed because of what the woman said: "He told me every-thing I have ever done." The Samaritans came to Jesus and begged him to stay with them. So he stayed there two days. Many more believed because of the things he said.

They said to the woman, "First we believed in Jesus because of what you told us. But now we believe because we heard him ourselves. We know that this man really is the Savior of the world."

More than 5,000 People Fed

After this, Jesus went across Lake Galilee. Many people followed him because they saw the miracles he did to heal the sick. Jesus went up on a hill and there sat down with his followers.

Jesus looked up and saw a large crowd coming toward him. He said to Philip, "Where can we buy bread for all these people to eat?" (Jesus asked Philip this question to test him. Jesus already knew what he planned to do.)

Philip answered, "We would all have to work a month to buy enough bread for each person here to have only a little piece."

Another follower there was Andrew. He was Simon Peter's brother. Andrew said, "Here is a boy with five loaves of barley bread and two little fish. But that is not enough for so many people."

Jesus said, "Tell the people to sit down." This was a very grassy place. There were about 5,000 men who sat down there. Then Jesus took the loaves of bread. He thanked God for the bread and gave it to the people who were sitting there. He did the same with the fish. He gave them as much as they wanted. They all had enough to eat.

Jesus, the Bread of Life

The next day came. The people found Jesus on the other side of the lake. They asked him, "Teacher, when did you come here?"

Jesus answered, "Are you looking for me because you saw me do miracles? No! I tell you the truth. You are looking for me because you ate the bread and were satisfied. Earthly food spoils and ruins. So don't work to get that kind of food. But work to get the food that stays good always and gives you eternal life. The Son of Man will give you that food. God the Father has shown that he is with the Son of Man."

The people asked Jesus, "What are the things God wants us to do?"

Jesus answered, "The work God wants you to do is this: to believe in the One that God sent."

Then Jesus said, "I am the bread that gives life. He who comes to me will never be hungry. He who believes in me will never be thirsty. I came down from heaven to do what God wants me to do. I did not come to do what I want to do. I must not lose even one of those that God has given me, but I must raise them up on the last day. This is what the One who sent me wants me to do. Everyone who sees the Son and believes in him has eternal life. I will raise him up on the last day. This is what my Father wants."

The Jews began to complain about Jesus. They complained because he said, "I am the bread that comes down from heaven." The Jews said, "This is Jesus. We know his father and mother. He is only Joseph's son. How can he say, 'I came down from heaven'?"

After Jesus said this, many of his followers left him. They stopped following him.

Jesus asked the 12 followers, "Do you want to leave, too?"

Simon Peter answered Jesus, "Lord, where would we go? You have the words that give eternal life. We believe in you. We know that you are the Holy One from God."

Then Jesus answered, "I chose all 12 of you. But 1 of you is a devil."

Jesus was talking about Judas, the son of Simon Iscariot. Judas was 1 of the 12. But later he was going to turn against Jesus.

Jesus Talks About the Spirit

Jesus went to the Temple and began to teach. Jesus stood up and said in a loud voice, "If anyone is thirsty, let him come to me and drink. If a person believes in me, rivers of living water will flow out from his heart. This is what the Scripture says." Jesus was talking about the Holy Spirit. The Spirit had not yet been given because Jesus had not yet been raised to glory. But later, those who believed in Jesus would receive the Spirit.

Later, Jesus talked to the people again. He said, "I am the light of the world. The person who follows me will never live in darkness. He will have the light that gives life."

Jesus Heals a Man Born Blind

As Jesus was walking along, he saw a man who had been born blind. His followers asked him, "Teacher, whose sin caused this man to be born blind — his own sin or his parents' sin?"

Jesus answered, "It is not this man's sin or his parents' sin that made him be blind. This man was born blind so that God's power could be shown in him. While it is daytime, we must continue doing the work of the One who sent me. The night is coming. And no one can work at night. While I am in the world, I am the light of the world."

After Jesus said this, he spit on the ground and made some mud with it. He put the mud on the man's eyes. Then he told the man, "Go and wash in the Pool of Siloam." So the man went to the pool. He washed and came back. And he was able to see.

Some people had seen this man begging before. They asked, "What happened? How did you get your sight?"

He answered, "The man named Jesus made some mud and put it on my eyes. Then he told me to go to Siloam and wash. So I went and washed and came back seeing."

Pharisees Question the Healing

Then the people took to the Pharisees the man who had been blind. The day Jesus had made mud and healed his eyes was a Sabbath day. So now some of the Pharisees were saying, "This man does not keep the Sabbath day. He is not from God!"

Others said, "But a man who is a sinner can't do miracles like these." So they could not agree with each other.

They asked the man again,

"What do you say about him? It was your eyes he opened."

The man answered, "He is a prophet."

The Jews did not believe that he had been blind and could now see again. So they sent for the man's parents and asked them, "Is this your son? You say that he was born blind. Then how does he see now?"

His parents answered, "We know that this is our son, and we know that he was born blind. But we don't know how he can see now. We don't know who opened his eyes. Ask him. He is old enough to answer for himself." His parents said this because they were afraid of the Jews. The Jews had already decided that anyone who said that Jesus was the Christ would be put out of the synagogue. That is why his parents said, "He is old enough. Ask him."

So for the second time, the Jewish leaders called the man who had been blind. They said, "You should give God the glory by telling the truth. We know that this man is a sinner."

He answered, "I don't know if he is a sinner. But one thing I do know. I was blind, and now I can see."

The Jewish leaders asked, "What did he do to you? How did he make you see again?"

He answered, "I have already told you that. But you would not listen to me. Why do you want to hear it again? Do you want to become his followers, too?"

Then they insulted him and said, "You are his follower. We are followers of Moses. We know that God spoke to Moses. But we don't even know where this man comes from!"

The man answered, "This is a very strange thing. You don't know where he comes from, and yet he opened my eyes. We all know that God does not listen to sinners. But God listens to anyone who worships and obeys him. Nobody has ever heard of anyone giving sight to a man born blind. If this man were not from God, he could do nothing."

They answered, "You were born full of sin! Are you trying to teach us?" And they threw the man out.

Jesus heard that they had thrown him out. So Jesus found him and said, "Do you believe in the Son of Man?"

He asked, "Who is the Son of Man, sir? Tell me, so I can believe in him!"

Jesus said to him, "You have already seen him. The Son of Man is the one talking with you now."

He said, "Yes, Lord, I believe!"

Then the man bowed and worshiped Jesus.

The Shepherd and His Sheep

Jesus said, "I tell you the truth. The man who does not enter the sheepfold by the door, but climbs in some other way, is a thief and a robber. The one who enters by the door is the shepherd of the sheep. The man who guards the door opens it for him. And the sheep listen to the voice of the shepherd. He calls his own sheep, using their names, and he leads them out. He brings all of his sheep out. Then he goes ahead of them and leads them. They follow him because they know his voice. But they will never follow a stranger. They will run away from him because they don't know his voice." Jesus told the people this story, but they did not understand what it meant.

Jesus Is the Good Shepherd

So Jesus said again, "I tell you the truth. I am the door for the sheep. All the people who came before me were thieves and robbers. The sheep did not listen to them. I am the door. The person who enters through me will be saved. He will be able to come in and go out and find pasture. A thief comes to steal and kill and destroy. But I came to give life — life in all its fullness.

"I am the good shepherd. The good shepherd gives his life for the sheep. The worker who is paid to keep the sheep is different from the shepherd who owns them. So when the worker sees a wolf coming, he runs away and leaves the sheep alone. Then the wolf attacks the sheep and scatters them. The man runs away because he is only a paid worker. He does not really care for the sheep.

"I am the good shepherd. I know my sheep, as the Father knows me. And my sheep know me, as I know the Father. I give my life for the sheep. I have other sheep that are not in this flock here. I must bring them also. They will listen to my voice, and there will be one flock and one shepherd. The Father loves me because I give my life. I give my life so that I can take it back again. No one takes it away from me. I give my own life freely. I have the right to give my life, and I have the right to take it back. This is what my Father commanded me to do."

The Death of Lazarus

There was a man named Lazarus who was sick. He lived in the town of Bethany, where Mary and her sister Martha lived. Mary is the woman who later put perfume on the Lord and wiped his feet with her hair. Mary's brother was Lazarus, the man who was now sick. So Mary and Martha sent someone to tell Jesus, "Lord, the one you love is sick."

Jesus loved Martha and her sister and Lazarus. But when he heard that Lazarus was sick, he stayed where he was for two more days. Then Jesus said to his followers, "Let us go back to Judea."

After Jesus said this, he added, "Our friend Lazarus has fallen asleep. But I am going there to wake him."

The followers said, "But Lord, if he can sleep, he will get well."

So then Jesus said plainly, "Lazarus is dead. And I am glad for your sakes that I was not there so that you may believe. But let us go to him now."

Jesus in Bethany

Jesus arrived in Bethany. There he learned that Lazarus had already been dead and in the tomb for four days. Bethany was about two miles from Jerusalem. Many Jews had come there to comfort Martha and Mary about their brother.

Martha heard that Jesus was coming, and she went out to meet him. But Mary stayed at home. Martha said to Jesus,

"Lord, if you had been here, my brother would not have died. But I know that even now God will give you anything you ask."

Jesus said, "Your brother will rise and live again."

Martha answered, "I know that he will rise and live again in the resurrection on the last day."

Jesus said to her, "I am the resurrection and the life. He who believes in me will have life even if he dies. And he who lives and believes in me will never die. Martha, do you believe this?"

Martha answered, "Yes, Lord. I believe that you are the Christ, the Son of God. You are the One who was coming to the world."

Jesus Cries

After Martha said this, she went back to her sister Mary. She talked to Mary alone. Martha said, "The Teacher is here and he is asking for you." When Mary heard this, she got up quickly and went to Jesus. When she saw him, she fell at his feet and said, "Lord, if you had been here, my brother would not have died."

Jesus saw that Mary was crying and that the Jews who came with her were crying, too. Jesus felt very sad in his heart and was deeply troubled. He asked, "Where did you bury him?"

"Come and see, Lord," they said.

Jesus cried.

So the Jews said, "See how much he loved him."

But some of them said, "If Jesus healed the eyes of the blind man, why didn't he keep Lazarus from dying?"

Jesus Raises Lazarus

Again Jesus felt very sad in his heart. He came to the tomb. The tomb was a cave with a large stone covering the entrance. Jesus said, "Move the stone away."

Martha said, "But, Lord, it has been four days since he died. There will be a bad smell."

Then Jesus said to her, "Didn't I tell you that if you believed, you would see the glory of God?"

So they moved the stone away from the entrance. Then Jesus looked up and said, "Father, I thank you that you heard me. I know that you always hear me. But I said these things because of the people here around me. I want them to believe that you sent me." After Jesus said this, he cried out in a loud voice, "Lazarus, come out!" The dead man came out. His hands and feet were wrapped with pieces of cloth, and he had a cloth around his face.

Jesus said to them, "Take the cloth off of him and let him go."

The Leaders Plan to Kill Jesus

There were many Jews who had come to visit Mary. They saw what Jesus did. And many of them believed in him. But some of the Jews went to the Pharisees. They told the Pharisees what Jesus had done. Then the leading priests and Pharisees called a meeting of the Jewish council. They asked, "What should we do? This man is doing many miracles. If we let him continue doing these things, everyone will believe in him. Then the Romans will come and take away our Temple and our nation."

That day the Jewish leaders started planning to kill Jesus.

Jesus with Friends in Bethany

Six days before the Passover Feast, Jesus went to Bethany, where Lazarus lived. There they had a dinner for Jesus. Martha served the food. Lazarus was one of the people eating with Jesus. Mary brought in a pint of very expensive perfume made from pure nard. She poured the perfume on Jesus' feet, and then she wiped his feet with her hair.

And the sweet smell from the perfume filled the whole house.

Judas Iscariot, one of Jesus' followers, was there. (He was the one who would later turn against Jesus.) Judas said, "This perfume was worth 300 silver coins. It should have been sold and the money given to the poor." But Judas did not really care about the poor. He said this because he was a thief. He was the one who kept the money box, and he often stole money from it.

Jesus answered, "Let her alone. It was right for her to save this perfume for today — the day for me to be prepared for burial. The poor will always be with you, but you will not always have me."

Jesus Washes His Followers' Feet

It was almost time for the Jewish Passover Feast. Jesus knew that it was time for him to leave this world and go back to the Father. He had always loved those who were his own in the world, and he loved them all the way to the end.

Jesus and his followers were at the evening meal. The devil had already persuaded Judas Iscariot to turn against Jesus. Jesus knew that the Father had given him power over every-thing. He also knew that he had come from God and was going back to God. So during the meal Jesus stood up and took off his outer clothing. Taking a towel, he wrapped it around his waist. Then he poured water into a bowl and began to wash the followers' feet. He dried them with the towel that was wrapped around him.

Jesus came to Simon Peter. But Peter said to Jesus, "Lord, are you going to wash my feet?"

Jesus answered, "You don't understand what I am doing now. But you will understand later."

Peter said, "No! You will never wash my feet."

Jesus answered, "If I don't wash your feet, then you are not one of my people."

When he had finished washing their feet, he put on his clothes and sat down again. Jesus asked, "Do you understand what I have just done for you? You call me 'Teacher' and 'Lord.' And this is right, because that is what I am. I, your Lord and Teacher, have washed your feet. So you also should wash each other's feet. I did this as an example for you.

"I give you a new command: Love each other. You must love each other as I have loved you. All people will know that you are my followers if you love each other."

Jesus Comforts His Followers

Jesus said, "Don't let your hearts be troubled. Trust in God. And trust in me. There are many rooms in my Father's house. I would not tell you this if it were not true. I am going there to prepare a place for you. After I go and prepare a place for you, I will come back. Then I will take you to be with me so that you may be where I am. You know the way to the place where I am going."

Thomas said to Jesus, "Lord, we don't know where you are going. So how can we know the way?"

Jesus answered, "I am the way. And I am the truth and the life. The only way to the Father is through me. Now you do know him, and you have seen him.

The Promise of the Holy Spirit

"If you love me, you will do the things I command. I will ask the Father, and he will give you another Helper. The Helper is the Spirit of truth. He lives with you and he will be in you.

"I will not leave you all alone like orphans. I will come back to you.

"I leave you peace. My peace I give you. I do not give it to you as the world does. So don't let your hearts be troubled. Don't be afraid. You heard me say to you, 'I am going, but I am coming back to you.' I have told you this now, before it happens. Then when it happens, you will believe.

Jesus Is Like a Vine

"I am the true vine. No branch can produce fruit alone. It must remain in the vine. It is the same with you. You cannot produce fruit alone. You must remain in me.

"I am the vine, and you are the branches. If anyone does not remain in me, then he is like a branch that is thrown away. That branch dies. People pick up dead branches, throw them into the fire, and burn them. Remain in me and follow my teachings. If you do this, then you can ask for anything you want, and it will be given to you.

Jesus Warns His Followers

"If the world hates you, remember that it hated me first. If you belonged to the world, then it would love you as it loves its own. But I have chosen you out of the world. So you don't belong to it. That is why the world hates you.

"I have told you these things to keep you from giving up.

"I have many more things to say to you, but they are too much for you now. But when the Spirit of truth comes he will lead you into all truth.

"I told you these things so that you can have peace in me. In this world you will have trouble. But be brave! I have defeated the world!"

Jesus Prays for His Followers

After Jesus said these things he looked toward heaven. Jesus prayed, "Father, the time has come. I finished the work you gave me to do. I brought you glory on earth. And now, Father, give me glory with you. Give me the glory I had with you before the world was made.

"You gave me some men from the world. I have shown them what you are like. Holy Father, keep them safe. Keep them safe by the power of your name (the name you gave me), so that they will be one, the same as you and I are one.

"I pray for these men. But I am also praying for all people who will believe in me because of the teaching of these men. Father, I pray that all people who believe in me can be one. You are in me and I am in you. I pray that these people can also be one in us, so that the world will believe that you sent me. I will be in them and you will be in me. So they will be completely one. Then the world will know that you loved these people the same as you loved me.

"Father, I want these people that you have given me to be with me in every place I am. I want them to see my glory. This is the glory you gave me because you loved me before the world was made. Father, you are the One who is good. The world does not know you, but I know you. And these people know that you sent me. I showed them what you are like. And again I will show them what you are like. Then they will have the same love that you have for me. And I will live in them."

Jesus Is Arrested

When Jesus finished praying, he left with his followers. They went across the Kidron Valley. On the other side there was a garden of olive trees. Jesus and his followers went there.

Judas knew where this place was, because Jesus met there often with his followers. Judas was the one who turned against Jesus. So Judas led a group of soldiers to the garden. Judas also brought some guards from the leading priests and the Pharisees. They were carrying torches, lanterns, and weapons.

Then the soldiers with their commander and the Jewish guards arrested Jesus.

Then the Jews led Jesus to the Roman governor's palace. Pilate went back inside the palace. He called Jesus to him and asked, "Are you the king of the Jews?"

Jesus said, "My kingdom does not belong to this world. If it belonged to this world, my servants would fight so that I would not be given over to the Jews. But my kingdom is from another place."

Pilate said, "So you are a king!"

Jesus answered, "You say that I am a king. That is true. I was born for this: to tell people about the truth. That is why I came into the world. And everyone who belongs to the truth listens to me."

Pilate said, "What is truth?" After he said this, he went out to the Jews again.

Pilate tried to let Jesus go free. But the Jews shouted, "Take him away! Take him away! Kill him on a cross!"

Pilate asked them, "Do you want me to kill your king on a cross?"

The leading priests answered, "The only king we have is Caesar!"

So Pilate gave Jesus to them to be killed on a cross.

Jesus Is Killed on a Cross

The soldiers took charge of Jesus. Carrying his own cross, Jesus went out to a place called The Place of the Skull. There they nailed Jesus to the cross.

After this, Jesus knew that everything had been done. He said, "I am thirsty." There was a jar full of vinegar there, so the soldiers soaked a sponge in it. Then they put the sponge on a branch of a hyssop plant and lifted it to Jesus' mouth. Jesus tasted the vinegar. Then he said, "It is finished." He bowed his head and died.

In the place where Jesus was killed, there was a garden. In the garden was a new tomb where no one had ever been buried. Men laid Jesus in that tomb because it was near, and the Jews were preparing to start their Sabbath day.

Jesus' Tomb Is Empty

Early on the first day of the week, Mary Magdalene went to the tomb. It was still dark. Mary saw that the large stone had been moved away from the tomb. So Mary ran to Simon Peter and the other follower (the one Jesus loved). Mary said, "They have taken the Lord out of the tomb. We don't know where they have put him."

Jesus Appears to His Followers

That evening the followers were together. The doors were locked, because they were afraid of the Jews. Then Jesus came and stood among them. He said, "Peace be with you!" After he said this, he showed them his hands and his side. The followers were very happy when they saw the Lord.

Jesus Appears to Thomas

Thomas was not with the followers when Jesus came. Thomas was 1 of the 12. The other followers told Thomas, "We saw the Lord."

But Thomas said, "I will not believe it until I see the nail marks in his hands. And I will not believe until I put my finger where the nails were and put my hand into his side."

A week later the followers were in the house again. Thomas was with them. The doors were locked, but Jesus came in and stood among them. He said, "Peace be with you!" Then he said to Thomas, "Put your finger here. Look at my hands. Put your hand here in my side. Stop doubting and believe."

Thomas said to him, "My Lord and my God!"

Then Jesus told him, "You believe because you see me. Those who believe without seeing me will be truly happy."

Why John Wrote This Book

Jesus did many other mira-

PAUSE & WONDER

God sent Someone to us who was a human being just like us. But that man — Jesus — was also God Himself. In the perfect and loving way that Jesus lived and died, I can see how perfect and loving God is. And in the mighty way that Jesus rose up from the dead, I can see the mighty power of God the Father.

cles before his followers that are not written in this book. But these are written so that you can believe that Jesus is the Christ, the Son of God. Then, by believing, you can have life through his name.

There are many other things that Jesus did. If every one of them were written down, I think the whole world would not be big enough for all the books that would be written.

WORTH WONDERING...

- If you could meet Lazarus today, what kind of questions would you like to ask him?
- What are your favorite things this book tells us about Jesus?
- What commands can you find in this book — things that God tells us to do or to be?
- What good example can you give of someone in this book who did what was right?
- What example can you give of someone in this book who did what was wrong?
- In this book of the Bible, how do you see that God is great? And how do you see that He is good?
- Think about some friends you have who might know very little about Jesus or the Bible. What parts of this book do you

think would be most interesting to them?

GREAT VERSES TO THINK ABOUT AGAIN...

Look back in John to see if you can find these verses:

- *I am the bread that gives life.*
- *I am the light of the world.*
- *I am the door for the sheep.*
- *I am the good shepherd.*
- *I am the resurrection and the life.*
- *I am the way. And I am the truth and the life.*
- *I am the vine, and you are the branches.*

AND THERE'S MORE...

John also tells in his own way many of the things about Jesus which are in the gospels of Matthew, Mark and Luke. When you read John in a full Bible, look also for...

- What Jesus said about having freedom from sin.
- Many more words of Jesus which He spoke to His 12 apostles the night before He was killed.

INTRODUCING...

ACTS

After Jesus rose from the dead and went back to heaven, His exciting story kept on going. Why? Because He sent His Holy Spirit to live inside His followers. And just as Jesus had promised, these followers saw amazing things happen. Because of the powerful things they did and the powerful words they spoke, the good news about Jesus began spreading far away to other lands. People everywhere accepted this good news. They agreed with the offer of never-ending life that God was making through His Son Jesus.

The Holy Spirit made them bold and brave. And with the Holy Spirit inside us, we can be bold and brave, too — wherever God sends us.

The Holy Spirit is God Himself living inside us!

The Book of
ACTS

The Good News
of Jesus Spreads

Looking forward to Acts...

"The Good News of Jesus Spreads"

The Church is born! And just as Jesus promised, His followers are given the Holy Spirit to make them strong and brave. Because of this, the good news about Jesus goes out to the world.

Peter and **John:** Leaders of the first church in Jerusalem.

Stephen: A man chosen by the church leaders to help provide food to widows in the church. He had great faith and was full of the Holy Spirit.

Saul (also called **Paul**): A Pharisee who was an enemy of Christians until Jesus appeared to him. The name Paul means "little."

Barnabas: One of those who helped spread the news about Jesus. His name means "Son of Encouragement."

Silas: One of Paul's helpers.

Damascus: The leading city of Syria, the country next to Israel on the north side.

Antioch: A city north of Syria. Paul and Barnabas were teachers in the church there. Then the Holy Spirit sent them to take the news of Jesus to other countries.

Corinth: A city in Greece where Paul spent two years preaching and teaching.

Caesarea: A city on the shore of the Mediterranean Sea. It was the headquarters for the Roman rulers of Judea and Samaria.

After Jesus went back to heaven, I wonder what His followers did next...

THE APOSTLES saw Jesus during the 40 days after he was raised from death. He spoke to them about the kingdom of God. He told them not to leave Jerusalem. He said, "The Father has made you a promise which I told you about before. Wait here to receive this promise. John baptized people with water, but in a few days you will be baptized with the Holy Spirit."

Jesus Is Taken Up into Heaven

The apostles were all together. They asked Jesus, "Lord, are you at this time going to give the kingdom back to Israel?"

Jesus said to them, "The Father is the only One who has the authority to decide dates and times. These things are not for you to know. But the Holy Spirit will come to you. Then you will receive power. You will be my witnesses — in Jerusalem, in all of Judea, in Samaria, and in every part of the world."

After he said this, as they were watching, he was lifted up. A cloud hid him from their sight. As he was going, they were looking into the sky. Suddenly, two men wearing white clothes stood beside them. They said, "Men of Galilee, why are you standing here looking into the sky? You saw Jesus taken away from you into heaven. He will come back in the same way you saw him go."

Then they went back to Jerusalem from the Mount of Olives. (This mountain is about half a mile from Jerusalem.) When they entered the city, they went to the upstairs room where they were staying. Peter, John, James, Andrew, Philip, Thomas, Bartholomew, Matthew, James son of Alphaeus, Simon (known as the Zealot), and Judas son of James were there. They all continued praying together. Some women, including Mary the mother of Jesus, and Jesus' brothers were also there with the apostles.

The Coming of the Holy Spirit

When the day of Pentecost came, they were all together in one place. Suddenly a noise came from heaven. It sounded like a strong wind blowing. This noise filled the whole house where they were sitting. They saw something that looked like flames of fire. The flames were separated and stood over each person there. They were all filled with the Holy Spirit, and they began to speak different languages. The Holy Spirit was giving them the power to speak these languages.

There were some religious Jews staying in Jerusalem who were from every country in the world. When they heard this noise, a crowd came together. They were all surprised, because each one heard them speaking in his own language. They were completely amazed at this. They asked each other, "What does this mean?"

Peter Speaks to the People

Peter stood up with the 11 apostles. In a loud voice he spoke to the crowd: "My fellow Jews, and all of you who are in Jerusalem, listen to me.

"Jesus from Nazareth was a very special man. God clearly showed this to you by the miracles, wonders, and signs God did through him. You all know this, because it happened right here among you. Jesus was given to you, and you killed him. With the help of evil men you nailed him to a cross. But God knew all this would happen. This was God's plan which he had made long ago. God raised Jesus from death. God set him free from the pain of death. Death could not hold him.

"So, all the people of Israel should know this truly: God has made Jesus both Lord and Christ. He is the man you nailed to the cross!"

When the people heard this, they were sick at heart. They

asked Peter and the other apostles, "What shall we do?"

Peter said to them, "Change your hearts and lives and be baptized, each one of you, in the name of Jesus Christ for the forgiveness of your sins. And you will receive the gift of the Holy Spirit. This promise is for you. It is also for your children and for all who are far away. It is for everyone the Lord our God calls to himself."

Peter warned them with many other words. He begged them, "Save yourselves from the evil of today's people!" Then those people who accepted what Peter said were baptized. About 3,000 people were added to the number of believers that day. They spent their time learning the apostles' teaching. And they continued to share, to break bread, and to pray together.

The Believers Share

The apostles were doing many miracles and signs. And everyone felt great respect for God. All the believers stayed together. They shared everything. They sold their land and the things they owned. Then they divided the money and gave it to those people who needed it. The believers met together in the Temple every day. They all had the same purpose. They broke bread in their homes, happy to share their food with joyful hearts. They praised God, and all the people liked them. More and more people were being saved every day; the Lord was adding those people to the group of believers.

Peter Heals a Crippled Man

One day Peter and John went to the Temple. There, at the Temple gate called Beautiful Gate, was a man who had been crippled all his life. Every day he was carried to this gate to beg. He would ask for money from the people going into the Temple. The man saw Peter and John going into the Temple and asked them for money. But Peter said, "I don't have any silver or gold, but I do have something else I can give you: By the power of Jesus Christ from Nazareth — stand up and walk!" Then Peter took the man's right hand and lifted him up. Immediately the man's feet and ankles became strong. He jumped up, stood on his feet, and began to walk. He went into the Temple with them, walking and jumping, and praising God. All the people recognized him. They could not understand how this could happen.

Peter Speaks to the People

All the people were amazed and ran to Peter and John at Solomon's Porch. When Peter saw this, he said to them, "Men of Israel, why are you surprised? You are looking at us as if it were our own power that made this man walk. Do you think this happened because we are good? No! The God of Abraham, Isaac and Jacob, the God of our ancestors, gave glory to Jesus, his servant. But you gave him up to be killed. Pilate decided to let him go free. But you told Pilate you did not want Jesus. He was pure and good, but you said you did not want him. And so you killed the One who gives life! But God raised him from death. We are witnesses to this. It was the power of Jesus that made this crippled man well. He was made completely well because of trust in Jesus. You all saw it happen!

"Brothers, I know you did those things to Jesus because you did not understand what you were doing. Your leaders did not understand either. God said this would happen. He said through the prophets that his Christ would suffer and die. And now God has made these things come true in this way. So you must change your hearts and lives! Come back to God, and he will forgive your sins. Then the Lord will give you times of spiritual rest. He will give you Jesus, the One he chose to be the Christ. He sent Jesus to bless you by turning each of you away from doing evil things."

Peter and John at the Council

While Peter and John were speaking to the people, a group of men came up to them. They were upset because the two apostles were teaching the people. Peter and John were preaching that people will rise from death through the power of Jesus. The Jewish leaders grabbed Peter and John and put them in jail. It was already night, so they kept them in jail until the next day. But many of those who heard Peter and John preach believed the things they said. There were now about 5,000 men in the group of believers.

The next day the Jewish leaders made Peter and John stand before them. The Jewish leaders asked them: "By what power or authority did you do this?"

Then Peter was filled with the Holy Spirit. He said to them, "Rulers of the people and you older leaders, are you questioning us about a good thing that was done to a crippled man? Are you asking us who made him well? We want all of you and all the Jewish people to know that this man was made well by the power of Jesus Christ from Nazareth! You nailed him to a cross, but God raised him from death.

"Jesus is the only One who can save people. His name is the only power in the world that has been given to save people. And we must be saved through him!"

The Jewish leaders saw that Peter and John were not afraid to speak. They understood that these men had no special training or education. So they were amazed. Then they realized that Peter and John had been with Jesus. They saw the crippled man standing there beside the two apostles. They saw that the man was healed. So they could say nothing against them. The Jewish leaders told them to leave the meeting. Then the leaders talked to each other about what they should do. They said, "What shall we do with these men? Everyone in Jerusalem knows that they have done a great miracle! We cannot say it is not true. But we must warn them not to talk to people anymore using that name. Then this

thing will not spread among the people."

So they called Peter and John in again. They told them not to speak or to teach at all in the name of Jesus. But Peter and John answered them, "What do you think is right? What would God want? Should we obey you or God? We cannot keep quiet. We must speak about what we have seen and heard." The Jewish leaders could not find a way to punish them because all the people were praising God for what had been done. So the Jewish leaders warned the apostles again and let them go free.

The Believers' Prayer

Peter and John left the meeting of Jewish leaders and went to their own group. They told them everything that the leading priests and the older Jewish leaders had said to them. When the believers heard this, they prayed to God with one purpose. They prayed, "Lord, you are the One who made the sky, the earth, the sea, and everything in the world. Herod, Pontius Pilate, the non-Jewish people, and the Jewish people all came together against Jesus here in Jerusalem. Jesus is your holy Servant. He is the One you made to be the Christ. These people made your plan happen; it happened because of your power and your will. And now, Lord, listen to what they are saying. They are trying to make us afraid! Lord, we are your servants. Help us to speak your word without fear. Help us to be brave by showing us your power; make sick people well, give proofs, and make miracles happen by the power of Jesus, your holy servant."

After they had prayed, the place where they were meeting was shaken. They were all filled with the Holy Spirit, and they spoke God's word without fear.

Sharing Everything

The group of believers were joined in their hearts, and they had the same spirit. No person in the group said that the things he had were his own. Instead, they shared everything. With great power the apostles were telling people that the Lord Jesus was truly raised from death. And God blessed all the believers very much. They all received the things they needed. Everyone that owned fields or houses sold them. They brought the money and gave it to the apostles. Then each person was given the things he needed.

The apostles did many signs and miracles among the people. All the people were saying good things about them. More and more men and women believed in the Lord and were added to the group of believers.

The Jews Against Stephen

Stephen was richly blessed by God. God gave him the power to do great miracles and signs among the people. But some Jews were against him.

So they paid some men to say, "We heard him say things against Moses and against God!"

This upset the people, the older Jewish leaders, and the teachers of the law. They came to Stephen, grabbed him and brought him to a meeting of the Jewish leaders. All the people in the meeting were watching Stephen closely. His face looked like the face of an angel.

The high priest said to Stephen, "Are these things true?"

Stephen answered, "Brothers and fathers, listen to me. You are always against what the Holy Spirit is trying to tell you. Your ancestors were like this, and you are just like them! Your fathers tried to hurt every prophet who ever lived. Those prophets said long ago that the Righteous One would come. But your fathers killed them. And now you have turned against the Righteous One and killed him. You received the law of Moses, which God gave you through his angels. But you don't obey it!"

Stephen Is Killed

When the Jewish leaders heard Stephen saying all these things, they became very angry. They were so mad that they were grinding their teeth at Stephen. But Stephen was full of the Holy Spirit. He looked up to heaven and saw the glory of God. He saw Jesus standing at God's right side. He said, "Look! I see heaven open. And I see the Son of Man standing at God's right side!"

Then the Jewish leaders all shouted loudly. They covered their ears with their hands and all ran at Stephen. They took him out of the city and threw stones at him until he was dead. The men who told lies against Stephen left their coats with a young man named Saul. While they were throwing stones, Stephen prayed, "Lord Jesus, receive my spirit!" He fell on his knees and cried in a loud voice, "Lord, do not hold this sin against them!" After Stephen said this, he died.

Saul agreed that the killing of Stephen was a good thing.

Saul Is Converted

In Jerusalem Saul was still trying to frighten the followers of the Lord by saying he would kill them. So he went to the high priest and asked him to write letters to the synagogues in the city of Damascus. Saul wanted the high priest to give him the authority to find people in Damascus who were followers of Christ's Way. If he found any there, men or women, he would arrest them and bring them back to Jerusalem.

So Saul went to Damascus. As he came near the city, a bright light from heaven suddenly flashed around him. Saul fell to the ground. He heard a voice saying to him, "Saul, Saul! Why are you doing things against me?"

Saul said, "Who are you, Lord?"

The voice answered, "I am Jesus. I am the One you are trying to hurt. Get up now and go into the city. Someone there will tell you what you must do."

The men traveling with Saul stood there, but they said nothing. They heard the voice, but they saw no one. Saul got up from the ground. He opened his eyes, but he could not see. So the men with Saul took his hand and led him into Damascus. For three days Saul could not see, and he did not eat or drink.

There was a follower of Jesus

in Damascus named Ananias. The Lord spoke to Ananias in a vision, "Ananias!"

Ananias answered, "Here I am, Lord."

The Lord said to him, "Get up and go to the street called Straight Street. Find the house of Judas. Ask for a man named Saul from the city of Tarsus. He is there now, praying. Saul has seen a vision. In it a man named Ananias comes to him and lays his hands on him. Then he sees again."

But Ananias answered, "Lord, many people have told me about this man and the terrible things he did to your people in Jerusalem. Now he has come here to Damascus. The leading priests have given him the power to arrest everyone who worships you."

But the Lord said to Ananias, "Go! I have chosen Saul for an important work. He must tell about me to non-Jews, to kings, and to the people of Israel. I will show him how much he must suffer for my name."

So Ananias went to the house of Judas. He laid his hands on Saul and said, "Brother Saul, the Lord Jesus sent me. He is the one you saw on the road on your way here. He sent me so that you can see again and be filled with the Holy Spirit." Immediately, something that looked like fish scales fell from Saul's eyes. He was able to see again! Then Saul got up and was baptized. After eating some food, his strength returned.

Saul Preaches in Damascus

Saul stayed with the followers of Jesus in Damascus for a few days. Soon he began to preach about Jesus in the synagogues, saying, "Jesus is the Son of God!"

All the people who heard him were amazed. They said, "This is the man who was in Jerusalem. He was trying to destroy those who trust in this name! He came here to do the same thing. He came here to arrest the followers of Jesus and take them back to the leading priests."

But Saul became more and more powerful. His proofs that Jesus is the Christ were so strong that the Jews in Damascus could not argue with him.

After many days, the Jews made plans to kill Saul. They were watching the city gates day and night. They wanted to kill him, but Saul learned about their plan. One night some followers of Saul helped him leave the city. They lowered him in a basket through an opening in the city wall.

Then Saul went to Jerusalem. He tried to join the group of followers, but they were all afraid of him. They did not believe that he was really a follower. But Barnabas accepted Saul and took him to the apostles. Barnabas told them that Saul had seen the Lord on the road. He explained how the Lord had spoken to Saul. Then he told them how boldly Saul had preached in the name of Jesus in Damascus.

And so Saul stayed with the followers. He went everywhere in Jerusalem, preaching boldly in the name of Jesus. He would often talk and argue with the Jews who spoke Greek. But they were trying to kill him. When the brothers learned about this, they took Saul to Tarsus.

Many of the believers were scattered by the terrible things that happened after Stephen was killed. Some of them went to places as far away as Phoenicia, Cyprus, and Antioch. When they came to Antioch, they spoke about the Lord Jesus. And a large group of people believed and turned to the Lord.

The church in Jerusalem heard about all of this, so they sent Barnabas to Antioch. Barnabas was a good man, full of the Holy Spirit and full of faith. When he reached Antioch and saw how God had blessed the people, he was glad. He encouraged all the believers in Antioch. He told them, "Never lose your faith. Always obey the Lord with all your hearts."

Then Barnabas went to the city of Tarsus to look for Saul. When he found Saul, he brought him to Antioch. And for a whole year Saul and Barnabas met with the church. They taught many people there. In Antioch the followers were called Christians for the first time.

Barnabas and Saul Are Chosen

In the church at Antioch there were prophets and teachers. They were all worshiping the Lord and giving up eating. The Holy Spirit said to them, "Give Barnabas and Saul to me to do a special work. I have chosen them for it."

So they gave up eating and prayed. They laid their hands on Barnabas and Saul and sent them out.

Barnabas and Saul in Cyprus

Barnabas and Saul were sent out by the Holy Spirit. They went to the island of Cyprus.

They went across the whole

island. Sergius Paulus, the governor, was a smart man. He asked Barnabas and Saul to come to him, because he wanted to hear the message of God. But Elymas, the magician, was against them. He tried to stop the governor from believing in Jesus. But Saul was filled with the Holy Spirit. (Saul's other name was Paul.) He looked straight at Elymas and said, "You son of the devil! You are an enemy of everything that is right! You are full of evil tricks and lies. You are always trying to change the Lord's truths into lies! Now the Lord will touch you, and you will be blind. For a time you will not be able to see anything — not even the light from the sun."

Then everything became dark for Elymas. He walked around, trying to find someone to lead him by the hand. When the governor saw this, he believed. He was amazed at the teaching about the Lord.

Paul and Barnabas Leave Cyprus

Paul and those with him sailed away to Pamphylia. But John Mark left them and returned to Jerusalem. They continued their trip to a city near Pisidia. On the Sabbath day they went into the synagogue.

Paul stood up. He raised his hand and said, "Men of Israel and you other people who worship God, please listen! The news about salvation has been sent to us. Those who live in Jerusalem and their leaders did not realize that Jesus was the Savior. They did not understand the words that the prophets wrote, which are read every Sabbath day. But they made them come true when they said Jesus was guilty. They could not find any real reason for Jesus to die, but they asked Pilate to have him killed. But God raised him up from death! We tell you the Good News about the promise God made to our ancestors. We are their children, and God has made this promise come true for us. God did this by raising Jesus from death. Brothers, you must understand what we are telling you: You can have forgiveness of your sins through Jesus."

While Paul and Barnabas were leaving the synagogue, the people asked them to tell them more about these things on the next Sabbath.

On the next Sabbath day, almost all the people in the city came to hear the word of the Lord. Seeing the crowd, the Jews became very jealous. They said insulting things and argued against what Paul said. But Paul and Barnabas spoke very boldly.

When the non-Jewish people heard Paul, many of the people believed the message. They were the ones chosen to have life forever.

And so the message of the Lord was spreading through the whole country. But the Jews started trouble against Paul and Barnabas and drove them out of their area.

Paul and Barnabas in Iconium

In Iconium, Paul and Barnabas went as usual to the Jewish synagogue. They spoke so well that a great many Jews and Greeks believed. But some of the Jews who did not believe excited the non-Jewish people and turned them against the believers. Paul and Barnabas stayed in Iconium a long time and spoke bravely for the Lord. The Lord showed that their message about his grace was true by giving them the power to work miracles and signs.

Some non-Jewish people, some Jews, and some of their rulers wanted to harm Paul and Barnabas by killing them with stones. When Paul and Barnabas learned about this, they went to Lystra and Derbe, and to the areas around those cities. They announced the Good News there, too.

Paul Is Nearly Killed

In Lystra some Jews persuaded the people to turn against Paul. And so they threw stones at Paul and dragged him out of town. They thought that they had killed him. But the followers gathered around him, and he got up and went back into the town. The next day, he and Barnabas left and went to the city of Derbe.

Paul and Barnabas told the Good News in Derbe and many became followers. And Paul and Barnabas made the followers of Jesus stronger. They helped them to stay in the faith. They said, "We must suffer many things to enter God's kingdom." They chose elders for each church, by praying and giving up eating.

The Return to Antioch in Syria

Then they sailed away to Antioch. This is where the believers had put them into God's care and had sent them out to do this work. And now they had finished the work.

When they arrived in Antioch, they gathered the church together. Paul and Barnabas told them all about what God had done with them.

Paul and Barnabas Separate

After some time, Paul said to Barnabas, "We preached the message of the Lord in many towns. We should go back to all those towns to visit the believers and see how they are doing."

Paul and Barnabas separated and went different ways. Barnabas sailed to Cyprus and took Mark with him. But Paul chose Silas and went through Syria and Cilicia, giving strength to the churches.

Paul and the men with him went to Troas. That night Paul had a vision. In the vision, a man from Macedonia came to him. The man stood there and begged, "Come over to Macedonia. Help us!" After Paul had seen the vision, we immediately prepared to leave for Macedonia. We understood that God had called us to tell the Good News to those people.

Paul and Silas in Jail

We left Troas in a ship, and we sailed to Neapolis. Then we went by land to Philippi, the leading city in that part of Macedonia.

Once, Roman officers tore the clothes of Paul and Silas and had them beaten with rods again and again. Then Paul and Silas were thrown into jail. The jailer was ordered to guard them carefully. When he heard this order, he put them far inside the jail. He pinned down their feet between large blocks of wood.

About midnight Paul and Silas were praying and singing songs to God. The other prisoners were listening to them. Suddenly, there was a big earthquake. It was so strong that it shook the foundation of the jail. Then all the doors of the jail broke open. All the prisoners were freed from their chains. The jailer woke up and saw that the jail doors were open. He thought that the prisoners had already escaped. So he got his sword and was about to kill himself. But Paul shouted, "Don't hurt yourself! We are all here!"

The jailer told someone to bring a light. Then he ran inside. Shaking with fear, he fell down before Paul and Silas. Then he brought them outside and said, "Men, what must I do to be saved?"

They said to him, "Believe in the Lord Jesus and you will be saved — you and all the people in your house." So Paul and Silas told the message of the Lord to the jailer and all the people in his house. At that hour of the night the jailer took Paul and Silas and washed their wounds. Then he and all his people were baptized immediately. After this the jailer took Paul and Silas home and gave them food. He and his family were very happy because they now believed in God.

Paul and Silas in Corinth

Paul and Silas traveled to Corinth. Paul used all his time telling people the Good News. He showed the Jews that Jesus is the Christ. But they would not accept Paul's teaching and said some evil things. So he said to them, "If you are not saved, it will be your own fault! I have done all I can do! After this, I will go only to non-Jewish people!" Many others in Corinth also listened to Paul. They believed and were baptized.

During the night, Paul had a vision. The Lord said to him, "Don't be afraid! Continue talking to people and don't be quiet! I am with you. No one will hurt you because many of my people are in this city." Paul stayed there for a year and a half, teaching God's word to the people.

Paul in Jerusalem

After these things, Paul made plans to go to Jerusalem. He said, "After I have been to Jerusalem, I must also visit Rome."

In Jerusalem some Jews from Asia saw Paul at the Temple. They caused all the people to be upset, and they grabbed Paul. They shouted, "Men of Israel, help us! This is the man who goes everywhere teaching things that are against the law of Moses, against our people, and against this Temple."

All the people in Jerusalem became very upset. They ran and took Paul and dragged him out of the Temple. The Temple doors were closed immediately. The people were about to kill Paul. Now the commander of the Roman army in Jerusalem learned that there was trouble in the whole city. Immediately he ran to the place where the crowd was gathered. He brought officers and soldiers with him, and the people saw them. So they stopped beating Paul. The commander went to Paul and arrested him.

The next night the Lord came and stood by Paul. He said, "Be brave! You have told people in Jerusalem about me. You must do the same in Rome also."

In the morning some of the Jews made a plan to kill Paul.

They made a promise that they would not eat or drink anything until they had killed him. There were more than 40 Jews who made this plan. They went and talked to the leading priests and the older Jewish leaders. They said, "We have made a promise to ourselves that we will not eat or drink until we have killed Paul! So this is what we want you to do: Send a message to the commander to bring Paul out to you. Tell him you want to ask Paul more questions. We will be waiting to kill him while he is on the way here."

But Paul's nephew heard about this plan. He went to the army building and told Paul about it. Then Paul called one of the officers and said, "Take this young man to the commander. He has a message for him."

So the officer brought Paul's nephew to the commander. The officer said, "The prisoner, Paul, asked me to bring this young man to you. He wants to tell you something."

The commander led the young man to a place where they could be alone. The commander asked, "What do you want to tell me?"

The young man said, "The Jews have decided to ask you to bring Paul down to their council meeting tomorrow. They want you to think that they are going to ask him more questions. But don't believe them! There are more than 40 men who are hiding and waiting to kill Paul. They have all made a promise not to eat or drink until they have killed him! Now they are waiting for you to agree."

The commander sent the young man away. He said to him, "Don't tell anyone that you have told me about their plan."

Paul Is Sent to Caesarea

The commander called two officers. He said to them, "I need some men to go to Caesarea. Get 200 soldiers ready. Also, get 70 horsemen and 200 men with spears. Be ready to leave at nine o'clock tonight. Get some horses for Paul to ride. He must be taken to Governor Felix safely." So the soldiers took Paul to Caesarea.

After some days Felix asked for Paul to be brought to him. He listened to Paul talk about believing in Christ Jesus. But Felix became afraid when Paul spoke about things like right living, self-control, and the time when God will judge the world. He said, "Go away now. When I have more time, I will call for you."

But after two years, Festus became governor. Felix was no longer governor, but he had left Paul in prison to please the Jews.

Paul Asks to See Caesar

Festus wanted to please the Jews. So he asked Paul, "Do you want to go to Jerusalem? Do you want me to judge you there on these charges?"

Paul said, "I have done nothing wrong to the Jews; you know this is true. If I have done something wrong and the law says I must die, I do not ask to be saved from death. But if these charges are not true, then no one can give me to them. No! I want Caesar to hear my case!"

Festus talked about this with the people who advised him. Then he said, "You have asked to see Caesar; so you will go to Caesar!"

Paul Sails for Rome

It was decided that we would sail for Italy.

We sailed slowly for many days. We had a hard time because the wind was blowing against us. Then we came to a place called Safe Harbors.

But we had lost much time. It was now dangerous to sail. So Paul warned them, "Men, I can see there will be a lot of trouble on this trip. The ship and the things in the ship will be lost. Even our lives may be lost!" But the captain and the owner of the ship did not agree with Paul. So most of the men decided that the ship should leave.

The Storm

Then a good wind began to blow from the south. The men on the ship thought, "This is the wind we wanted, and now we have it!" So they pulled up the anchor. We sailed very close to the island of Crete. But then a very strong wind named the "Northeaster" came from the island. This wind took the ship and carried it away. The ship could not sail against it. So we stopped trying and let the wind blow us. The next day the storm was blowing us so hard that the men threw out some of the cargo. A day later they threw out the ship's equipment. For many days we could not see the sun or the stars. The storm was very bad. We lost all hope of staying alive — we thought we would die.

Then one day Paul stood up before them and said, "Men, I tell you to cheer up. None of you will die! But the ship will be lost. Last night an angel from God came to me. This is the God I worship. I am his. God's angel said, 'Paul, do not be afraid! You must stand before Caesar. And

God has given you this promise: He will save the lives of all those men sailing with you.' So men, be cheerful! I trust in God. Everything will happen as his angel told me. But we will crash on an island."

The Ship Is Destroyed

When daylight came, the sailors saw land. They did not know what land it was, but they saw a bay with a beach. They wanted to sail the ship to the beach, if they could. So they cut the ropes to the anchors and left the anchors in the sea. At the same time, they untied the ropes that were holding the rudders. Then they raised the front sail into the wind and sailed toward the beach. But the ship hit a sandbank. The front of the ship stuck there and could not move. Then the big waves began to break the back of the ship to pieces.

The soldiers decided to kill the prisoners so that none of them could swim away and escape. But Julius, the officer, wanted to let Paul live. He did not allow the soldiers to kill the prisoners. Instead he ordered everyone who could swim to jump into the water and swim to land. The rest used wooden boards or pieces of the ship. And this is how all the people made it safely to land.

Paul on the Island of Malta

When we were safe on land, we learned that the island was called Malta. It was raining and very cold. But the people who lived there were very good to us. They made us a fire and welcomed all of us. Paul gathered a pile of sticks for the fire. He was putting them on the fire when a poisonous snake came out because of the heat and bit him on the hand. The people living on the island saw the snake hanging from Paul's hand. They said to each other, "This man must be a murderer! He did not die in the sea, but Justice does not want him to live." But Paul shook the snake off into the fire. He was not hurt. The people thought that Paul would swell up or fall down dead. The people waited and watched him for a long time, but nothing bad happened to him. So they changed their minds about Paul. Now they said, "He is a god!"

There were some fields around there owned by a very important man on the island. His name was Publius. He welcomed us into his home and was very good to us. We stayed in his house for three days. Publius' father was very sick with a fever and dysentery. But

Paul went to him and prayed. Then he put his hands on the man and healed him. After this, all the other sick people on the island came to Paul, and he healed them, too. The people on the island gave us many honors. We stayed there three months. When we were ready to leave, they gave us the things we needed.

Paul in Rome

Finally, we came to Rome. The believers in Rome heard that we were there. They came out to meet us. When Paul saw them, he was encouraged and thanked God.

Paul was allowed to live alone. But a soldier stayed with him to guard him. Paul stayed two full years in his own rented house. He welcomed all people who came and visited him. He preached about the kingdom of God and taught about the Lord Jesus Christ. He was very bold, and no one tried to stop him from speaking.

WORTH WONDERING...

- What do you learn about the Holy Spirit in the book of Acts?
- If you could meet Paul today, what kind of questions would you like to ask him?
- What good example can you give of someone in this book who did what was right?
- What example can you give of someone in this book who did what was wrong?
- In Acts, how do you see that God is great? And how do you see that He is good?

A GREAT VERSE TO THINK ABOUT AGAIN...

Look back in Acts to find this important verse:

- *The Holy Spirit will come to you. Then you will receive power. You will be my witnesses — in Jerusalem, in all of Judea, in Samaria, and in every part of the world.*

AND THERE'S MORE...

When you read Acts in a full Bible, look especially for...

- The story of Ananias and Sapphira, two people who tried to lie to God.
- Stories about Philip as he preached the good news.
- How God showed Peter in a dream that he must tell the news about Jesus to everyone — and not just Jews.
- How an angel got Peter out of jail.

INTRODUCING...

ROMANS • 1 and 2 CORINTHIANS • GALATIANS
EPHESIANS • PHILIPPIANS • COLOSSIANS
1 and 2 THESSALONIANS • 1 and 2 TIMOTHY
TITUS • PHILEMON

The next part of the Bible is made up of *letters* that were written by men we sometimes call "apostles." These men were God's messengers and leaders for the new Christian church that was spreading around the world.

The Gospels tell us *what Jesus did,* while the letters tell us *what that means for you and me.* They teach us what to believe and how to live.

These letters are arranged in the Bible according to who wrote them. The first 13 letters are all by Paul, whose exciting story is such a big part of the book of Acts. Paul wrote many of these letters while he was in prison.

His first nine letters in the New Testament were written to Christians in different places. These are the books from Romans through First and Second Thessalonians. The next four letters were written by Paul to men who were Christian workers. Two of these letters were to his helper Timothy. Another was to his helper Titus, and the last one was to his friend Philemon.

In these letters Paul reminded his readers again and again that God is our loving Father. In His love God created you and me and the world around us. And also in His love He sent us His Son Jesus. That makes it possible for us to be *new creations,* living in love with God forever.

That's why it's good to think of these books as personal letters from God to you and me.

Paul's Letter to the
ROMANS

God's Plan
to Save Us

Looking forward to Romans...

"God's Plan to Save Us"

In this letter, Paul explains carefully what the good news of Jesus really means for us. He says we were enemies with God — but now, because of what Jesus has done, we can have peace with God.

Rome was the largest and richest city in the world at this time. Rome was the greatest city the world had ever known. It was the capital of the great Roman Empire.

I wonder why the good news of Jesus is so important...

FROM PAUL, a servant of Christ Jesus. God called me to be an apostle and chose me to tell the Good News. This letter is to all of you in Rome whom God loves and has called to be his holy people. May God our Father and the Lord Jesus Christ show you kindness and give you peace.

A Prayer of Thanks

First I want to say that I thank my God through Jesus Christ for all of you. I thank God because people everywhere in the world are talking about your great faith.

God knows that every time I pray I always mention you. God is the One I serve with my whole heart by telling the Good News about his Son. I pray that I will be allowed to come to you, and this will happen if God wants it. I want very much to see you, to give you some spiritual gift to make you strong. I mean that I want us to help each other with the faith that we have. Your faith will help me, and my faith will help you. Brothers, I want you to know that I planned many times to come to you. But this has not been possible.

I must serve all people — Greeks and non-Greeks, the wise and the foolish. That is why I want so much to preach the Good News to you in Rome.

I am proud of the Good News. It is the power God uses to save everyone who believes. The Good News shows how God makes people right with himself. God's way of making people right with him begins and ends with faith.

All People Have Done Wrong

There are things about God that people cannot see — his eternal power and all the things that make him God. But since the beginning of the world those things have been easy to understand. They are made clear by what God has made. So people have no excuse for the bad things they do. They knew God. But they did not give glory to God, and they did not thank him. Their thinking became useless. Their foolish minds were filled with darkness. They said they were wise, but they became fools. They gave up the glory of God who lives forever. They traded that glory for the worship of idols made to look like earthly people. They traded God's glory for things that look like birds, animals, and snakes.

People did not think it was important to have a true knowledge of God. So God left them and allowed them to have their own worthless thinking. And so those people do the things that they should not do. They are filled with every kind of sin, evil, selfishness, and hatred. They are full of jealousy, murder, fighting, lying, and thinking the worst about each other. They gossip and say evil things about each other. They hate God. They are rude and conceited and brag about themselves. They invent ways of doing evil. They do not obey their parents. They are foolish, they do not keep their promises, and they show no kindness or mercy to other people. They know God's law

PAUSE & WONDER

Paul says here in Romans that certain things about God are easy to understand by looking at what He has made. When God created the world, He built in some great clues to help me be sure that He's the One who really made it. I want to keep my eyes open for these clues!

says that those who live like this should die. But they continue to do these evil things. And they also feel that those who do these things are doing right.

How God Makes People Right

People who have God's law and those who have never heard of the law are all the same when they sin. Hearing the law does not make people right with God. The law makes people right with God only if they obey what the law says.

So Jews and non-Jews are the same. They are all guilty of sin. No one can be made right with God by following the law. The law only shows us our sin.

But God has a way to make people right with him without the law. And God has now shown us that way which the law and the prophets told us about. God makes people right with himself through their faith in Jesus Christ. This is true for all who believe in Christ, because all are the same. All people have sinned and are not good enough for God's glory. People are made right with God by his grace, which is a free gift. They are made right with God by being made free from sin through Jesus Christ. God gave Jesus as a way to forgive sin through faith. And all of this is because of the blood of Jesus' death. This showed that God always does what is right and fair.

So do we have a reason to brag about ourselves? No! A person is made right with God through faith, not through what he does to follow the law.

The Example of Abraham

What about Abraham, the father of our people? What did he learn about faith? If Abraham was made right by the things he did, then he had a reason to brag. But he could not brag before God. The Scripture says, "Abraham believed God. And that faith made him right with God."

There was no hope that Abraham would have children. But Abraham believed God and continued hoping. And that is why he became the father of many nations. As God told him, "Your descendants will also be too many to count." Abraham was almost 100 years old, much past the age for having children. Also, Sarah could not have children. Abraham thought about all this. But he never doubted that God would keep his promise. Abraham never stopped believing. He grew stronger in his faith and gave praise to God. Abraham felt sure that God was able to do the thing that God promised. So, "God accepted Abraham's faith, and that made him right with God." God will accept us also because we believe. We believe in the One who raised Jesus our Lord from death. Jesus was given to die for our sins. And he was raised from death to make us right with God.

Right with God

We have been made right with God because of our faith. So we have peace with God through our Lord Jesus Christ. And we are happy because of the hope we have of sharing God's glory. And we also have joy with our troubles because we know that these troubles produce patience. And patience produces character, and character produces hope. And this hope will never disappoint us, because God has poured out his love to fill our hearts.

Christ died for us while we were still weak. We were living against God, but at the right time, Christ died for us. Very few people will die to save the life of someone else. Although perhaps for a good man someone might possibly die. But Christ died for us while we were still sinners. In this way God shows his great love for us.

Life in the Spirit

So now, those who are in Christ Jesus are not judged guilty. God did what the law could not do. He sent his own Son to earth with the same human life that others use for sin. He sent his Son to be an offering to pay for sin. So God used a human life to destroy sin. Now we do not live following our sinful selves, but we live following the Spirit.

If a person's thinking is controlled by his sinful self, then there is death. But if his thinking is controlled by the Spirit, then there is life and peace. This is true because if a person's thinking is controlled by his sinful self, then he is against God.

So, my brothers, we must not be ruled by our sinful selves. We must not live the way our sinful selves want. If you use your lives to do the wrong things your sinful selves want, then you will die spiritually. But if you use the Spirit's help to stop doing the wrong things you do with your body, then you will have true life.

The true children of God are those who let God's Spirit lead them. If we are God's children, then we will receive the blessings

God has for us. We will receive these things from God together with Christ. But we must suffer as Christ suffered, and then we will have glory as Christ has glory.

Our Future Glory

We have sufferings now. But the sufferings we have now are nothing compared to the great glory that will be given to us.

We are very weak, but the Spirit helps us with our weakness. We do not know how to pray as we should. But the Spirit himself speaks to God for us, even begs God for us. The Spirit speaks to God with deep feelings that words cannot explain. God can see what is in people's hearts. And he knows what is in the mind of the Spirit, because the Spirit speaks to God for his people in the way that God wants.

We know that in everything God works for the good of those who love him. They are the people God called, because that was his plan. God knew them before he made the world. And God decided that they would be like his Son.

God's Love in Christ Jesus

So what should we say about this? If God is with us, then no one can defeat us. God let even his own Son suffer for us. God gave his Son for us all. So with Jesus, God will surely give us all things. Who can accuse the people that God has chosen? No one! God is the One who makes them right. Who can say that God's people are guilty? No one! Christ Jesus died, but that is not all. He was also raised from death. Can anything separate us from the love Christ has for us? Can troubles or problems or sufferings? If we have no food or clothes, if we are in danger, or even if death comes — can any of these things separate us from Christ's love?

In all these things we have full victory through God who showed his love for us. Yes, I am sure that nothing can separate us from the love God has for us. Not death, not life, not angels, not ruling spirits, nothing now, nothing in the future, no powers, nothing above us, nothing below us, or anything else in the whole world will ever be able to separate us from the love of God that is in Christ Jesus our Lord.

Give Your Lives to God

So brothers, since God has shown us great mercy, I beg you to offer your lives as a living sacrifice to him. Your offering must be only for God and pleasing to him. This is the spiritual way for you to worship. Do not change yourselves to be like the people of this world. But be changed within by a new way of thinking. Then you will be able to decide what God wants for you. And you will be able to know what is good and pleasing to God and what is perfect.

Your love must be real. Hate what is evil. Hold on to what is good. Love each other like brothers and sisters. Give your brothers and sisters more honor than you want for yourselves. Do not be lazy but work hard. Serve the Lord with all your heart. Be joyful because you have hope. Be patient when trouble comes. Pray at all times. Share with God's people who need help. Bring strangers in need into your homes.

Wish good for those who do bad things to you. Wish them well and do not curse them. Be happy with those who are happy. Be sad with those who are sad. Live together in peace with each other. Do not be proud, but make friends with those who seem unimportant. Do not think how smart you are.

If someone does wrong to you, do not pay him back by doing wrong to him. Try to do what everyone thinks is right. Do your best to live in peace with everyone. My friends, do not try to punish others when they wrong you. Wait for God to punish them with his anger. Do not let evil defeat you. Defeat evil by doing good.

Christians Should Obey the Law

All of you must obey the government rulers. No one rules unless God has given him the power to rule. And no one rules now without that power from

God. So if anyone is against the government, he is really against what God has commanded. You must obey not only because you might be punished, but because you know it is the right thing to do.

Loving Others

Do not owe people anything. But you will always owe love to each other. The person who loves others has obeyed all the law.

The law says, "You must not murder anyone. You must not steal. You must not want to take your neighbor's things." All these commands and all others are really only one rule: "Love your neighbor as you love yourself." Love never hurts a neighbor. So loving is obeying all the law.

I say this because we live in an important time. Yes, it is now time for you to wake up from your sleep. Our salvation is nearer now than when we first believed. The "night" is almost finished. The "day" is almost here. So we should stop doing things that belong to darkness and take up the weapons used for fighting in the light. Let us live in a right way, like people who belong to the day. We should not have wild parties or get drunk. There should be no fighting or jealousy. But clothe yourselves with the Lord Jesus Christ. Forget about satisfying your sinful self.

We who are strong in faith should help those who are weak. We should help them with their weaknesses, and not please only ourselves. Let each of us please his neighbor for his good, to help him be stronger in faith. Even Christ did not live to please himself. It was as the Scriptures said: "When people insult you, it hurts me." Everything that was written in the past was written to teach us, so that we could have hope. That hope comes from the patience and encouragement that the Scriptures give us.

Patience and encouragement come from God. And I pray that God will help you all agree with each other the way Christ Jesus wants. Then you will all be joined together, and you will give glory to God the Father of our Lord Jesus Christ. Christ accepted you, so you should accept each other. This will bring glory to God.

WORTH WONDERING...

■ What *promises* from God can you find in this book — something that He says He will do for us?

- What commands can you find in this book — things that God tells us to do or to be?

- Suppose a friend asked you this question: Why did Jesus have to die? As you remember what you read in the book of Romans, how would you answer your friend?

- In this book of the Bible, how do you see that God is great? And how do you see that He is good?

- Suppose you were in the Roman church when this letter arrived from Paul. You listened while the letter was read aloud to everyone. Which parts of this letter do you think would be the most important to you?

- Which parts of this book do you think the devil would most like you NOT to understand and obey?

- Jesus said (in the book of Matthew) that everyone who hears His words and obeys them is like a wise man who built his house on rock. Which words in this book do you think are the most important for you to obey right now?

GREAT VERSES TO THINK ABOUT AGAIN...

Look back in Romans to see if you can find these verses:

- *We know that in everything God works for the good of those who love him.*

- *We have been made right with God because of our faith. So we have peace with God through our Lord Jesus Christ.*

- *Love each other like brothers and sisters. Give your brothers and sisters more honor than you want for yourselves.*

- *We live in an important time. Yes, it is now time for you to wake up from your sleep. Our salvation is nearer now than when we first believed.*

- *I am proud of the Good News. It is the power God uses to save everyone who believes.*

- *I am sure that nothing can separate us from the love God has for us.*

AND THERE'S MORE...

When you read Romans in a full Bible, look especially for...

- Why Paul was thankful for the Roman Christians.

- What Paul says about God's future plan for the Jews.

Paul's First Letter to the
CORINTHIANS

Help for a Church
with Problems

Looking forward to 1 Corinthians...

"Help for a Church with Problems"

The church in Corinth had many problems. Paul talked about these problems in this letter.

One of the problems was that some people in the church were boasting about being followers of this or that different leader. But Paul says that what really matters is to be a follower of Jesus. And we do that by having the Holy Spirit control how we live. The best proof that we are living by the Holy Spirit is when we truly love other people.

Corinth was a seaport and the most important city in Achaia. Achaia is the southern part of what is today the country of Greece. The people who lived in Corinth came from all over the Roman Empire.

Paul spent two years in Corinth, teaching and preaching in the church.

I wonder how I can live by God's Holy Spirit...

DEAR BROTHERS, when I came to you, I did not come as a proud man. I preached God's truth, but not with fancy words or a show of great learning. I decided that while I was with you I would forget about everything except Jesus Christ and his death on the cross.

When I came to you, I was weak and shook with fear. My teaching and my speaking were not with wise words that persuade people. But the proof of my teaching was the power that the Spirit gives. I did this so that your faith would be in God's power, not in the wisdom of a man.

Following Men Is Wrong

The teaching I gave you was like milk, not solid food. I did this because you were not ready for solid food. And even now you are not ready. You are still not spiritual. You have jealousy and arguing among you. This shows that you are not spiritual. You are acting like people of the world. One of you says, "I follow Paul," and another says, "I follow Apollos." When you say things like this, you are acting like worldly people.

Is Apollos important? No! Is Paul important? No! We are only servants of God who helped you believe. Each one of us did the work God gave us to do. I planted the seed of the teaching in you, and Apollos watered it. But God is the One who made the seed grow. We are workers together for God.

And you are a house that belongs to God. Like an expert builder I built the foundation of that house. I used the gift that God gave me to do this. Others are building on that foundation. But everyone should be careful how he builds. The foundation that has already been laid is Jesus Christ. Anyone can build on that foundation, using gold, silver, jewels, wood, grass, or straw. But the work that each person does will be clearly seen, because the Day will make it plain. That Day will appear with fire, and the fire will test every man's work.

You should know that you yourselves are God's temple. God's Spirit lives in you. If anyone destroys God's temple, God will destroy him, because God's temple is holy. You yourselves are God's temple.

Use Your Bodies for God's Glory

"I am allowed to do all things." But all things are not good for me to do. "I am allowed to do all things." But I must not do those things that will make me their slave. "Food is for the stomach, and the stomach for food." Yes. But God will destroy them both. The body is for the Lord, and the Lord is for the body.

You should know that your body is a temple for the Holy Spirit. The Holy Spirit is in you. You have received the Holy Spirit from God. You do not own yourselves. You were bought by God for a price. So honor God with your bodies.

Love

I may speak in different languages of men or even angels. But if I do not have love, then I am only a noisy bell or a ringing cymbal. I may have the gift of prophecy; I may under-stand all the secret things of God and all knowledge; and I may have faith so great that I can move mountains. But even with all these things, if I do not have love, then I am nothing. I may give everything I have to feed the poor. And I may even give my body as an offering to be burned. But I gain nothing by doing these things if I do not have love.

Love is patient and kind. Love is not jealous, it does not brag, and it is not proud. Love is not rude, is not selfish, and does not become angry easily. Love does not remember wrongs done against it. Love is not happy with evil, but is happy with the truth. Love patiently accepts all things. It always trusts, always hopes, and always continues strong.

Love never ends. There are gifts of prophecy, but they will be ended. There are gifts of speaking in different languages, but those gifts will end. There is the gift of knowledge, but it will be ended. These things will end, because this knowledge and these prophecies we have are not complete. But when perfection comes, the things that are not complete will end. When I was a child, I talked like a child; I thought like a child; I made plans like a child. When I became a man, I stopped those childish ways. It is the same with us. Now we see as if we are looking into a dark mirror. But at that time, in the future, we shall see clearly. Now I know only a part. But at that time I will know fully, as God has known me. So these three things continue forever: faith, hope and love. And the greatest of these is love.

We Will Be Raised from Death

When Christ comes again, those who belong to him will be raised to life. Then the end will come.

But someone may ask, "What kind of body will they have?"

The body is raised to a life that cannot be destroyed. It is raised in glory. When it is raised, it has power, it is a spiritual body.

I tell you this secret: We will not all die, but we will all be changed. It will only take a second. We will be changed as quickly as an eye blinks. This will happen when the last trumpet sounds.

The trumpet will sound and those who have died will be raised to live forever. And we will all be changed. This body that will ruin must clothe itself with something that will never ruin. And this body that dies must clothe itself with something that will never die.

Death's power to hurt is sin. But we thank God! He gives us the victory through our Lord Jesus Christ.

So my dear brothers, stand strong. Do not let anything change you. Always give yourselves fully to the work of the Lord. You know that your work in the Lord is never wasted.

Be careful. Continue strong in the faith. Have courage, and be strong. Do everything in love.

■ What promises from God can you find in this book — things that He says He will do for us?

■ What commands can you find in this book — things that God tells us to do or to be?

■ Suppose you were in the Corinthian church when this letter arrived from Paul. You listened while the letter was read aloud to everyone. Which parts of this letter do you think would be the most important to you?

■ Which parts of this book do you think the devil would most like you NOT to understand and obey?

■ Jesus said (in the book of Matthew) that everyone who hears His words and obeys them is like a wise man who built his house on rock. Which words in this book do you think are the most important for you to obey right now?

GREAT VERSES TO THINK ABOUT AGAIN...

Look back in First Corinthians to see if you can find these verses:

■ *You should know that your body is a temple for the Holy Spirit. The Holy Spirit is in you. You have received the Holy Spirit from God. You do not own your-*selves. *You were bought by God for a price. So honor God with your bodies.*

■ *Always give yourselves fully to the work of the Lord. You know that your work in the Lord is never wasted.*

■ *Love patiently accepts all things. It always trusts, always hopes, and always continues strong.*

AND THERE'S MORE...

When you read First Corinthians in a full Bible, look especially for...

■ What Paul says about other problems and questions in the Corinthian church.

■ Why Paul was thankful for the Corinthians.

■ What Paul says about the gifts given to us by the Holy Spirit.

Paul's Second Letter to the
CORINTHIANS

Paul Answers Those Who Accuse Him

Looking forward to 2 Corinthians...

WHAT'S IT ABOUT?

"Paul Answers Those Who Accuse Him"

SIGNS AND WONDERS

Helping other people follow Jesus is wonderful work — and also a great honor. Paul talks about that in this second letter to the Corinthians.

Paul was often needy and in trouble. And people in the church sometimes accused him of this or that. But Paul didn't want people to look down on him, because of the work God gave him to do.

FACES AND PLACES

Corinth was a seaport and the most important city in Achaia. Achaia is the southern part of what is today the country of Greece. The people who lived in Corinth came from all over the Roman Empire.

Paul spent two years in Corinth, teaching and preaching in the church.

I wonder what it means to be God's worker...

BROTHERS, we want you to know about the trouble we suffered in the country of Asia. We had great burdens there that were greater than our own strength. We even gave up hope for life. Truly, in our own hearts we believed that we would die.

But this happened so that we would not trust in ourselves. It happened so that we would trust in God, who raises people from death. God saved us from these great dangers of death. And he will continue to save us.

God is the One who makes you and us strong in Christ. God made us his chosen people. He put his mark on us to show that we are his. And he put his Spirit in our hearts to be a guarantee for all he has promised.

Victory Through Christ

Thanks be to God, who always leads us in victory through Christ.

We have troubles all around us, but we are not defeated. We do not know what to do, but we do not give up. We are persecuted, but God does not leave us. We are hurt sometimes, but we are not destroyed. We carry the death of Jesus in our own bodies, so that the life of Jesus can also be seen in our bodies.

So we do not give up. Our physical body is becoming older and weaker, but our spirit inside us is made new every day. We have small troubles for a while now, but they are helping us gain an eternal glory. That glory is much greater than the troubles. So we set our eyes not on what we see but on what we cannot see. What we see will last only a short time. But what we cannot see will last forever.

We know that God will have a house for us to live in. It will be a home in heaven that will last forever. This is what God made us for. And he has given us the Spirit to be a guarantee for this new life.

So we always have courage. We live by what we believe, not by what we can see. Our only goal is to please God. We want to please him whether we live here or there. For we must all stand before Christ to be judged. Each one will receive what he should get — good or bad — for the things he did when he lived in the earthly body.

The love of Christ controls us. Because we know that Christ died for all so that those who live would not continue to live for themselves. He died for them and was raised from death so that they would live for him.

If anyone belongs to Christ, then he is made new. The old things have gone; everything is made new! All this is from God. Through Christ, God made peace between us and himself. And he gave us this message of peace. So we have been sent to speak for Christ. It is as if God is calling to you through us. We speak for Christ when we beg you to be at peace with God. Christ had no sin. But God made him become sin. God did this for us so that in Christ we could become right with God.

PAUSE & WONDER

The New Testament Letters — the books from Romans to Jude — all reflect the light of Jesus to me. (They're like the moon or the planets, which reflect the light of the sun.) These letters teach me the meaning of what Jesus did. They teach me what Jesus is doing now. And they tell me what Jesus will do in the future — how He'll come back for me, and let me live in His heaven.

We are workers together with God. So we beg you: Do not let the grace that you received from God be for nothing. God says, "I heard your prayers at the right time, and I gave you help on the day of salvation."

I tell you that the "right time" is now. The "day of salvation" is now.

Warning About Non-Christians

You are not the same as those who do not believe. So do not join yourselves to them. Good and bad do not belong together. Light and darkness cannot share together. What can a believer have together with a non-believer?

So we should make ourselves pure — free from anything that makes body or soul unclean. We should try to become perfect in the way we live, because we respect God.

Paul Tells About His Sufferings

Many people are bragging about their lives in the world. So I will brag, too.

I have worked much harder than they. I have been in prison more often. I have been hurt more in beatings. I have been near death many times. Five times the Jews have given me their punishment of 39 lashes with a whip. Three different times I was beaten with rods. One time they tried to kill me with stones. Three times I was in ships that were wrecked, and one of those times I spent the night and the next day in the sea. I have gone on many travels. And I have been in danger from rivers, from thieves, from my own people, the Jews, and from those who are not Jews. I have been in danger in cities, in places where no one lives, and on the sea. And I have been in danger with false brothers. I have done hard and tiring work, and many times I did not sleep. I have been hungry and thirsty. Many times I have been without food. I have been cold and without clothes. Besides all this, there is on me every day the load of my concern for all the churches. I feel weak every time someone is weak. I feel upset every time someone is led into sin.

If I must brag, I will brag about the things that show I am weak. God knows that I am not lying. I do not want people to think more of me than what they see me do or hear me say.

A painful problem was given to me. This problem is a messenger from Satan. It is sent to beat me and keep me from being too proud. I begged the

Lord three times to take this problem away from me. But the Lord said to me, "My grace is enough for you. When you are weak, then my power is made perfect in you." So I am very happy to brag about my weaknesses. Then Christ's power can live in me. So I am happy when I have weaknesses, insults, hard times, sufferings, and all kinds of troubles. All these things are for Christ. And I am happy, because when I am weak, then I am truly strong.

WORTH WONDERING...

- What promises from God can you find in this book — things that He says He will do for us?

- What commands can you find in this book — things that God tells us to do or to be?

- Suppose a friend asked you this question: Why did Jesus have to die? As you remember what you read in the book of Second Corinthians, how would you answer your friend?

- Suppose God had written this book of the Bible only for you. Which words or sentences do you think He might have underlined, because He especially wanted you to notice them?

GREAT VERSES TO THINK ABOUT AGAIN...

Look back in Second Corinthians to see if you can find these verses:

- *What we see will last only a short time. But what we cannot see will last forever.*

- *Thanks be to God, who always leads us in victory through Christ.*

- *Christ had no sin. But God made him become sin. God did this for us so that in Christ we could become right with God.*

- *Our only goal is to please God. We want to please him whether we live here or there. For we must all stand before Christ to be judged.*

AND THERE'S MORE...

When you read Second Corinthians in a full Bible, look especially for...

- How we can give money for God's work, and the right way to do it.

- How Paul had a vision in which he was taken up to heaven, and saw things that he is not able to explain.

- Why Paul loves the Corinthians.

Paul's Letter to the
GALATIANS

Christians Are Saved
by Grace

Looking forward to Galatians...

"Christians Are Saved by Grace"

SIGNS AND WONDERS

Jesus gives us freedom! We don't have to be slaves to anyone or anything when we live for Jesus. And we live for Him when the Holy Spirit is in control of our lives.

Paul was afraid that the Christians in Galatia were becoming slaves, instead of enjoying the freedom that Jesus gives. The Galatians were actually following rules instead of following Jesus. These rules were found in the Old Testament law. The Galatians thought that by following these rules, they would be saved.

FACES AND PLACES

Galatia: This large area today is a part of the country of Turkey.

Paul had visited Galatia on his missionary trips. He had started many churches there.

I wonder how I can be truly free...

I WAS NOT CHOSEN to be an apostle by men. It was Jesus Christ and God the Father who made me an apostle.

I pray that God our Father and the Lord Jesus Christ will be good to you and give you peace. Jesus gave himself for our sins to free us from this evil world we live in. This is what God the Father wanted.

The Only Good News

A short time ago God called you to follow him. He called you by his grace that came through Christ. But now I am amazed at you! You are already turning away and believing something different than the Good News. Some people are confusing you and want to change the Good News of Christ. I said this before. Now I say it again: You have already accepted the Good News. If anyone tells you another way to be saved, he should be condemned!

Paul's Authority Is from God

Brothers, I want you to know that the Good News I preached to you was not made by men. I did not get it from men, nor did any man teach it to me. Jesus Christ showed it to me.

You have heard about my past life. I belonged to the Jewish religion. I hurt the church of God very much and tried to destroy it. I was becoming a leader in the Jewish religion. I did better than most other Jews of my age. I tried harder than anyone else to follow the old rules. These rules were the customs handed down by our ancestors.

But God had special plans for me even before I was born. So he called me through his grace that I might tell the Good News about his Son to the non-Jewish people. So God showed me about his Son. When God called me, I did not get advice or help from any man. I did not go to Jerusalem to see those who were apostles before I was. But, without waiting, I went away to Arabia and later went back to Damascus.

After three years I went to Jerusalem to meet Peter and stayed with him for 15 days. In Judea the churches in Christ had never met me. They had only heard this about me: "This man was trying to hurt us. But now he is preaching the same faith that he once tried to destroy." And these believers praised God because of me.

Other Apostles Accepted Paul

After 14 years, I went to Jerusalem again, this time with Barnabas. I also took Titus with me. I went because God showed me that I should go. I met with those men who were the leaders of the believers. When we were alone, I told them the Good News that I preach to the non-Jewish people. I did not want my past work and the work I am now doing to be wasted.

Those men saw that God had given me special work, just as he had to Peter. God gave Peter the work of telling the Good News to the Jews. But God gave me the

---

P A U S E & W O N D E R

I can think of God's grace and mercy in this way: God's GRACE means giving me what I don't deserve. (What I don't deserve is a home in heaven forever.) And God's MERCY means not getting what I do deserve. (Because of my sin, what I deserve is to be sent to the prison of hell, far away from God's light and love.) God wants me to become the perfect person He created me to be. His love and grace and mercy reach out to me to make it happen.

work of telling the Good News to the non-Jewish people. James, Peter, and John saw that God had given me this special grace. So they said, "Paul and Barnabas, we agree that you should go to the people who are not Jews. We will go to the Jews." They asked us to do only one thing — to remember to help the poor. And this was something that I really wanted to do.

We know that a person is not made right with God by following the law. No! It is trusting in Jesus Christ that makes a person right with God. So we, too, have put our faith in Christ Jesus, that we might be made right with God. And we are right with God because we trusted in Christ — not because we followed the law. For no one can be made right with God by following the law.

I would really be wrong to begin teaching again those things of the Law of Moses that I gave up. I stopped living for the law. I died to the law so that I can now live for God. I was put to death on the cross with Christ. I do not live anymore — it is Christ living in me. I still live in my body, but I live by faith in the Son of God. He loved me and gave himself to save me. This gift is from God, and it is very important to me.

Keep Your Freedom

You were running a good race. You were obeying the truth. Who stopped you from following the true way? I trust in the Lord that you will not believe those different ideas. Someone is confusing you with such ideas. And he will be punished, whoever he is.

My brothers, God called you to be free. But do not use your freedom as an excuse to do the things that please your sinful self. Serve each other with love. The whole law is made complete in this one command: "Love your neighbor as you love yourself." If you go on hurting each other and tearing each other apart, be careful! You will completely destroy each other.

The Spirit and Human Nature

So I tell you: Live by following the Spirit. Then you will not do what your sinful selves want. Our sinful selves want what is against the Spirit. The Spirit wants what is against our sinful selves. The two are against each other.

The wrong things the sinful self does are clear: not being pure, worshiping false gods, doing witchcraft, hating, making trouble, being jealous, being angry, being selfish, making people angry with each other, causing divisions among people, having envy, being drunk, having wild and wasteful parties, and doing other things like this. I warn you now as I warned you before: Those who do these things will not be in God's kingdom. But the Spirit gives love, joy, peace, patience, kindness, goodness, faithfulness, gentleness, self-control. Those who belong to Christ Jesus have crucified their own sinful selves. They have given up their old selfish feelings and the evil things they wanted to do. We get our new life from the Spirit. So we should follow the Spirit.

Life Is Like Planting a Field

Do not be fooled: You cannot cheat God. A person harvests only what he plants. If he plants to satisfy his sinful self, his sinful self will bring him eternal death. But if he plants to please the Spirit, he will receive eternal life from the Spirit. We must not become tired of doing good. We will receive our harvest of eternal life at the right time. We must not give up! When we have the opportunity to help anyone, we should do it. But we should give special attention to those who are in the family of believers.

WORTH WONDERING...

■ What did Paul want the Galatians to understand about his past life?

■ Why does God let us into heaven — because we believe in Jesus, or because we do good things and follow good rules?

■ How do we know if we are living by the Holy Spirit?

GREAT VERSES TO THINK ABOUT AGAIN...

Look back in Galatians to see if you can find these verses:

■ *Do not use your freedom as an excuse to do the things that please your sinful self.*

■ *I was put to death on the cross with Christ. I do not live anymore — it is Christ living in me. I still live in my body, but I live by faith in the Son of God.*

AND THERE'S MORE...

When you read Galatians in a full Bible, look especially for...

■ How Paul showed that Peter was wrong about something.

■ Why God gave His people the Old Testament law.

Paul's Letter to the
EPHESIANS

We Are One
in Christ

Looking forward to Ephesians...

"We Are One in Christ"

We are rich in Jesus! He has given heaven's riches to all Christians. And He has made all of us a part of one Church. All Christians are our brothers and sisters.

Ephesus: This important city was a place where many people served idols and false gods. A huge, beautiful temple was built here for the goddess Diana. Thousands of people from all over the world came to visit. Ephesus was a place of great spiritual darkness. So the Christians there were like a light shining in the night.

Paul spent three years as a preacher and teacher in Ephesus.

I wonder how I can be a stronger Christian...

IN CHRIST we are set free by the blood of his death. And so we have forgiveness of sins because of God's rich grace. God gave us that grace fully and freely. God, with full wisdom and understanding, let us know his secret purpose. His goal was to carry out his plan when the right time came. He planned that all things in heaven and on earth would be joined together in Christ as the head.

From Death to Life

In the past your spiritual lives were dead because of your sins and the things you did wrong against God. Yes, in the past you lived the way the world lives. You followed the ruler of the evil powers that are above the earth. We lived trying to please our sinful selves. We were the same as all other people.

But God's mercy is great, and he loved us very much. God gave us new life with Christ. You have been saved by God's grace. And he raised us up with Christ and gave us a seat with him in the heavens. You did not save yourselves. It was a gift from God. You cannot brag that you are saved by the work you have done. God has made us what we are. In Christ Jesus, God made us new people so that we would do good works. God had planned in advance those good works for us. He had planned for us to live our lives doing them.

The Love of Christ

So I bow in prayer before the Father. I ask the Father in his great glory to give you the power to be strong in spirit. He will give you that strength through his Spirit. I pray that Christ will live in your hearts because of your faith. I pray that your life will be strong in love and be built on love. And I pray that you and all God's holy people will have the power to understand the greatness of Christ's love. I pray that you can understand how wide and how long and how high and how deep that love is. Christ's love is greater than any person can ever know. But I pray that you will be able to know that love. Then you can be filled with the fullness of God.

With God's power working in us, God can do much, much more than anything we can ask or think of. To him be glory in the church and in Christ Jesus, forever and ever. Amen.

The Unity of the Body

I tell you now to live the way God's people should live. Always be humble and gentle. Be patient and accept each other with love. You are joined together with peace through the Spirit. Do all you can to continue together in this way. Let peace hold you together.

So you must stop telling lies. Tell each other the truth because we all belong to each other in the same body.

When you talk, do not say harmful things. But say what people need — words that will help others become stronger. Then what you say will help those who listen to you. And do not make the Holy Spirit sad. The Spirit is God's proof that you belong to him. God gave you the Spirit to show that God will make you free when the time comes. Do not be bitter or angry or mad. Never shout angrily or say things to hurt others. Never do anything evil. Be kind and loving to each other. Forgive each other just as God forgave you in Christ.

Living in the Light

You are God's children whom he loves. So try to be like God. Live a life of love. Love other people just as Christ loved us.

In the past you were full of darkness, but now you are full of light in the Lord. So live like children who belong to the light. Light brings every kind of goodness, right living, and truth. Try to learn what pleases the Lord. Do not do the things that people in darkness do.

So be very careful how you live. Do not live like those who are not wise. Live wisely. I mean that you should use every chance you have for doing good, because these are evil times. So do not be foolish with your lives. But learn what the Lord wants you to do. Do not be drunk with wine. That will ruin you spiritually. But be filled with the Spirit. Speak to each other with psalms, hymns, and spiritual songs. Sing and make music in your hearts to the Lord. Always give thanks to God the Father for everything, in the name of our Lord Jesus Christ.

Children and Parents

Children, obey your parents the way the Lord wants. This is the right thing to do. The command says, "Honor your father and mother." This is the first command that has a promise with it. The promise is: "Then everything will be well with you, and you will have a long life on the earth."

Fathers, do not make your children angry, but raise them with the training and teaching of the Lord.

Wear the Full Armor of God

Finally, be strong in the Lord and in his great power. Wear the full armor of God. Wear God's armor so that you can fight against the devil's evil tricks. Our fight is not against people on earth. We are fighting against the rulers and authorities and the powers of this world's darkness. We are fighting against the spiritual powers of evil in the heavenly world. That is why you need to get God's full armor. Then on the day of evil you will be able to stand strong. And when you have finished the whole fight, you will still be standing. So stand strong, with the belt of truth tied around your waist. And on your chest wear the protection of right living. And on your feet wear the Good News of peace to help you stand strong. And also use the shield of faith. With that you can stop all the burning arrows of the Evil One. Accept God's salvation to be your helmet. And take the sword of the Spirit — that sword is the teaching of God. Pray in the Spirit at all times. Pray with all kinds of prayers, and ask for everything you need. To do this you must always be ready. Never give up. Always pray for all God's people.

WORTH WONDERING...

- Why should Christians get along with one another?

- What promises from God can you find in this book — something that He says He will do for us?

- What commands can you find in this book — things that God tells us to do or to be?

- Which parts of this book do you think the devil would most like you NOT to understand and obey?

- Suppose God had written this book of the Bible only for you. Which words or sentences do you think He might have underlined, because He especially wanted you to notice them?

GREAT VERSES TO THINK ABOUT AGAIN...

Look back in Ephesians to see if you can find these verses:

- *God made us new people so that we would do good works.*

- *You did not save yourselves. It was a gift from God.*

- *You cannot brag that you are saved by the work you have done. God has made us what we are.*

- *Christ's love is greater than any person can ever know. But I pray that you will be able to know that love. Then you can be filled with the fullness of God.*

AND THERE'S MORE...

When you read Ephesians in a full Bible, look especially for...

- How God brings together Jews and non-Jews. He brings them together in Christ.

- How wives and husbands should love one another.

- How slaves and masters should behave toward one another.

Paul's Letter to the
PHILIPPIANS

Serve Others
with Joy

Looking forward to Philippians...

"Serve Others with Joy"

Jesus gives us true joy, even when we face hardships. Philippi was the city where Paul and Silas had been singing in jail one night. Then God sent an earthquake to set them free.

As he writes this letter, Paul is behind bars again. He is in prison in Rome. But as you can see, he knows how to find joy even in prison.

Philippi was an important city in the country of Macedonia. Today this area is in the northern part of Greece.
Paul began the church in Philippi on one of his missionary trips.

I wonder how I can stay happy, even when things go wrong...

BROTHERS, I want you to know that what has happened to me has helped to spread the Good News. I am in prison because I am a believer in Christ. All the palace guards and everyone else knows this. I am still in prison, but most of the believers feel better about it now. And so they are much braver about telling the Good News about Christ.

You are praying for me, and the Spirit of Jesus Christ helps me. So I know that this trouble will bring my freedom. The thing I want and hope for is that I will not fail Christ in anything. I hope that I will have the courage now, as always, to show the greatness of Christ in my life here on earth. I want to do that

if I die or if I live. To me the only important thing about living is Christ.

Be sure that you live in a way that brings honor to the Good News of Christ. Then whether I come and visit you or am away from you, I will hear good things about you. I will hear that you continue strong with one purpose and that you work together as a team for the faith of the Good News.

Does your life in Christ give you strength? Does his love comfort you? Do we share together in the Spirit? Do you have mercy and kindness? If so, make me very happy by having the same thoughts, sharing the same love, and having one mind and purpose. When you do things, do not let selfishness or pride be your guide. Be humble and give more honor to others than to yourselves. Do not be interested only in your own life, but be interested in the lives of others.

Be Unselfish Like Christ

In your lives you must think and act like Christ Jesus. Christ himself was like God in everything. He was equal with God. But he did not think that being equal with God was something to be held on to. He gave up his place with God and made himself nothing. He was born to be a man and became like a servant. And when he was living as a man, he humbled himself and was fully obedient to God. He obeyed even when that caused his death — death on a cross. So God raised Christ to the highest place. God made the name of Christ greater than every other name. God wants every knee to bow to Jesus — everyone in heaven, on earth, and under the earth. Everyone will say, "Jesus Christ is Lord" and bring glory to God the Father.

Be the People God Wants You to Be

It is even more important that you obey now while I am not with you. Keep on working to complete your salvation, and do it with fear and trembling. Yes, God is working in you to help you want to do what pleases him. Then he gives you the power to do it.

Do everything without complaining or arguing. You will be God's children without fault. But you are living with crooked and mean people all around you. Among them you shine like stars in the dark world. You offer to them the teaching that gives life.

The Importance of Christ

We worship God through his Spirit. We are proud to be in Christ Jesus. And we do not trust in ourselves or anything we can do. Even if I am able to trust in myself, still I do not. If anyone thinks that he has a reason to trust in himself, he should know that I have greater reason for trusting in myself. I am a Hebrew, and my parents were Hebrews. The law of Moses was very important to me. That is why I became a Pharisee. No one could find fault with the way I obeyed the law of Moses. At one time all these things were important to me.

But now I think those things are worth nothing because of

Christ. Not only those things, but I think that all things are worth nothing compared with the greatness of knowing Christ Jesus my Lord. Because of Christ, I have lost all those things. And now I know that all those things are worthless trash. This allows me to have Christ and to belong to him.

All I want is to know Christ and the power of his rising from death. I want to share in Christ's sufferings and become like him in his death. If I have those things, then I have hope that I myself will be raised from death.

I do not mean that I am already as God wants me to be. I have not yet reached that goal. But I continue trying to reach it and to make it mine. I forget the things that are past. I try as hard as I can to reach the goal and get the prize. That prize is mine because God called me through Christ to the life above.

What the Christians Are to Do

Be full of joy in the Lord always. I will say again, be full of joy.

Let all men see that you are gentle and kind. The Lord is coming soon. Do not worry about anything. But pray and ask God for everything you need. And when you pray, always give thanks. And God's peace will keep your hearts and minds in Christ Jesus. The peace that God gives is so great that we cannot understand it.

Brothers, continue to think about the things that are good and worthy of praise. Think about the things that are true and honorable and right and pure and beautiful and respected. And do what you learned and received from me. Do what I told you and what you saw me do. And the God who gives peace will be with you.

WORTH WONDERING...

■ Paul talks in this letter about the goals in his life — what he wants to do or to become. What are his goals?

■ What can we think about to help us be unselfish?

■ Can you find any promises from God in this book — something that He says He will do for us?

■ What commands can you find in this book — something that God tells us to do or to be?

■ Suppose an angel appeared to you right now. The angel said that God was glad you were reading the book of Philippians. And he said that there were a few words or sentences in this book that God wanted you to especially think about right now. Which words or sentences do you think those might be?

■ Which parts of this book do you think the devil would most like you NOT to understand and obey?

GREAT VERSES TO THINK ABOUT AGAIN...

Look back in Philippians to see if you can find these verses:

■ *God made the name of Christ greater than every other name. God wants every knee to bow to Jesus — everyone in heaven, on earth, and under the earth. Everyone will say, "Jesus Christ is Lord" and bring glory to God the Father.*

■ *All I want is to know Christ and the power of his rising from death. I want to share in Christ's sufferings and become like him in his death.*

■ *To me the only important thing about living is Christ.*

■ *Continue to think about the things that are good and worthy of praise. Think about the things that are true and honorable and right and pure and beautiful and respected.*

■ *God is working in you to help you want to do what pleases*

him. Then he gives you the power to do it.

AND THERE'S MORE...

When you read Philippians in a full Bible, look especially for...

■ Paul's prayer for the Philippians.

■ How Paul is sending two of his helpers to the Philippians.

Paul's Letter to the
COLOSSIANS

Jesus Is
Above All Things

Looking forward to Colossians...

WHAT'S IT ABOUT?

"Jesus Is Above All Things"

SIGNS AND WONDERS

Jesus is perfectly God, and He is our perfect Leader. Some wrong teachers in the church in Colosse did not think that these things were true. So Paul wrote this letter to help them see the truth.

FACES AND PLACES

Colosse was a smaller city in what is today the country of Turkey.
Paul had never visited this city.

I wonder how much Jesus is God, and how much He is man?...

IN OUR PRAYERS for you we always thank God, the Father of our Lord Jesus Christ. We thank God because we have heard about the faith you have in Christ Jesus and the love you have for all of God's people. You have this faith and love because of your hope, and what you hope for is saved for you in heaven.

You learned about this hope when you heard the true teaching, the Good News that was told to you. Everywhere in the world that Good News is bringing blessings and is growing. This has happened with you, too, since you heard the Good News and understood the truth about the grace of God.

Since the day we heard this about you, we have continued praying for you. We ask God that you will know fully what God wants. We pray that you will also have great wisdom and understanding in spiritual things. Then you will live the kind of life that honors and pleases the Lord in every way. You will produce fruit in every good work and grow in the knowledge of God.

Then God will strengthen you with his own great power. And you will not give up when troubles come, but you will be patient. Then you will joyfully give thanks to the Father. He has made you able to have all that he has prepared for his people who live in the light. God made us free from the power of darkness, and he brought us into the kingdom of his dear Son. The Son paid for our sins, and in him we have forgiveness.

The Importance of Christ

No one has seen God, but Jesus is exactly like him. Christ ranks higher than all the things that have been made. Through his power all things were made — things in heaven and on earth. All things were made through Christ and for Christ. Christ was there before anything was made. And all things continue because of him. He is the head of the body. (The body is the church.) Everything comes from him.

At one time you were separated from God. You were God's enemies in your minds because the evil deeds you did were against God. But now Christ has made you God's friends again. He did this by his death while he was in the body, that he might bring you into God's presence. He brings you before God as people who are holy, with no wrong in you, and with nothing that God can judge you guilty of. And Christ will do this if you continue to believe in the Good News you heard. You must continue strong and sure in your faith. You must not be moved away from the hope that Good News gave you. That same Good News has been told to everyone in the world. I, Paul, help in preaching that Good News.

Paul's Work for the Church

God gave me a special work to do that helps you. My work is to tell fully the teaching of God. This teaching is the secret truth that was hidden since the beginning of time.

This truth is Christ himself, who is in you. He is our only hope for glory. So we continue to preach Christ to all men. We use all wisdom to warn and to teach everyone.

We are trying to bring each one into God's presence as a mature person in Christ. To do this, I work and struggle, using Christ's great strength that works so powerfully in me.

I want you to know that I am trying very hard to help you. And I am trying to help others who have never seen me. I want them to be strengthened and joined together with love.

Continue to Live in Christ

As you received Christ Jesus the Lord, so continue to live in him. Keep your roots deep in him and have your lives built on him. Be strong in the faith, just as you were taught. And always be thankful.

Be sure that no one leads you away with false ideas and words that mean nothing. Those ideas come from men. They are the worthless ideas of this world. They are not from Christ. All of God lives in Christ fully (even when Christ was on earth). And in him you have a full and true life. He is ruler over all rulers and powers.

In Christ you were made free from the power of your sinful self. When you were baptized, you were buried with Christ and you were raised up with Christ because of your faith in God's power. That power was shown when he raised Christ from death. You were spiritually dead because of your sins and because you were not free from the power of your sinful self. But God made you alive with Christ. And God forgave all our sins. We owed a debt because we broke God's laws. That debt listed all the rules we failed to follow. But God forgave us that debt. He took away that debt and nailed it to the cross. God defeated the spiritual rulers and powers. With the cross God won the victory and defeated them.

He showed the world that they were powerless.

Your New Life in Christ

You were raised from death with Christ. So aim at what is in heaven, where Christ is sitting at the right hand of God. Think only about the things in heaven, not the things on earth. Your old sinful self has died, and your new life is kept with Christ in God. Christ is your life. When he comes again, you will share in his glory.

So put all evil things out of your life: doing evil, letting evil thoughts control you, wanting things that are evil, and always selfishly wanting more and more. In your evil life in the past, you also did these things.

But now put these things out of your life: anger, bad temper, doing or saying things to hurt others, and using evil words when you talk. Do not lie to each other.

God has chosen you and made you his holy people. He loves you. So always do these things: Show mercy to others; be kind, humble, gentle, and patient. Do not be angry with each other, but forgive each other. If someone does wrong to you, then forgive him. Forgive each other because the Lord forgave you. Do all these things; but most important, love each other. Love is what holds you all together in perfect unity. Let the peace that Christ gives control your thinking. Always be thankful. Let the teaching of Christ live in you richly. Everything you say and everything you do should all be done for Jesus your Lord. And in all you do, give thanks to God the Father through Jesus.

WORTH WONDERING...

- What does Paul want us to understand most about Jesus Christ?

- How does Paul show in this letter that Jesus really is God?

- What promises from God can you find in this book — things that He says He will do for us?

- What commands can you find in this book — things that God tells us to do or to be?

- Suppose you were one of the teachers in the Colossian church who were teaching wrong things about Jesus. When this letter arrived from Paul, you listened while it was read aloud to everyone. Which parts of this letter do you think would be the most important to you?

- Which parts of this book do

you think the devil would most like you NOT to understand and obey?

GREAT VERSES TO THINK ABOUT AGAIN...

Look back in Colossians to see if you can find these verses:

- *No one has seen God, but Jesus is exactly like him.*

- *As you received Christ Jesus the Lord, so continue to live in him. Keep your roots deep in him and have your lives built on him.*

- *Think only about the things in heaven, not the things on earth.*

AND THERE'S MORE...

When you read Colossians in a full Bible, look especially for...

- How to live God's way, instead of following the rules of people.

Paul's First Letter to the
THESSALONIANS

Encouragement
for New Christians

Looking forward to 1 Thessalonians...

WHAT'S IT ABOUT?

"Encouragement for New Christians"

SIGNS AND WONDERS

We have something BIG to look forward to! Jesus is coming back to earth.

FACES AND PLACES

Thessalonica was a city in Macedonia, in what is today northern Greece.

Paul had started the church in Thessalonica on a missionary trip to that area.

When Jesus comes back to earth, I wonder what will happen to Christians who are no longer alive...

WHEN WE PRAY to God our Father, we always thank him that you continue to be strong in our Lord Jesus Christ.

We brought the Good News to you. But we did not use only words. We brought the Good News with power, with the Holy Spirit, and with sure knowledge that it is true. Also you know how we lived when we were with you. We lived that way to help you.

We were very gentle with you. We were like a mother caring for her little children. Because we loved you, we were happy to share God's Good News with you.

You know that we treated each of you as a father treats his own children. We strengthened you, we comforted you, and we told you to live good lives for God.

Also, we always thank God because of the way you accepted his message. You heard his message from us, and you accepted it as the word of God, not the words of men. And it really is God's message.

A Life that Pleases God

Brothers, now I have some other things to tell you.

Do all you can to live a peaceful life. Take care of your own business. Do your own work. We have already told you to do these things. If you do, then people who are not

521

believers will respect you. And you will not have to depend on others for what you need.

The Lord's Coming

Brothers, we want you to know about those who have died. We do not want you to be sad as others who have no hope. We who are living now may still be living when the Lord comes again. We will be with the Lord, but not before those who have already died. The Lord himself will come down from heaven. There will be a loud command with the voice of the archangel and with the trumpet call of God. And those who have died and were in Christ will rise first. After that, those who are still alive at that time will be gathered up with them. We will be taken up in the clouds to meet the Lord in the air. And we will be with the Lord forever. So comfort each other with these words.

Jesus died for us so that we can live together with him. It is not important if we are alive or dead when Jesus comes. So comfort each other and give each other strength, just as you are doing now.

Final Words

Now, brothers, we ask you to respect those people who work hard with you, who lead you in the Lord and teach you. Respect them with a very special love because of the work they do with you.

Always be happy. Never stop praying. Give thanks whatever happens. That is what God wants for you in Christ Jesus.

WORTH WONDERING...

- When Jesus comes back to earth, what will happen to Christians who have already died?

- What commands can you find in this book — things that God tells us to do or to be?

GREAT VERSES TO THINK ABOUT AGAIN...

Look back in First Thessalonians to see if you can find these verses:

- *Because we loved you, we were happy to share God's Good News with you.*

- *Give thanks whatever happens.*

AND THERE'S MORE...

When you read First Thessalonians in a full Bible, look especially for...

- Paul's words about why he wants to visit them again.

- More about what will happen when Jesus returns to earth.

Paul's Second Letter to the
THESSALONIANS

Looking Again
to the Future

Looking forward to 2 Thessalonians...

WHAT'S IT ABOUT?

"Looking Again to the Future"

SIGNS AND WONDERS

We can find comfort in the Lord right now, as we wait for Him to come back to earth. When He comes, He will bring terrible punishment to the people who don't believe in Him.

FACES AND PLACES

Thessalonica was a city in Macedonia, in what is today northern Greece.
Paul had started the church in Thessalonica on a missionary trip to that area.

I wonder what it will be like when Jesus comes back...

W E MUST ALWAYS thank God for you. And we should do this because it is right. It is right because your faith is growing more and more. And the love that every one of you has for each other is also growing. So we brag about you to the other churches of God. We tell them about the way you continue to be strong and have faith. You are being treated badly and are suffering many troubles, but you continue with strength and faith.

God will do what is right. He will give trouble to those who trouble you. And he will give peace to you people who are troubled and to us also. God will give us this help when the Lord Jesus is shown to us from heaven with his powerful angels. He will come from heaven with burning fire to punish those who do not know God. He will punish those who do not obey the Good News of our Lord Jesus Christ. Those people will be punished with a destruction that continues forever. They will not be allowed to be with the Lord, and they will be kept away from his great power. This will happen on the day when the Lord Jesus comes to receive glory with his holy people. And all the people who have believed will be amazed at Jesus. You will be in that group of believers because you believed what we told you.

That is why we always pray

for you. We ask our God to help you live the good way that he called you to live. We pray that the Lord Jesus Christ himself and God our Father will comfort you and strengthen you in every good thing you do and say.

And now, brothers, pray for us. Pray that the Lord's teaching will continue to spread quickly.

The Lord is faithful. He will give you strength and protect you from the Evil One.

WORTH WONDERING...

■ Think back to what you have seen in both this book and First Thessalonians. What does Paul really like about the Christians he is writing to in this church? And what does he pray for them?

■ When Jesus comes back to the earth, what does Paul say will happen to people who don't believe in Him?

■ What promises from God can you find in this book — things that He says He will do for us?

■ What commands do you see in this book — things that He tells us to do or to be?

■ Which parts of this book do you think the devil would most like you NOT to understand and obey?

A GREAT VERSE TO THINK ABOUT AGAIN...

Look back in Second Thessalonians to find this verse:

■ *The Lord is faithful. He will give you strength and protect you from the Evil One.*

AND THERE'S MORE...

When you read Second Thessalonians in a full Bible, look especially for...

■ How important it is to work and not be lazy.

Paul's First Letter to
TIMOTHY

Advice to a
Young Preacher

Looking forward to 1 Timothy...

"Advice to a Young Preacher"

Paul tells his young helper Timothy how to be protected from false teachers.

Timothy was a young man whom Paul met on one of his missionary trips. They became workers together for the Lord, and their love for one another grew. Paul thought of Timothy as a son, and as a fellow soldier for the Lord.

I wonder what Christians are supposed to know about false teachers...

TIMOTHY, you are like a son to me. I tell you this so that you can fight the good fight of faith. Continue to have faith and do what you know is right.

First, I tell you to pray for all people. Ask God for the things people need, and be thankful to him. You should pray for kings and for all who have authority. Pray for the leaders so that we can have quiet and peaceful lives — lives full of worship and respect for God. This is good, and it pleases God our Savior. God wants all people to be saved. And he wants everyone to know the truth. There is only one God. And there is only one way that people can reach God. That way is through Jesus Christ, who is also a man. Jesus gave himself to pay for the sins of all people. Jesus is proof that God wants all people to be saved.

Be a Good Servant of Christ

Command and teach these things. You are young, but do not let anyone treat you as if you were not important. Be an example to show the believers how they should live. Show them with your words, with the way you live, with your love, with your faith, and with your pure life. Continue to read the Scriptures to the people, strengthen them, and teach them. Do not speak angrily to an older man, but talk to him as if he were your father. Treat younger men like brothers. Treat older women like mothers, and younger women like sisters. Always treat them in a pure way.

When we came into the world, we brought nothing. And when we die, we can take nothing out. So, if we have food and clothes, we will be satisfied with that. Those who want to become rich bring temptation to themselves. They are caught in a trap. They begin to want many foolish things that will hurt them, things that ruin and destroy people. The love of money causes all kinds of evil. Some people have left the true faith because they want to get more and more money. But they have caused themselves much sorrow.

But you are a man of God. So you should stay away from all those things. Try to live in the right way, serve God, have faith, love, patience, and gentleness. Keeping your faith is like running a race. Try as hard as you can to win.

WORTH WONDERING...

■ What are the most important things that Paul wants Timothy to do?

■ Suppose you were Timothy, and you received this letter from Paul. Now you've decided to write a letter back to him. What kind of questions and comments would you write in your letter? What would you say?

GREAT VERSES TO THINK ABOUT AGAIN...

Look back in First Timothy to see if you can find these verses:

■ *Continue to have faith and do what you know is right.*

■ *There is only one way that people can reach God. That way is through Jesus Christ.*

■ *The love of money causes all kinds of evil.*

AND THERE'S MORE...

When you read First Timothy in a full Bible, look especially for...

■ How church leaders should be chosen

■ How the church should treat widows.

Paul's Second Letter to
TIMOTHY

Encouragement for a Soldier of Christ

Looking forward to 2 Timothy...

"Encouragement for a Soldier of Christ"

Be a good soldier of Jesus Christ! This is Paul's final message to Timothy. Paul is in prison in Rome. He knows he will soon be killed. In his letter to Timothy, he puts it this way: "The time has come for me to leave this life."

Now that his life is nearly over, Paul can look back and not be disappointed. He can say that he hadn't lost his faith. He can say that he has not stopped living for Jesus. And he knows that a reward in heaven is waiting for him.

When it is time for your life to come to an end...will you be able to say the same things?

Timothy was a young man whom Paul met on one of his missionary trips. They became workers together for the Lord, and their love for one another grew. Paul thought of Timothy as a son, and as a fellow soldier for the Lord.

I wonder how the great apostle Paul felt when he knew it was time for him to die...

TIMOTHY, I always remember you in my prayers, day and night. And I thank God for you in these prayers. I remember that you cried for me. And I want very much to see you so that I can be filled with joy.

I remember your true faith. That kind of faith first belonged to your grandmother Lois and to your mother Eunice. And I know that you now have that same faith. That is why I remind you to use the gift God gave you. God gave you that gift when I laid my hands on you. Now let it grow, as a small flame grows into a fire. God did not give us a spirit that makes us afraid. He gave us a spirit of power and love and self-control.

So do not be ashamed to tell people about our Lord Jesus. And do not be ashamed of me. I am in prison for the Lord. But suffer with me for the Good News. God gives us the strength to do that. God saved us and made us his holy people. That was not because of anything we did ourselves but because of what he wanted and because of his grace.

That grace was given to us through Christ Jesus before time began. It was not shown to us until our Savior Christ Jesus came. Jesus destroyed death. And through the Good News, he showed us the way to have life that cannot be destroyed.

I was chosen to tell that Good News and to be an apostle

and a teacher. And I suffer now because I tell the Good News.

But I am not ashamed. I know Jesus, the One I have believed in. And I am sure that he is able to protect what he has trusted me with. Follow the true teachings you heard from me. Follow them as an example of the faith and love we have in Christ Jesus. Protect the truth that you were given. Protect it with the help of the Holy Spirit who lives in us.

A Loyal Soldier of Christ Jesus

Timothy, you are like a son to me. Be strong in the grace that we have in Christ Jesus. You and many others have heard what I have taught. You should teach the same thing to some people you can trust. Then they will be able to teach it to others. Share in the troubles that we have. Accept them like a true soldier of Christ Jesus. A soldier wants to please his commanding officer, so he does not waste his time doing the things that most people do. If an athlete is running a race, he must obey all the rules in order to win. The farmer who works hard should be the first person to get some of the food that he grew. Think about these things that I am saying. The Lord will give you the ability to understand all these things.

Remember Jesus Christ. He is from the family of David. After Jesus died, he was raised from death. This is the Good News that I preach, and I am suffering because of that Good News. I am even bound with chains like a criminal. But God's teaching is not in chains. So I patiently accept all these troubles.

I do this so that those whom God has chosen can have the salvation that is in Christ Jesus. With that salvation comes glory that never ends.

This teaching is true: If we died with him, then we will also live with him. If we accept suffering, then we will also rule with him. If we refuse to accept him, then he will refuse to accept us. If we are not faithful, he will still be faithful, because he cannot be false to himself.

A Worker Pleasing to God

Do the best you can to be the kind of person that God will accept, and give yourself to him. Be a worker who is not ashamed of his work — a worker who uses the true teaching in the right way.

Stay away from the evil things young people love to do. Try hard to live right and to have faith, love, and peace. Work for these things together with those who have pure hearts and who trust in the Lord.

The Last Days

Remember this! There will be many troubles in the last days. In those times people will love only themselves and money. They will brag and be proud. They will say evil things against others. They will not obey their parents. People will not be thankful or be the kind of people God wants. They will not have love for others. They will refuse to forgive others and will speak bad things. They will not control themselves. They will be cruel and will hate what is good. In the last days, people will turn against their friends. They will do foolish things without thinking. They will be conceited and proud. They will love pleasure. They will not love God.

Obey the Teachings

But you know all about me. You know what I teach and the way I live. You know my goal in life. You know my faith, my patience, and my love. You know that I never stop trying. You know how I have been hurt and have suffered. You know all that happened to me in Antioch, Iconium, and Lystra. You know the hurts I suffered in those places. But the Lord saved me from all those troubles. Everyone who wants to live the way God wants, in Christ Jesus, will be hurt. People who are evil and cheat other people will go from bad to worse. They will fool others, but they will also be fooling themselves.

But you should continue following the teachings that you

PAUSE & WONDER

This book tells me that all Scripture is given by God. It is useful for teaching me and for showing me what is wrong in my life. It is useful for correcting my faults and teaching me how to live right. Using the Scriptures, I can be ready to serve God, and I will have everything I need to do every good work.

learned. You know that these teachings are true. And you know you can trust those who taught you. You have known the Holy Scriptures since you were a child. The Scriptures are able to make you wise. And that wisdom leads to salvation through faith in Christ Jesus. All Scripture is given by God and is useful for teaching and for showing people what is wrong in their lives. It is useful for correcting faults and teaching how to live right. Using the Scriptures, the person who serves God will be ready and will have everything he needs to do every good work.

My life is being given as an offering to God. The time has come for me to leave this life. I have fought the good fight. I have finished the race. I have kept the faith. Now, a crown is waiting for me. I will get that crown for being right with God. The Lord will give that crown not only to me but to all those who have waited with love for him to come again.

WORTH WONDERING...

■ From what Paul says in this letter, what will life be like for the person who follows Jesus?

■ Suppose you were Timothy, and you received this letter from Paul. Now you've decided to write a letter back to him. What kind of questions and comments would you write in your letter? What would you say?

■ Which parts of this book do you think the devil would most like you NOT to understand and obey?

GREAT VERSES TO THINK ABOUT AGAIN...

Look back in Second Timothy to see if you can find these verses:

■ *God did not give us a spirit that makes us afraid. He gave us a spirit of power and love and self-control.*

■ *Remember this! There will be many troubles in the last days.*

■ *I have fought the good fight. I have finished the race. I have kept the faith.*

AND THERE'S MORE...

When you read Second Timothy in a full Bible, look especially for...

■ Paul's words about Demas, a man who left Paul "because he loved this world too much."

■ More about the last days.

Paul's Letter to
TITUS

Instructions for Doing Good

Looking forward to Titus...

"Instructions for Doing Good"

God's grace comes to us through Jesus Christ. And when we learn to live by that grace, we can live a truly good life.

Titus, like Timothy, was a young man who worked with Paul. Titus was a pastor to the church in Crete. Crete is an island in the Mediterranean Sea, south of Greece.

I wonder what it means for a Christian to live a good life...

I WAS SENT to help the faith of God's chosen people. I was sent to help them to know the truth. And that truth shows people how to serve God. That faith and that knowledge come from our hope for life forever. God promised that life to us before time began, and God does not lie.

At the right time God let the world know about that life through preaching. He trusted me with that work, and I preached because God our Savior commanded me to.

Titus, you are like a true son to me in the faith we share. I left you in Crete so that you could finish doing the things that still needed to be done. You should do good deeds to be an example in every way.

Following the True Teaching

You must speak things that make the true teaching attractive. Teach older men to have self-control, to be serious, and to be wise. They should be strong in faith, strong in love, and strong in patience.

Also, teach older women to be holy in the way they live. Teach them not to speak against others or have the habit of drinking too much wine. They should teach what is good. In that way they can teach younger women to love their husbands and children. They can teach younger women to be wise and pure, to take care of their homes, to be kind, and to obey their husbands. Then no one will be able to criticize the teaching God gave us.

In the same way, tell young men to be wise. You should do good deeds to be an example in every way for young men. When you teach, be honest and serious. And when you speak, speak the truth so that you cannot be criticized. Then anyone who is against you will be ashamed because there is nothing bad that he can say against us.

God's grace has come. That grace can save every person. It teaches us not to live against God and not to do the evil things the world wants to do. That grace teaches us to live on earth now in a wise and right way — a way that shows that we serve God. We should live like that while we are waiting for the coming of our great God and Savior Jesus Christ. He will come with glory. He gave himself for us; he died to free us from all evil. He died to make us pure people who belong only to him — people who are always wanting to do good things.

He saved us because of his mercy, not because of good deeds we did to be right with God. He saved us by making us new through the Holy Spirit. God poured out to us that Holy Spirit fully through Jesus Christ our Savior. We were made right with God by His grace. And God gave us the Spirit so that we could receive the life that never ends.

WORTH WONDERING...

- If someone told you that he wanted to live "a good life," what would that mean to you?
- What does God's grace do for us?

A GREAT VERSE TO THINK ABOUT AGAIN...

Look back in Titus to find these words:

- *He saved us because of his mercy, not because of good deeds we did to be right with God. He saved us by making us new through the Holy Spirit.*

AND THERE'S MORE...

When you read Titus in a full Bible, look especially for...

- How to choose leaders for the church.
- How people in Crete were known for being liars and lazy people.

Paul's Letter to
PHILEMON

A Slave Is Now
a Christian

Looking forward to Philemon...

WHAT'S IT ABOUT?

"A Slave Is Now a Christian"

SIGNS AND WONDERS

Paul asks his friend Philemon to practice forgiveness. And God asks you to practice forgiveness as well.

FACES AND PLACES

Philemon: A rich man, and a member of the Colossian church. He was a friend of Paul's. If he caught one of his runaway slaves, Roman law called for him to punish that slave severely.

Onesimus: The slave of Philemon. He may have stolen money from Philemon. Then he ran away to Rome. In Rome he met Paul, and became a Christian.

**Suppose I were a runaway slave
who had met Paul and become a Christian.
I wonder what would happen if Paul
wanted me to go back to my master...**

TO PHILEMON, our dear friend and worker: Grace and peace to you from God our Father and the Lord Jesus Christ.

Philemon's Love and Faith

I remember you in my prayers. And I always thank my God for you. I hear about the love you have for all God's holy people and the faith you have in the Lord Jesus. I pray that the faith you share will make you understand every blessing that we have in Christ. My brother, you have shown love to God's people. You have made them feel happy. This has given me great joy and comfort.

Accept Onesimus as a Brother

There is something that you should do. And because of your love in Christ, I feel free to order you to do it. But because I love you, I am asking you instead. I, Paul, am an old man now, and a prisoner for Christ Jesus. I am asking you a favor for my son Onesimus. He became my son while I was in prison. He has become useful for both you and me.

I am sending him back to you, and with him I am sending my own heart. I wanted to keep him with me to help me while I am in prison for the Good News. By helping me he would be serving you. But I did not want to do anything without asking you first. Then any favor you do for me will be because you want to do it, not because I forced you to do it.

Onesimus was separated from you for a short time. Maybe that happened so that you could have him back forever — not to be a slave, but better than a slave, to be a loved brother. I love him very much. But you will love him even more. You will love him as a man and as a brother in the Lord.

If you think of me as your friend, then accept Onesimus back. Welcome him as you would welcome me. If Onesimus has done anything wrong to you, charge that to me. If he owes you anything, charge that to me. I will pay back anything Onesimus owes. And I will say nothing about what you owe me for your own life. So, my brother, I ask that you do this for me in the Lord. Comfort my heart in Christ. I write this letter, knowing that you will do what I ask you and even more.

Also, please prepare a room for me to stay in. I hope that God will answer your prayers and I will be able to come to you.

The grace of our Lord Jesus Christ be with your spirit.

WORTH WONDERING...

■ What did Paul want Philemon to do with Onesimus?

■ From what Paul says, what kind of man was Onesimus?

■ Suppose you were Philemon, and you received this letter from Paul. Now you've decided to write a letter back to him. What kind of questions and comments would you write in your letter? What would you say?

GREAT VERSES TO THINK ABOUT AGAIN...

Look back in Philemon to see if you can find these verses:

■ *My brother, you have shown love to God's people. You have made them feel happy.*

■ *Grace and peace to you from God our Father and the Lord Jesus Christ.*

INTRODUCING...

HEBREWS • JAMES • 1 AND 2 PETER
1, 2, AND 3 JOHN • JUDE

After Paul's letters, the next part of the Bible is another group of letters. Just like Paul's letters, they help us understand what to believe and how to live. They explain how we can follow Jesus every day.

We don't know for sure who wrote the first letter in this part of the Bible. This is the letter we call the book of Hebrews, because it was written to Jewish Christians — Hebrews who believed in Jesus.

Each of the next seven letters is named for the man who wrote it. We have one letter from James, two from Peter, three from John, and one from Jude.

Like the ones Paul wrote, all these letters were written to churches and Christian workers. These Christians sometimes felt like sheep among wolves. They faced difficult problems and questions. And they needed encouragement — just as Christians do today. The men who wrote these letters were God's messengers with God's wise answers for all who would read them. That's why these letters are still so rich and powerful for us, hundreds of years later.

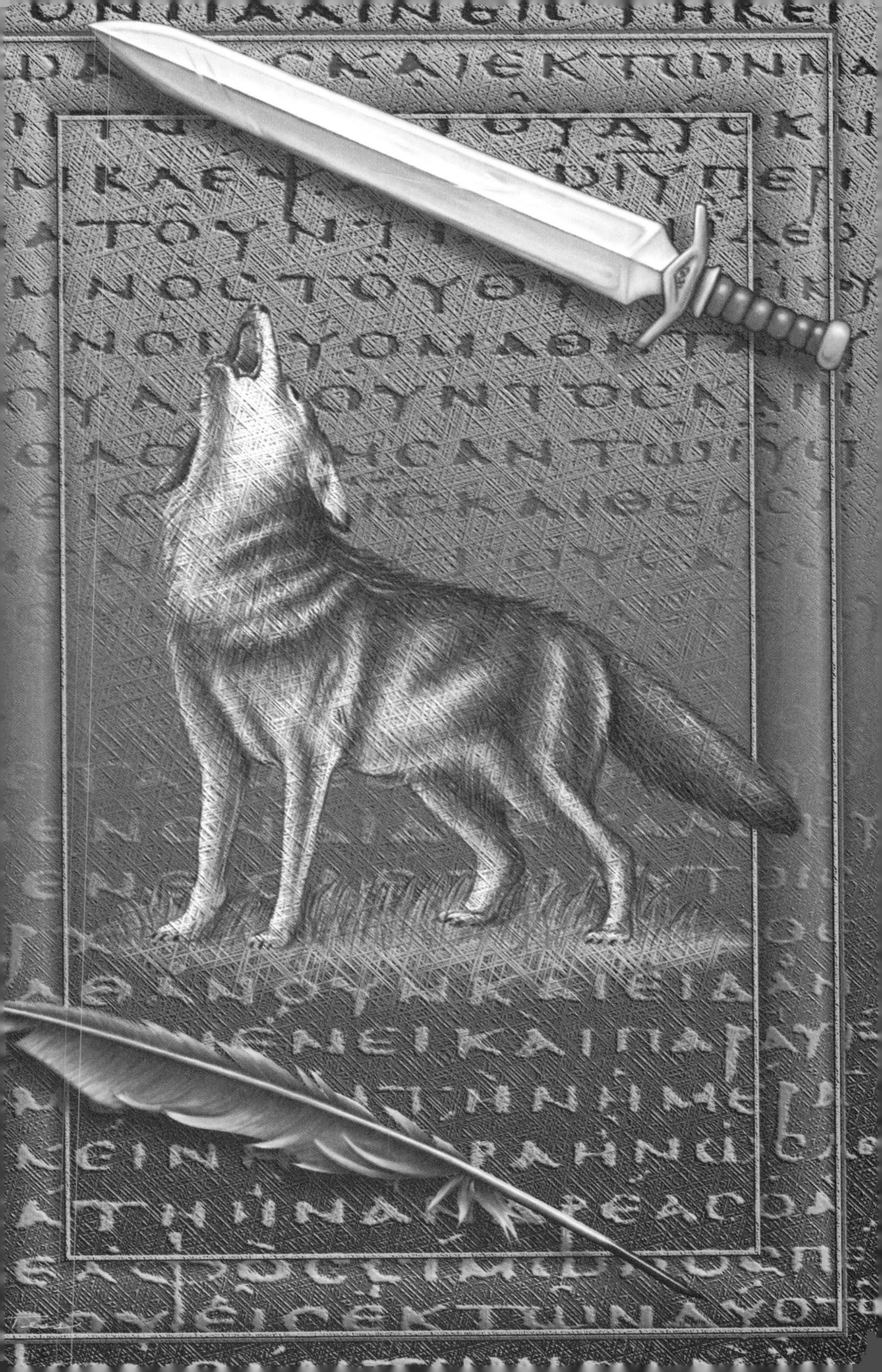

The Letter to the
HEBREWS

A Better Life through Christ

Looking forward to Hebrews...

WHAT'S IT ABOUT?

"A Better Life through Christ"

SIGNS AND WONDERS

The book of Hebrews shows the greatness of Christ. It shows how He is greater than angels, greater than Moses, and greater than the Old Testament way of worshiping God with sacrifices in the Temple. Jesus is everything we need Him to be. He is our Great High Priest in heaven.

Since this is true, how should we live? We should live by faith. The book of Hebrews tells us what faith is.

FACES AND PLACES

Hebrews: The Jews. This book is written to Jews who believe in Christ. They are called Hebrew Christians.

I wonder what it means that Jesus is our priest...

IN THE PAST God spoke to our ancestors through the prophets. And now in these last days God has spoken to us through his Son. God has chosen his Son to own all things. And he made the world through the Son. The Son reflects the glory of God. He is an exact copy of God's nature. He holds everything together with his powerful word. The Son made people clean from their sins. Then he sat down at the right side of God, the Great One in heaven.

Christ Became Like Men

Jesus became like men and died so that he could free them. They were like slaves all their lives because of their fear of death. For this reason Jesus had to be made like his brothers in every way. He became like men so that he could be their merciful and faithful high priest in service to God. Then Jesus could bring forgiveness for their sins. And now he can help those who are tempted. He is able to help because he himself suffered and was tempted.

We Must Continue to Follow God

So encourage each other every day. Help each other so that none of you will become hardened because of sin and its tricks. This is what the Scripture says: "Today listen to what he says. Do not be stubborn."

God's word is alive and working. It is sharper than a sword sharpened on both sides. It cuts all the way into us, where the soul and the spirit are joined. It cuts to the center of our joints and our bones. And God's word judges the thoughts and feelings in our hearts. Nothing in all the world can be hidden from God. Everything is clear and lies open before him. And to him we must explain the way we have lived.

Christ's Death Takes Away Sins

Christ was offered as a sacrifice one time to take away the sins of many people. And he will come a second time, but not to offer himself for sin. He will come again to bring salvation to those who are waiting for him.

So, brothers, let us come near to God with a sincere heart and a sure faith. We are people who have faith and are saved.

Faith

Faith means being sure of the things we hope for. And faith means knowing that something is real even if we do not see it. People who lived in the past became famous because of faith.

By faith we understand that the whole world was made by God's command. This means that what we see was made by something that cannot be seen.

By faith Abel offered God a better sacrifice than Cain did.

By faith Enoch was taken to heaven. He never died. He could not be found, because God had taken him away. Before he was taken, the Scripture says that he was a man who truly pleased God. Without faith no one can please God. Anyone who comes to God must believe that he is real and that he rewards those who truly want to find him.

By faith Noah heard God's warnings about things that he could not yet see. He obeyed God and built a large boat to save his family.

By faith Abraham obeyed God's call to go to another place that God promised to give him. He left his own country, not knowing where he was to go.

By faith Abraham was made able to become a father. Abraham trusted God to do what he had promised. This man was so old that he was almost dead. But from him came as many descendants as there are stars in the sky. They are as many as the grains of sand on the seashore that cannot be counted.

By faith Abraham offered his son Isaac as a sacrifice. God tested him. Abraham believed that God could raise the dead. And really, it was as if Abraham got Isaac back from death.

By faith Moses' parents hid him for three months after he was born. They saw that Moses was a beautiful baby. And they were not afraid to disobey the king's order.

By faith Moses, when he grew up, refused to be called the son of the king of Egypt's daughter. He chose to suffer with God's people instead of enjoying sin for a short time. He was looking only for God's reward. By faith Moses prepared the Passover and spread the blood on the doors.

By faith the people crossed the Red Sea as if it were dry land. The Egyptians also tried to do it, but they were drowned.

By faith the walls of Jericho fell. They fell after the people had marched around the walls of Jericho for seven days.

Follow Jesus' Example

So we have many people of faith around us. Their lives tell us what faith means. So let us run the race that is before us and never give up. We should remove from our lives anything that would get in the way. And we should remove the sin that so easily catches us. Let us look only to Jesus. He is the one who began our faith, and he makes our faith perfect. Jesus suffered death on the cross. But he accepted the shame of the cross as if it were nothing. He did this because of the joy that God put before him. And now he is sitting at the right side of God's throne. Think about Jesus. He held on patiently while sinful men were doing evil things against him. Look at Jesus' example so that you will not get tired and stop trying.

God Is Like a Father

Accept your sufferings as if they were a father's punishment. God does these things to you as a father punishing his sons. God punishes us to help us, so that we can become holy as he is. We do not enjoy punishment. Being punished is painful. But later, after we have learned from being punished, we have peace, because we start living in the right way.

Be Careful How You Live

Try to live in peace with all people. And try to live lives free from sin. If anyone's life is not holy, he will never see the Lord.

We should worship God in a way that pleases him. So let us worship him with respect and fear, because our God is like a fire that burns things up.

Keep on loving each other as brothers in Christ. Remember to welcome strangers into your homes. Some people have done this and have welcomed angels without knowing it.

Keep your lives free from the love of money. And be satisfied with what you have.

Obey your leaders and be under their authority. These men are watching you because they are responsible for your souls. Obey them so that they will do this work with joy, not sadness. It will not help you to make their work hard.

WORTH WONDERING...

■ Why does God sometimes discipline us? And how does He discipline us?

■ Why is Jesus coming again to the earth?

■ Think about what you read in this book about faith. If a person truly has faith in God, how would other people be able to tell?

GREAT VERSES TO THINK ABOUT AGAIN...

Look back in Hebrews to see if you can find these verses:

■ *God's word is alive and working.*

It is sharper than a sword sharpened on both sides.

■ *Accept your sufferings as if they were a father's punishment. God does these things to you as a father punishing his sons. God punishes us to help us, so that we can become holy as he is.*

■ *Let us look only to Jesus. He is the one who began our faith, and he makes our faith perfect.*

AND THERE'S MORE...

When you read Hebrews in a full Bible, look especially for...

■ How Christ was like Melchizedek. This man was a king and a priest in the book of Genesis. And Abraham gave an offering to him.

■ More details of how what Jesus has done is better than the sacrifices in the Temple.

The Letter of
JAMES

How to Live as a Christian

Looking forward to James...

WHAT'S IT ABOUT?

"How to Live as a Christian"

SIGNS AND WONDERS

Our faith must be alive. Our faith must show itself in the way we live. Faith is not just accepting something that we think is true. Faith is doing something because we believe the truth.

FACES AND PLACES

James: He was a brother of Jesus. He was the son of Mary and Joseph of Nazareth. He became a leader in the church in Jerusalem.

I wonder how I can put my faith to work...

MY BROTHERS, you will have many kinds of troubles. But when these things happen, you should be very happy. You know that these things are testing your faith. And this will give you patience.

Let your patience show itself perfectly in what you do. Then you will be perfect and complete. You will have everything you need. But if any of you needs wisdom, you should ask God for it. God is generous. He enjoys giving to all people, so God will give you wisdom.

Every good action and every perfect gift is from God. These good gifts come down from the Creator of the sun, moon, and stars. God does not change like their shifting shadows. God decided to give us life through the word of truth. He wanted us to be the most important of all the things he made.

Listening and Obeying

Do what God's teaching says; do not just listen and do nothing. When you only sit and listen, you are fooling yourselves. A person who hears God's teaching and does nothing is like a man looking in a mirror. He sees his face, then goes away and quickly forgets what he looked like. But the truly happy person is the one who carefully studies God's perfect law that makes people free. He continues to study it. He listens to God's teaching and does not forget what he heard. Then he obeys what God's teaching says. When he does this, it makes him happy.

Love All People

My dear brothers, you are believers in our glorious Lord Jesus Christ. So never think that some people are more important than others. Suppose someone comes into your church meeting wearing very nice clothes and a gold ring. At the same time a poor man comes in wearing old, dirty clothes. You show special attention to the one wearing nice clothes. You say, "Please, sit here in this good seat." But you say to the poor man, "Stand over there," or "Sit on the floor by my feet!" What are you doing? You are making some people more important than others. With evil thoughts you are deciding which person is better.

One law rules over all other laws. This royal law is found in the Scriptures: "Love your neighbor as you love yourself." If you obey this law, then you are doing right. But if you are treating one person as if he were more important than another, then you are sinning.

Yes, you must show mercy to others, or God will not show mercy to you when he judges you. But the person who shows mercy can stand without fear when he is judged.

Faith and Good Works

My brothers, if someone says he has faith, but does nothing, his faith is worth nothing. Can faith like that save him? A

PAUSE & WONDER

Do I believe in Jesus? My faith in Him will prove itself if I don't let troubles make me sad. My faith in Him will prove itself if I don't easily become angry. My faith in Him will prove itself if I treat everyone fairly and with respect. My faith in Him will prove itself if I help others who are in need. My faith in Him will prove itself if I control what I say. My faith in Him will prove itself if I don't get into fights and arguments. Do I believe in Jesus? My life gives the answer.

brother or sister in Christ might need clothes or might need food. And you say to him, "God be with you! I hope you stay warm and get plenty to eat." You say this, but you do not give that person the things he needs. Unless you help him, your words are worth nothing. It is the same with faith. If faith does nothing, then that faith is dead, because it is alone. Faith that does nothing is dead!

Controlling the Things We Say

If there were a person who never said anything wrong, he would be perfect. He would be able to control his whole body, too. A big forest fire can be started with only a little flame. And the tongue is like a fire. It starts a fire that influences all of life. The tongue gets this fire from hell. People can tame every kind of wild animal, bird, reptile, and fish. But no one can tame the tongue. It is wild and evil. It is full of poison that can kill.

True Wisdom

Is there anyone among you who is truly wise and under-standing? Then he should show his wisdom by living right. He should do good things without being proud. A wise person does not brag. But if you are selfish and have bitter jealousy in your hearts, you have no reason to brag. Your bragging is a lie that hides the truth. That kind of "wisdom" does not come from God. That "wisdom" comes from the world. It is not spiritual. It is from the devil. Where there is jealousy and selfishness, there will be confusion and every kind of evil. But the wisdom that comes from God is like this: First, it is pure. Then it is also peaceful, gentle, and easy to please. This wisdom is always ready to help those who are troubled and to do good for others. This wisdom is always fair and honest. When people work for peace in a peaceful way, they receive the good result of their right-living.

Give Yourselves to God

Do you know where your fights and arguments come from? They come from the selfish desires that make war inside you. You want things, but you do not have them. So you are ready to kill and are jealous of other people. But you still cannot get what you want. So you argue and fight. You do not get what you want because you do not ask God. Or when you ask, you do not receive because the reason you ask is wrong. You want things only so that you can use them for your own pleasures.

So give yourselves to God. Stand against the devil, and the devil will run away from you. Come near to God, and God will come near to you. Clean sin out of your lives. Don't be too proud before the Lord, and he will make you great.

You Are Not the Judge

Brothers, do not say bad things about each other. God is the only Judge. He is the only One who can save and destroy. So it is not right for you to judge your neighbor.

Be Patient

Brothers, be patient until the Lord comes again. A farmer is patient. He waits for his valuable crop to grow from the earth. He waits patiently for it to receive the first rain and the last rain. You, too, must be patient. Do not give up hope. The Lord is coming soon.

WORTH WONDERING...

■ What commands can you find in this book — things that God tells us to do or to be?

■ What promises from God can you find in this book — things that He says He will do for us?

■ Suppose God had written this book of the Bible only for you. Which words or sentences do you think He might have underlined, because He especially wanted you to notice them?

■ Which parts of this book do you think the devil would most like you NOT to understand and obey?

GREAT VERSES TO THINK ABOUT AGAIN...

Look back in James to see if you can find these verses:

■ *Faith that does nothing is dead!*

■ *Do you know where your fights and arguments come from? They come from the selfish desires that make war inside you.*

■ *Give yourselves to God. Stand against the devil, and the devil will run away from you.*

AND THERE'S MORE...

When you read James in a full Bible, look especially for...

■ Warnings to those who are rich.

■ Abraham's example of faith.

■ Rahab's example of faith.

■ Job's example of patience.

■ Elijah's example of prayer.

The First Letter of
PETER

Encouragement for Suffering Christians

Looking forward to 1 Peter...

WHAT'S IT ABOUT?

WHAT'S IT ABOUT?

"Encouragement for Suffering Christians"

SIGNS AND WONDERS

As time went by, the number of Christians grew throughout the Roman Empire. But more and more people tried to hurt Christians. Many times, Christians were killed just because they believed in Christ. This was what the world was like as Peter wrote this letter.

FACES AND PLACES

Peter: He was one of the 12 apostles Jesus chose. After Jesus went up to heaven, Peter became one of the leaders of the church in Jerusalem. His name means "rock." Jesus gave him this name.

I wonder if I'll ever have to suffer as a Christian...

GOD PLANNED long ago to choose you by making you his holy people. Making you holy is the Spirit's work. God wanted you to be made clean by the blood of the death of Jesus Christ.

Suffering for Doing Right

A person might have to suffer even when he has done nothing wrong. But if he thinks of God and bears the pain, this pleases God. If you are punished for doing wrong, there is no reason to praise you for bearing punishment. But if you suffer for doing good, and you are patient, then that pleases God. That is what you were called to do. Christ suffered for you. He gave you an example to follow. So you should do as he did.

People insulted Christ, but he did not insult them in return. Christ suffered, but he did not threaten. He let God take care of him. God is the One who judges rightly. Christ carried our sins in his body on the cross. He did this so that we would stop living for sin and start living for what is right. And we are healed because of his wounds. You were like sheep that went the wrong way. But now you have come back to the Shepherd and Protector of your souls.

All of you should live together in peace. Try to understand each other. Love each other as brothers. Be kind and humble. Do not do wrong to a person to pay him back for doing wrong to you. Or do not insult someone to pay him back for insulting you. But ask God to bless that person.

Stand Strong

And all of you should be very humble with each other. "God is against the proud, but he gives grace to the humble."

So be humble under God's powerful hand. Then he will lift you up when the right time comes. Give all your worries to him, because he cares for you.

Control yourselves and be careful! The devil is your enemy. And he goes around like a roaring lion looking for someone to eat. Refuse to give in to the devil. Stand strong in your faith. You know that your Christian brothers and sisters all over the world are having the same sufferings you have.

Yes, you will suffer for a short time. But after that, God will make everything right. He called you to share in his glory in Christ. That glory will continue forever.

WORTH WONDERING...

■ What promises from God can you find in this book — things that He says He will do for us?

■ What commands can you find in this book — things that God tells us to do or to be?

■ Jesus said (in the book of Matthew) that everyone who hears His words and obeys them is like a wise man who built his house on rock. Which words in this book do you think are the most important for you to obey right now?

GREAT VERSES TO THINK ABOUT AGAIN...

Look back in First Peter to see if you can find these verses:

■ *Christ suffered for you. He gave you an example to follow. So you should do as he did.*

■ *Yes, you will suffer for a short time. But after that, God will make everything right.*

AND THERE'S MORE...

When you read First Peter in a full Bible, look especially for...

■ Rules for wives and husbands.

■ Why we should obey human authorities.

■ Why we should live holy lives.

The Second Letter of
PETER

Correcting
False Teachings

Looking forward to 2 Peter...

WHAT'S IT ABOUT?

"Correcting False Teachings"

SIGNS AND WONDERS

Dangers were growing for the Christian churches in the world. There were more and more false teachers. They were leading people away from Christ, and into the arms of the devil.

Peter tells us how to escape this danger. And he looks ahead to the coming end of the world.

FACES AND PLACES

Peter: He was one of the 12 apostles Jesus chose. After Jesus went up to heaven, Peter became one of the leaders of the church in Jerusalem. His name means "rock." Jesus gave him this name.

I wonder how I can be ready for the end of the world...

THERE USED TO BE false prophets among God's people, just as there are now. And you will have some false teachers in your group. They will secretly teach things that are wrong — teachings that will cause people to be lost. They will even refuse to accept the Master, Jesus, who bought their freedom. And so they will quickly destroy themselves.

The Lord knows how to save those who serve him. He will save them when troubles come. And the Lord will hold evil people and punish them, while waiting for the Judgment Day.

These false teachers do anything they want and brag about it. They are like animals that act without thinking. They have caused many people to suffer; so they themselves will suffer. That is their pay for what they have done. They take pleasure in doing evil things openly. So they are like dirty spots and stains among you. They lead weak people into the trap of sin. They have taught their hearts to be selfish. God will punish them.

Jesus Will Come Again

It is important for you to understand what will happen in the last days. People will laugh at you. They will live doing the evil things they want to do. They will say, "Jesus promised to come again. Where is he?" But they do not want to remember what happened long ago. God spoke and made heaven and earth. He made the earth from water and with water. Then the world was flooded and destroyed with water. And that same word of God is keeping heaven and earth that we have now. They are being kept to be destroyed by fire. They are being kept for the Judgment Day and the destruction of all who are against God.

But do not forget this one thing, dear friends: To the Lord one day is as a thousand years, and a thousand years is as one day. The Lord is not slow in doing what he promised — the way some people understand slowness. But God is being patient with you. He does not want anyone to be lost. He wants everyone to change his heart and life.

But the day the Lord comes again will be a surprise, like a thief. The skies will disappear with a loud noise. Everything in the skies will be destroyed by fire. And the earth and everything in it will be burned up. In that way everything will be destroyed. So what kind of people should you be? You should live holy lives and serve God. You should wait for the day of God and look forward to its coming.

WORTH WONDERING...

■ What will happen at the end of the world?

■ What commands do you see in this book?

■ What promises from God do you see in this book?

A GREAT VERSE TO THINK ABOUT AGAIN...

Look back in Second Peter to find these words:

■ *You should live holy lives and serve God. You should wait for the day of God and look forward to its coming.*

AND THERE'S MORE...

When you read Second Peter in a full Bible, look especially for...

■ More about false teachers.

■ How Peter saw the glory of Jesus.

■ Why we can trust the Scriptures.

The First Letter of
JOHN

Love One Another

Looking forward to
1 John...

WHAT'S IT ABOUT?

"Love One Another"

SIGNS AND WONDERS

This is a book of love, faith, and light.

FACES AND PLACES

John was one of the twelve disciples. He also wrote the gospel of John and the book of Revelation. John's name means "God is gracious." John was an old man when he wrote his letters which are in the Bible.

I wonder what love is all about...

GOD IS LIGHT, and in him there is no darkness at all. We should live in the light, too. If we live in the light, the blood of the death of Jesus, God's Son, is making us clean from every sin.

If we say that we have no sin, we are fooling ourselves, and the truth is not in us. But if we confess our sins, he will forgive our sins. We can trust God. He does what is right. He will make us clean from all the wrongs we have done. Jesus is the way our sins are taken away.

We Are God's Children

The Father has loved us so much! He loved us so much that we are called children of God. And we really are his children.

This is the teaching you have heard from the beginning: We must love each other. This is how we know what real love is: Jesus gave his life for us. So we should give our lives for our brothers. My children, our love should not be only words and talk. Our love must be true love. And we should show that love by what we do.

Whoever does not love does not know God, because God is love. This is how God showed his love to us: He sent his only Son into the world to give us life through him. True love is God's love for us, not our love for God.

God sent his Son to be the way to take away our sins. That

is how much God loved us, dear friends! So we also must love each other.

Where God's love is, there is no fear, because God's perfect love takes away fear. It is punishment that makes a person fear. So love is not made perfect in the person who has fear.

If someone says, "I love God," but hates his brother, he is a liar. He can see his brother, but he hates him. So he cannot love God, whom he has never seen. And God gave us this command: Whoever loves God must also love his brother.

Faith in the Son of God

Everyone who believes that Jesus is the Christ is God's child. How do we know that we love God's children? We know because we love God and we obey his commands. Loving God means obeying his commands. And God's commands are not too hard for us. Everyone who is a child of God has the power to win against the world. It is our faith that wins the victory against the world. So the one who wins against the world is the person who believes that Jesus is the Son of God.

We Have Eternal Life Now

This is what God told us: God has given us eternal life, and this life is in his Son. Whoever has the Son has life. But the person who does not have the Son of God does not have life.

I write this letter to you who believe in the Son of God. I write so that you will know that you have eternal life now.

WORTH WONDERING...

- How many times do you see the word love in this book?
- What commands do you see in First John?
- What promises from God do you see in First John?

A GREAT VERSE TO THINK ABOUT AGAIN...

Look back in First John to find these words:

- *He loved us so much that we are called children of God. And we really are his children.*

AND THERE'S MORE...

When you read First John in a full Bible, look especially for...
- Warnings against false teachers.
- How we can have victory over the devil.

The Second Letter of
JOHN

Do Not Help
False Teachers

Looking forward to 2 John...

"Do Not Help False Teachers"

John warns against teachers who go far away from the teachings of Christ.

John knows that the truth in Jesus is all about love and obedience. Love for others and obedience to God will help us keep away from false teaching.

John was one of the twelve disciples. He also wrote the gospel of John and the book of Revelation. John's name means "God is gracious." John was an old man when he wrote his letters which are in the Bible.

I wonder what I should know about false teachers...

TO THE CHOSEN LADY and to her children: I was very happy to learn about some of your children. I am happy that they are following the way of truth, as the Father commanded us. And now, dear lady, I tell you: We should all love each other. This is not a new command. It is the same command we have had from the beginning. And loving means living the way he commanded us to live. And God's command is this: that you live a life of love.

False Teachers

Many false teachers are in the world now. They refuse to say that Jesus Christ came to earth and became a man.

Anyone who refuses to say this is a false teacher and an enemy of Christ. Be careful! Do not lose the reward that you have worked for. Be careful, so that you will receive your full reward.

Follow the Teaching of Christ

A person must continue to follow only the teaching of Christ. If he goes beyond Christ's teaching, then he does not have God. But if he continues following the teaching of Christ, then he has both the Father and the Son.

If someone comes to you, but does not bring this teaching, then do not accept him into your house. Do not welcome him. If you accept him, you are helping him with his evil work.

I have much to say to you, but I do not want to use paper and ink. Instead, I hope to come visit you. Then we can be together and talk. That will make us very happy.

WORTH WONDERING...

■ Suppose you were the "chosen lady" who received this letter from John. Now you've decided to write a letter back to him. What kind of questions and comments would you write in your letter? What would you say?

A GREAT VERSE TO THINK ABOUT AGAIN...

Look back in Second John to find these words:

■ *God's command is this: that you live a life of love.*

The Third Letter of
JOHN

Help Christians
Who Teach Truth

Looking forward to 3 John...

WHAT'S IT ABOUT?

"Help Christians Who Teach Truth"

SIGNS AND WONDERS

Like John's other letters, Third John is about love, truth, and obedience.

FACES AND PLACES

John was one of the twelve disciples. He also wrote the gospel of John and the book of Revelation. John's name means "God is gracious." John was an old man when he wrote his letters which are in the Bible.

I wonder how I can help those who teach the truth about Jesus...

TO MY DEAR friend Gaius whom I love in the truth: My dear friend, I know your soul is doing well. I pray that you are doing fine in every way and that your health is good. Some brothers in Christ came and told me about the truth in your life. They said that you are following the way of truth. This made me very happy. It always gives me the greatest joy when I hear that my children are following the way of truth.

My dear friend, it is good that you continue to help the brothers. You are helping those that you do not even know! These brothers told the church about the love you have. Please help them to continue their trip.

Help them in a way that will please God. They started out on their trip to serve Christ. They did not accept any help from those who are not believers. So we should help these brothers. And when we do, we share in their work for the truth.

I wrote a letter to the church. But Diotrephes will not listen to what we say. He always wants to be their leader. When I come, I will talk about what Diotrephes is doing. He lies and says evil things about us. But that is not all he does. He refuses to help those who are working to serve Christ. He also stops those who want to help the brothers and puts them out of the church.

My dear friend, do not follow

what is bad; follow what is good. He who does what is good is from God. But he who does evil has never known God.

I have many things I want to tell you, but I do not want to use pen and ink. I hope to visit you soon. Then we can be together and talk. Please give our love to each one of the friends there.

WORTH WONDERING...

■ Suppose you were Gaius, the person whom John sent this letter to. Now you've decided to write a letter back to John. What kind of questions and comments would you write in your letter? What would you say?

A GREAT VERSE TO THINK ABOUT AGAIN...

Look back in Third John to find these words:

■ *It always gives me the greatest joy when I hear that my children are following the way of truth.*

The Letter of
JUDE

Warnings about
False Teachers

Looking forward to Jude...

"Warnings about False Teachers"

Once again, God tells one of his messengers to write against false teachers. Jude wanted to write about our salvation, but the danger from the false teachers was growing.

Jude: He was a brother of Jesus, just like the writer of the book of James.

I wonder how I can watch out for false teachers...

DEAR FRIENDS, I wanted very much to write to you about the salvation we all share together. But I felt the need to write to you about something else: I want to encourage you to fight hard for the faith that God gave his holy people.

God gave this faith once, and it is good for all time. Some people have secretly entered your group. They have already been judged guilty for the things they are doing. Long ago the prophets wrote about these people. They are against God. They have used the grace of our God in the wrong way — to do sinful things. They refuse to accept Jesus Christ, our only Master and Lord.

God Will Punish Sinners

I want to remind you of some things that you already know: Remember that the Lord saved his people by bringing them out of the land of Egypt. But later the Lord destroyed all those who did not believe. Also remember the cities of Sodom and Gomorrah and the other towns around them. They did not obey God. Their towns were full of sin. They suffer the punishment of eternal fire, as an example for all to see.

It is the same with these people who have entered your group. They are guided by dreams. They make themselves dirty with sin. They reject God's authority and say bad things against the glorious angels. These people say bad things about what they do not understand. They understand things not by thinking, but by feeling, the way dumb animals understand things. And these are the very things that destroy them.

It will be bad for them. They have followed the way that Cain went. To make money, they have given themselves to doing the wrong that Balaam did. They have fought against God as Korah did. And like Korah, they will be destroyed.

They are like dirty spots in the special meals you share together. They eat with you and have no fear. They take care of only themselves. They are clouds without rain. The wind blows them around. They are trees that have no fruit when it is time and are pulled out of the ground. So they are dead two times. They are like wild waves in the sea. These people do shameful things in the same way waves make foam. They are like stars that wander in the sky. A place in the blackest darkness has been kept for them forever.

Enoch, the seventh descendant from Adam, said this about these people: "Look, the Lord is coming with thousands and thousands of his holy angels. The Lord will judge every person. He is coming to judge everyone and to punish all who are against God. He will punish them for all the evil they have done against him. And he will punish the sinners who are against God. He will punish them for all the evil things they have said against him."

These people always complain and blame others. They always do the evil things they want to do. They brag about themselves. The only reason they say good things about other people is to get what they want.

A Warning and Things to Do

Dear friends, remember what the apostles of our Lord Jesus Christ said before. They said to you, "In the last times there will be people who laugh about God. They will do only what they want to do — things that are against God." These are the people who divide you. They do only what their sinful selves want. They do not have the Spirit.

But dear friends, use your most holy faith to build yourselves up strong. Pray with the Holy Spirit. Keep yourselves in God's love. Wait for the Lord

Jesus Christ with his mercy to give you life forever.

Show mercy to people who have doubts. Save them. Take them out of the fire. Show mercy mixed with fear to others. Hate even their clothes which are dirty from sin.

Praise God

God is strong and can help you not to fall. He can bring you before his glory without any wrong in you and give you great joy. He is the only God. He is the One who saves us. To him be glory, greatness, power, and authority through Jesus Christ our Lord for all time past, now, and forever. Amen.

WORTH WONDERING...

- What would you say is the biggest thing that Jude wants us to know about false teachers?
- What commands does Jude give in this letter?

GREAT VERSES TO THINK ABOUT AGAIN...

Look back in Jude to see if you can find these verses:

- *Use your most holy faith to build yourselves up strong. Pray with the Holy Spirit. Keep yourselves in God's love.*
- *God is strong and can help you not to fall. He can bring you before his glory without any wrong in you and give you great joy.*

INTRODUCING...

REVELATION

If you thought of the Bible as a long and winding river, then the book of Revelation would be like the ocean that the river flows into. When you stand on the seashore and look out on the ocean, it seems to go on forever. But if you *really* want to see forever, this last book of the Bible is the best place to look.

In Revelation, it's as if God drew back a curtain so we can all see our forever-future.

Revelation is written in a sort of picture-language. It's running over with exciting pictures you can fill your imagination with. It reads like a dream...because it *is* a dream, actually. And someday it will be a dream-come-true.

Revelation was written for us by the apostle John when he was an old man. The Christians in those days were being attacked by the enemies of God. These enemies held John as a prisoner on a rugged little island called Patmos.

One Sunday, there on Patmos, the Lord gave him a vision — a dream. John heard a loud voice that sounded like a trumpet. The voice told him to write down what he was seeing in the vision. John turned to look at whoever was speaking to him. And there before his eyes was the Lord Jesus Himself in glory, with His face as bright as the sun.

In the rest of the dream, John saw amazing and wonderful things. And he wrote them down for us to read and understand and obey.

The Book of
REVELATION

Christ Will Win
Over Evil

Looking forward to Revelation...

"Christ Will Win over Evil"

The first pages of the Bible — the opening pages in the book of Genesis — tell us how the first man and woman enjoyed a perfect paradise. The last pages of the Bible — the closing paragraphs in Revelation — tell us about the NEW perfect paradise God is creating for His chosen people from throughout the world's history. The Bible ends where it begins — with no sin, no death, no sorrow.

John: He was one of the 12 apostles.
Patmos: This is a small, rocky island. It is in the Aegean Sea, which is the part of the Mediterranean Sea that lies between Greece and Turkey.
Heaven: More than any other part of the Bible, Revelation is our book of heaven. John saw that everything is always new there. It's a place where there is no crying or hurting or darkness. Heaven is pure and beautiful and bright, like a bride in her wedding gown.

I wonder how everything will end...

THIS IS the revelation of Jesus Christ. God gave this revelation to show what must soon happen. The one who reads the words of God's message is happy. And the people who hear this message and do what is written in it are happy. The time is near when all of this will happen.

John Sees Jesus

I am John, and I am your brother in Christ. I was on the island of Patmos. On the Lord's day the Spirit took control of me. I heard a loud voice behind me that sounded like a trumpet. The voice said, "Write what you see."

I turned to see who was talking to me. When I turned, I saw seven golden lampstands. I saw someone among the lampstands who was like a Son of Man. He was dressed in a long robe. He had a gold band around his chest. His head and hair were white like wool, as white as snow. His eyes were like flames of fire. His feet were like bronze that glows hot in a furnace. His voice was like the noise of flooding water. He held seven stars in his right hand. A sharp two-edged sword came out of his mouth. He looked like the sun shining at its brightest time.

When I saw him, I fell down at his feet like a dead man. He put his right hand on me and said, "Do not be afraid! I am the First and the Last. I am the One who lives. I was dead, but look: I am alive forever and ever! And I hold the keys of death and where the dead are. So write the things you see, what is now and what will happen later."

John Sees Heaven

After this I looked, and there before me was an open door in heaven. And I heard the voice that sounded like a trumpet. The voice said, "Come up here, and I will show you what must happen after this." Then the Spirit took control of me. There before me was a throne in heaven. Someone was sitting on the throne. The One who sat on the throne looked like precious stones, like jasper and carnelian. All around the throne was a rainbow the color of an emerald. Around the throne there were 24 other thrones. There were 24 elders sitting on the 24 thrones. The elders were dressed in white, and they had golden crowns on their heads. Lightning flashes and noises of thunder came from the throne. Before the throne there were seven lamps burning. Also before the throne there was something that looked like a sea of glass. It was clear like crystal.

Around the throne, on each side, there were four living things. These living things had eyes all over them, in front and in back. The first living thing was like a lion. The second was like a calf. The third had a face like a man. The fourth was like a flying eagle. Each of these four living things had six wings. The living things were covered all over with eyes, inside and out. Day and night they never stop saying: "Holy, holy, holy is the Lord God All-Powerful. He was, he is, and he is coming."

These living things give glory and honor and thanks to the One who sits on the throne. And every time the living things do this, the 24 elders bow down before the One who sits on the throne. The elders put their crowns down before the throne and say: "Our Lord and God! You are worthy to receive glory and honor and power. You made all things. Everything existed and was made because you wanted it."

Then I saw a scroll in the right hand of the One sitting on the throne. The scroll had writing on both sides. It was kept closed with seven seals. And I saw a powerful angel. He called in a loud voice, "Who is worthy to break the seals and open the scroll?" But there was no one in heaven or on earth or under the earth who could open the scroll or look inside it. I cried and cried because there was no one who was worthy to open the scroll or look inside. But one of the elders said to me, "Do not cry! The Lion from the tribe of Judah has won the victory. He is David's descendant. He is able to open the scroll and its seven seals."

Then I saw a Lamb standing in the center of the throne with the four living things around it. The elders were also around the Lamb. The Lamb looked as if he had been killed. The Lamb came and took the scroll from the right hand of the One sitting on the throne. After he took the scroll, the four living things and the 24 elders bowed down before the Lamb. Each one of them had a harp. Also, they were holding golden bowls full of incense. These bowls of incense are the prayers of God's holy people. And they all sang a new song to the Lamb: "You are worthy to take the scroll and to open its seals, because you were killed; and with the blood of your death you bought men for God from every tribe, language, people, and nation. You made them to be a kingdom of priests for our God. And they will rule on the earth."

Then I looked, and I heard the voices of many angels. The angels were around the throne, the four living things, and the elders. There were thousands and thousands of angels — there were 10,000 times 10,000. The angels said in a loud voice: "The Lamb who was killed is worthy to receive power, wealth, wisdom and strength, honor, glory, and praise!"

Then I heard every living thing in heaven and on earth and under the earth and in the sea. I heard every thing in all these places, saying: "All praise and honor and glory and power forever and ever to the One who sits on the throne and to the Lamb!"

Then I watched while the

PAUSE & WONDER

The more I understand the Bible, the more I love it. And the more I love it, the more I love the One who wrote it — because I know He loves me. It makes me want to obey Him with all my heart and soul and mind and strength.

Lamb opened the first of the seven seals. I looked and there before me was a white horse. The rider on the horse held a bow, and he was given a crown. And he rode out, defeating the enemy. He rode out to win the victory.

The Lamb opened the second seal. Then another horse came out. This was a red horse. Its rider was given power to take away peace from the earth. He was given power to make people kill each other. And he was given a big sword.

The Lamb opened the third seal. I looked, and there before me was a black horse. Its rider held a pair of scales in his hand.

The Lamb opened the fourth seal. I looked, and there before me was a pale horse. Its rider was named death.

The Lamb opened the fifth seal. Then I saw some souls under the altar. They were the souls of those who had been killed because they were faithful to God's message and to the truth they had received. These souls shouted in a loud voice, "Holy and true Lord, how long until you judge the people of the earth and punish them for killing us?" Then each one of these souls was given a white robe. They were told to wait a short time longer. There were still some of their brothers in the service of Christ who must be killed as they were. They were told to wait until all of this killing was finished.

Then I watched while the Lamb opened the sixth seal. There was a great earthquake. The sun became black like rough black cloth. The full moon became red like blood. The stars in the sky fell to the earth like figs falling from a fig tree when the wind blows. The sky disappeared. It was rolled up like a scroll. And every mountain and island was moved from its place.

Then all people hid in caves and behind the rocks on the mountains. There were the kings of the earth, the rulers, the generals, the rich people and the powerful people. Everyone, slave and free, hid himself. They called to the mountains and the rocks, "Fall on us. Hide us from the face of the One who sits on the throne. Hide us from the anger of the Lamb! The great day for their anger has come. Who can stand against it?"

The Great Crowd

Then I looked, and there was a great number of people. There were so many people that no one could count them. They were from every nation, tribe, people, and language of the earth. They were all standing before the throne and before the Lamb. They wore white robes and had palm branches in their hands. They were shouting in a loud voice, "Salvation belongs to our God, who sits on the throne, and to the Lamb." The elders and the four living things were there. All the angels were standing around them and the throne. The angels bowed down on their faces before the throne and worshiped God. They were saying, "Amen! Praise, glory, wisdom, thanks, honor, power, and strength belong to our God forever and ever. Amen!"

Then one of the elders said, "These are the people who have come out of the great suffering. They have washed their robes with the blood of the Lamb. Now they are clean and white. And they are before the throne of God. They worship God day and night in his temple. And the One who sits on the throne will protect them. Those people will never be hungry again. They will never be thirsty again. The sun will not hurt them. No heat will burn them. For the Lamb at the center of the throne will be their shepherd. He will lead them to springs of water that give life. And God will wipe away every tear from their eyes."

The Seventh Seal

The Lamb opened the seventh seal. Then there was silence in heaven for about half an hour. And I saw the seven angels who stand before God. They were given seven trumpets.

The Seven Angels and Trumpets

Then the seven angels who had the seven trumpets prepared to blow them.

Then hail and fire mixed with blood was poured down on the earth. Something that looked like a big mountain burning with fire was thrown into the sea. A large star, burning like a torch, fell from the sky. It fell on a third of the rivers and on the springs of water. And a third of all the water became bitter. Many people died from drinking the water that was bitter.

While I watched, I heard an eagle that was flying high in the air. The eagle said with a loud voice, "Trouble! Trouble! Trouble for those who live on the earth!"

Then I saw a deep hole that leads down to the bottomless pit. Smoke came up from the hole like smoke from a big furnace. The sun and sky became dark because of the smoke from the hole. Then locusts came down to the earth out of the smoke. They were given the power to sting like scorpions. They were told not to harm the grass on the earth or any plant or tree. They could harm only the people who did not have the sign of God on their foreheads.

In my vision I saw horses and riders. The heads of the horses looked like heads of lions. The horses had fire, smoke, and sulfur coming out of their mouths. A third of all the people on earth were killed by the fire, the smoke, and the sulfur. The horses' power was in their mouths and also in their tails. Their tails were like snakes that have heads to bite and hurt people.

The other people on the earth were not killed by these terrible things. But they still did not change their hearts and turn away from what they had made with their own hands. They did not stop worshiping demons and idols made of gold, silver, bronze, stone, and wood — things that cannot see or hear or walk. These people did not change their hearts and turn away from their sins.

Then there were loud voices in heaven. The voices said: "The power to rule the world now belongs to our Lord and his Christ. And he will rule forever and ever."

The 24 elders bowed down on their faces and worshiped God. They said: "We give thanks to you, Lord God All-Powerful. You are the One who is and who was. We thank you because you have used your great power and have begun to rule! The people of the world were angry; but now is the time for your anger. Now is the time for the dead to be judged. It is time to reward your servants the prophets and to reward your holy people, all who respect you, great and small. It is time to destroy those who destroy the earth!"

Then God's temple in heaven was opened. The Holy Box that holds the agreement that God gave to his people could be seen in his temple. Then there were flashes of lightning, noises, thunder, an earthquake, and a great hailstorm.

The Two Beasts

Then I saw a beast coming up out of the sea. This beast looked like a leopard, with feet like a bear's feet. He had a mouth like a lion's mouth. The whole world was amazed and followed the beast. People also worshiped the beast. They asked, "Who is as powerful as the beast? Who can make war against him?"

The beast was allowed to say proud words and words against

God. He was allowed to use his power for 42 months. He spoke against God's name, against the place where God lives, and against all those who live in heaven. He was given power to make war against God's holy people and to defeat them. He was given power over every tribe, people, language, and nation. All who live on earth will worship the beast. These are all the people since the beginning of the world whose names are not written in the Lamb's book of life.

If anyone has ears, he should listen: If anyone is to be a prisoner, then he will be a prisoner. If anyone is to be killed with the sword, then he will be killed with the sword. This means that God's holy people must have patience and faith.

Then I saw another beast coming up out of the earth. This second beast fools those who live on earth. He ordered people to make an idol to honor the first beast. The second beast was given power to give life to the idol. Then the idol could speak and order all who did not worship it to be killed. The second animal also forced all people, small and great, rich and poor, free and slave, to have a mark on their right hand or on their forehead. No one could buy or sell without this mark. This mark is the name of the beast or the number of his name. This number is 666.

The Earth Is Harvested

Then I saw another angel flying high in the air. The angel had the eternal Good News to preach to those who live on earth — to every nation, tribe, language, and people. The angel said in a loud voice, "Fear God and give him praise. The time has come for God to judge all people. Worship God. He made the heavens, the earth, the sea, and the springs of water."

I looked and there before me was a white cloud. Sitting on the white cloud was One who looked like a Son of Man. He had a gold crown on his head and a sharp sickle in his hand. Then another angel came out of the temple. This angel called to the One who was sitting on the cloud, "Take your sickle and gather from the earth. The time to harvest has come. The fruit of the earth is ripe." So the One that was sitting on the cloud swung his sickle over the earth. And the earth was harvested.

Then another angel came out of the temple in heaven. This angel also had a sharp sickle. And then another said, "Take your sharp sickle and gather the bunches of grapes from the earth's vine. The earth's grapes are ripe." The angel swung his sickle over the earth. He gathered the earth's grapes and threw them into the great winepress of God's anger. The grapes were crushed in the winepress outside the city. And blood flowed out of the winepress. It rose as high as the heads of the horses for a distance of 200 miles.

The Last Troubles

Then I saw another wonder in heaven. It was great and amazing. There were seven angels bringing seven troubles. These are the last troubles, because after these troubles God's anger is finished.

I saw what looked like a sea of glass mixed with fire. All of those who had won the victory over the beast and his idol and over the number of his name were standing by the sea. They had harps that God had given them. They sang the song of Moses, the servant of God, and the song of the Lamb: "You do great and wonderful things. Everything the Lord does is right and true. Everyone will respect you, Lord. They will honor you. All people will come and worship you."

After this I saw the temple (the Tent of the Agreement) in heaven. The temple was opened. And the seven angels bringing the seven troubles came out of the temple. They were dressed in clean, shining linen. They wore golden bands tied around their chests. Then one of the four living things gave seven golden bowls to the seven angels. The bowls were filled with the anger of God, who lives forever and ever. The temple was filled with smoke from the glory and the power of God. No one could enter the temple until the seven troubles of the seven angels were finished.

The Bowls of God's Anger

Then I heard a loud voice from the temple. The voice said to the seven angels, "Go and pour out the seven bowls of God's anger on the earth."

Then a loud voice came out of the temple from the throne. The voice said, "It is finished!" Then there were flashes of lightning, noises, thunder, and a big earthquake. This was the worst earthquake that has ever happened since people have been on earth. The cities of the nations were destroyed. Every island disappeared, and there were no more mountains. Giant hailstones fell on people from the sky. The hailstones weighed about 100 pounds each. People cursed God because of the hail. This trouble was a terrible thing.

People in Heaven Praise God

After this I heard what sounded like a great many people in heaven. They were saying: "Hallelujah! Salvation, glory, and power belong to our God. His judgments are true and right."

Then the 24 elders and the four living things said: "Amen, Hallelujah!"

A voice came from the throne: "Praise our God, all you who serve him! Praise our God, all you who honor him, both small and great!"

Then I heard what sounded like a great many people. It sounded like the noise of flooding water and like loud thunder. The people were saying: "Hallelujah! Our Lord God rules. He is the All-Powerful. Let us rejoice and be happy and give God glory! Give God glory, because the wedding of the Lamb has come. And the Lamb's bride has made herself ready. Fine linen was given to the bride for her to wear. The linen was bright and clean."

(The fine linen means the good things done by God's holy people.)

Then the angel said to me, "Write this: Those who are invited to the wedding meal of the Lamb are happy!" Then the angel said, "These are the true words of God."

The Rider on the White Horse

Then I saw heaven open. There before me was a white horse. The rider on the horse is called Faithful and True. He is right when he judges and makes war. His eyes are like burning fire, and on his head are many crowns. He is dressed in a robe dipped in blood. His name is the Word of God. The armies of heaven were following him on white horses. They were dressed in fine linen, white and clean. A sharp sword comes out of the rider's mouth. He will use this sword to defeat the nations. On his robe and on his leg was written this name: "KING OF KINGS AND LORD OF LORDS."

Then I saw the beast and the kings of the earth. Their armies were gathered together to make war against the rider on the horse and his army. But the beast was captured and thrown alive into the lake of fire that burns with sulfur. Their armies were killed with the sword that came out of the mouth of the rider on the horse.

The 1,000 Years

I saw an angel coming down from heaven. He had the key to the bottomless pit. He also held a large chain in his hand. The angel grabbed the dragon, that old snake who is the devil. The angel tied him up for 1,000 years. Then he threw him into the bottomless pit and closed it and locked it over him. The angel did this so that he could not trick the people of the earth anymore until the 1,000 years were ended. After 1,000 years he must be set free for a short time.

Then I saw some thrones and people sitting on them. They had been given the power to judge. And I saw the souls of those who had been killed because they were faithful to the truth of Jesus and the message from God. They had not worshiped the beast or his idol. They had not received the mark of the beast on their foreheads or on their hands. They came back to life and ruled with Christ for 1,000 years.

When the 1,000 years are over, Satan will be set free from his prison. He will go out to trick the nations in all the earth. Satan will gather them for battle. There will be so many people that they will be like sand on the seashore. And Satan's army marched across the earth and gathered around the camp of God's people and the city that God loves. But fire came down from heaven and burned them up. And Satan, who tricked them, was thrown into the lake of burning sulfur with the beast. There they will be punished day and night forever and ever.

People of the World Are Judged

Then I saw a great white throne and the One who was sitting on it. Earth and sky disappeared. And I saw the dead, great and small, standing before the throne. And the book of life was opened. There were also other books opened. The dead were judged by what they had done, which was written in the books. Each person was judged by what he had done. And if anyone's name was not found written in the book of life, he was thrown into the lake of fire.

The New Jerusalem

Then I saw a new heaven and a new earth. And I saw the holy city coming down out of heaven from God. This holy city is the new Jerusalem. It was prepared like a bride dressed for her husband. I heard a loud voice from the throne. The voice said, "Now God's home is with men. He will live with them, and they will be his people. God himself will be with them and will be their God. He will wipe away every tear from their eyes. There will be no more death, sadness, crying, or pain. All the old ways are gone."

The One who was sitting on the throne said, "Look! I am making everything new! I will give free water from the spring of the water of life to anyone who is thirsty. Anyone who wins the victory will receive this. And I will be his God, and he will be my son."

One of the angels carried me to a very large and high mountain. He showed me the holy city, Jerusalem. It was shining with the glory of God. It was shining bright like a very expensive jewel. It was clear as crystal. The street of the city was made of pure gold. The gold was clear as glass.

I did not see a temple in the city. The Lord God All-Powerful and the Lamb are the city's temple. The city does not need the sun or the moon to shine on it. The glory of God is its light. Nothing unclean will ever enter the city. No one who does shameful things or tells lies will ever go into it. Only those whose names are written in the Lamb's book of life will enter the city.

Then the angel showed me the river of the water of life. The river was shining like crystal. It flows from the throne of God and of the Lamb down the middle of the street of the city. The tree of life was on each side of the river. It produces fruit 12 times a year, once each month. The leaves of the tree are for the healing of all people.

Nothing that God judges guilty will be in that city. And God's servants will worship him. They will see his face, and his name will be written on their foreheads. There will never be night again. They will not need the light of a lamp or the light of the sun. The Lord God will give them light. And they will rule like kings forever and ever.

"Listen! I am coming soon! I will bring rewards with me. I will repay each one for what he has done. I am the First and the Last, the Beginning and the End.

"I, Jesus, have sent my angel to tell you these things for the churches. I am the descendant from the family of David. I am the bright morning star."

Jesus is the One who says that these things are true. Now he says, "Yes, I am coming soon."

Amen. Come, Lord Jesus!

WORTH WONDERING...

- What does this book tell you about heaven?
- What warnings did you notice in the book of Revelation?
- If you could meet the apostle John today, what kind of questions would you like to ask him? Which parts of this book would you most like to know more about?
- In this book of the Bible, how do you see that God is great? And how do you see that He is good?
- What promises from God can you find in this book — things that He says He will do for us?
- Suppose you were a famous artist. Someone has asked you

to paint a picture showing something that happens in this book of Revelation. What person or event from this book would you choose to paint?

■ Which parts of this book do you think the devil would most like you NOT to understand and obey?

■ What do you think are the most important things this book tells us about Jesus?

GREAT VERSES TO THINK ABOUT AGAIN...

Look back in Revelation to see if you can find these verses:

■ *Look! I am making everything new!*

■ *On his robe and on his leg was written this name: "KING OF KINGS AND LORD OF LORDS."*

■ *I was dead, but look: I am alive forever and ever! And I hold the keys of death.*

■ *Those who are invited to the wedding meal of the Lamb are happy!*

■ *The power to rule the world now belongs to our Lord and his Christ. And he will rule forever and ever.*

AND THERE'S MORE...

When you read Revelation in a full Bible, look especially for...

■ Seven "letters" which Jesus tells John to give to seven different churches. In these letters Jesus tells us what is good and what is not good in each church.

■ A dragon and a woman who was giving birth to a son. The dragon wanted to eat the baby as soon as it was born.

■ An angel announcing destruction for the city of Babylon.

Where to Find Your Favorite Bible Characters

AARON .... in Exodus
ABEDNEGO .... in Daniel
ABEL .... in Genesis
ABRAHAM .... in Genesis
ADAM .... in Genesis
ANNA .... in Luke
BALAAM .... in Numbers
BARNABAS .... in Acts
BOAZ .... in Ruth
CALEB .... in Numbers
DANIEL .... in Daniel
DAVID .... in 1 & 2 Samuel, 1 Chronicles, Psalms
DEBORAH .... in Judges
ELIJAH .... in 1 Kings
ELISHA .... in 1 & 2 Kings
ELIZABETH .... in Luke
ESAU .... in Exodus
ESTHER .... in Esther
EVE .... in Genesis
EZEKIEL .... in Ezekiel
EZRA .... in Ezra & Nehemiah
GABRIEL .... in Luke
GIDEON .... in Judges
GOLIATH .... in 1 Samuel
GOOD SAMARITAN .... in Luke
HANNAH .... in 1 Samuel
HEROD .... in Matthew & Luke
HEZEKIAH .... in 2 Kings, 2 Chronicles, & Isaiah
ISAAC .... in Genesis
JACOB .... in Genesis
JEREMIAH .... in Jeremiah
JESUS .... throughout the Bible, and especially in the Gospels, Acts, & Revelation
JOHN the Apostle .... in the Gospels, Acts, & Revelation

JOHN the Baptist .... in the Gospels
JONAH .... in Jonah
JONATHAN .... in 1 Samuel
JOSEPH, husband of Mary .... in Matthew & Luke
JOSEPH, son of Jacob .... in Genesis
JOSHUA .... in Joshua
JOSIAH .... in 2 Kings & 2 Chronicles
LAZARUS .... in John
MARY & MARTHA .... in Luke & John
MARY, mother of Jesus .... in Matthew & Luke
MATTHEW .... in Matthew
MESHACH .... in Daniel
MORDECAI .... in Esther
MOSES .... in Exodus, Leviticus, Numbers &
Deuteronomy
NAAMAN .... in 2 Kings
NAOMI .... in Ruth
NEBUCHADNEZZAR .... in Daniel
NEHEMIAH .... in Nehemiah
NICODEMUS .... in John
NOAH .... in Genesis
PAUL .... in Acts and his Letters
PETER .... in the Gospels & Acts
PRODIGAL SON .... in Luke
RACHEL .... in Genesis
RAHAB .... in Joshua
REBEKAH .... in Genesis
RUTH .... in Ruth
SAMSON .... in Judges
SAMUEL .... in 1 Samuel
SARAH .... in Genesis
SAUL the king .... in 1 Samuel
SHADRACH .... in Daniel
SILAS .... in Acts
SIMEON .... in Luke
SOLOMON .... in 2 Kings, 2 Chronicles, Proverbs,
Ecclesiastes, & Song of Solomon
STEPHEN .... in Acts
THOMAS .... in John
WISE MEN .... in Matthew
ZACCHAEUS .... in Luke